Money and Culture

Fiona Cox
Hans-Walter Schmidt-Hannisa
(eds.)

Money and Culture

PETER LANG
Frankfurt am Main · Berlin · Bern · Bruxelles · New York · Oxford · Wien

Bibliographic Information published by the Deutsche Nationalbibliothek
The Deutsche Nationalbibliothek lists this publication in the Deutsche Nationalbibliografie; detailed bibliographic data is available in the internet at <http://www.d-nb.de>.

Cover design:
Olaf Glöckler, Atelier Platen (Friedberg)

ISBN 978-3-631-56790-6

www.peterlang.de

TABLE OF CONTENTS

Acknowledgements

The editors would like to thank Artificial Eye Film Company Limited, London, for permission to reproduce stills from Robert Bresson's film *L'Argent*.

We would like to acknowledge, also, generous financial support from the College of Arts, Celtic Studies and Social Sciences at the National University of Ireland, Cork.

Introduction

Of all the forces that govern our lives money is the most protean. The essays in this volume, which for the most part stem from a conference on *Money and Culture* organised by the editors in 2005,[1] analyse exemplary instances of the many transformations that money has taken over centuries and across cultures. These twenty five essays show the metamorphoses of money from hard gold to the intangible but inexorable force of a virtual economy; from works of art to the lots in a casino; from the socio-economic forces that create and smash identities to human hair and teeth and flesh. Inevitably many of the same themes recur in different guises according to the light cast on them by a specific age or culture; the interface between art and money, the religious status enjoyed by money, the paradoxical emptiness of money and the interplay between society and money are all dominant themes within the volume. The essays could have been organised according to theme, but it seemed to us to be more cohesive to arrange them chronologically.

The symbiosis of money and culture means that, even as money shapes the conditions by which and in which we live, it also serves as a mirror in which each society sees itself reflected. Michael Hutter analyses the ways in which two thousand years of British history are charted in the transformations of the figure of Britannia on British currency from just after the Roman invasion onwards, and shows us how Britannia herself functioned as a model for British ideals of feminine beauty. Michael Shields demonstrates the potency of mirror imagery to mediaeval society in Germany, as he probes the tension between knightly values and financial values in the second half of the thirteenth century and demonstrates how courtly culture was dependent on economic considerations. He shows that in this world where creativity is so tightly bound up with money, both song and coin function as a mirror of the self.

Cordula Politis argues that the text of *Fortunatus* which dates from the end of the fifteenth century looks back to the Biblical *exemplum* of Solomon who chooses wisdom over riches. *Fortunatus*, however, presents money as a value-neutral commodity whose impact on a person's life depends on their aptitude for using it. In this way money reflects a personality, and the wisdom of Solomon is replaced by *experienz*.

---

1 Money and Culture. XIII Annual Conference of the School of Language and Literature (An Scoil Teanga agus Litríochta) on Cross-Currents in Literature, Film and the Visual Arts. National University of Ireland, University College Cork, 6-8 May 2005.

Michael Fodor analyses an 18th century representation of money in Diderot's *Le Neveu de Rameau* where the pantomime of money opens up a world of possibility as it ceases to resemble itself but instead resembles the goods and services that it purchases. William Carter's reading of *Faust II* offers further insights into the world of money in the 18th century by showing us Goethe in his role as senior adviser to Duke Carl August. Goethe's fascination with taxes offered him new insights into the interdependence between state and citizen, and also enabled him to forecast the political economy in Germany.

As Anders Mortensen studies the neglected Romantic critics of political economy, he develops and discusses a trope of mutually excluding aesthetic and economic values in a range of Romantic writings. Sheila Dickson examines the significance of money in the work of Achim von Arnim who straddles the 18th and 19th centuries, the enlightened and the romantic discourse, and shows how his writings strive for the utopia that is the harmonious reconciliation of love and riches, the dual meanings of *Schatz*.

Armin Schäfer analyses money and madness within *Moby Dick,* as he demonstrates the monomaniacal tendencies of Captain Ahab who sees himself reflected within the doubloon, itself hosting a proliferation of significations.

Kirill Postoutenko compares the way in which Chichikov seems to perform the role of money in Gogol's *Dead Souls*, while money inversely poses as a *picaro,* or rogue, in Marx's writings, and uses this interplay as a means of thinking about *abstractio* in European culture. Niamh Sweeney employs the theories of Baudrillard and Derrida as she elucidates Baudelaire's presentation of the delicate contract between the French bourgeois consumers of art and the demands of the marketplace. Fiona Cox examines the figure of the prostitute in Hugo's *Les Misérables*, arguing that it is the harsh economics of 19th century France that colour Hugo's subversion of the myth of Pygmalion as he charts the inevitable fall of Fantine.

Dick Collins shows the near-absence of money from the Classical Gothic, while in the Gothic's urchin child, the Victorian Penny Dreadful, it is ubiquitous; paradoxically in the latter, money represents the absence or degradation of human values, while at the same time it is held up as the ultimate aspiration of the reader. Mary Pierse points out that direct references to money are understated in mainstream Victorian fiction. She argues that Arthur Conan-Doyle and George Moore both inherit a reticence about referring directly to money, but that a close reading of their novels reveals that both writers are determined to challenge late Victorian opinions and to prompt debate on the financial and social implications of having, getting and spending.

Hans-Walter Schmidt-Hannisa's article investigates the role of money in relationships between men and women, as represented in selected novellas by

Arthur Schnitzler. Schnitzler turns out to be an author obsessed by the question what money can buy in such relationships. What is the nature of such love that is 'for sale'?

In her study of the autobiographies of John D. Rockefeller (1909) and Andrew Carnegie (1920) Christina Oldman shows how both business tycoons drew on established notions of masculinity to construct confidence-inspiring identities that could counter-balance the fluid, shifting world of money.

Brian Moloney analyses the double identity of the Italian novelist Italo Svevo who also worked as a businessman and published articles on commerce under the name of Ettore Schmidt. Moloney argues that the language of transaction infiltrates the post First-World-War fiction of Svevo and, through his reading of Maynard Keynes, shows that these later narrative works are the ironic expression of one aspect of the chaotic economic consequences of peace.

Guy Snaith takes us to the world of francophone Canada during the Second World War, the setting of Gabrielle Roy's *Bonheur d'occasion* (1945). Roy uses the novel to raise her voice against the model of the United States of America where value is established through consumer spending. Snaith argues that her depiction of ordinary people struggling to make ends meet in desperate times is as relevant today as in 1945, chillingly reminding us of the boost to the stockmarket from the war in Iraq.

Cinema has offered new ways of thinking about, and of representing, money in the modern world. Ekkehard Knörer argues that in his film *L'Argent* (1983) the director Robert Bresson links the representation of money to Jansenist aesthetics and gives us a cinematographic vision of the miracle of transubstantiation. Money is the prime example of the counterfeit sign, a sinfully false simulation of the world which itself is in need of redemption from these simulations.

Ailbhe Thunder probes the unacknowledged but extensive network of links between Ben Younger's film *Boiler Room* (2000) and Oliver Stone's *Wall Street* (1987). She sees *Boiler Room* functioning as a counterfeit copy of *Wall Street* and links this relationship to the depiction of virtual, electronic money, claiming that the endlessly deferred cybercapital of the virtual economy mirrors the crisis of representation in postmodern theory.

Joyce Goggin also examines the crisis of representation with regard to money, using the work of Baudrillard to argue that Steven Soderbergh's *Ocean's Eleven* shows us a world of postmodern finance where the notion of value has become abstract, where paper money is no longer a guarantee of a certain quantity of precious metal, but rather just a promise of a replica of itself. On this reading paper money has taken on what she calls a false indexicality as an ersatz gold standard.

Michael Bzdak shows us a different form of 'money in the bank' by analysing the image projected by leading banks in the United States who integrate works of art into their corporate culture. He demonstrates that the history of twentieth century art is incomplete if we don't understand the influence of business on the art world. Matthias Weiss shows a different side of this interplay between the world of art and the world of commerce by arguing that the trading floor itself becomes a work of art as it is transformed into a stage ready for the worship of money. The façade of the New York stock exchange resembles a temple from antiquity, and stock exchange capitalism is depicted as a source of redemption while the onlooker is exhorted to have faith in speculative investment. Mary O'Neill also examines the interface between commerce and culture as she explores the different challenges posed by the Brazilian artist Lygia Clark and the German artists Hans Haacke and Gustav Metzger to the invisible ways in which public opinion is manipulated by multi-national corporations in order to create an image of humane and enlightened cultural values.

Sina Vatanpour explores Paul Auster's treatment of money in *The New York Trilogy* (1990). He shows how money is used as a mechanism to blur identity, as a transfer of money becomes a transfer of meaning and consciousness. Ultimately, however, both money and language are empty ciphers, leaving us in a 'city of ghosts' as the American national identity ends up being anchored in an absence of identity.

In the final chapter of this volume Joachim Schwend also examines the way in which a national identity is forged through its attitude to money, as he depicts the time-poor but money-rich Ireland of the twenty first century, where the choice of brand privileges sign over use and where the shopping mall has replaced the Celtic Stone Circle.

This metamorphosis of a religious cult into the cult of money is simply the last depiction in the volume of the transformative powers of money, powers that have shown us money as works of art, as gold doubloon, as pound of human flesh or as signs that vanish without trace into cyberspace. The essays have taken us from Roman Britain to twenty first century Ireland, via Germany, France, Italy, Russia, the USA and Canada. Their richness and variety testify to our perennial fascination in the way in which money forges our identities, both national and individual, and in the constant dynamism and creative interplay that exists between money and culture.

Cork / Galway Fiona Cox / Hans-Walter Schmidt-Hannisa

Michael Hutter

Visual Credit: The Britannia Vignette on the Notes of the Bank of England*

1. Putting a Seal into circulation

On 30 July of the year 1694, the directors of the newly incorporated Bank of England held one of their first regular meetings. One item of business on that day was a decision on the Common Seal of the new bank. The seal was to be placed on all forms of public communication by the bank, including the notes which it was permitted to issue. The minutes record the directors' decision that the Common seal should represent "Britannia sitting and looking on a Bank of mony".[1]

The vignette of the Seal was printed on the front side of virtually all the notes issued by the Bank from 1694 to 1961. Even today, a version of the image survives on all denominations of British paper currency.

FIGURE 1: 1694 vignette

* The support of the Getty Research Institute is gratefully acknowledged.

1 Quoted in Virginia Hewitt and J.M. Keyworth, *As Good as Gold. 300 Years of British Bank Note Design* (London: British Museum, 1987), p. 22.

The original vignette, executed in several variations, shows a dressed, bare-headed female figure on a throne, with various insignia, looking onto a heap of coins, each marked with a cross.

What are the reasons for the extraordinary persistence of this particular image on a bank note, and what does such persistence tell us about the effect of artistic expression on economic development and growth?

2. From Athena to Britannia: the deviations of accumulated meaning

In choosing the figure of Britannia, the directors appropriated a symbol whose meaning was charged with power. The symbol had accumulated that meaning in the political sphere over the course of the previous century. Now, it was to be used to certify the abilities of a private venture – a corporation of bankers and money-lenders which happened to have the Treasury of the Crown as its major creditor.

To display Britannia with a pile of coins minted from precious metal or specie[2] implied a bold deviation from traditional reproductions of the image. To appreciate the boldness and the consequences of that deviation, we must take a closer look at the cultural history of the Britannia figure.

a) Britannia ruling

In 1660, Charles II. came to power. After more than a decade of civil war, he was able to succeed his father to a throne which from now on had to share part of its power with Parliament. The provision of the kingdom with coins for commercial transactions was failing, private tradesmen's tokens had become customary for low denominations.[3] In 1665, Charles had urged England into war with the Dutch States over the control of trade routes to West Africa. The same year, he ordered the minting of copper farthings and half-pennies. After 1672, the use of private tokens was sanctioned with capital punishment. It took a few years for the private tokens to disappear, only to be replaced by tokens which forged the official copper coins of the Crown.

---

2 At the end of the 17th century, silver still played a relevant role. In the following centuries, gold became the dominating material while the value of silver continued to decline.

3 C. Peck, *English Copper, Tin and Bronze Coins in the British Museum, 1558-1958* (London: British Museum, 1964), p. 104.

Copper and tin coins were never considered part of the Mint's assets. They were excluded from the annual accounts of the Mint.[4] They were a service of the Crown to the populace which involved considerable expense in purchasing the raw metal and in processing it. The fact that these editions in copper and tin were not perceived as "serious money" probably accounts for the fact that their design involved novelties which would not have been permitted on the precious metal coins.

FIGURE 2: Half-Penny 1672, reverse side

The coins show the head of Charles II. on the front, and the figure of Britannia on the reverse. Britannia sits on a globe, holding an olive branch and a spear.[5] Britannia was used by Charles to signal Power and Virtue, the core qualities of a political sovereign, to the coin-using population. The coins were used as propaganda tokens for the ambitions of the King.[6] Jan Roettier, the King's master die-maker, was able to draw on a cultural tradition reaching back to Roman times.

After England had been occupied by Roman forces, Roman Emperors presented the island as a female, unarmed figure named "Britannia". We will

4 ibid., p. 106.

5 What she is looking at can be identified by comparison with Royal medals that bore the same image, plus the legend: "Quattuor Maria Vindico" ("I rule the four Seas"), see ibid., p. 107.

6 J. E. Elliott, "The walls of Ecbatana and the aging queen: notes toward an optics of money", in: *Word & Image* 15,3 (1999), pp. 199-216, here: p. 205.

investigate this design more closely in the next section. After Rome's decline, the image disappeared, but reemerged in the 13th century in the context of the religious worship of the Virgin Mary. It experienced a new peak of popularity under the reign of Elizabeth I.[7] Visual representations took their cues from renaissance allegories of abundance and show Britannia on a throne, facing the viewer, carrying sceptre and cornucopia, with ships out at sea in the background.

FIGURE 3: Michael Drayton: Frontispiece of „Poly-Olbion“ (1612)

In the literary field, Edmund Spencer's canonical epic of the period, *The Fairie Queene*, conflated Britannia with the ruling Queen, summarizing the themes of patriotism, honor and idealism. By now, the once subservient figure had acquired qualities of virtue and power. These qualities were part of the cultural repertoire of meaning when Charles decided to use them on his edition of copper coins.

For the immediate artistic pattern, Roettier referred to the original Roman coins. However, he did so indirectly because he used an oil on canvas portrait of a living person for his design. The model was Frances Stewart, one of Charles II.'s

7 Roy T. Matthews, "Britannia and John Bull: From Birth to Maturity", in: *Historian*, summer 2000, web-version: http://www.encyclopedia.com/doc/1G1-64910240.html.

major mistresses, as painted by Peter Lily, the court painter, in the early 1660s. Roettier turns the figure, the spear is held in front, hiding the olive branch. She sits on a shore, looking out on a sea dominated by an English ship of war. The crest displays the crosses of St. George and St. Andrew. In this medal, minted in 1667 on the occasion of a victory in the Dutch War, the likeness to an actual woman becomes visible, but disappears again in the design of the coin destined for public circulation.

FIGURE 4: Roettier medal 1667, reverse side

The design of Britannia sitting on a globe remained on all the copper coin editions of succeeding kings and queens until the second half of the 20th century. This is the pattern after which the Bank of England Seal was fashioned. But before we turn to its use and its effects, we will pursue the accumulation of meaning in this seated female figure further into the depths of history.

b) Britannia ruled

The Roman coins mentioned above date to the reigns of the emperors Hadrian and Antoninus. After Roman troops had occupied Britain as far north as the isthmus of Tyne and Solvay, Emperor Hadrian ordered the construction of a protective stone wall in 122 AD. His successor Antoninus added a further earthen wall some years later. They commemorated their feat of power and virtue in copper coins with their portrait on the front, and a figure lettered "Britannia" on the reverse side. Britannia is without armour and helmet. She sits next to or on a structure of rocks, signifying Hadrian's wall.

FIGURE 5: Antoninus sestercius 172, reverse side

Roman emperors used the same visual strategy to advertise their victories over other territories. There are coins minted by Trajan showing a female figure named "Hispania" (Spain) or one named "Dacia" (today's Romania). In all these cases, the reference pattern is a female figure that wears a helmet as a sign of armour. That figure is frequently called "Roma", in some cases "Minerva".[8] Minerva is the protector goddess of Rome and signifies the imperial power of the city. By showing Britannia and the other territorial allegories in flowing garments and without helmet, the relationship between dominating and dominated power is expressed.

c) Before Britannia

Minerva is an adoption of the Greek goddess Athena. The image of Minerva or Roma seated on a throne has its immediate predecessor in Greek coinage. A silver tetradrachm minted in Thrace in 287 BC shows Athena seated on a throne, assuming the same position as the Roman Minerva. Thracian coins, in turn, trace their development to the early coins of classical Greece. The most successful of

8 There are many variations of this basic form, particularly in later Imperial times. For instance, the figure is named "Fortuna" when she holds a cornucopia, or "Securitas" when she holds a genius instead of the standard.

these coins were the drachms minted by the city of Athens. They display the head of Athena on the front and an owl, the archaic Athenean totem animal on the reverse side. The Athenean 'owls' were the first coins which moved the older totem design to the reverse side and filled the front side with the image of a universal deity that was accepted throughout the currency area. Their circulation in all economies around the Mediterranean Sea and far into the depths of Asia marked the beginning of an age of international trade and financial services.

FIGURE 6: Tetradrachm Thrace 287 BC, reverse side

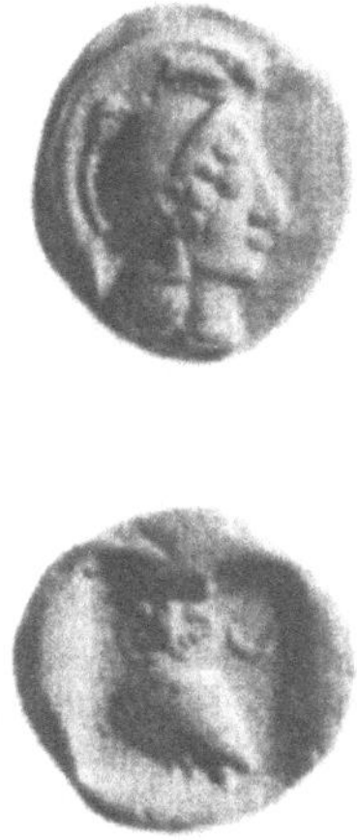

FIGURE 7: Tetradrachm Athens 522 BC, front and reverse side

Two features of this early paradigmatic form are worth mentioning. First, there is the movement of a visual pattern from the front to the reverse side of the token. The owl, like other totem animals in the Greek archipelago, helped to ascertain the integrity of the coin's value. The coin stood for a certain weight in silver, electron or gold. The metaphysical reference gave authority to the claim, and it increased the hesitation to "open" and thus violate the coin. When the animal images slipped to the reverse – which, up to that time, had been filled with geometric patterns –, they continued to literally "back" the value of the tokens, but left the front message to a more widely understood, but still religiously defined image.[9] When the Romans adopted Greek figures, both religious and economic meanings took second rank to political meanings. Roman coins were made of copper, so the forgery problem was less acute. Also, their economy depended more strongly on military command than on commercial interaction. For that reason as well, acceptance of a coin was less in doubt. As a result, the role of the coin as the most widely copied form of advertising or announcement took precedence, particularly in Imperial times.

Secondly, it can be observed that, despite all the variations, a female head or figure is chosen. Therefore the female, in consequence, must be seen as a central aspect of the message. She signifies a counterpart to the male side of power. She stands for procreation, for protection of wealth, for security. This helps to convey the fundamental paradox of the performance of money signs across: a presence of value which is not asserted actively and aggressively, but passively and protectively.[10] We will return to this aspect much later in the story.

Now that we have traced the image that became the vignette on the Bank of England notes all the way to its origins in ancient Greek culture, it becomes apparent that the history of the Britannia figure is a history of deviations: (1) the power of the goddess is crossed with human power by seating her on a throne – (2) The power of a force in Greek religion is crossed with the power of Rome's military force – (3) the power of Rome is increased by generating tamed versions for occupied territories – (4) the tamed version, revived after more than a thousand years, is reversed again, to signify that the former ruling power, Rome, is now dominated by a new ruling power, England. The representation of the aspiring political, imperial power is grounded in its military ability to rule land and water. This sets the stage for the next deviation, the one in which we are primarily interested.

---

9 Michael Hutter, "The Early Form of Money", in Dirk Baecker (ed.), *Problems of Form* (Stanford: Stanford UP, 1999), pp. 107-120.

10 Virginia Hewitt, *Beauty and the Banknote. Images of Women on Paper Money* (London: British Museum, 1994).

3. The effect of bank note circulation on the volume of market transactions

Circulating paper bank notes are among the major social inventions of Western Europe.[11] The supply of money units has to be scarce in order to communicate the scarcity value of a commodity purchased or sold. Such scarcity seems guaranteed in the case of precious metal: the belief in the value of the metal is so strong that it is used to signify preciousness itself. Precious metal comes in two varieties, gold and silver. For more than two thousand years, gold and silver were minted for purposes of economic transaction. The amount of minted metal, countable in weight units, determined the amount of signs available for transactions on open markets.[12]

In times of economic prosperity, development was notoriously hampered by the constant unavailability of money tokens. Furthermore, the manipulation or forgery of coins held profitable opportunities for individual gain. Consequently, the value attributed to the circulating token supply was higher than the weighable value of the metal contained in the coins, but the ease of inspection held such expansion within narrow limits.

Paper money began to be used in Europe in the form of written contracts between a creditor and a debtor. By the late 17th century, the major varieties were promissory notes exchanged between merchants, and deposit slips issued by a bank holding a deposit. Both kinds of paper were customarily "endorsable" by a number of persons beyond the original contractors. The circulation of promissory notes and deposit slips between five to seven persons, usually within the span of a few months, increased the availability of money units, at least in the larger commercial centers, like Genoa, Venice, Amsterdam or London. The custom generated a run of a few stations during which the note, like electricity, charged transactions with economic value.

The use of the early notes illuminates the central point: money is a form of credit, and credit is a social relation. That relation between the giver and the receiver of credit has to be experienced in a convincing manner. Such is the case

---

11 It is true that "flying paper" was invented much earlier in China; see Richard von Glahn, "The Origins of Paper Money in China", in W. Goetzman and K.G. Rouwenhorst (eds.), *The Origins of Value* (Oxford: Oxford University Press, 2005), pp. 65-89. But the key difference is the decentralized fashion in which Western paper money operates. As the Chinese development shows, paper slips which depend on the political authority of a ruler lose their value with the demise of the ruler and do not constitute an autonomous development.

12 To compute the total volume, one has to add book money, i.e. wealth transfers in deposits.

when the paper token is credibly linked to "real", that is material value in the shape of gold and silver. Only a fraction of those who utilize money notes issued by a bank will want to convert their notes into metal at any given time. If it is possible to keep the conversion rate low, and to keep confidence in the solvency of the bank high, then the circulation of money can be expanded considerably. The longer the notes circulate, the higher is the volume available for payment purposes.

Bank notes provided the communicative basis for the expansion of the feasible volume of market transactions. Their introduction and institutionalization constituted the core of the "financial revolution" in England during the first third of the 18th century.[13] The second third was characterized by the "consumer revolution".[14] These two developments were the basis for the "industrial revolution"" that came to prominence in the last third of the century.

4. The emergence of the Bank of England

A crucial factor in the development of paper money is the emergence and success of the particular version issued by the Bank of England.

That emergence seems inevitable and coincidental at the same time. On the one hand, the major London banks had developed their deposit slips into running cash notes, and the success of the Bank of Amsterdam – a "public bank" into which the major merchants of the Dutch States deposited – had instigated a lively English discussion on the merits of such a bank. Furthermore, the Treasury was desperately seeking ways to use future tax payments as collateral for present loans. On the other hand, we have a meticulous account of the improbable odds against which the Bank was chartered and survived the first decade of its existence.

The original purpose for establishing the Bank was the raising of a loan to the Treasury in the amount of 1.2 million pounds, to be serviced by the Treasury with interest payments in perpetuity. That project was one of many that Charles Montagu, First Lord of the Treasury and since 1694 Chancellor of the Exchequer, had to execute in order to pay for the wartime expenditures of William III. It was presented in 1694 among projects for lotteries or for annuity schemes. The project was approved for a sum of 1.5 million pounds, to be paid in part, at an interest

13 P.G.M. Dickson, *The Financial Revolution in England. A study in the development of public credit 1688-1756* (London: Macmillan, 1967).

14 John Brewer, *The Pleasures of the Imagination. English culture in the eighteenth Century* (New York: Farrar, Straus, Giroux, 1997).

rate of 6% p.a., against the collateral of the Crown's ships' tonnage and liquor duties. The privilege to issue notes was mentioned only in passing in a clause of the Act of Parliament that led to the grant of charter on 27 July 1694.

The group of men behind the Bank project were established members of the financial community. The only outsider was William Paterson, the Scottish projector who had been in charge of the active promotion of the Bill. He was voted out of the Board nine months after its inception. That group was successful in subscribing the required sum for the loan within 12 days, and it easily filled the quota of actual deposits. Five days after the signing of the charter, the new Bank paid 112.000 pounds into the Exchequer, "which they did by their bank bills, sealed with the seal of their corporation, being the Britannia sitting on a bank of money."[15]

At the same time, the King began to use the Bank for making payments to allies in his wars with France, and the Bank was able to engage in further loans. The loans of the Bank were paid out in notes. These notes were much more easily exchanged than the formal sealed bills given to the Exchequer. By September, the directors decided on three ways of paying: account statements, personal checks and "notes payable to bearer".

The scheme succeeded beyond expectations because a crucial trigger in generating "immaterial credit" had been hit, almost by accident. That trigger was the issue of notes based on future payments of the State, or "Public Credit".

5. The Evolution of the Britannia vignette

The first notes of the new bank came in two varieties. The first were "sealed bills", which were promissory notes that had to show the name of the person in whose favor they were drawn, the time period during which the note was valid, and the seal of the bank. It was the seal, not the signature, which bestowed the legal sanction upon the contract. The second were "running cash notes" which were deposit slips, issued in irregular amounts, sometimes with interest payments added. Ten years later, round amounts had become the rule. From the beginning, the running cash notes, with the seal, were printed as copper engravings, leaving space for names, amounts and the cashier's signature. Before the end of 1694, the two kinds of notes were merged into one under the name of Bank-note. 1695 brought an experiment with a telling result: "Lettered notes", which featured a watermark ranging from A to H, were issued. The notes did not bear a seal. Two

[15] Quoted in John Clapham, *The Bank of England. A History* (Cambridge: Cambridge University Press, 1944), 2 vols., p. 20.

months later it was decided to withdraw them because the public did not accept them.[16]

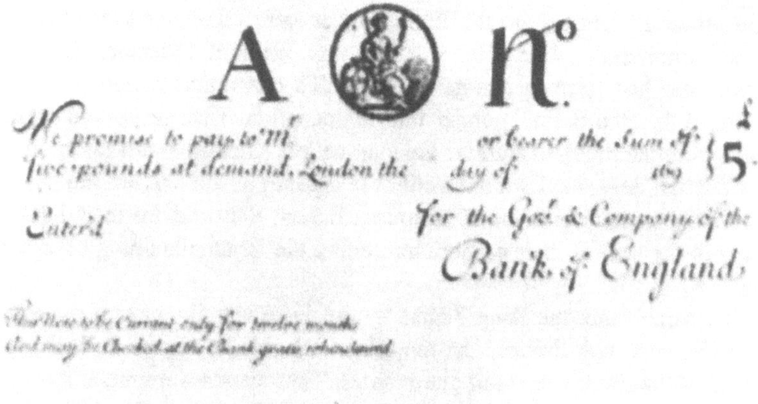

FIGURE 8: Running cash note 1697

The running cash note blank of 1697 reflects the two sources that charge the meaning of the paper slip. One is the legal language that formulates the contract between the Bank and its creditor. The other is the visual language of the vignette. The figure, with bare feet and flowing garment, turns toward the right, while the model on the Stuart coin turned toward the left. She is still supported by a crest with a single English cross. She holds the conventional spear in her left hand, the right hand holds the olive branch, symbol of wisdom and fertility. New is the bank of minted coins to her right. The power and virtue claimed by the figure in the seal is not based on political and military power, but on peaceful commerce and, above all, on the reserves of bullion and precious coins in the vaults of the bank issuing the notes on which the vignettes are printed.

The contemporary observers, published in the (broadsheet) print media, noticed right away that the new Bank was extending "Credit beyond the intention of the Act".[17] At the same time, another competing project, the national Land Bank, was approved by Parliament. Then, on 6 May 1696, the Bank experienced its first bank run. Two days before, clipped silver coins had lost their currency.[18]

---

16 W. R. Bisschop, *The Rise of the London Money Market 1640-1826* (London: Cass & Co., 1968), p. 94.

17 Clapham, *The Bank of England*, p. 22.

18 On the advice of John Locke, all silver coins were recalled and reminted in 1696, thus cutting the nominal volume of available coin money in half.

People were scrambling for full value coin, and they called in their notes. Cash payments had to be partially suspended, the interest rate reached 24% in early 1697. The Bank survived on the strength of reserves from the original loan deposit, and the issue of a new "specie note" which guaranteed repayment in newly minted money. The pressure on the Bank subsided only after the successful passing of a bill which enlarged the collateral base of the Bank, raised the interest paid to 8%, established that no other joint-stock bank was to be erected during "the Continuance of the Bank of England" and sanctioned forgery of the Bank's notes with death – the penalty for clipping or counterfeiting the king's money.[19] A private institution carried out the business of transforming public credit by issuing paper notes which were almost, but not quite, the king's money. A balance had been found which preserved the commercial autonomy of money issue, yet placed it under the surveillance and support of the political authority.

During this first decade, the visual signature of the bank note stabilized as much as the variations of notes stabilized. In the early years, short-lived variations were printed. A particularly rich example is the specie note of 1697. The vignette is open, the closure of the seal is not yet established. The note is assigned an irregular amount of "new money", i.e. it was paid and will be paid in the reminted coins which are as good as specie. The winner in this competition of forms was the running cash note with the closed vignette shown as figure 8.

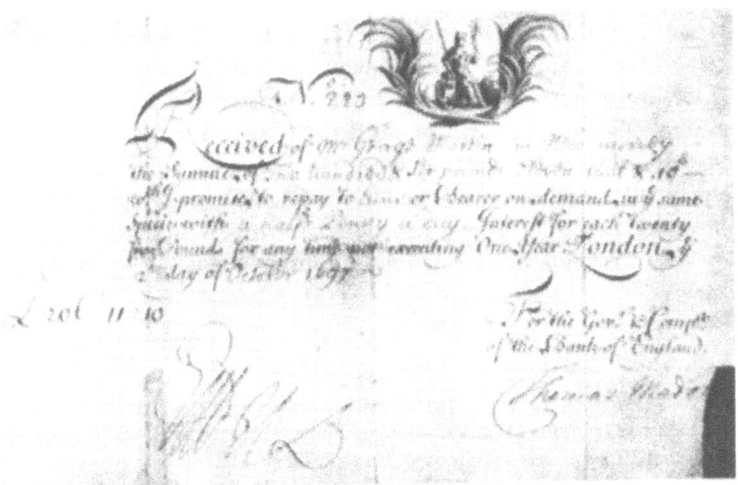

Figure 9: specie note 1697

[19] Clapham, *The Bank of England*, p. 50.

Within the next hundred years, the Bank experienced an amazing career from a "shady deal between some projectors and a penniless government"[20] to the most powerful financial institution in England. In 1708, on the occasion of the charter's first renewal, an act of Parliament specified the Bank's monopoly as a joint-stock corporation. In 1720, the Crown supported the Bank when it had lost parts of its assets in the crash of the South Sea Company.[21] By 1762, 70% of state debt (77 million pounds) was handled by the Bank. After 1781, all the Exchequer's money business was done at the Bank. In turn, the Prime Minister, who now carried political power, demanded an extension of credit when the circumstances called for it. The balance between the Prime Minister who used the institution like a national bank and the stockholders of the Bank corporation was still precarious.

During these years, the appearance of the note changed in a number of respects. The vignette wandered to the upper left corner. Britannia turns toward the left, the olive branch has become more prominent, while the bank of money is placed far at the back. A new visual device was the introduction of an intricately patterned block into which the number value of the note was inscribed. The "sum block" demanded technical skills in printing that discouraged counterfeiting.

A watershed came in 1797 when Parliament suspended cash payments at the Bank, due to the expenses of the war with France. As a reaction, specie was hoarded by merchants and households. In turn, the Bank increased its volume of note issue from 11 million pounds in 1790 to 17 million pounds in 1804. A quarter of the volume came from newly issued one- and five-pound notes. In 1793, the war events which led up to the restriction had prompted the Bank to issue, first, five-pound notes and then one- and two-pound notes. The issues, greatly expanded after 1797, forced a much wider portion of the population, largely illiterate, to use paper money. At the same time, hundreds of country banks sprung up, contributing at times more than 4 million pounds in issued notes. The economy was about to shift from a gold-using to a gold-based currency.

---

20 Raymond de Roover, "New Interpretations in the History of Banking", in: J. Kirshner (ed.), *Business, Banking, and Economic Thought in Late Medieval and Early Modern Europe* (Chicago: Univ. of Chicago Press, 1974) p. 231.

21 The South Sea Company, founded in 1711, was a serious competitor to the Bank of England. It took over 9.5 million pounds in Public Debt against the privilege of free commercial intercourse with the countries in the South Seas. In 1720, it was charged to take over the entire Public Debt, but crashed due to fraudulent schemes of its directors (Bisshop, *The Rise of the London Money Market*, p. 133). Thus, another possible "evolutionary variation" was eliminated.

FIGURE 10: 90 pound note, 1757

The design of the new notes was highly conservative. Although counterfeiting increased rapidly after 1797 as a side effect to issuing notes in low denominations to illiterates, all the plans to change to a more sophisticated, inimitable design for the notes, both in technical and in artistic terms, were refused. Despite the deleterious effects, the Bank tolerated the counterfeit notes rather than change the pictorial and the textual content. Britannia moved only slightly during these years. In most designs after 1793 she is shown full face, confronting the viewer. The crest to her right is placed at such an angle that it appears to be only a baroque ornament. To the left, items that appear to be heaps or hives are indicated. The bank of money seems to be substituted by beehives – a change that does not become apparent until the introduction of a new note in 1855. The notes continued to be printed as copper engravings. Only the quality of the custom-made watermarked paper was improved.

After the end of the restriction period, the Bank continued its development toward a new type of "Bank of banks." In 1833 the notes of the Bank of England became legal tender. In 1844 the Bank Charter Act split the Bank into an issue and a banking department. The Bank was granted a monopoly to note issue in Great Britain, and it was obliged to purchase gold at a fixed price per ounce. The Bank had become a central bank.

FIGURE 11: 5-pound note, 1838. The design is identical to the 5-pound note of 1793.

Eleven years after this decisive structural change, the only major change in the appearance of the note during the entire century took place. Since 1855, all denominations of notes were issued with a newly designed Britannia, displaying a large beehive.[22]

FIGURE 12: five-pound note, 1857

The figure signifies no longer the seal of a corporation, but the image of a nation's identity. The piece of paper no longer needs to be protected by an adapted goddess sitting on gold. Its value flows from the productive force of agriculture and industry which is represented by the beehive. Britannia has changed her appearance to a fictional Saxon princess. Such personages were fashionable inventions by contemporary Pre-Raphaelite painters.

6. The retreat of Britannia, and of paper money

The Bank weathered the violent financial crises of the second half of the century, and it emerged as the leading international financial institution. Until 1931, it "anchored" the international monetary system. After the Bretton Woods agreement in 1947, the Bank became one of the major players in the concerted effort of central banks around the globe – most of them patterned after its role model – to stabilize the supply of currencies and their exchange rates. While the steady supply of cash money remained an important task of central banks, such issues do not play a major role in the total volume of money active in contemporary economies.

With the emergency issues of the First World War, Britannia began to withdraw from the Bank of England notes. In 1914, when the Bank was again forced to issue one-pound notes in times of war, it reduced the dimension of the note and it re-used the pre-1855 version of Britannia. Other issues used entirely different designs, like St. George slaying the dragon.

When new one-pound notes – which by now had become customary – were introduced in 1928, the Maclise vignette and the Sum Block were given equal size. The notes' features were extended to colors and to an architectural and ornamental design on the reverse side. These notes were withdrawn in 1961.

[22] Reportedly, the author of the new vignette, Daniel Maclise, was paid 100 pounds for his commission. See Hewitt/Keyworth, *As Good as Gold*, p. 1987.

FIGURE 13: one-pound note, pattern of a 1917 issue

FIGURE 14: one-pound-note 1928

The one-pound note introduced in 1960 displayed a portrait of Elizabeth II. on the front side, while the reverse side showed Britannia turning to the left, displaying a palm branch in a forward reaching gesture. Next to her, a pile of small round objects suggests a return to the original historical rendering of the Bank's seal.

FIGURE 15: one pound note after 1960, reverse side

Notes of all denominations issued between 1970 and 2000 featured a tiny Britannia, turning to the left, situated in a small vignette on the bottom of the front side of the notes.

FIGURE 16: Vignette on notes until 2000

Notes issued after 2000 document a further shift: Britannia can be seen, alternating with the number of the denomination, in a hologram stamp on the front side of the notes.

7. Conclusion: The visualization of Public Credit

The case of the Britannia vignette allows us to observe an unusually long stretch of development. That feature is particularly valuable because processes of evolution are measured in centuries. Not only can we trace the image on the notes for more than 300 years; thanks to the durability of coins, we can also pursue the preceding evolution for another 2000 years.

The vignette appeared on the first notes of the Bank, and it has not left them since. The technical quality of the notes improved, but the visual appearance remained very static. There were always several slight variations current, but, as in an animated sequence, we perceive how the design slowly changes. The frame, at first often open, closes and becomes intricately scrolled and crowned in the Maclise version. The female figure changes her clothing little. She begins facing right, turns 90° to face the viewer by 1793, and turns left after 1960. The attributes which surround her lose significance. The crest, without St. Andrew's Cross, is turned sideways. The spear becomes a purely compositional element. The olive branch changes only in the late reverse side version, but its interpretation shifts from promise to fertility to honesty, then to productivity and on to peace – hence the switch from olive to palm branch in the 1960 issue. The feature indicating the source of the note's commercial value is initially denoted as a pile of marked items. By 1855, at the latest, the feature has turned into a beehive. The attribute remains until the vignette begins its movement first to the reverse side, then to a framed quotation on the front side, now to one of two states of a light-fractioning device stamped onto the note.[23]

The design was not changed when the credibility of the Bank was in doubt. It was changed in quiet times, in a manner which adjusted technical and visual features with the least possible degree of alteration. The experimentation with new images and new combinations took place in the note issues of small rural banks. The Bank of England had a different task. It had to set the standard of stability for the value of the currency in a continuously turbulent financial market.

---

[23] Another development and reversion of the Britannia image, not to be pursued here, is the goddess of liberty, which was adopted by the emerging United States as a representation of their new identity. See John Higham, *Hanging Together. Unity and Diversity in American Culture* (New Haven: Yale Univ. Press, 2002), p. 31.

It had to set the standard in visual representation as well. The Britannia image had been charged with the veneration addressed to the goddess of knowledge, and then with the trust in a political power that had moved beyond the walls of its ancient colonizers and had succeeded in controlling the seas.

The Bank had been able to transfer the credibility of the image to its own products. The Bank had been permitted to use Britannia in the first place because the State was its major creditor. In a sense, then, the feature indicating the source of value is not only the pile of minted gold accumulated by the Bank's depositors and stockholders, but also and foremost Britannia herself, in her role as Public Credit.[24] She remains on the vignette, becomes even more prominent by facing the viewer, while the accompanying feature mutates to a symbol of natural productivity.

The visual representation changed its role when the volume of the monetary expansion in the 20th century was stabilized by other means. The mint authority of the State, combined with the practice of handling commercial bills and extending credit through notes drawn on the Bank became one integrated institution – a complex, yet manageable organizational machinery which gave hope to generations of economists that economies could be fine-tuned with the aid of a consistent monetary policy.

Under the new regime, the surfaces of the notes did not need to persuade the user of their validity anymore. They could now be used for new technical features to discourage forgery, and for images promoting the glory of the Nation. The vignette turned into a historical item, with all the correct historical attributes. It had crossed from being a figure of meaning to being an ornament of meaning.[25]

How does the evolution of the Britannia fit into an argument that claims the relevance of aesthetic innovation for economic innovation? It does so in a curiously inverted manner. The economic dimension of this case lies in the provision of a means of credit which, in a next step, enables people to become commercially active. Without reliable credit circulation, economic activity is severely restricted in space, in time and in the circle of actors who can be involved. Therefore, the visualization of such credit must follow the opposite rules: it must not be perceived as new, because validity implies absence of change. The user must not hesitate, he or she 'must not think twice' in using a

24 Defoe calls Public Credit a "fickle lady" – again a female figure that generates value, emphasizing her volatility. See Daniel Defoe, *An Essay upon Public Credit* (London, 1710).

25 In the new Euro notes, the only "figure of meaning" that has survived as an ornament is the signature of the cashier – the third element besides the visual and the textual design.

note. It must, like the use of a language, seem self-evident in all respects. As soon as the user hesitates, the circulation falters and, at worst, breaks down. The image must also not be of apparent aesthetic value, because the source of the note's value does not lie in its artistic qualities but in financial claims and precious reserves. Rather, the image represents archetypes of perception, in a rendering which reflects nothing more than the state of the craft in copper engraving or steel etching, without artistic ambition.

The archetype is female at the primary, unchanging level. The gender signifies the counterpart, the complementary side of commercial action. The female procreates, protects and supports. On the second level, the archetype is a ruling figure identified with the realm of currency. The figure changes, together with shifts in national self-interpretation, during the course of centuries. On a third level, the archetypes signify the ability to "pay the bearer on demand". Crest, spear and branch, gold hoards and beehives all belong to the arsenal of visual symbols that enable communication about properties that guarantee payment, without being able to spell out the properties and without the necessity of reading them.

The visual form of the bank note, continuing the visual form of the coin, had an impact on the "reverse side" of economic transactions. During the years when its charge of meaning was relevant, it did not irritate and stimulate the form of commercial ventures, but it supported all the forms of payment in which such ventures were couched. The task of the note designs was not to trigger new interpretations, but to provide stable valuations while irritations of all sorts, due to external shocks, invention and deception, impacted on economic transactions.

Cordula Politis

Wisdom vs. Riches: The Discourse on Money in *Fortunatus*

I.

The prose narrative *Fortunatus*, widely regarded as one of the first original works of fiction composed in the German vernacular, chronicles the economic success-story of its eponymous hero and the subsequent decline of his less fortunate sons. The precise origins of this so-called *Volksbuch* (chapbook) lie somewhat in the dark. Written towards the end of the fifteenth century in a southern German trade town, probably Nuremberg or Augsburg,[1] *Fortunatus* appears to have been authored by a member of the newly prospering bourgeois classes. Earliest surviving prints date to 1509 (Augsburg); subsequently, *Fortunatus* was translated into numerous European languages and enjoyed enduring popularity for centuries, before being rediscovered in the nineteenth century by the Romantics, most notably Ludwig Tieck and Adelbert von Chamisso.[2]

The time and place of *Fortunatus*' genesis indicate decisive factors as to its background. By the end of the fifteenth century, the disintegration of the feudal order, which had shaped society throughout the Middle Ages, was well under way in Germany. Structures of society generally became more permeable; a person's position at birth no longer defined their situation for life. The aristocracy's hegemony was challenged, as non-aristocratic citizens, often merchants and self-made entrepreneurs, were gradually able to rise beyond the status conferred on them by birth and enter a higher stratum of society. A famous example of this is the prominence of the Fugger dynasty in Augsburg. Brought to prominence by Jakob Fugger (1459-1525), nicknamed *The Rich*, the Fugger family amassed a huge fortune by investing in the mining industry. The originally non-aristocratic Fugger exerted enormous influence on Emperors Maximilian I

---

1 For an overview of the discussion on *Fortunatus*' place of publication, see Dietrich Huschenbett, "Fortunatus aus Augsburg" *Zeitschrift für Deutsches Altertum und Deutsche Literatur* 130 (2001): pp. 431-434. Huschenbett ultimately subscribes to the argument that *Fortunatus* was written and originally published in Augsburg.

2 E.g. Ludwig Tieck's *Fortunat* and Adelbert von Chamisso's *Peter Schlemihls wundersame Geschichte*. On the latter, see Annemarie Wambach, "'Fortunati Wünschhütlein und Glücksäckel' in neuem Gewand: Adelbert von Chamissos *Peter Schlemihl*", *German Quarterly* 67 (1994): pp. 173-184.

and Karl V by financing their military projects. In return, Emperor Maximilian elevated the family's status to that of count.

Such changes in society were complemented by radical developments in the economic situation. The canonical ban on interest, which had been in existence throughout medieval times, was finally being challenged by representatives of the new economic order. This was especially the case in the trade centres of Southern Germany, within whose radius *Fortunatus* originated. An important figure here is the humanist Conrad Peutinger, town clerk of Augsburg. In 1499, Peutinger wrote the first of many treatises in defence of entrepreneurship.[3] Crucially, he insisted on the individual's right to accumulate monetary riches, as opposed to mere possessions. Peutinger's endeavours were complemented by those of well-known theologian Johannes Eck, whom the Fugger had instructed to write a testimonial in defence of the profit derived from interest. The eventual abolition of the interest ban gave an enormous boost to the financial sector. The possibility of having money itself work for one, rather than people, substantially aided the rise of the self-made entrepreneur and paved the way for early forms of capitalism.

Against the background of socio-economic and cultural changes that mark the turn from fifteenth to sixteenth century as an age of transition, the narrative *Fortunatus* poses vital questions on the role of money in human life: can money buy happiness, love, or at least peace of mind? How should we rank money in the hierarchy of earthly goods, and is our desire for money good or bad? The implications of these questions, which in themselves suggest why this anonymous work ought to occupy a crucial place in any cultural history of money, are two-fold; they may be divided into economic implications on the one hand, and poetical ones on the other. Here, I will deal mainly with the economic aspect of Fortunatus' selection of riches over wisdom, setting this against a more traditional template for this particular choice. Furthermore, I will consider the poetical implications of the new economic situation as reflected in the narrative. I argue that the unconventional nature of Fortunatus' choice on an economic level is complemented by profound shifts in the composition of the narrative, which are indicative of the shape in which the modern novel was to evolve.

---

3 See Johannes Janota, "*Fortunatus*" in *Große Werke der Literatur* III, ed. H.-V. Geppert (Tübingen, Basel: Francke, 1993), pp. 49-56, here: p. 55.

II.

The story begins with Fortunatus' father Theodorus. Theodorus, "a noble burgher of long-established lineage",[4] manages to squander the wealth amassed by his parents. Faced with penury, Theodorus' son, Fortunatus,[5] decides to make his fortune elsewhere and leaves his native Cyprus in the service of the count of Flanders. Initially, devotion to his master and excellence in chivalric pursuits pay off, and Fortunatus enjoys a pleasant life as the count's favourite. Soon, however, his fellow servants are unwilling to tolerate such favouritism, and trick Fortunatus into leaving his master for good. Having exchanged Flanders for London, Fortunatus falls in with a rather undesirable crowd, in whose company he uses up all his earnings. The last straw comes when he finally becomes embroiled in a murder case; Fortunatus flees London and crosses over to France. Losing his way "in a big, wild forest"[6] he reaches breaking-point. Famished and penniless, cut off from family and friends, he is at the end of his tether and fears for his life. Unable to make his way out of the forest, Fortunatus is forced to spend the night there, only to find himself threatened by wild animals, from which he seeks rescue in a tree.

Following this state of crisis, Fortunatus encounters the apparition of "a very beautiful woman".[7] The lady refers to herself as "Lady Luck"[8] and explains her power as follows:

> Through the influence of heaven and the stars/and the planets I have been given six virtues/ which I may pass on to a human being/ [...] in accordance with the reign of the planets. They are wisdom/ riches/ strength/ health/ beauty and long life".[9]

---

4 "ein edler purger/ altz herkommens". All quotations taken from *Fortunatus*, ed. Hans-Gert Roloff (Stuttgart: Reclam, 1981), here: p. 5

5 The name Fortunatus of course points to the goddess Fortuna, who was traditionally seen to bestow material advantages on man. Dieter Kartschoke points out the mercantile aspect of the Fortuna-conception in the narrative. See Dieter Kartschoke, "Weisheit oder Reichtum? Zum Volksbuch von Fortunatus und seinen Söhnen" in *Literatur im Feudalismus*, ed. Dieter Richter (Stuttgart: Metzler, 1975), pp. 213-259; see esp. pp. 244f.

6 "in aynen großsenn wilden wald", p. 42.

7 "ain gar schoenes weibs bild", p. 45.

8 "junckfraw des glücks", p. 46.

9 "durch die einfliessung des himels und der sternen/ und der planeten So ist mir verlihen sechs tugendt/ die ich fürter verleühen mag/ [...] nach den stunden und regirung der planeten. Das ist weyßhait/ Reichtumb/ Stercke/ Gesundthait/ Schoene/ und langs leben (p. 46).

From out of these attributes, Fortunatus is quick to choose wealth: "I desire wealth, so that I may always have enough money".[10] He promptly receives a purse that provides him with an infinite supply of money in any given currency. The *junckfraw* subsequently disappears for good.

Fortunatus' choice calls up a parallel situation in the Old Testament, where King Solomon is confronted with a similar choice. Originally found in 1 Kings (3, 3.5ff.), King Solomon's choice was a commonplace of devotional literature in the Middle Ages. In the Biblical original, God appears to Solomon in a dream with the words "Ask what I shall give thee". In response, Solomon asks for "an understanding heart to judge [God's] people, that [he] may discern between good and bad". Pleased that Solomon did not seek material goods like long life or riches, God's reward is to grant him not only a wise heart, but also that which he did not ask for, i.e. riches and honour. Evoked by the parallels in Fortunatus' situation, this exemplum would certainly have been at the back of the contemporary audience's mind. In addition, the narrator explicitly establishes reference to it in the epilogue, where he advises the reader not to follow Fortunatus, but to choose wisdom over riches, "as did Solomon, which is how he became the richest king on earth".[11]

How does Fortunatus' choice relate to the precedent set by Solomon? By choosing wisdom, Solomon displays moral righteousness and fear of God. According to his example, wisdom is the only acceptable choice. Fortunatus subverts this orthodox view by choosing riches and thereby simultaneously rejecting wisdom. Does this automatically set him up for a fall? Where Solomon conforms to the existing system that purports to hold spiritual above material values, Fortunatus breaks a taboo by inverting the traditional hierarchy. What is more, Fortunatus' selfish concerns – after all, his wealth is to be used for personal gain only – set him apart from the publicly minded Solomon who asks for a gift that will enable him to better rule his people. Such contrast may lead the reader to expect a higher authority, God, to punish Fortunatus for his unconventional behaviour. But, whether his subversion of traditional values will prove to be fatal or, rather, successful can only be judged from the outcome of Fortunatus' subsequent development.

Let us consider, then, how Fortunatus fares with his newly acquired riches. Following the *junckfraw*'s departure, he leaves the forest and frequents the nearest inn in order to recuperate. But when he tries to buy a number of valuable horses from the local count, this raises suspicion as to the whereabouts of his

10 "so beger ich reichtumb/ das ich alweg gelts gnuog hab", p. 46.

11 "Als auch gethon hat Salomon/ dardurch er der reichest künig der erden wordenn ist", p. 195.

wealth. The count threatens to kill him, prompting Fortunatus to regret the choice of riches after barely twenty-four hours (p.51). However, he is spared on this occasion and subsequently learns to handle the magic purse to his advantage by using it in a discreet and circumspect fashion.

Together with his faithful servant Lüpoldus, Fortunatus sets about travelling the world. Through Germany, Flanders, England and Scotland, from there on to France, Spain, Portugal, back through France to Italy, Sicily, Greece, Cyprus, Jerusalem, and Alexandria, until his travels finally take him to Constantinople, Fortunatus explores the *orbis christianus* in its entirety. On his journey, he repeatedly finds himself at the mercy of envious people who try to rob him of the magic purse. Losing his purse temporarily to a thief briefly causes him to regret his choice once more, while Lüpoldus' accidental killing of an intruder leads to a rather tricky situation for both master and servant.

However, the companions are able to overcome any difficulties and, after further travels in Eastern Europe, Fortunatus eventually returns to his native Cyprus. Bearing the outward signs of great wealth he is welcomed enthusiastically by his country's high and mighty. While sad to learn that both his parents have died during his absence, Fortunatus sets about establishing an emporium of his own. He buys his family house as well as several others, has them demolished and erects a lavish palace. The trappings of success are complemented by a more spiritual dimension, when he builds a church complete with thirteen adjoining houses and installs a cathedral dean and twelve chaplains. Building work completed, Fortunatus decides it is time to take a wife and weds the beautiful and aristocratic Cassandra in a ceremony attended by the king of Cyprus. She duly bears him two sons, and the family spend their time in contented luxury.

But Fortunatus' contentment does not last. After twelve years, a feeling of restlessness causes him to leave his family behind in order to explore the Far East. Having silenced Cassandra's protestations with the generous provision of funds, Fortunatus travels to the outer reaches of India. On the way, he stops in Alexandria, and there sets up a prospering merchant business. His business achievements bring him to the attention of the Sultan, who shows him his most prized possession, a magic cap (*wünschhüetlin*; p.113) that enables the wearer to be transported to wherever he wishes to be, literally at the drop of a hat. Unfortunately for the Sultan, Fortunatus steals the cap from him, never again to return it. The *wünschhüetlin* complements the magic purse in the most wonderful way, pairing as it does unlimited wealth with unlimited mobility.

When he has finally explored the known world and amassed a sufficient fortune, Fortunatus returns home. Subsequent years are spent in the pleasant company of his sons and wife. But, this life "in all joys"[12] comes to an abrupt halt when Cassandra falls seriously ill. Although Fortunatus spares no expense, he cannot save his wife, and she succumbs to a swift death. From then on he is deprived of all joy. Realizing the futility of money in the face of death (p. 121), Fortunatus falls into deep depression that brings on a bout of illness from which he is never to recover. Again, the very best doctors, despite charging exorbitant sums, can do nothing to ward off death, and soon he passes away.

On balance, does the gift of wealth turn out to be a genuine one for Fortunatus? Fortunatus certainly reaps substantial benefits from his riches; he is able to build a lavish palace and church, find a beautiful wife with whom he has a family, establish an extremely successful business, and indulge his passion for travelling. Hence the unconventional choice proves to work to his general advantage, not least because it enables him to rise from utter destitution to the upper echelons of society. Yet Fortunatus temporarily regrets not having chosen wisdom (pp. 51; 70). While some of the complications arising from the magic purse can be explained by his temporary ineptitude in dealing with the newly found wealth, a deeper problem appears to be attached to the possession of great riches. Throughout the narrative, Fortunatus experiences increased vulnerability to crime on the one hand, and a sense of isolation from his fellow human beings on the other. While he is able to master the practical implications of wealth and thus achieve lasting prosperity, he can do nothing to overcome the state of isolation. For in order to protect the magic purse, it is imperative that Fortunatus tell no one about this possession, not even his wife. Such secrecy condemns him to a degree of loneliness and mistrust even of those closest to him (see p. 76). Indeed, this sense of isolation may qualify this protagonist as a precursor of the modern novel's hero, for whom the experience of isolation would come to be a defining characteristic.

We must note, however, that Fortunatus ultimately does not question his choice. Notably, his last words to his sons concern their use of the magic purse, and he implores them to exercise prudence in order not to forfeit this gift (p. 122f.). Therefore, the narrative presents as genuine the possibility that Fortunatus' choice should turn out to be positive overall, and this suggests that divergence from Solomon's example does not necessarily induce ruin, not psychologically and certainly not financially. Fortunatus' successful preoccupation with money reflects a new reality in contemporary sixteenth

---

12 "in allen freüden", p. 120.

century society. Whether the focus on money allows one to find happiness is a different matter, however, and one that is not entirely resolved.[13]

Fortunatus' story contrasts with that of his sons Ampedo and Andolosia, neither of whom are able to handle the possession of wealth successfully. Andolosia, the more active of the two, persuades his brother to entrust him with the magic purse and leaves home in the hope of emulating his father's adventures. His first stop is France, where he leads an extravagant and morally dubious life-style that pays no respect to the privilege of old aristocracy. As a result, he is forced to move on. In London, he falls in love with the king's daughter Agripina, and tries to buy his way into the king's favour by mounting absurdly expensive spectacles designed to demonstrate his wealth. Foolishly, he then betrays the source of his wealth to Agripina, who promptly cheats him out of his most prized possession. Having eventually managed to win back the magic purse, Andolosia returns to Cyprus, where he brokers the marriage between princess Agripina and the Cypriot crown prince. Held in high esteem by the King of Cyprus, who comes to depend on his financial assistance, Andolosia's prominent position and lavish life-style soon cause rivals at court to envy his position. Before long, he is captured by two jealous counts, divulges the purse's secret under torture and is killed.

Andolosia's brother Ampedo fares no better by comparison. Early on, Ampedo chooses to enjoy the wealth he has inherited within the confines of his luxurious home. On hearing of his brother's disappearance, he destroys the magic cap, even though this might have offered a way of rescuing Andolosia, and promptly succumbs to a deathly disease. Hence both brothers go to ruin. But, their ruin is not a punishment meted out by a superhuman authority; they perish because of their own mistakes. If only they had handled their wealth in accordance with their father's explicit advice and exercised prudence, things might have turned out very differently. The brothers maintain neither secrecy nor discretion, despite having been told to do so *expressis verbis*, and so their downfall seems both inevitable and entirely self-inflicted.

This indicates that a choice such as Fortunatus' may result in success *or* failure, which emphasizes the importance of individual effort and the possibilities inherent in it. Rather than affirming Solomon's choice as the only feasible one after all, the sons' story merely demonstrates that Fortunatus' material success is

---

13 For Haubrichs, this question is answered in the negative. He sees the author's response to life of the early bourgeoisie of the big German towns as "characterized by a strongly felt resignation", and generally regards *Fortunatus* to be "a story of the impossibility of happiness". Wolfgang Haubrichs, "Glück und Ratio im *Fortunatus*. Der Begriff des Glücks zwischen Magie und städtischer Ökonomie", *Zeitschrift für Literaturwissenschaft und Linguistik* 50 (1983): pp. 28-47, here: p. 47.

not a given, and this again reflects the economic realities of the time.[14] The protagonists' outcome proves to be determined not by whether Fortunatus' choice is right or wrong *per se*, but by whether each character has the right or wrong way of realizing it and carrying it out.

III.

Finally, in view of the contrasting development of Fortunatus and his sons, we need to consider the epilogue that concludes the narrative. It reinforces the need to follow Solomon's example, and thus takes us back to the divergence between Fortunatus' choice and its successful outcome, and the Biblical precedent:

> We should note the following about the preceding story:/ if only young Fortunatus had chosen wisdom/ as opposed to riches/ he would have received plenty of it/ and no one would have been able to deprive him of this treasure. Further, through wisdom and reason/ he would have been able to attain worldly goods/ sustenance and great possessions. But because, in his youthfulness and in his quest for lust and joy, he desired worldly riches most of all (as undoubtedly many today would choose a magic purse over all the wisdom in the world), he created trouble and bitterness for himself and his sons/ and although they were able to lead a sweet and pleasant life for a brief while/ they met the end/ that you have all heard about. Consequently, everyone faced with such a choice/ should not consider long/ but follow reason and not his impudent and foolish mind/ and choose wisdom over riches. As did Solomon,/ who as a result became the richest king on earth. [15]

---

14 For Albrecht Classen, *Fortunatus* may serve as an example of the history of mentalities and every-day life in the early modern period in Germany. See Albrecht Classen, "Mentalitäts- und Alltagsgeschichte in der frühen Neuzeit: *Fortunatus*", *Monatshefte* 86, no. 1 (1994), pp. 22-44.

15 "Bey dieser hystoria ist tzu vermercken/ hette der jung Fortunatus im walde betrachtlichen Weißhait/ für den seckel der reichtumb/ [...] erwoelt und begert/ sy waere ym auch mit hauffen gegeben worden/ den selben schatz ym nyemandt hett mügen enpfieren. Durch welliche weißhait unnd vernunfft/ er auch tzeitlich guot/ eerliche narung und grosse hab/ het muegen erlangen. So aber er ym dotzumal in seiner jugent umb freüd und wollust willen/ der weltt reichtumb und guot am maysten liebet und geviele (als ungezweiffelt noch von manigem ain solcher seckel für alle vernuft begert wurd) schuoff er im selbs und seinen sünen mye und bitterkait der gallen/ und wiewol ynen etliche wenig tzeit/ sueß und lieblich was/ nam es doch ain sollich ennd/ wie ir hyerinn vernommen habt. Dem nach ain ygklicher dem solliche wal gegeben wurde/ bedencke sich nit lang/ volge der vernunfft und nit seinem frechen torechten gemuet/ und erkyeß Weißhayt für reichtumb. Als auch gethon hat Salomon/ dardurch er der reichest künig der erdenn wordenn ist." (p. 194f.)

On first sight, this appears to be an outright condemnation of Fortunatus' choice. But, although Fortunatus temporarily regrets his decision, his eventual success may be seen to validate it objectively. How, then, are we to interpret the relation between epilogue and preceding narrative? Proven inaccurate by the preceding story, the epilogue's admonition would seem to be not much more than a formality. In other words, the narrator may have felt the need to pay lip service to traditional standards, while at the same time showing that they have become superseded by a new reality.[16] For the situation in which Fortunatus finds himself is so different from that of Solomon and the hegemony of aristocrats he represents that a new model of shaping one's life may indeed be called for. Notably, both figures occupy a very different place in genealogy. While Solomon succeeds his father David to the throne, Fortunatus' father provides but a negative role model. While Solomon has a place in the world, Fortunatus does not, and his endeavour to find one prompts him to use unconventional means, after more conventional attempts to secure prosperity have been frustrated early on. Solomon's example is a static one, in symmetry with the static nature of medieval society, which seeks to retain a comfortable status quo. By contrast Fortunatus, having hit rock bottom socially and financially, is determined to change his situation. His provocative choice comes with a dynamic of its own, which reflects the dynamics of early modern society.[17]

Fortunatus' choice radically undermines the given paradigm and thus negates tradition. The fact that he succeeds nevertheless generates a sense of unpredictability within the narrative; the rigid template of Solomon's choice is discarded in favour of a more fluid pattern. Such unpredictability not only reflects a new trend in the urban society of the fifteenth and sixteenth centuries, it also was to emerge as an innovative characteristic of fictional literature from this time onwards.[18]

---

16 Jan-Dirk Müller points out that divine influence in the narrative is limited to a restricted area, outside of which other entities are in power, even though this may not always be apparent. See Jan-Dirk Müller, "Die Fortuna des Fortunatus. Zur Auflösung mittelalterlicher Sinndeutungen des Sinnlosen", in *Fortuna*, ed. W. Haug und B. Wachinger (Tübingen: Niemeyer, 1995), pp. 216-238, here: p. 226.

17 Bachorski points out that the individual's struggle for his or her social identity is central not only to *Fortunatus*, but indeed to a number of fifteenth and sixteenth century prose narratives. See Hans-Jürgen Bachorski, *Geld und soziale Identität im "Fortunatus". Studien zur literarischen Bewältigung frühbürgerlicher Widersprüche* (Göppingen: Kümmerle, 1983), p. 39.

18 For an overview of the history of ideas bearing on German literature in the sixteenth century, see Barbara Könneker, "Deutsche Literatur im Zeitalter des Humanismus und der Reformation" in *Renaissance und Barock* (Teil II), *Neues Handbuch der*

While Fortunatus' success appears to justify the choice of riches, this is set against the fate of his sons, and heirs of the magic purse, who go to ruin. One might ask whether, considering this divergence in terms of patterns of success and failure, the sons' negative development should validate the normative example of Solomon after all. Should the choice have been wisdom, which, according to the epilogue would have generated *grosse hab*, great goods, anyway? Not necessarily. The example of a hermit encountered by Andolosia (p. 152f.) suggests that wisdom without riches may not lead to prosperity either. Besides, and more importantly, it is clear that Ampedo and Andolosia perish because they personally are unable to handle the riches at their disposal – not because this is impossible *per se*. And while money can be of no use without a certain degree of wisdom, this does not negate the value of money as such. Although Fortunatus manages to acquire this quality of knowledge over time, his sons do not, in spite of their father's warnings. As we have seen, it is as a result of their own shortcomings that they perish as they do.

Opposing endings for Fortunatus and his sons mean that the narrative ends on a note of ambivalence. Thus the teleological approach of medieval fiction, which sees a narrative development frequently predetermined by programmatic ideas that override individually motivated concerns, is abandoned in favour of a more open and more 'modern' approach. Instead of adhering to a predictable pattern, i.e. Solomon's precedent, the outcome is determined individually, and spontaneously here by the characters' individual talent for dealing with money.

IV.

By resorting to the image of the magic purse, *Fortunatus* represents the source of money in the protagonists' lives in terms of a fairy-tale. Nevertheless, the narrative explores the phenomenon of money in the society of the late fifteenth and early sixteenth centuries in what appears to be a reasonably realistic way. The representation of money in *Fortunatus* gives expression to a new view of money as a value-neutral commodity, whose impact on a person's life depends on their aptitude for using it. *Fortunatus* explores the role of money as a facilitator of social change, and in doing so posits a new literary and socio-economic model, that of the *Aufsteiger*, who may rise in society regardless of his background, provided he respects the privilege and power of the existing aristocracy.

Literaturwissenschaft, vol. 10, ed. A. Buck (Frankfurt a.M.: Athenaion, 1972), pp. 145-176.

The new role of money necessitates a change of paradigm where the definition of wisdom is concerned. Instead of the traditional definition with its strong spiritual component manifest (e.g. in Solomon's example), wisdom is substituted by *experienz*, knowledge acquired through practical experience. Notably, the knowledgeable use of wealth entails knowing when to deceive, or even kill someone, as Fortunatus' encounters show; hence this form of wisdom has lost its ethical component and may take on an almost Machiavellian shape. Equally affected by the depletion of spiritual content in the presence of money is the area of religion. In the example of Fortunatus, we may observe a new manifestation of piety, which is founded on material potency alone. This is evident in the way in which the protagonist's travel itinerary merely ticks off crucial stations of Christian pilgrimage without, it seems, ever pausing to dwell on their spiritual importance (pp. 63-65); it is also apparent when Fortunatus establishes his religious credentials by way of erecting a church, enabled simply by his financial prowess. Thus the narrative hints at the general impact which the excessive presence of money may have on spiritual values, and this in turn could represent a subtle criticism of divergence from Solomon's example after all.

Fortunatus' main achievement, however, is to transcend existing parameters in the discourse on money. Through challenging the example of Solomon this narrative reflects a new economic situation, the outcome of which is by no means certain for the individual. In doing so, the narrative experiments with open possibilities. This has poetical consequences of its own, as the constraints of teleology, characteristic of medieval literature, are loosened. Ultimately, "wisdom versus riches" may turn out not to provide a genuine alternative any more, as the protagonists' experiences indicate how riches must be accompanied by wisdom in some form so as to bear fruit. By demonstrating how traditional patterns of discourse are no longer sufficient to capture a newly unfolding economic reality, *Fortunatus* illustrates the impact of money on human life with new complexity, while simultaneously contributing to a substantial shift in the dynamics of early sixteenth century narrative.

Michael Shields

Songs and Money as a Mirror of the Self. Reflections on Ehrenbote von Rhein's *Spiegelweise*

My paper has two aims. On the one hand it tries to construct a coherent reading of a song which, though apparently famous in the 13th century, has not been much read or understood since. This provides an opportunity, on the other, to make an excursion into the fairly stable though changing cultural and literary conventions within which the text had meaning. According to these conventions, singers supplied "êre" (honour, or rather its commodified equivalent "image" in the form of songs) to their patrons in exchange for "guot" (wealth, for example money, goods or houses). Singers were at pains to show that this was more than just a symbiotic relationship between patrons and propaganda agents. In practice, 13th-century singers seem to have been defined (along with other less reputable travelling entertainers) in terms of this arrangement, as "those who take *guot* in exchange for *êre*".[1] I will try to show that this song deals with the complex relationship between patrons and the money they spend on enhancing their *êre* in song.

I.

The song, a riddle, is a single twelve-line stanza (melodies were frequently long enough for a single stanza to form a song in its own right) set to a melody known as the *Spiegelweise* ('mirror').

> Young man, I will show you a mirror
> in which you shall espy yourself; towards which you should bow down.
> If you have any moral pockmarks then you should scrape them off.
> Look over, look back, look into the world at large!
> and purify yourself of anything that is unbecoming in what is of low worth,
> and strive zealously after that which best becomes what is good.

---

[1] According to the first codification of 13th-century German law (written in 1220-1235), those who took "guot" in return for "êre" had no legal rights, or more precisely and picturesquely, they had "shadow rights": compensation for damages was to be symbolically exacted from a shadow of what they had lost, cf. *Sachsenspiegel. Landrecht*, ed. Karl August Eckhart (Göttingen, Berlin: Musterschmidt, ²1955), p. 108 (section I, 50, §2); p. 234 (section III, 45, §9).

What could be a better mirror?
For gold presents a brilliant appearance,
and copper twinkles nicely.
We recognize the good man by the bad –
God himself says "He who practises virtues is the one we should call noble."
A king's child is anything but noble if he strives for what is not virtuous.[2]

The composer and – by convention – owner of the melody is a professional singer, Ehrenbote vom Rhein (the "messenger of honour from the Rhine"). He almost certainly wrote the text as well, as the melody is believed to have derived its name from its mirror theme (comparable practices have been observed in other songs such as Kelin's *Hundsweise*, named after a stanza about a dog). Apart from this, textual echoes link it to other 13th-century songs,[3] but it is only preserved in a 15th-century manuscript alongside later texts set to the same melody. Little is known about Ehrenbote except that he was highly rated as a singer of "Sprüche" (moral, political and religious songs performed throughout Germany by travelling singers[4]) well into the 14th century: a Franconian, Lupold Hornburg (writing ca. 1348), lists him together with Walther von der Vogelweide, Wolfram von Eschenbach, Konrad von Würzburg, Frauenlob and seven others as one of the twelve masters. His reputation for not mincing his words was still known: "Ehrenbote's song was forthright" ("Des Erenboten sang was sleht").[5]

---

2 Text in *Die Gedichte Reinmars von Zweter*, ed. Gustav Roethe (Leipzig: Hirzel, 1887), p. 537; notes pp. 171-75 and p. 628. This edition will be referred to as "Roethe, *Reinmar von Zweter*" in the remaining footnotes. The only text source is the Colmar Manuscript, Munich, Bayerische Staatsbibilothek cgm 4997, fol.721v-722r. Here and throughout, translations are my own unless indicated otherwise.

3 Compare for example Roethe, *Reinmar von Zweter*, p. 450-51 (no. 79, v. 9-10: "You shall hear who is noble: the man who acts nobly, he whose nobility cannot be led astray or destroyed in any way by a base desire" ("wer edel sî, daz sult ir hoeren:/ daz ist, der edellîchen tuot/ dem niht unedellîcher muot/ sîn edele mac zervüeren noch zerstoeren.") and no. 80, v. 12: "No-one is noble unless he acts nobly" – "nieman ist edel, ern tuo dan edellîchen").

4 Helmut Tervooren, *Sangspruchdichtung* (Stuttgart, Weimar: Metzler ²2001) is an excellent introduction. For an account of the singers see Sylvia Ranawake, "German 'Minstrels' and their Travels", *Forum for Modern Language Studies* 36/1 (2000), pp. 49-62.

5 Text and translation in *Epochen der deutschen Lyrik 1300-1500*, ed. Eva Kiepe, Hansjürgen Kiepe (Nördlingen: Beck/dtv, 1982), pp. 86-88. For an account of the "old masters" in Meistersang see Horst Brunner, *Die alten Meister* (Munich: Beck, 1975).

Unlike other singers, such as Reinmar von Zweter, whose extensive oeuvre happens to have survived reasonably intact, virtually no original texts exist to the three melodies ('Töne') by Ehrenbote that survive. (A 'Ton', the combination of a particular metric scheme with its melody, could continue to be used for the performance of later texts.) In fact, it has been argued that this is one of only two *Spiegelweise* stanzas that can be dated with reasonable certainty to the 13th century, though there may be others. Stylistically and thematically they could belong to the 13th century, but Burghart Wachinger, the author of the most recent survey, thinks they are later, conservative imitations.[6] The *Spiegelweise* was

6 Burghart Wachinger, "Ehrenbote", in Kurt Ruh (ed.), *Die deutsche Literatur des Mittelalters: Verfasserlexikon* (Berlin 1978ff.), vol. 2 (1980), pp. 387-389. The 'genuine' stanzas are Roethe, *Reinmar von Zweter*, p. 537, p. 560 (nos. 255 and 305). Often the quickest and clearest way of referring to Spruch texts is via the *Repertorium der Sangsprüche und Meisterlieder des 12. bis 18. Jahrhunderts*, ed. Horst Brunner

apparently Ehrenbote's most important *Ton* (according to Wachinger perhaps the only genuine surviving *Ton*) and presumably that to which he composed a significant body of texts. Their loss can be attributed to the vagaries of textual transmission rather than to the singer's lack of merit as an author. However, it does mean that the surviving texts are a bit like the tip of an iceberg that has melted below water level.

If this is one reason why the stanza has been ignored, another is that Ehrenbote's existence was wrongly denied in Gustav Roethe's edition of the songs in 1887. Formal and thematic similarities suggest that Ehrenbote's songs were influenced by those of Reinmar von Zweter.[7] This fact, not in itself surprising, led Roethe, who produced what is still the standard edition of the texts, to conclude that there was no such singer and that Ehrenbote's songs were by Reinmar. Wachinger advances two arguments against this: the surviving *Spiegelton* texts may echo Reinmar, but they have a strikingly distinct style unlike Reinmar's, and their melody has a structure typical of the period after Reinmar.[8] As Roethe offers what is still the only interpretation of the text in the notes to his edition, I will outline it briefly; subsequent accounts of the text do not propose alternatives to Roethe's reading.[9]

The stanza engages in the widespread medieval didactic practice of offering a behavioural role-model, a "mirror" for the edification of the young. Roethe observes that the unusual thing about this particular mirror is that unlike most medieval *specula* it contains bad things as well as exemplary ones. He adverts indirectly to the poem's riddle structure (what is the mirror?) by pointing out the unexpectedness of the solution, which he thinks is delivered immediately in lines

---

and Burkhart Wachinger (Tübingen: Niemeyer, 1986-2006), 16 vols., here vols. 3-5, *Katalog der Texte. Älterer Teil*, ed. Frieder Schanze and Burghart Wachinger (1986-91), here referred to by its standard abbreviation "RSM". The abovementioned texts are: RSM [1]Ehrb/1/1a, RSM [1]Ehrb/1/502a/1). In fact, at least one other stanza, (Roethe, *Reinmar von Zweter*, pp. 537-38, no. 256; RSM [1]Ehrb/1/501a/3) looks just as old; the fact that Roethe declared it unauthentic because it was not "Reinmarisch" in sentiment actually speaks in favour of authorship by Ehrenbote. Michael Baldzuhn, *Vom Sangspruch zum Meisterlied* (Tübingen: Niemeyer, 2002), pp.482-486, argues for an early dating of all *Spiegelweise* stanzas but reserves judgement on their authorship.

7 Metrically the *Spiegelweise* resembles Reinmar's *Frauen-Ehren-Ton*. Imitations of this kind between singers were not unusual; cf. Roethe, *Reinmar von Zweter*, pp. 171-175 and p. 376. For some textual parallels see footnote 3.

8 It has a third *Stollen*, ie the musical and metric section (*Stollen* or *pes*) repeated at the beginning is sung a third time at the end of the Ton, resulting in a musical structure AABA.

9 Roethe, *Reinmar von Zweter*, pp. 173, 628. The text summary in RSM [1]Ehrb/1/502a is a replication of Roethe's reading.

4-6. The young man's mirror is the world at large: he is to learn from it with open eyes by studying the contrast between good and evil which he will find in the world. This idea is picked up (if ambiguously) in lines 8-9 by the proverbial observation that even when it is (deceptively?) shiny, copper can be identified as a baser metal by being compared directly with gold. Roethe quotes a number of parallel usages of the proverb in late 13th-century German texts to support this reading, for example in the song by Rumelant von Sachsen: "brass can be detected when seen alongside real gold".[10] At the end of the stanza the young man who is its addressee is left with the choice of being ignoble or noble; Roethe compares the closing, "democratic" idea that true nobility is a question of behaviour, not of birth, with stanzas by Reinmar von Zweter.[11] In fact, the idea is not peculiar to Reinmar and is articulated clearly elsewhere, as in a stanza by Bruder Wernher which I will discuss below.[12] Roethe is irritated by its presentation as a biblical quotation ("God himself says...") because there is no such passage in the Bible. In fact the text may be paraphrasing the Bible, though not verbatim.

Roethe's reading is unconvincing in a number of ways: it selectively avoids interpreting some lines, and the structure of the resulting selection is arbitrary. If the text really means what Roethe says, then it is interlarded with images that distract from the message or go beyond it. Why is the young man to "bow down" to what he sees in the mirror if it is so faulty? If what he sees is the world (lines 4-6), why has it been implied in line 3 that he sees himself? Why is he looking at two things as well as at the world (line 4)? It is possible that the stanza suggests young men should learn from observing the real world (line 4) – this topos is found in 13th-century German literature.[13] But it certainly isn't the whole

---

10 "doch sô wirt gemerket missinc bî dem gold." Roethe, *Reinmar von Zweter*, p. 628.

11 Roethe, *Reinmar von Zweter*, p.450 no. 79, v. 9-10: "wer edel sî, daz sult ir hoeren:/ daz ist, der edellîchen tuot/ dem niht unedellîcher muot/ sîn edele mac zervüeren noch zerstoeren." ("I will tell you who is noble – it's the man who acts nobly and does not allow any ignoble desire to tear or destroy his nobility"); no. 80, v. 12: "nieman ist edel, ern tuo dan edellîchen" ("No-one is noble unless he acts nobly.").

12 Anton E. Schönbach, "Die Sprüche des Bruder Wernher" in *Sitzungsberichte der Kaiserlichen Akademie der Wissenschaften in Wien, philologisch-historische Klasse* 148/7 (1904) and 150/1 (1905), here 148/7, pp. 55-6 (abbreviated below as "Schönbach, *Bruder Wernher*"). Schönbach identifies the proverbs of Bede as the source of the phrase "nobilis ille, qui vivit nobiliter".

13 Hans-Joachim Behr, "Welterfahrung als Beglaubigung. Überlegungen zu einem Argumentationsmuster in der deutschen Lyrik des 12. und 13. Jahrhunderts", in *Reisen und Welterfahrung in der deutschen Literatur des Mittelalters*, ed. Dietrich

message. Why is it delivered at the beginning of the stanza? This isn't how riddles are usually structured – normally the audience is left to guess the solution, not told the answer before the song is even half over. If we are looking at one of Ehrenbote's better texts then the second half of the stanza is unlikely to be just padding and repetition. Keeping for the moment to Roethe's reading, the adage about copper and gold (lines 8 and 9) seems unmotivated unless one is to conclude that it refers to the king's child (line 12) who is copper pretending to be gold. For the argument to add up, one would need to find a link between the king's child at the end of the stanza and the person addressed at the beginning, the young man studying his blemishes as he peers into a mirror which either contains a reflection of his (future?) self or of the world (in which he will ultimately prove to be made either of copper or gold). The text encourages the listener to make conflicting but interesting equations, and one could argue that it is like a mirror because different people see different things in it. The mirror contains the young man's potentially spotted reflection, but may also contain other things, since a mirror is capable of mirroring the entire world (a frequent topos in these texts), and this is one of the reasons why mirrors fascinate: when a mirror is broken into a thousand pieces each piece can reflect everything (another topos); or perhaps the prince will produce his own "reflection" in the world when he makes his mark in the course of his subsequent life (not a topos).

Closer reading shows that the text does not have the straightforward clarity suggested by Roethe's observations, but is deliberately ambiguous in at least three places.

1) The command "you should bow down towards it" ("dar gein soltû dich nîgen") does not make it clear whether the young man is leaning towards the mirror for a better view of his own spots, or bowing down to pay his respects to it.

2) Gold and copper, which one would expect to be presented as positively and negatively connotated opposites, are here both attractively shiny, so that the listener is tempted to accept that each is desirable in its way. Moreover, gold and copper can either be read as concrete examples of the mirror which the listener is guessing at, or as examples of things that are inferior to the mirror (despite their attractive shininess).

3) Similarly, in line 10 "vrum" and "boese", which I have translated as "good" and "bad", need not necessarily be opposites, but might be complementary properties on a scale of values. (This depends how you understand the word "by" ("bî"), which can mean "alongside" or "by means of".)

Huschenbett and John Margetts (Würzburg: Königshausen & Neumann, 1991), pp. 85-95.

Although in my translation I have followed Roethe in reading the line as a conventional restatement of the idea that bad things are recognised by contrast with good ones, it might simply mean "both the good man and the man of low status should be recognised", in which case the line belongs with lines 11 and 12 and has lost the connection with lines 7-9. Formally this reading has the advantage that it is supported by the music structure; the melody of lines 10-12 is a third *Stollen* (*pes*), ie another repetition of the opening musical and metric unit (lines 1-3, 4-6).

If the mirror is not "the world", what is it? After listing objections to Roethe's explanation I ought to be able to suggest a preliminary alternative that is not at odds with the text, even if it isn't the only possible answer. One clue seems to lie in the stage directions given in the text. The stanza is preoccupied with the act of looking at things, and it seems the answer lay in whatever it was the singer showed the young man (and the audience) during the performance. Was the singer holding something mirror-like, or miming the act of holding a mirror in his hand? Was he in fact enacting the role of a fortune-teller? Other 13th-century singers including Walther von der Vogelweide, Frauenlob and Dietmar der Setzer apparently made use of soothsaying as a role in performance, and pope John XXII. banned the use of mirrors for fortunetelling in 1318 and 1326/7.[14] But a modern performer could also explain the mirror *and* the money reference of lines 8-9 in a different and somewhat witty answer by holding his hands out to the audience for money, or holding a coin ready in each hand. Looking into the singer's hand (line 7), the young man and other members of the audience would then realize that it contained his reflection: his *êre* was being measured in terms of what he was supposed put in the singer's hand. Showing what this hypothetical performance might actually have meant to 13th-century audiences in the context of their literary and cultural experience is rather more complex.

---

[14] Cf. Walther's song "Einen tiufel ich beswuor", in *Gedichte Walthers von der Vogelweide*, ed. Karl Lachmann and Carl von Kraus (Berlin: de Gruyter, [8]1923) p. xxviii (title abbreviated below as "Lachmann, *Walther von der Vogelweide*"; songs are identified by the page and line number of the first edition); also Frauenlob's song "Ich hete in einem swerte/ von aventiure einen geist" in Frauenlob (Heinrich von Meißen), *Leichs, Sangsprüche, Lieder*, ed. Karl Stackmann and Karl Bertau (Göttingen: Vandenhoeck & Ruprecht, 1981) I, p. 479 (title abbreviated below as "Stackmann, *Frauenlob*"); and the supernatural anecdote about Setzer in *Chronicon Colmariense*, ed. G.H. Pertz (Hannover: Hahn, 1861), p. 253. On fortune-telling by mirrors cf. Bieler, "Spiegel" in *Handwörterbuch des deutschen Aberglaubens*, vol. IX, ed. Hanns Bächtold-Stäubli (Berlin: de Gruyter, 1941/2000), pp. 547-577, here p. 555 and p. 563. In the 18th and 19th centuries, magic mirrors were provided with a cover that could be opened and closed.

II.

References to money and coin imagery are not infrequent in medieval European literatures. In Latin these tend to be condemnations of corrupt (mainly Roman) clerical practices, for example in song 1 of the *Carmina Burana*.

> A hand that bears gifts makes a saint of a murderer. Coin seals the truce, coin gives persuasive advice, coin makes the rough smooth, coin ends the war. A coin in a priest's hand is enough for the law. You who sit in judgement, you give the coin pride of place.[15]

Vernacular texts are more diverse as they cater for different social classes. What they share with the Latin texts is a strongly outraged sense that it is wrong to convert ethical value systems into financial terms which will destroy them, but the systems are often secular rather than ecclesiastical. The fact that value systems seemed increasingly to be translateable into money terms only made it more necessary to reassert their integrity. When Bertran de Born, a troubadour knight from Périgord, composed a song in the Winter of 1182/83 objecting to a truce between the French and English kings, some of the reasons he gave were financial (while receiving English money the French king lost other revenues as well as military power), but the argument he uses stigmatizes the use of monetary discourse in war negotiations. (One of the conditions of the peace was that Philippe Auguste's widowed sister Margaret was to receive an annuity of 2750 Angevine pounds, calculated at a fixed exchange rate of 53 Angevine solidi against 13 1/3 Sterling solidi, or 4:1.[16]) Real knights don't forego their inheritance for such dirty money settlements.

> Since this peace the two kings have made
> irritates the barons in their thoughts,
> I'll make such a song that once they hear of it
> they will all be impatient to go to war.
> I don't like a disinherited king who stays at peace
> and loses his right,
> until he takes by force what he has demanded.
>
> People think it is vile of each
> to have made a deal that dirties both.

---

15 "Manus ferens munera/ pium facit impium;/ nummus iungit federa, nummus dat consilium;/ nummus lenit aspera, nummus sedat prelium./ nummus in prelatis/ est pro jure satis;/ nummo locum datis/ vos, qui iudicatis." In *Carmina Burana*, vol. I, ed. A. Hilka and O. Schumann (Heidelberg: Carl Winter, 1930), p. 6.

16 For a lively summary of the negotiations see Karl Heinrich Bertau, *Deutsche Literatur im europäischen Mittelalter* (Munich: Beck, 1972), pp. 657-661.

The French crown has five duchies,
and if you count them now, three are missing.
The king is losing the taxes and revenue of Gisors,
and down here Quercy is still in disorder,
as are Brittany and the land of Angumois.

[...]

If the English king gave King Philip a gift and showed him *milte*,
it is proper for him to thank him for it:
he has had so much English coin delivered
that in France he has raised the price of straps and bags to hold it.
Not men of Anjou or Maine,
but sterling coins, were the first troops
to defeat the men of Champagne. [17]

After this portrayal of an unequal battle of men against a supernatural host of sterlings, Bertran concludes with the observation that Philip should attack rather than negotiate in a dishonourable fashion when he could have fought; however, the Burgundians and French have "traded in *êre* for greed" ("Ben ant camjat honor per cobeesa").

The idea that negotiating like merchants for money is not for knights is reformulated in Hartmann von Aue's Arthurian romance *Iwein*. One description of a single combat is dressed up, with somewhat heavy-handed word play, in financial metaphors. The joke exploits the contrast between combat (the currency used by Gawein and Iwein) and money:

> Now I will tell you what happened when the two experienced knights [Iwein and Gawein] faced each other. They husbanded the iron armour that was protecting their bodies, but there was no question of them sparing the swords. With these they displayed great generosity towards the shields, that is, they lavished blows upon them.

---

17 "1. Pois als baros enoia en lur pesa/ D'aqesta patz q'ant faicha li doi rei,/ Farai chansson tal que qand er apresa/ A cada un sera tart que gerrei./ E no m'es bel de rei q'en patz estei/ Deseretatz, ni qe perda son drei/ Tro la demanda q'a fait'a conquesa.
2. Ad ambedos ten hom ad avolesa/ Car ant fait plaich don qecs de lor sordei./ Cinc ducatz a la corona francesa,/ E si.ls comtatz, son a dire li trei./ E de Giortz pert lo ces e l'esplei,/ E Caersins reman sai en trepei,/ E Bretaigna e la terr'engolmesa.
[...]
4. Si.l reis engles li fetz don ni larguesa/ Al rei Felip, dreitz es q'el l'en mercei!/ Q'el fetz liurar la moneda englesa,/ Q'en Franssa.n son carzit sac e correi./ E no foron Angevin ni Mansei,/ Qe d'esterlins foro.ill primier conrei/ Qe desconfiron la gen campanesa. [...]" Translation adapted from *The Poems of the Troubadour Bertran de Born*, ed. William D. Paden, Tilde Sankovitch and Patricia H. Stäblein (Berkeley: University of California Press, 1986), pp. 364-369.

> Each of the knights thought: "What is the use of my effort? As long as he keeps carrying the shield in front of him he is safe." So they hacked the shields away. [...] They lent out more powerful blows than I can tell without asking for any guarantor or pawn, and repayment was made straight away by the other. It is a good thing if someone is eager to pay off his debts at once, for if he wants to borrow he shall get a loan easily. But the two of them had to worry that someone who borrows without repaying the loan is likely to pay for it! They feared that they would have to pay for it if they borrowed but didn't pay it back. For the one who doesn't repay his loans must often suffer for it. They would have had to suffer had they not paid off their loan. Therefore each of them paid it back in such a way that he wouldn't have to pay for it with his reputation. And it was a lot that they had to repay in order to escape a pillorying from death and from those who call out the names of bad debtors. Both granted loans very generously but never sent for repayment because they had brought more than enough principal to the battlefield and also paid back on the spot more than was requested, and sooner. (*Iwein*, 7125-7170)[18]

The portrayal of the give and take of blows as a kind of money-lending is given added point by the fact that there is money on the fight, since the combat has been organised to decide the outcome of an inheritance dispute between a girl and her greedy elder sister – though the knights themselves will not be rewarded except by the enhancement of their reputations. The scene has the effect of asserting the independence of knightly from financial values while showing that this is an unattainable construct in a financial world. Also lurking behind this description is the stereotype (one that would outlast the middle ages) of an aristocrat who runs up unmanageable debts and goes into battle to repay them. Perhaps the implied joke is that sword-blows are the only debts such a knight will repay. Elsewhere in *Iwein* we are given other examples of how courtly culture is dependent on economic considerations. In one episode a chastelain apparently relies disgracefully on the income from a factory of enslaved noblewomen to maintain a courtly lifestyle that has literature as one of its cultural trappings. Generally it is clear that like reading and writing, money dealings are not suitable activities for knights. When Gawein is accused of being a forger in another story (Wolfram von Eschenbach's *Parzival*) this is an attack of the worst kind upon his honour as a knight. When Gawein rejects the accusation by saying that accusers will not find a minting-hammer in his luggage, Wolfram's audience probably laughed at the ridiculousness of the idea. In literature, the currency upon which knights depend is their reputation – their "êre", a combination of their rating on the scales of military prowess ("manheit") and generosity ("milte", Provençal "larguesa"), displayed at festivals and other public events, but also of their ability to conform

---

18 Hartmann von Aue, *Iwein*, ed. G.F. Beneke, K. Lachmann and L. Wolff (Berlin, New York: de Gruyter, [7]1968), pp. 171-72 (title abbreviated below as "*Iwein*").

to aristocratic codes of well-bred behaviour ("zuht") and to protect their dependents from others.

In songs, the references to money are usually about coins as metaphors for moral realities, for example when Frauenlob quotes a proverb about forgery to illustrate a point about political deception at court: "The purer the gold from which a coin is minted, the quicker forgeries will be made of it." ("Je reiner golt, je sneller valsch")[19]; Literary references to forged coin make it clear that it was a familiar enough part of life. Perhaps it is worth remembering that coinage was a more localized commodity in the 13th century, and could be produced by people one possibly knew, such as the local bishop, rather than by an abstract and anonymous authority (we don't normally entertain the possibility of meeting a man who makes our money nowadays). Money was also more transient: bracteates (pennies thin enough for the image imprinted on the front also to be found as a mirror image on the obverse side) were the normal currency in many parts of 13th-century Germany, and because they wore out quickly they were reissued frequently (twice yearly in many parts of Germany[20]), so that it was advisable to spend them rather than hold on to them after they had become invalid as currency.

Singers are not afraid to ask for payment in the texts of their songs. We already find begging stanzas in the earliest surviving German Spruch texts, those of two travelling singers nicknamed Spervogel ("bird of passage") and Herger ("sir beggar"?) dated around the year 1173. These are complaints about the poverty of the singer and his lack of success in finding patronage. The demands for payment still lack self-assurance and compensate for this by resorting to humour. This fits well with the fact that travelling singers had no legal rights.[21] Here the phrase "taking *guot* in exchange for *êre*" still seems to mean that the singer loses *êre* without conferring it upon his patron. In one song Spervogel is tantalised by a kind of beggar's hell: "I was very hungry and entered a garden in which there was fruit. But I wasn't able to get any of it. It was bad luck. Again and again I shook the branches: I never got a single piece of fruit."[22] In another: "It pains me that I have bad luck: this is why I had to depart without taking a drink from a lake, from which a cool spring was flowing with great and mighty

---

19 Stackmann, *Frauenlob*, p. 431.

20 P. Berghaus, "Münzverrufung", in *Lexikon des Mittelalters*, (Zürich 1999), vol. 6, col. 936.

21 See footnote 1.

22 *Des Minnesangs Frühling*, ed. Hugo Moser and Helmut Tervooren, (Stuttgart: S. Hirzel, [36]1977), p. 53. Songs are conventionally identified by the page and line number of the first edition (here 29,13-19).

force, from which many people were quenching their thirst, and were well satisfied. But no matter how often I held out my bowl, it never even got wet."[23] Whether the singers wanted money or some other form of tip is not specified. As the 13th century progresses, singers become more self-confident as a group, elaborating a body of socially justified arguments why they should be rewarded for their services.

The first surviving songs that make more aggressive demands for payment are those of Walther von der Vogelweide. (Around the same time, we find a minnesinger in Vienna, Neidhart von Reuental, asking his patron for a house, in a song that is given the name "Neidhart's shilling".) As well as being an innovative writer of love songs Walther has been credited with transforming the German Spruch into a powerful propaganda tool which he placed at the disposal of imperial politics, so it is not surprising if he looked for a premium fee.[24] Walther did acquire a place he could call home from emperor Frederick II, some time before 1220, and wrote a gleeful song about it:

> Look, world, I have my fiefdom, I have my fiefdom! Now I do not fear the frost on my toes and need not implore stingy lords. The noble, generous king has provided for me so that I will have air in Summer and heat in Winter. Now I think myself better than my neighbours, they no longer look askance at me as they used to. I was poor far too long, through no fault of my own; I was so full of complaining that my breath stank; now the king has freshened it, and freshened up my song.[25]

The key word here is "generous". Demonstrating the right degree of generosity (*milte*) enabled a feudal lord to maintain the bonds between himself and his

---

23 "Mich hungerte harte./ ich steic in einen garten./ dâ was obez innen,/ des moht ich niht gewinnen./ Daz kom von unheile./ dicke wégt ích den ast./ mir wart des óbezìs nie niht ze teile." "Daz ich ungelücke hân, daz tuot mir wê./ des muos ich ungetrunken gân von einem sê,/ dar ûz ein schoener brunne vlôz,/ der was michel unde grôz./ dar kam vil der vremden diet, die wurden hôh gesetzet./ ich bôt dar dicke mînen napf, der wart mir nie genetzet." *Des Minnesangs Frühling*, ed. Hugo Moser and Helmut Tervooren, (Stuttgart: S. Hirzel, 36 1977), p. 45 (23,13-19). Other singers use similar images.

24 Hedwig Herger, *Das Lebenszeugnis Walthers von der Vogelweide. Die Reiserechnungen des Passauer Bischofs Wolfger von Erla* (Vienna: Schendl, 1970), p. 81 and p. 208.

25 "Ich hân mîn lehen, al die werlt, ich hân mîn lêhen./ nû envürhte ich niht den hornunc an die zêhen,/ und will alle bœse hêrren dester minre vlêhen./ Der edel künec, der milte künec hât mich berâten,/ daz ich den sumer luft und in dem winter hitze hân./ mîn nâhgebûren dunke ich verre baz getân:/ si sehent mich niht mêr an in butzen wîs alsô si tâten./ ich bin ze lange arm gewesen ân mînen danc./ ich was sô voller scheltens daz mîn âtem stanc:/ daz hât der künec gemachet reine, und dar zuo mînen sanc." Lachmann, *Walther von der Vogelweide*, 29,15.

vassals, and lords were expected to display it at public events. Their *milte* is described in protracted detail in Arthurian romances and town chronicles as well as by singers. 13th-century references to *milte* are unquestioning: it needed no rational justification in financial terms. (If it did, it would be rejected: extravagant displays of generosity were not justifiable from an economic point of view.) Like any dominant cultural practice, the exercise of *milte* is indispensible for as long as there is an awareness that society could not function without it. If one is to believe the Spruch texts, *milte* is sustainable because it generates generosity like chain letters: there will always be more where that came from. The argument is directed formulaically against those who spend their money maintaining their own property ("dem hûse leben") instead of keeping open house[26]. Such home birds are contrasted with paragons of *milte* such as Alexander the Great and Saladin, who never stopped distributing gifts and consequently were able to conquer the world.[27] The ideal governor was expected to find a moderate balance between economy and *milte*: but where a course of action implies a choice between the two, the songs consistently argue that the courtly values bound up in *milte* (for example trust, loyalty, friendship and respect) are the more important.

Singers had a private interest in encouraging potential patrons to be generous, and this could undermine the objectivity and authority of their moral stance. In the following late 13th-century stanza, the anonymous author was clearly annoyed when Rudolf von Habsburg didn't reward him, but his annoyance renders the criticism of Rudolf less authoritative. Apparently the singer is picking up on a habit of Rudolf's of repeating himself: here Rudolf has apparently said "ich engibe niht" ("I've nothing for you") to begging singers often enough and mechanically enough for it to become a leitmotif.

> The king of Rome gives nothing, though he has a king's possessions; he gives nothing, truly he has the heart of a lion; he gives nothing, he is completely chaste; he gives nothing, but is free of fickleness. He gives nothing, he loves God and honours chaste women; he gives nothing, no man was ever so perfect. He gives nothing, he's free of scandal; he gives nothing, he is wise and pure. He gives nothing, his courts are just; he gives nothing, he loves loyalty and honour. He gives nothing, he's full of virtues; alas, he'll never give anybody anything, why go on talking about it! He gives nothing, he is

---

26 *Iwein*, line 2812. Singers played with the ambiguous term "hûsêre" ("reputation for hospitality" but also "control of domestic finances"). The singer Dietmar der Setzer criticises mean patrons' obsession with "heim" ("home"), cf. *Deutsche Liederdichter des 13. Jahrhunderts*, ed. Karl von Craus (Tübingen: Niemeyer, ²1978), p. 53.

27 Lachmann, *Walther von der Vogelweide*, 19,17f. and 16,36f.

> a warrior with many joyful virtues. He gives nothing, our King Rudolf, no matter what you sing or say of him.[28]

French singers expressed similar dissatisfaction with Philippe Auguste's miserliness.

19th- and 20th-century readers of Sprüche have had problems coming to terms with the amount of time singers devoted to the base activity of begging, and urging their patrons to *milte*. Singers sometimes seem so obsessed by it that one might wonder why they were listened to at all. Some analysis of this has been done in the case of Walther von der Vogelweide, whose work has been more extensively discussed than that of any other singer. Christa Ortmann and Ulrich Baltzer describe the problem as a conflict between the ethos of Walther's poetic persona and the need to look for payment: how can Walther give impartial political advice about the future of the Empire if he is in the pay of one particular camp?[29] According to Baltzer's analysis, Walther hides his dependency on patronage by reversing his formulation of the relationship between poet and patron. Patrons should show *milte* to poets, not because the poet needs money, but because the patron needs an occasion to evince *êre* by demonstrating his capacity for generosity. By supporting Walther the patron reinforces the fabric of society and strengthens the reputation on which his power is based. The goods acquired by the singer are not a reward for his song but rather an expression both of the esteem in which his work is held and of the patron's *milte*, proof that he is acting according to the dictates of fairness by giving the singer, whose status is unjustly low, his due. Baltzer notes that Walther's appeals for *milte* are never found in isolation but always bedded into a network of values: "êre" ("reputation"), "triuwe" ("loyalty"), "zuht" ("good breeding"), and so forth. This

---

28 "Der künic von Rôme ne gît ouch niht, unde hat doch küniges guot/ ern gît ouch niht, erst werlich reht alsô ein lewe gemuot/ ern gît ouch niht, er ist kiusche gar/ ern gît ouch niht, und ist doch wandels eine./ern gît ouch niht; er minnet got, und êret reiniu wîp./ ern gît ouch niht, ez engewan nie man so vollekomenen lîp./ ern gît ouch niht, erst schanden bâr, ern gît ouch niht, er ist wîs unde reine./ ern gît ouch niht, er rihtet wol;/ ern gît ouch niht, er minnet triuwe und êre./ ern gît ouch niht, erst tugende vol,/ ern gît ouch leider nieman niht, was sol der rede mere!/ ern gît ouch niht, er ist ein helt mit zuhten wol gemeit./ ern gît ouch niht, der künic Ruodolf, swaz ie man von im singet oder geseit." RSM [1]Stol/11. Compare the similar song by Unverzagter, "Der künic Ruodolf minnet got und ist an triuwen staete", RSM [1]Unv/3/1.

29 Christa Ortmann, "Der Spruchdichter am Hof. Zur Funktion der Walther-Rolle in Sangsprüchen mit milte-Thematik" in *Walther von der Vogelweide*, ed. Danielle Buschinger and Wolfgang Spiewok (Greifsawld: Reineke-Verlag, 1989), pp. 17-35; Ulrich Baltzer, "Strategien der Persuasion in den Sangsprüchen Walthers von der Vogelweide" in *Zeitschrift für deutsches Altertum* 120 (1991), pp. 119-139.

is true of later singers as well. However, Walther's elite status and proximity to the imperial court mean that he is not the best example to use. There is another singer who discussed the problems of patronage more representatively. Bruder Wernher wrote a particularly high number of begging songs in which he carps at the stinginess of patrons and their inability to distinguish good singers from bad; the verb "twingen", used by Wernher to describe this activity, could be translated as 'hectoring'.[30] There is some justification for thinking that Wernher (active in Austria-Swabia, ca. 1225-1250) gained a certain reputation because his *twingen* benefited singers generally. Another 13th-century singer, Robin, praises him as one of five dead singers[31]: "I will lament Bruder Wernher./ He will give us pleasure for a long time,/ a good hunter who was well able to extract/ property [from patrons] by his forceful singing."[32]. Apart from this it is clear from his songs that Wernher was prepared to commit himself to firm political positions in negotiating the relationship between the empire and the papacy, and he may have been regarded as an honest broker in public life. A feature of Wernher's songs is that he uses the topos of social decline to describe a social transition away from ethical and towards financial codes of behaviour; his *twingen* can be read as part of an attempt to prevent the collapse of social structures. Other better-class singers later in the century continue to justify the exchange of *êre* for *guot* in a similar vein, notably Friedrich von Sonnenburg, who argues that the singer-patron relationship is exactly analogous with that between man and God.

> The man is a liar who says that those who give *guot* in exchange for *êre* are committing a sin, unless He who gives most of all likewise sins in doing so. He gives Christians, Jews and heathen wealth and happy times; He gives us five senses, good fortune, our soul and body, the joy of children, wealth, wisdom, and loving women; this is how forthcoming we find Him. Truly, everything that lives enjoys life by His

---

30 There is no adequate account of Wernher's *twingen* to date. Udo Gerdes, *Bruder Wernher. Beiträge zur Deutung seiner Sprüche* (Göppingen: Kümmerle, 1973), avoids analysing the begging theme and plays down the political dimension of the songs. Cf. the review by Eva Kiepe-Willms in *Zeitschrift für deutsche Philologie* 99 (1976), pp. 118-123.

31 RSM [1]Rob/2. Wernher is dead in the version of the song preserved in the Jena MS, but it is possible that it was originally either a celebration of the fact that Wernher was still alive, unlike the other singers mentioned, or of his recent death. The other singers are: Reinmar [von Hagenau], Walther [von der Vogelweide], Stolle, Neidhart.

32 "... muoz ich klagen/ Bruoder Wernheren lange/ muoz er uns wol behagen./ Er hetzing mit getwange/ kunde wol guot bejagen", RSM [1]Rob/2.

gift. He gives the whole kingdom of heaven to the elect in exchange for His *êre*; that's how lavish He is with gifts.[33]

One of the stanzas in Ehrenbote's *Spiegelweise* complains about God's unfair distribution of *êre* and *guot* and the evils of wealth and may be linked with Sonnenburg's text.[34]

Before returning to the 'mirror' stanza it is worth looking at two of Wernher's songs. The first articulates the fundamental problem of the paid singer's credibility:

> How can a singer survive, since people now take his praise for flattery, his exempla for a joke, his criticisms for the scolding [of an unpaid singer]? Any lord who doesn't follow this fashion will live honourably, and singers will offer him good teaching if he chooses the right ones. What does he really know, the man who says that my praise is lies and calls my criticism scolding? He wants to do without my friendship and wants me to do without his. He should have wiped it off the slate; why is he making me pay for it? God knows that I have always spoken well of upright people, and that I didn't do this out of deceitfulness. I thought I was doing the right thing![35]

As in Walther's songs, the power relations have been inverted and the patron is being threatened with loss of the singer's support. The other song situates *milte* in the midst of other values in much the same way as Walther has done, but spells it out much more clearly. As in the scheme outlined by Baltzer, *milte* is inseparable from honour and singers are the noble poor who by deserve the support of lords.

> They say that nobody is noble ("edel") unless he behaves in a noble fashion ("edellîche"); if that is true, then there are plenty of lords who will have to be

---

33 "Swer giht, der guot durch êre gebe,/ daz sich der sünde sêre,/ der liuget, alder ez sündet der,/ der aller meist dâ gît./ Dem kristen, juden, sô gît er/ dem heiden, merket mêre,/ dem ketzer ouch, swie schande er lebe,/ guot unde guote zît./ Fünf sinne, saelde, sêle unt lîp/ gît er uns, fröude an kinden,/ rîchtuom, wîsheit unt liebiu wîp;/ sus gebende er sich lât vinden./ swaz lenendec ist, daz hât für wâr/ von sîner gâbe daz leben./ er gît daz himelrîche gar/ der rehten diet durch êre sîn; sus kan er rîlich geben.", *Die Sprüche Friedrichs von Sonnenburg*, ed. Achim Masser (Tübingen: Niemeyer, 1979), no. 68.

34 Roethe, *Gedichte*, p.537, no. 256.

35 "Waz sol ein singer sich bewarn,/ sît man diu lop vür smeichen hât/ und ouch diu bîspel vür ein spot, vür schelten twingen zelt?/ Swelch hêrre sich dar niht enlât,/ der mac mit êren wol gevarn;/ dem sîn ouch singer guote zuht, ob er die rehten welt./ Waz weiz an sîme herzen der,/ der mir mîn lop ze lôsen giht, mîn twingen zeime schelten?/ der wil, daz er mîn und ich sîn ze vriunde enber./ daz solte er ab den holzen slân, wes lât ers mich engelten?/ got weiz daz wol, deich den biderben guotez nâch gesprochen hân,/ daz ich daz niht durch lôsen tet; ich wânde, ich haete rehte und wol getân." Schönbach, *Wernher* vol. II, pp. 21-22, no. 45.

ashamed; they have certainly not protected themselves from disgrace ("schande"). Falsehood ("valsch") and stinginess ("erge") live with them. Those two destroy generosity ("milte"), honour ("êre") and the reputation of being noble ("den edelen namen"). Woe to the man that ever had wealth, if he lets himself be pushed by disgrace and stinginess out of a position of high honour ("von hôhen êren")! He should look at poor men of noble desires ("die armen hôchgemuoten") who are able, by using the complete set of courtly virtues ("mit ganzer hübscheit"), to strive for honour ("êre"). A poor man is well-born who behaves in a proper and virtuous way; the man is completely boorish and low-born ("ungeslacht"), no matter how rich he is, who is on the side of disgrace ("schande").[36]

For poor men, exercising virtue means upholding courtly values; for rich men it is expressed through support of the virtuous poor, resulting in a rise in *êre* for the lord and his court. Wernher deliberately portrays *milte* as a manly virtue; the "false" and "stingy" man has been pushed aside as a weakling.

Returning now to Ehrenbote's mirror riddle, it becomes apparent that the singer is using an abbreviated version of the same argument. The rich young man's most important virtue, that which will enhance his *êre* and his survival chances in political life, is his ability to promote virtue in the world by being generous. Whether or not the motto in line 11 ("He who practices virtues is the one we should call noble") is a direct reference to Wernher and/or to Reinmar von Zweter, and/or to its Latin source,[37] there can be little doubt that audiences conditioned by songs like Wernher's could see that its theme was *milte*. As already noted, an advantage of this reading is that it gives point to the reference to copper and gold in lines 7-8: each metal, good in its way, is the singer's index of his patron's virtue. In reality, almost all coinage in 13th-century Germany was copper or silver.[38]

Reviving my earlier speculation (while remembering that it is still exactly that): if the 'mirror' were a coin hidden in the singer's hand, or even perhaps a forged coin, or a coin with the young man's image stamped upon it, the

---

36 Schönbach, *Wernher*, vol. I, pp. 55-57, no. 22. My translation follows the version found in the Jena MS, fol.8^{v}, not that of the Manesse MS favoured by Schönbach: "Man seit daz nieman edele si . nicht wen der edeliche tuot . unde ist daz war des mugen sich genuge herren schamen D[i]e nicht vuor schanden sint behuot . den wonet ouch valsch . und irge bi . die dri vuor terben milte unde ere . und ouch den edelen namen We im daz er ie guot gewan . der sich die schande unde irge lat von hohen eren dringen Her solte sehen die armen hoch gemuoten an . die da mit gantzer hubescheit . kunden wol nach eren ringen Des ist ein armer wol geborn . der truwe . milte . und ere hat . so ist er ein ungeslachter gar swie riche er si der scanden bi gestat ."

37 See footnote 12.

38 Philip Grierson, *Coins of Medieval Europe* (London: B.A. Seaby, 1991), p. 122.

performance situation could develop a number of small jokes that fit together. The young man is perhaps being judged not only by his ability to put coins in his singers' palms but by the quality of the coinage issued by his mint. There is a suggestion in line 3 that it might be deficient: bowing down to look at the mirror image (of his own face?) stamped upon the coin, the young man discovers pockmarks on it – the efflorescence that pits a coin when it contains too much base metal and not enough silver. Another singer, Rumelant von Sachsen (dateable between 1273 and 1276), complains about the copper spots on French "tornoise" (large silver coins named after the town of Tours) and equates them with the falsehood of great lords ("der grozen herren valsch"), to which the honest copper of "heller" and "berner" (coins from Hall and Bern) is preferable.[39] Perhaps the young man has just begun to rule, as it was usual to mark a new reign by issuing fresh coin.[40] Having reached this numismatic hypothesis, it seems academically prudent not to take it further (for example by becoming more specific about which man, or which coins, Ehrenbote may have been referring to), since I have no way of dating or locating the song or its author accurately.

Besides, the fact that the song has survived in a 15th-century manuscript is evidence that later readers found it of more than just ephemeral interest, perhaps because it was seen to comment wittily on the importance of issuing hard currencies, or because it explores parallels between the tangible values of coinage, the *êre* of a ruler, and his song policy. The stanza closes with the observation that a false king's son is like a bad penny. This could be a variation on the idea "render unto Caesar what is Caesar's" – in a way the king's coins are his children, and the ruler who issued good coins was performing an act of *milte*. Walther von der Vogelweide's version of the parable of the coin (Mat. 22, 18-22) adapts the biblical text to the needs of his audience by giving Christ a minting-hammer instead of a coin.[41] Another subsidiary meaning which might be expanded is that the relationship between a king's character and that of his money is analogous to his relationship with his songs. Finally – and this takes my reading back from the realms of financial speculation – the riddle is also self-referential. The mirror is song itself, and its image is revealed to the young man as the *Spiegelweise* is being sung. What he sees in the reflection of song, whether he likes it or not, is his public self.

---

39 RSM [1]Rum/7/3.

40 Cf. for example *Das Stadtrechtsbuch von Sillein*, ed. I.T. Piirainen (Berlin, New York: de Gruyter, 1972), p. 113: "New pence shall be issued when a new lord comes." ("Phenninge sol man vorneuwen wenn ein neuwe herr chümt").

41 Lachmann, *Walther von der Vogelweide*, 11,18.

Michael Fodor

Diderot and the Play of Money

Economic debates dominated the third quarter of the 18th century in France.[1] In 1751 Vincent de Gournay became Intendant of commerce and spearheaded a movement of commercial liberalism, engaged both in administration and in the translation of foreign economic works.[2] In 1756, the future leader of the Physiocrats, François Quesnay, published his first *Encyclopédie* articles. By the 1760s the Physiocratic school was hogging the political conversation with a steady stream of both books and articles in the periodicals they controlled, advocating laissez-faire in the sphere of grain pricing and distribution.[3] By 1774 the economic turn had culminated in Turgot's ministry, which devoted itself, albeit unsuccessfully, to deregulating both grain pricing and guild organisation.[4] Diderot was an agent in and of this economic turn.[5] His *Lettre sur le commerce de la librairie* of 1763 took up the issue of liberalism in the publishing sector; the *Apologie de l'abbé Galiani* of 1770 was a defense of Galiani's attack on the grain liberalism of the Physiocrats. In 1773, he was invited to Russia by Catherine II and two works of political reflection resulted from that sojourn: the *Observations sur le Nakaz* and the *Mélanges pour Catherine II*. During this period, he also completed versions of two of his greatest fictional works, *Le Neveu de Rameau* and *Jacques le fataliste*. Money is present in these two fictional works and in the Russian political works. It serves as form for the fiction and as content for the politics. As fictional form and political content, two monies emerge: in the

---

1 See Catherine Larrère, *L'Invention de l'économie au XVIIIème siècle* (Paris: PUF, 1992).

2 See Takumi Tsuda, "Un économiste trahi, Vincent de Gournay (1712-1759)" in *Traités sur le commerce de Josiah Child avec les Remarques inédites de Vincent de Gournay*, ed. T. Tsuda (Tokyo: Kiokuniya Company Ltd., 1983), pp. 445-485.

3 The bibliography on the Physiocrats is very extensive. For a recent critical synthesis with an excellent bibliography see Yves Citton, *Portrait de l'économiste en physiocrate: Critique littéraire de l'économie politique* (Paris: L'Harmattan, 2000).

4 For a detailed account see Edgar Faure, *La Disgrâce de Turgot* (Paris: Gallimard, 1961).

5 Relatively little attention has been devoted to Diderot's political economy. But see Anthony Strugnell's work and in particular his "Diderot on Luxury, Commerce and the Merchant", *Studies on Voltaire and the Eighteenth Century*, 217 (1985), pp. 83-95.

fiction, the play of money is allowed to develop; in the politics, it must be suppressed.

Le Neveu de Rameau presents the confrontation of two world-views: on the one hand that of the nephew, an unabashed hedonist and on the other, that of Moi, a more ascetic *philosophe*. The nephew's moral philosophy is presented during a discussion on what constitutes a good education. According to the nephew, the ultimate good is sensual pleasure ("jouissances" in French) since a good education is one that "leads to all sorts of pleasures with no risks or downsides".[6] As for the means to pleasure that the good education must focus on, the nephew maintains that it is financial power, symbolised by gold:

> Gold is everything and the rest without gold is nothing. And so rather than stuffing the child's head with maxims, which he would have to forget unless he wanted to become a pauper, what I do is when I have a louis (which is not often) I stand in front of him, I take the louis out of my pocket, I show it admiringly to him, I raise my eyes to heaven, I kiss the louis...[7]

In this world-view, money has become God and the nephew is one of his priests. The passage drives this point home with the gestures employed by the nephew who admires, lifts, and kisses the louis just as a priest would admire, lift and kiss the host. With the nephew then, money has replaced the host and sensual gratification has displaced divine grace.

This shift embodied in Diderot's character ties in remarkably with the theses of Jochen Hörisch. In his trilogy on the poetics of communion, money and media, Hörisch argues for three phases, or what he calls onto-semiologies, in the structuring of European civilisation.[8] Hörisch's historical schema has a theological onto-semiology being replaced around the 18th century by a monetary onto-semiology which in the latter half of the 20th century gives way to a digital one. The second volume on the poetics of money focuses on the advent of the monetary onto-semiology. As Hörisch summarises it, "the monetary orientation to the world succeeds the religious and fulfills its functions precisely, and not

---

6 "Sans péril et sans inconvénient." Diderot, *Oeuvres*, ed. André Billy (Paris: Gallimard "La Pléiade", 1957), p. 494. All translations of Diderot are my own.

7 "L'or est tout; et le reste, sans or, n'est rien. Aussi, au lieu de lui farcir la tête de belles maximes qui'il faudrait qu'il oubliât sous peine de n'être qu'un gueux, lorsque je possède un louis, ce qui ne m'arrive pas souvent, je me plante devant lui. je tire le louis de ma poche, je le lui montre avec admiration, j'élève les yeux au ciel, je baise le louis devant lui." Diderot, *Oeuvres*, p. 491.

8 *Brot und Wein: Die Poesie des Abendmahls* (Frankfurt a.M.: Suhrkamp, 1992); *Kopf oder Zahl: Die Poesie des Geldes* (Frankfurt a.M.: Suhrkamp, 1996); *Ende der Vorstellung: Die Poesie der Medien* (Frankfurt a.M.: Suhrkamp, 1999).

metaphorically but analytically: the coin is heir to the Host, money becomes the God term of modernity".[9] The nephew functions as a fictional embodiment of this onto-semiological shift. As a hoister not of the host but of the coin, he serves as Diderot's representative of the displacement of the divine by the monetary, of the communion coin by the financial coin.

As just shown, Rameau's nephew is a character obsessed by money but perhaps even more remarkably, he is a character that resembles money. He wants to have money, but in another remarkable way, he is money. How so? Via pantomime, which is arguably the most striking feature of the nephew. At different moments, during the dialogue, the nephew mimes colorful people, famous actors or musicians. In other words, at these striking times he is other than himself. An opening description by Moi prepares the reader for this problematic nature of the nephew's identity: "nothing disresembles him more than himself".[10] This disresemblance, this lack of identity, this extraordinary capacity to be other, are also what characterises money. Money understood as purchasing power is indeed ultimately other than itself because it is ultimately the good or service which it purchases. Like the pantomimic nephew, money is disresembling itself and resembling the goods and services it purchases. Functioning money, that is to say circulating money, is transforming itself into the goods or services that it purchases. Conversely, when money ceases to circulate, that is to say when it ceases to disresemble itself, when it ceases to be pantomimic, then it has become dysfunctional money, the money of the miser. The miser in not spending his money, in not transforming his money into goods and services grants money an undue self-resemblance.[11] Or to build on a concept that Hörisch has used in a more recent article, that of convertibility (of religions, of currencies and of electronic data)[12], the miser's perversion of money lies in his refusal of conversion, his refusal to convert money into goods or services. So at the heart of the nephew and of functional money lie a propensity to become other, a willingness to be converted (via pantomime and commercial transactions respectively). In this way, *Le Neveu de Rameau* foregrounds the issue of otherwardness; the nephew and money share what I will call an allological (my neologism: allo-, Greek for other) nature. There is in the nephew as in money a

---

9 Jochen Hörisch, *Heads or Tails: The Poetics of Money*, transl. Amy Horning Marschall (Detroit: Wayne State University Press, 2000), p. 168.

10 "Rien ne dissemble plus de lui que lui-même." Diderot, *Oeuvres*, p. 426.

11 Molière's *The Miser* is the theatrical treatment of this issue.

12 Jochen Hörisch. "Konversionen: Ver-wandlungen von Glaube, Geld und Daten", in *Der blaue Reiter: Journal für Philosophie*, 11 (2000), pp. 10-14.

refusal of self-resemblance, of the same, of tauto-logy. Allo-logy, that would be the name for the play of money and of the nephew.

That allology is also a-logical in the sense that it tends to overcome words. Pantomime is that theatrical art which does without words; money, while perhaps not speechless, is said to speak louder than words. Money and pantomime then both want to speak wordlessly. This marginalisation of words was already potentially present in the nephew's liturgy: a ceremony which begins by replacing the Host, that is to say the body of God, could very well continue by silencing the voice of the body, that is to say the word of God! Add pantomime to the liturgy and that trick is turned. In light of the nephew's and money's allology, Hörisch's onto-semiological shift can be retranslated: in the Bible, God says: "I am that I am" (Exodus 3:14; King James version); in *Le Neveu de Rameau*, a pantomime, like money, speaks wordlessly: it is what it is not.

Diderot's longer novel *Jacques le fataliste* is another occasion for the personification of money. As indicated by the title, determinism constitutes the central issue in the novel and the relationship of the two main characters, Jacques and his master, is one major locus of indeterminacy. That indeterminacy is specified in monetary terms:

Jacques:	It was decreed that you would have the titles (*les titres*) and I would have the substance (*la chose*).
The master:	But in such an accounting I have only to take your place and put you in mine.
Jacques:	You would lose the title and would not gain the substance. Let us remain as we are, we go well together, and let the remainder of our life be devoted to making a proverb.
The master:	What proverb?
Jacques:	Jacques leads his master...[13]

This exchange foregrounds what Marc Shell has conceptualised as the relationship of the inscription and the inscribed. In the chapter "What is Truth: Lessing's Numismatics and Heidegger's Alchemy" of *Money, Language and Thought*, Shell analyzes the question of monetary value as the interaction of

[13] "J.: Il fut arrêté que vous auriez les titres et que j'aurais la chose. Le M.: Mais, à ce compte, ton lot vaudrait mieux que le mien. J.: Qui vous le dispute? Le M.: Mais, à ce compte, je n'ai qu'à prendre ta place et te mettre à la mienne. J.: Savez-vous ce qui en arriverait? Vous y perdriez le titre et vous n'auriez pas la chose. Restons comme nous sommes, nous sommes fort bien tous deux; et que le reste de notre vie soit employé à faire un proverbe. La M.: Quel proverbe? J.: Jacques mène son maître..." Diderot, *Oeuvres*, p. 646.

matter and of form, of precious metal and of institutional signature.[14] In his conceptualisation, the matter becomes the inscribed thing and the institutional signature becomes the inscription. The logic of money then becomes "the logic of the relationship between the inscription and the inscribed thing".[15] When it comes to reading eighteenth century French authors, Shell prefers to read Rousseau rather than Diderot[16] but we can read Diderot in Shell's terms. Diderot's *titre* functions as Shell's inscription on the one hand, Diderot's *chose*, as Shell's inscribed thing on the other. The logic of the relationship of Jacques and his master is the logic of the relationship of inscription and of inscribed thing. The play in that relationship allows for, on the one hand, metallism or substantivism, that is to say the belief that value derives from the inscribed thing, the metal and on the other, nominalism or functionalism, that is to say the belief that monetary value derives from the inscription. The play in the relationship can be paired up with the play in Diderot's novel. The digressions, the authorial interjections, the introduction of possible worlds have enabled critics to characterise *Jacques the Fatalist* as an anti-novel.[17] A monetary realist, reading this anti-novel, would argue that when the inscribed does not found value you get anti-money, and since as in the above passage, the inscribed *qua chose* is not unreservedly masterful you can expect to get an anti-novel. Monetary nominalists on the other hand, would approve of the anti-novel *Jacques le fataliste*. At the least, the inscription has become a player in the game; emitting institutions, be they monetary or literary authorities, have their say. Through *Jacques le fataliste*, literary realism becomes as unrealistic as monetary realism, saying as weighty as assaying.

There is another type of inscription that features prominently in the novel. Jacques is a fatalist because he believes that everything that occurs is preordained: the site of this predestination is "the great register up there" in which everything is inscribed.[18] These inscriptions in the great register are interesting in at least two regards. The first concerns the comparison of monetary and

---

14 Marc Shell, *Money, Language and Thought* (Baltimore: Johns Hopkins University Press, 1982), pp. 156-177.

15 ibid., p. 157.

16 Marc Shell, "The Lie of the Fox: Rousseau's Theory of Verbal Monetary and Political Representation" in *The Economy of Literature* (Baltimore: Johns Hopkins University Press, 1978), pp. 89-122.

17 See Richard G. Hodgson, "The Parody of Traditional Narrative Structures in the French Anti-Novel from Charles Sorel to Diderot", *Neophilologus* 66, no 3 (1982), pp. 340-348.

18 Diderot, *Oeuvres*, p. 514.

registerial inscription. How does Jacques' register function, what do its inscriptions do? Whenever an event occurs, more often unhappy than happy, Jacques accepts it by asserting that it was inscribed in the register. Here then inscription marks the events as necessary. From a logical standpoint, the modality of registerial inscription is necessity. If we turn now to monetary inscription, the signature of the emitting institution (typically the state) makes the metal or paper legal tender. In effect, what monetary inscription does is open up the sphere of purchasing possibility. With money much, perhaps everything, is possible. From a logical standpoint then, the modality of money is possibility. As we have seen, that modality is also that of the antinovel. The evocation of other possibilities, of other possible worlds contributes to the antiness of this anti-novel. Much as money can buy different goods, Diderot's narrator can tell different tales. A purchased good could have been some other good because the money which allowed its purchase could have been used for some other purchase; the tale could have been some other tale. By insisting on possibility rather than necessity the narrator can be said to be a monetary one.

There is a second way in which Jacques's fatalistic inscriptions are thought-provoking. On face value, Jacques's fatalism leads to a dualistic world view of maximal necessity and contingency, or absolute predictability and unpredictability. Now what such a view leaves out is the possibility of a relative predictability. This is where we enter the realm of probability, that is to say the scientific technique of statistics and the business technique of insurance. Now, *Jacques le fataliste* is a novel in which thefts and other business catastrophes abound: most notably, the life-path of Jacques's master is dictated by a swindle. After a business catastrophe (e.g. shipwreck) an eighteenth-century merchant could say that thankfully he was insured or that unluckily he did not insure himself. But Jacques does not reason in such an insurance-framed manner, his reaction is that it was written in the register. A fatalist then does not think in terms of insurance. As it were, fatalism occupies an intermediate position on the historical spectrum that runs from ancient tragedy to modern insurance. Jacques' fatalism amounts to more than tragedy but less than insurance. More than tragedy because personable gods have been replaced by a single and impersonal register, a pre-completed accounting journal if you will. Less than insurance because Jacques does not think in terms of anticipating possible loss and of compensating for such a loss. Godful ancients had tragedy, godless moderns will have actuarial tables, Jacques has a hybrid of immanence (a register) and transcendence (up above). In this way, Jacques reminds us of the nephew's liturgy: with the nephew, we have a coin, that is lifted up but that is not yet inconvertible paper money; with Jacques, we have a register, that is up above but that is not yet a set of actuarial tables.

After having completed the first draft of *Jacques the Fatalist* in 1771 and having revised *Rameau's Nephew* in 1772, Diderot was called to Russia by the Empress Catherine II in 1773. This contact with the Empress resulted in two works: the *Mélanges pour Catherine II* and the *Observations sur le Nakaz* which, while of a fragmentary nature, provide his most extended comments on political administration. Commercial, fiscal and monetary policies are discussed in both works. The most general discussion of money occurs in the *Observations sur le Nakaz*, specifically in observations 138 and 139.[19] Diderot's preoccupation with the problematic of the sign and the thing makes its return here, albeit in a slightly different form than in *Jacques the Fatalist*. Whereas there the problematic focuses on the theoretical origin of value, in the *Observations* it focuses on value-producing economic sectors. In *Jacques* the question pointed to was what gives money its value, the matter or the form, the inscribed or the inscription. The Russian question is whether wealth is increased by producing agricultural goods or monetary goods, grain or guineas. Diderot is hereby positioning himself in the central contemporary debate on whether only land can generate a surplus (the position of the Physiocrats) or whether manufacturing and commerce are capable of doing so (the position of Gournay's followers and of Forbonnais among others). In the first move of Diderot's argument, agricultural goods are granted the status of things and monetary goods those of signs. In the second move, Diderot proceeds to downgrade the status of signs. He argues first that an agricultural country has access to both things (grain) and signs (money) via the sale of things, whereas a pecuniary land has only the sign which, Diderot postulates, it will in the long run have to turn over completely to the agricultural country. In the final paragraph he moves on to the mines of Peru and argues that this metallic extraction amounts only to an increase in the quantity of signs and that in turn leads to a decrease in the value of the sign. The last line reads as a marriage of Voltaire (who in *Candide* famously defended the value of cultivation) and Quesnay (whose agricultural realm was a realm of fields): "Fools, we have enough gold and silver or signs; close down your mines and start cultivating fields".[20]

How does Diderot's political prescription relate to his fictional practice? How does the prescriptive money relate to the imaginary money? Whereas in the fictional works, there is a certain *laissez-faire* with regard to monetary signs, embodied in the nephew's pantomime or in the fatalist's use of the play of title and thing, in the political works Diderot argues for sign control. The monetary

---

19 Diderot, *Oeuvres (Tome 3, Politique)*, ed. L. Versini, (Paris: Robert Laffont), pp. 574-575.

20 ibid., p. 575.

sign must follow the agricultural thing and more unambiguously than the Master follows Jacques. Monetary signs must not be allowed to proliferate, unlike the alternative narratives in *Jacques*. In Observation 138 this semiophobia is extra-monetary – monetary signs are compared to non-sign things and the comparison has agricultural things dominating monetary signs. In Observation 104[21], the semiophobia takes an intra-monetary turn: here it is different forms of currency that are compared. Cash is assimilated to a thing, credit to a sign, and the relationship of sign to thing has become unhinged. Specifically, Diderot is addressing the problem of high prices in Russia and explains this phenomenon by the fact that since debtors often default, merchants feel forced to post a high price. The surpluses generated by high-priced cash payments should, according to the merchants's calculations, cover the defaults in credit payments. Here then, bills do not function as a trustworthy sign of coin; the sign, soft bills, is less than the thing, hard cash. To bring signs under control, to make signs as good as the thing, Diderot proposes a nationalisation of the credit recovery system. So, be it from an intra- or extra-monetary standpoint, the political entails a semiophobia: Diderot frets over the refusal to transform sign into thing (pay the bill at due date) or the temptation to forget things for signs (to forget agriculture for commerce).

One other moment of monetary insecurity is worth scrutiny. Note 40 in the *Mélanges pour Catherine II*[22] is entitled "About monies". While the title would lead one to expect economic prescription the content is in fact aesthetic. Rather than offering up monetary policy, Diderot advises the empress to pay greater attention to the beauty of the coins that she mints! He explains that coins, more even than public monuments, serve as the archeological touchstone of a civilisation. In this sense, the record of a sovereign is only as good as her coins. And so Diderot enjoins Catherine to foster "beautiful, sublime monies".[23] Here two aspects of money are being addressed and indeed revised: money's temporality and money's purpose. Traditionally the monetary arrow of time points from present to future. That direction is embodied in the traditional third function of money, the reserve function, which has money function as a store of value from present into the future. In Note 40, Diderot is suggesting a reversal of the direction: money looks backward in time rather than forward; it does not buy something in the future, it tells us something about the past. Much like the temporality of money is reversed, so is its purpose. Money is not a fount of purchasing power but a mark of aesthetic achievement. The inscription, a

---

21 ibid., pp. 557-558.

22 "Des monnaies", ibid., p. 328. Observation 103, while less extensive, is similar in content, see ibid., p. 557.

23 "Ah! madame, de belles, de sublimes monnaies.", ibid., p. 328.

potential source of value uncertainty, has in effect been de-monetised; the coin is here metamorphosed into sculpture. Note 40 serves to aestheticise the monetary. Coming back to the issue of political semiophobia, to Diderot's unease over money as a site for the anarchy of signs, Note 40 begins to appear as a form of wishful money-laundering. The arrow of money has been reversed and unbarbed...

Money then, through the problematic of thing and sign, inhabits the texts of Diderot. Money gives birth to two Diderots, based on varying valence granted to the possibility of disresemblance (to use the defining characteristic of the nephew). In politics, Diderot prefers a very short leash so as not to let the sign wander. He advises the Russian sovereign to restrain the play of money. In poetics though, money is allowed to play. It is that play of money which makes for the enchantments of those personifications of money, the nephew, Jacques and the master.

William H. Carter

"Uralte und nie gehobne Beschweerde": Goethe, *Faust*, and Taxes

> Our new constitution is now established, and has an appearance that promises permanency: but in this world nothing can be said to be certain, except death and taxes!
>
> Benjamin Franklin[1]

Benjamin Franklin's equation of death and taxes remains an age-old adage for good reason. The uncertain world has become no more reassuring, and one can still count on two things: the guaranteed end to all things living and regular, eternally recurring taxation. On a more positive note, performing one's civic duty by paying taxes contributes to the welfare of the state, providing a fleeting sense of solidarity with fellow taxpayers and, perhaps, momentary solace in an insecure world. Yet, one rarely has the time to reflect upon taxation because taxes continue to accrue – even after death. Franklin, in fact, was not the first to connect death and taxes. In 1762, Daniel Defoe writes: "things as certain as death and taxes, can be more firmly believed. The Devil does not have a cloven foot!"[2] Although the devil's appearance might seem out of place here, the mention of taxes is what stands in relief. The quotation comes from a chapter titled "Of the extraordinary appearance of the Devil, and particularly of the cloven foot" in Defoe's lesser-known *The History of the Devil*. As devilish dealings are by no means limited to any given genre, their histories must accordingly consider their various transactions, including taxation. Just prior to equating death and taxes, Defoe names the well-known account of Dr. Faustus, thus allowing the Faust legend to usher in the proverbial certainties and all the questions surrounding them.

By the time Defoe published *The History of the Devil* in 1762, Goethe had already begun his engagement with the Faust tradition, one that famously lasted a

---

1 Benjamin Franklin, Letter to Jean-Baptiste Le Roy (13 November 1789), in *The Private Correspondence of Benjamin Franklin* [...], 3rd ed., vol. 1 (London: H. Colburn, 1818), p. 259.

2 Daniel Defoe, *The History of the Devil* [...], 6th ed. (Boston: C.D. Strong, 1848), p. 207.

lifetime. What has received considerably less attention is Goethe's equally longstanding interest in matters of taxation, which also began during his childhood as he describes in book I of *Aus meinem Leben. Dichtung und Wahrheit* (*From my Life: Poetry and Truth* [1811]), and which culminates in the final scene he wrote for *Faust II*. Taxation traverses Goethe's literary corpus, as Alfons Pausch demonstrates in *Goethe und die Steuern*, where he catalogues the many scenes in Goethe's œuvre that refer to taxation. They range from *Götz von Berlichingen* and *Egmont* to the *Wilhelm Meister* novels and, of course, *Faust*.[3] Pausch exhibits his enthusiasm for the topic of taxation when he characterises Goethe's "human tragedy" [Menschentragödie] as a "tax tragedy" [Steuertragödie].[4] Perhaps not surprisingly, he also wrote a book called *Schiller und die Steuern*. While Pausch's zeal for taxation clearly colours his reading of *Faust*, his overstated remark underscores an overlooked aspect of Goethe's literary work, namely, the role that Goethe's decade-long experience in Weimar as a senior advisor to Duke Carl August plays in *Faust*, not only in the background but also in the specific, official language Goethe chooses. One scene in *Faust II* deserves a closer reading in light of Goethe's tax writings around 1785. In "The Anti-Emperor's Tent" ("Des Gegenkaisers Zelt"), the final scene of Act IV, Goethe repeatedly names different types of taxes, both legitimate and illegitimate, within both secular and sacred contexts. In the scene, Goethe raises issues of credit due and debt incurred, gold coins and the Golden Bull, along with questions of inheritance and its relevant taxation.

"The Anti-Emperor's Tent" begins with some comic relief by the couple Quickloot [Eilebeute] and Get-Quick [Habebald].[5] In contrast to their allegorical counterparts in the masque scene of Act I, Quickloot and Get-Quick are described by the Emperor's guards as "ghost-like" [gespensterhaft] (10836), while the currency they deal with is material: gold coins rather than paper money, or "phantom money" [Papiergespenst der Gulden] (6198), as Mephistopheles calls it. In Act I, Mephistopheles promotes the new currency for its convenience and ease of use: "These notes, when used in lieu of gold and pearls, / are handy, too;

---

3 Alfons Pausch, *Goethe und die Steuern* (Stuttgart: Fachverlag für Wirtschafts- und Steuerrecht, 1961), pp. 43-59.

4 ibid., p. 54. All undocumented translations are my own.

5 Johann Wolfgang von Goethe, *Faust*, ed. Albrecht Schöne, 4th rev. ed., vol. 1 (Frankfurt a.M.: Deutscher Klassiker Verlag, 1999). Translation: Johann Wolfgang von Goethe, *Faust I & II*, ed. and trans. Stuart Atkins (Princeton: Princeton UP, 1994). All quotes are from these editions.

you know right off how much you own."[6] Carrying money's weight in gold, however, is no simple task as Quickloot discovers when she attempts to lift a treasure chest full of it: "This is a fiendishly great weight! / I cannot lift or carry it."[7] Even with the encouragement of her partner in crime, who reminds her to lift with her legs, the weight of their loot proves more than she can handle. The chest falls to the ground and bursts open. Her attempt to gather its loose contents also fails as coins fall through a hole in her apron. When the Emperor's guards enter the tent and inquire into the couple's intentions, Quickloot and Get-Quick explain that as victorious soldiers they are simply liberating well-deserved spoils from the conquered Emperor. One of the guards deems their actions a blatant disregard for the chain of command and unbecoming of a soldier, to which Get-Quick rejoins that any question of honesty should be reconsidered within the context of taxation: "We know your kind of honesty, / you call it requisitioning!"[8] Goethe mentions here for the first time a specific type of tax. *Kontribution* was protection money paid to conquering armies or lands in order to prevent plundering and was a particular burden in the 18th century, as Ulrich Gaier points out.[9] Get-Quick sees no substantial difference between their crude collection attempt and its sanctioned, stately equivalent. The slapstick comedy that introduces this scene then turns to the pomp and circumstance associated with the new governing body.[10]

The Emperor and his four princes enter conversing about their expeditious triumph. Concerned less with the means employed in his service than with tending to its rewards, the Emperor's first order of business is to secure his

---

6 "Ein solch Papier, an Gold und Perlen statt, / Ist so bequem, man weiβ doch was man hat." (6119-20)

7 "Das hat ein mörderisch Gewicht, / Ich heb es nicht, ich trag es nicht." (10803-04).

8 "Die Redlichkeit die kennt man schon. / Sie heiβet: Kontribution." (10827-28)

9 "Beginning in the middle of the 18th century, [requisitioning] becomes an increasingly heavy burden on the population of a large part of Europe. In Lessing's *Minna von Barnhelm*, Tellheim's desperate situation occurs as a result of his attempt to avoid paying the excessive contributions extorted from the estates of defeated Saxony." ["Seit Mitte 18. Jh.s ein immer schwerer werdender Druck auf die Bevölkerung groβer Theils Europas. In Lessings *Minna von Barnhelm* entsteht Tellheims verzweifelte Lage nur dadurch, daß er es sich ersparen wollte, die überhöhten Kontributionen von den Ständen des besiegten Sachsen abzupressen."] Johann Wolfgang von Goethe, *Faust-Dichtungen*, ed. Ulrich Gaier, vol. 2 (Stuttgart: Reclam, 1999), pp. 1015-16.

10 Cf. Shakespeare's *Othello*: "Farewell the neighing steed, and the shrill trump, / The spirit-stirring drum, th'ear-piercing fife, / The royal banner, and all quality, / Pride, pomp, and circumstance of glorious war!" (III.iii. 353-356) William Shakespeare, *The Complete Works* ed. John Dover Wilson (London: Octopus Books Ltd, 1981), p. 973.

legacy: "To make secure forthwith my line, this court, our realm, / I join my lot with that of you four worthy men".[11] He awards the princes titles and duties corresponding to the imperial Golden Bull, the 1356 decree regulating the procedure for the election of the German King as well as extending privilege and indisputable inheritance.[12] The Emperor first appoints the *Erzmarschall* [Arch-Marshal], or *Erbmarschall* [Inheritance-Marshal] as Albrecht Schöne's version has it.[13] '*Erbmarschall*' may well be one of the numerous 'mistakes' in the scene, but it resonates with the central role that inheritance plays in both this scene and *Faust* in general. The Emperor's next appointments are the *Erzkämmerer* [Arch-Chamberlain] as head of domestic staff and the *Erztruchsess* [Arch-Steward] in charge of the grounds and hunting grounds. To the fourth prince, the Emperor awards the title of *Erzschenk* [Arch-Cupbearer], overseer of the realm's wine cellars. He adds that while the appointees should in no way doubt his trust and confidence in them, giving his word does not suffice:

> The Emperor's word alone enforces these donations,
> but to attest the fact a formal deed's required
> that bears his signature.[14]

---

11 "Deshalb denn ungesäumt, verbind' ich mich sogleich / Mit euch Vier Würdigen, für Haus und Hof und Reich" (10871-72)

12 Goethe first encountered the Golden Bull as a child in city hall, where a 1766 painting by Johann Daniel von Olenschlager hung. In book I of *Aus meinem Leben. Dichtung und Wahrheit*, Goethe recalls the work by the councilman and mayor of Frankfurt am Main. Later in book IV he remembers being around as Olenschlager wrote his *New commentary on the Golden Bull of Emperor Carl IV* (*Neue Erläuterung der Goldenen Bulle Kaisers Carl IV*). Goethe consults this book in July 1831 while preparing "The Anti-Emperor's Tent". Albrecht Schöne underscores the importance of the Golden Bull as a model for the scene and notes that instead of appointing the seven Electors mandated by the Golden Bull, Goethe's version has only five with the Archbishop representing three clergymen. Cf. Albrecht Schöne, *Faust Kommentare*, 4th rev. ed., vol. 2 (Frankfurt a.M.: Deutscher Klassiker Verlag, 1999), p. 689.

13 Schöne remarks: "The symbolic posts of the Electors for the imperial leader are also described in the following as *arch*-posts, which later became *heritable*-posts in noble families for their areas of rule and are also named as such in the coronation report in *Truth and Poetry*." ("Auch im folgenden werden diese symbolischen Dienste der Kurfürsten für das Reichsoberhaupt als *Erz*-Ämter bezeichnet – die später zu *Erb*-Ämter in Adelsgeschlechtern ihres Herrschaftsbereichs wurden, im Krönungsbericht in *Dichtung und Wahrheit* auch so benannt sind." Ibid., p. 696).

14 "Des Kaisers Wort ist groß und sichert jede Gift, / Doch zur Bekräftigung bedarfs der edlen Schrift, / Bedarfs der Signatur." (10927-29)

As the Emperor begins to explain the necessity and benefits of setting his wishes down in writing, he sees the Chancellor-Archbishop [*Erzbischof / Erzkanzler*] approaching. He is just the right person to oversee the traditional formalities that command various forms of donation and taxation.

In order to insure the Emperor's legacy and their own, the five electoral princes will have complete authority over the empire and maintain all territorial rights. Accordingly, they shall collect all the proceeds of the land:

> All taxes, tributes, rents, safe-conducts, tolls, and fiefs,
> the royalties of mines, salt-works, and mints, are yours.[15]

In addition to the various forms of taxation, they will benefit from natural resources and have the right to issue hard currency. The materiality of coins, based not on a signature alone but on their substance, again sharply contrasts with the issuing and circulation of paper money in Act I. Wolf Kittler demonstrates in his reading of Goethe's *Fairy Tale* (*Märchen*) that Goethe deals with coins and, specifically, their intrinsic value in an official report dated 5 November 1793.[16] In the coin report, Goethe writes: "money is not money because of the stamp, rather because of the certain intrinsic value."[17] The question of intrinsic value is fundamental to Goethe's tax concept as well, as we shall see.

More than a decade earlier in 1782, Goethe prepared a *Short History of Taxes in Saxony* (*Kurze Geschichte der Abgaben in Sachsen*) that underscores various forms of taxation. Safe-conducts [*Geleit*], tolls [*Zoll*], and rents [*Landbethen*] count among the oldest, undated original taxes [*Urabgaben*]. Following these are a number of taxes that date from the fifteenth century and include taxes on goods, beer, and income. Goethe notes that since the fourteenth century taxes have been paid in kind – generally ten percent – rather than in coin, a practice that continued well into the late-eighteenth century.[18] Moving ahead to the seventeenth century,

---

15 "Dann Steuer, Zins und Beet, Lehn und Geleit und Zoll, / Berg-, Salz- und Münzregal Euch angehören soll." (10947-48)

16 Wolf Kittler, *Die Geburt des Partisanen aus dem Geist der Poesie: Heinrich von Kleist und die Strategie der Befreiungskriege* (Freiburg: Rombach, 1987), pp. 150-62.

17 "[D]as Geld (sey) nicht durch den Stempel, sondern durch den innerlichen gewissen Werth Geld." Johann Wolfgang Goethe, *Amtliche Schriften*, ed. Helma Dahl, vol. 2, 1 (Weimar: Hermann Böhlaus Nachfolger, 1968), p. 379.

18 To this day, tax payments in kind continue to be an option in certain parts of the world. Consider the case in Russia. *The Economist* reports: "Investigators appointed by the president revealed that Russia's biggest enterprises ignored 29% of their taxes and paid another 63% in kind, with goods and services the government might or might not want. In lieu of $80,000 in taxes, one company reportedly offered the government ten tonnes of toxic chemicals". "Simplifying Tax Systems", *The Economist*, April 16, 2005, p. 61.

he introduces the state and correlates its needs with the taxes it levies: "In the seventeenth century, the needs [*Bedürfnisse*] of the state increased and correspondingly taxes [*Abgaben*], especially consumption and trade taxes."[19] Throughout his tax writings, Goethe frequently addresses the dyad of *Abgaben* and *Bedürfnisse* from the perspective of both the subject and the state. Though it may appear naïve, Goethe forecasts the nineteenth-century emergence of "political economy" [*Nationalökonomie*] in Germany, which as Keith Tribe explains, "was concerned with the general principles of economic life which governed the matter in which needs arose, were satisfied, and in so doing contributed to the progress of popular wealth."[20]

In 1785, Goethe wrote an extensive report on the tax situation in a local farming community, in which he presents the following view on taxes:

> Taxes are such fees, which have been imposed by sovereign princes to maintain and protect the state, deter common peril, [and] promote general wellbeing, which should also be levied with universal equality whenever possible. The foundation upon which they rest is an intrinsic value of goods; they stand in relation to the yield itself.[21]

Taxes [*Steuern*] number among the many fees [*Abgaben*] that Goethe notes in his *Short History of Taxes in Saxony*, but they also encompass the broader notion of taxation, both in Goethe's time and now.[22] In his view of taxation, Goethe emphasizes the interdependence between state and subject and reiterates that the state's needs stand in mutual, corresponding relationship to those of its subjects. Taxes provide the state with the means to protect itself as well as to "deter common peril" and "promote general wellbeing". Goethe's employment of "an intrinsic value of goods" is unique in his tax writings up to this point and

---

19 Johann Wolfgang Goethe, *Amtliche Schriften*, ed. Reinhard Kluge, vol. 1 (Frankfurt a. M.: Deutscher Klassiker Verlag, 1998), p. 158.

20 Keith Tribe, *Governing Economy: The Reformation of German Economic Discourse 1750-1840* (New York: Cambridge UP, 1988), p. 174.

21 "Steuern [sind] solche Abgaben die von dem Landesherren zur Erhaltung und Beschützung des Staats, zu Abwendung gemeiner Noth, zu Förderung gemeinsamen Bestens auferlegt worden, die denn auch mit einer allgemeinen Gleichheit womöglich erhoben werden sollen. Das Fundament worauf sie ruhen, ist ein innrer Werth der Güter, sie haben ein Verhältniß zu dem Ertrag derselben." Goethe, *Amtliche Schriften*, op. cit., p. 272.

22 In his very detailed discussion of finances up to Goethe's 1783 reform, Fritz Hartung writes: "A property tax, simply called tax, constituted the foundation of the tax system in all three regions." ["Die Grundlage des Steuersystems bildete in allen drei Landschaften eine Grundsteuer, schlechthin die Steuer genannt."] Fritz Hartung, *Das Großherzogtum Sachsen unter der Regierung Carl Augusts 1775-1832* (Weimar: Hermann Böhlaus Nachfolger, 1923), p. 44.

contributes to a long tradition of philosophical and economic debate on the subject. The discussion of intrinsic value dates back as far as Plato and Aristotle. Jean-Joseph Goux contrasts their respective views on money and its intrinsic value:

> Aristotle [...] maintained that money is not without an intrinsic value, that it is marked with the sign of its value. For Plato, value is thus fundamentally separate from monetary value, and he defends the notion of money as *arbitrary*, a notion that, through Berkeley and Steuart, will typify the idealist tendency in philosophical and political economy [...].[23]

Intrinsic value remains fundamental to economic discussions in France and Italy well into the eighteenth century, as Foucault reminds us in *The Order of Things*.[24] Late eighteenth-century Germany, however, was slow to import the latest economic theories, with the exception of those by Sir James Steuart. The prominent Scottish economist and contemporary of Adam Smith wrote extensively about intrinsic value during his stay in Tübingen, where he lived for a number of years beginning in 1757 and where he wrote a dissertation on the German coin in 1761 dedicated to the Duke of Württemberg. Goethe's use of intrinsic value in his tax report and monetary writings reflects both contemporaneous economic theory and his own practical experience in taxation and finance matters in Weimar for almost a decade at this point, his most productive year as a public official.[25]

---

23 Jean-Joseph Goux, *Symbolic Economies: After Marx and Freud*, trans. Jennifer Curtiss Gage (Ithaca: Cornell UP, 1990), pp. 95-96.

24 Michel Foucault, *The Order of Things: An Archeology of the Human Sciences* (New York: Vintage, 1994), pp. 174-80.

25 1785 was a significant year in terms of Goethe's production of official writings: "In 1785 Goethe reaches the remarkable peak of 91 pages, whereas the 16 pages from 1786 already announce his lack of enthusiasm and the flight to Italy." ["Das Jahr 1785 bildet einen einsamen Gipfel mit 91 Seiten, während sich in den 16 Seiten des Jahres 1786 schon Goethes Unlust und die Flucht nach Italien ankündigt."] Friedrich Sengle, *Das Genie und Sein Fürst: Die Geschichte der Lebensgemeinschaft Goethes mit dem Herzog Carl August von Sachsen-Weimar-Eisenach. Ein Beitrag zum Spätfeudalismus und zu einem vernachlässigten Thema der Goetheforschung* (Weimar: J. B. Metzler, 1993), p. 14. The same year that Goethe includes "an intrinsic value of goods" ["ein innrer Werth der Güter"] in his tax report, Kant also writes of the "intrinsic value of the person" ["innere[r] Werte der Person"] in the first section of *Grundlegung zur Metaphysik der Sitten* (*Foundations of the Metaphysics of Morals*). Cf. Immanuel Kant, *Grundlegung zur Metaphysik der Sitten*, ed. Karl Vorländer, 7th rev. ed. (Hamburg: Felix Meiner, 1994), p. 11. A comparison of the two theories of value shall be the subject of another study.

Let us return to "The Anti-Emperor's Tent", where the Emperor continues with the topic of succession. Although he is full of life, he must consider the future and calls upon those present to name the heir to his throne, when the time comes. The Archbishop affirms this wish, and the Emperor emphasizes the line of inheritance: "However you increase what you've received from us, / it shall descend upon your eldest sons entire."[26] Having declared his legacy, all that remains is its commitment to paper and the Emperor's signature. After he dismisses the princes, so that they may reflect on the day's events, the Chancellor-Archbishop remains. He tells the Emperor: "The Chancellor withdrew. The Bishop still remains."[27] And as the latter, he voices fatherly concerns about his son's devilish dealings. The Bishop warns of the Pope's likely reaction when he gets word of the Emperor's recent, demonically facilitated success (10982). Needless to say, the Pope will not be pleased:

> The Pope, once he's informed, will pass a penal judgment
> that shall with sacred bolts destroy your sinful realm.[28]

That is, unless the Emperor donates land to the Church. He hastily agrees, and as soon as the Archbishop begins the process of absolution, the Emperor feels immediate release from his sins. The Archbishop, returning to the role of Chancellor, reminds the Emperor that certain documentation is required to finalize the process, and the Emperor readily agrees to sign a deed of transfer. As the Archbishop begins to leave, he pauses to add the following:

> You will, besides, devote to the work's furtherance,
> in perpetuity, all local revenues:
> tithes, tribute, rents.[29]

The Emperor has agreed to contribute not only his property but also its tax proceeds. They shall fund the construction, maintenance, and management costs of the Church's new property "für ewig". Not surprisingly, the Emperor curses the day he engaged the services of the devil. While pacts with the devil frequently end in either death or renunciation, the Emperor's repudiation comes with the arrival of the taxman, as it were. Before the Archbishop makes his final exit, he

26 "Und wie ihr auch vermehrt was ihr von uns empfangen, / Es soll's der ältste Sohn in gleichem Maβ erlangen." (10969-70)

27 "Der Kanzler ging hinweg der Bischof ist geblieben." (10977)

28 "Wenn dieser es erfährt schnell wird er sträflich richten, / Mit heiligem Strahl dein Reich das sündige zu vernichten." (10985-86)

29 "Dann widmest du zugleich dem Werke, wie's entsteht, / Gesamte Landsgefälle: / Zehnten, Zinsen, Beet / Für ewig." (11023-25)

has just a few more conditions. As part of the Emperor's absolution, the Church will also profit from taxes levied on the stretch of coastal land that the Emperor granted to Faust:

> Your pardon, Sire! That man of dubious character
> received in fief our coasts; on them the ban will fall
> unless, in penitence, to our consistory
> there too you cede the tithes, the rents, the dues, the taxes.[30]

For the fourth time in the scene, Goethe names specific taxes. The fees [*Abgaben*] listed now include: requisitioning [*Kontribution*], tax [*Steuer*], rents [*Zins*], tribute [*Beet*], fiefs [*Lehn*], safe-conduct [*Geleit*], tolls [*Zoll*], tithes [*Zehnten*], dues [*Gaben*], and taxes [*Gefälle*]. During his first decade in Weimar, especially leading up to the trip to Italy, Goethe dealt extensively and repeatedly with taxation, which he at one point in his official writings describes as the "ancient and never withdrawn complaint" ["*uralte und nie gehobne Beschweerde*"].[31] The subject of taxation developed into a lasting engagement that pervades Goethe's literary corpus and concludes with this final scene that he composed for his "main business".[32]

"The Anti-Emperor's Tent" and Act IV conclude with a dejected Emperor agreeing to advance tax revenues yet to be levied on land that does not yet exist: "The land does not exist, it's only high sea still."[33] Even in this case, the Archbishop responds, taxation is only a matter of time: "The right time always comes for patient and just causes."[34] There is, however, one consolation for the Emperor. The collection of future taxes does not require any further paperwork. His word will suffice, but he will be held to it: "For our part, we expect your promise to be valid."[35] In this scene nothing was signed after all, just signed

---

30 "Verzeih o Herr! Es ward dem sehr verrufnen Mann / Des Reiches Strand verliehn; doch diesen trifft der Bann: / Verleihst du reuig nicht der hohen Kirchenstelle, / Auch dort, den Zehnten, Zins und Gaben und Gefälle." (11035-38)

31 Goethe, *Amtliche Schriften*, op. cit., p. 69.

32 "The scene composed and concluded in July 1831, including minor additions, is the very last piece of *Faust*. (Diary 22 July 1831: "The main business has been managed. Final fair copy. All corrections filed')". – "Die im Juli 1831 verfaßte, bis auf geringfügige Nachträge noch im gleichen Monat abgeschlossene Szene (Tagebuch 22. 7. 1831: 'Das Hauptgeschäft zu Stande gebracht. Letztes Mundum. Alles rein Geschriebene eingeheftet') ist das zuallerletzt geschriebene Stück der Faust-Dichtung." (Schöne, *Faust Kommentare*, op. cit., p. 688.)

33 "Das Land ist noch nicht da, im Meere liegt es breit." (11039)

34 "Wer's Recht hat und Geduld für den kommt auch die Zeit." (11040)

35 "Für uns mög Euer Wort in seinen Kräften bleiben!" (11041)

away – like losing a bet by the toss of a coin. Alone at last, the Emperor has time to reflect upon his recent conquest or, rather, defeat: "At this rate I'll have soon signed all my realm away."[36] The verb used here *verschreiben* ('to sign away') in its reflexive form denotes the slip of the pen, writing in the wrong place or at the wrong time, perhaps signing on the wrong line, all of which may lead to the signing away of something dearly valued. *Verschreiben* is also used to describe the selling of the self or soul to the devil: '*sich/seine Seele dem Teufel verschreiben*'. While the terms and conditions of such exchanges vary, in the final scene of Goethe's "main business", Faust's deal with the devil becomes leverage for the levying of taxes. All proceeds, ill gotten or otherwise, are ultimately subject to taxation in some form or other, by someone or some governing body. Goethe learned this lesson early on and elaborates on it throughout his literary career. Up to the point when Goethe dedicated himself entirely to the completion of *Faust*, he had still planned a volume of *Dichtung und Wahrheit* recounting his time in Weimar from 1775 until the summer of 1786, when he left for Italy. Having completed *Faust* in July of 1831, he continued to work on *Dichtung und Wahrheit*. While part IV was finished just prior to his death, the account of his public service must be read in his official writings and in works such as *Faust*.

---

36 "So könnt' ich wohl zunächst das ganze Reich verschreiben." (11042)

Anders Mortensen

Romantic Critics of Political Economy

This paper deals with problems and examples from my *work in progress*, entitled *Poetic versus economic value,* which contains a number of studies of an anti-monetary tradition in Romantic and Modernist literature. But let us begin at an early stage in our chronology, in a passage from the *Satyricon*. The passage is the most well-known of the story. It is from the end of the gloriously entertaining episode called *Cena Trimalchionis, the Feast of Trimalchio,* handed down to our own time through a sole manuscript found in Dalmatia, a region in today's Croatia, in the middle of the 17th century. The manuscript was marked with the author's name, *Petronius arbiter*, identified as the nobleman responsible for luxury and taste at the court of emperor Nero around the year AD 60. This fragmented novel is also known through the excellent film by Federico Fellini.

The two poets Enkolpios and Eumolpos have just escaped from the abundant but humiliating feast in the grand villa of the rich *parvenu* Trimalchio. Endlessly exhausted and drunk the older and, to all appearances, dying Eumolpos speaks to Enkolpios, thereby delivering his poetic will – in my rough translation:

> If I was rich like Trimalchio I would give you a manor, or a ship. But I can only give you what I have. I give you the poetry, and the seasons, especially spring and summer. I give you the wind and the sun. You shall have the sea, the good sea, and the soil, the mountains... the streams and the rivers... the proud and easy clouds, sailing through the sky. You shall look at them, and then, maybe, you will remember our short friendship. And I give you the trees and their swift, winged inhabitants. The sounds, the songs, the human voices – the most beautiful music. That I give to you.

Eumolpos is giving away things that cannot be possessed, things that have no value in the prevalent economy, in the value system where the tycoon Trimalchio rules. But Eumolpos' words concern a different kind of possession, a kind of wealth, which it is possible for even poor and destitute people to attain. In fact, this different kind of riches becomes more evident, when the usual kind of possession simply is not there. The riches of this poetic possession have their gold standard in another world, or let us say, in a belief that Eumolpos and Enkolpios share, in a value system different to that of the prevalent economy. Against the value of money Eumolpos sets the value of beauty, which can be spotted more easily when there is no real money around.

The same idea, and the same rhetorical trope, can frequently be found in Goethe's *Faust*, which to a considerable extent deals with questions of economy and value – especially the second part of the play from 1831. As the Poet says in the beginning, in the *Vorspiel auf dem Theater*: "Ich hatte nichts, und doch genug". (I had nothing, and yet enough.)[1]

I designate this rhetorical construction *the trope of mutually excluding values*. It can be regarded as commonplace in Romantic writings. But its way of putting monetary and aesthetic values together, and showing that there must either be fortune or beauty, does in most cases not primarily try to convince us that "you must be poor to experience beauty", or similar foolishness. Rather, the trope strongly implies that there is this different value system of beauty, which can supply you with enough resources to be free from the power of money or even the spell of greed.

Every chapter of my book deals with this trope, in different historical and literary contexts.

However, before we move on, I want to apologize for not telling you the whole truth. The quotation I made is correct, but it was not from *Satyricon* by Petronius, but from the film by Federico Fellini. The sequence of *The Feast of Trimalchio* which is approximately 18 minutes long in the film is fairly faithful to the text of the Latin original, and never openly anachronistic – except for this scene.[2] Fellini must have felt something essential was missing in the text – to him, in his time. But his Eumolpos speaks like a true Romantic poet, that is, like a poet from the last two and a half centuries. The trope of mutually excluding values is modern.

* * *

The book I am working on focusses on the belief, so commonly held among Romanticist and Modernist writers, that literature – and in a broader sense art and aesthetics – constitutes a value system that is analogous to, in conflict with, and furthermore has priority over the value system of money. Thereby literature takes over the mission of Christianity to guard Man from greed and Mammon. The study examines the anti-monetary tendency in a number of literary works, and shows why it must be considered a major aspect of the aesthetic ideology of the era. The book contains chapters on Charles Dickens, Charles Baudelaire and Arthur Rimbaud, Ezra Pound and High Modernism, and also deals with Swedish

---

1 Johann Wolfgang von Goethe, *Faust*, in *Werke*, ed. Erich Trunz (Hamburg: Christian Wegner Verlag, 1966), vol. 3, p. 14.

2 My "rough translation" of Eumolpos' speech thus concerns Fellini's *Satyricon* (Italy 1969).

writers like Carl Jonas Love Almqvist and August Strindberg. The opening part of the book, however, concerns the emergence of the analogies between aesthetic and economic value in the development of Aesthetics and Political Economy as disciplines in the 18th century. The achievements of the Scottish Enlightenment – Frances Hutcheson, David Hume, Adam Smith – are decisive for this development in Western thought. In the Scottish reflections upon value and the aesthetics of utility, and in the ensuing Romantic development of aesthetic autonomy, the still-ongoing struggle, which Barbara Herrnstein Smith calls the double discourse of value, originates.

The path that I have been following into this area of research stems from an old fascination linked to the Romantic ambitions of the early 20th century *High Modernism*. In the first Dada-manifesto from 1916 the chieftain of the movement, Hugo Ball, declares that the new ambition is not only to write "with words" but to write "the word", that is to say: to invent new words and create a new language, since the old one is "damned". This damnation is caused by the language being "soiled like the worn-out coins in the broker's hands."[3] The Modernist idea, tremendously important since Baudelaire, that language must be purified, is given an apparent economic motivation in Ball's manifesto, hostile to the bourgeois market – just like the writings of Baudelaire. In the High Modernist era a major mission is to challenge the prevalent political-economic order with art. To Ezra Pound, this task is *the* main ambition: the power of the usurers, of the Usurocracy, must be destroyed. His major work, the *Cantos*, deals with this desire; the poems are in a sense to be apprehended as acts of war, as aesthetic weapons against Usurocracy. In the first surrealist manifesto from 1924 the leader of the surrealist movement, André Breton, prophecies about the day when poetry "will proclaim the end of money, and will itself break the bread of heaven on earth!"[4] At the same time similar thoughts were being discussed in Germany in the circle of Stefan George and Hugo von Hofmannsthal.

The anti-monetary aspect is valuable to anyone trying to to understand the characteristics of High Modernism as both an artistic and an anti-bourgeois

3 Hugo Ball, "Manifest zum 1. Dada-Abend in Zürich 1916", in *Literaturrevolution 1910-1925. Dokumente – Manifeste – Programme. II. Zur Begriffsbestimmung der Ismen*, ed. Paul Pörtner (Neuwied am Rhein & Berlin-Spandau: Luchterhand, 1961), pp. 477-8: "[...] verehrteste Dichter, die ihr immer mit Worten, nie aber das Wort selber gedichtet haben. [...] Diese vermaleidete Sprache, an der Schmutz klebt wie von Maklerhänden, die die Münzen abgegriffen haben. Das Wort will ich haben, wo es aufhört und wo es anfängt."

4 André Breton, "Manifeste du surréalisme" (1924), in *Manifestes du surréalisme* (Paris: Gallimard, 1985), p. 28: "Le temps vienne où elle [la poésie] décrète la fin de l'argent et rompe seule le pain du ciel pour la terre!"

activist movement. A recurrent strain in this aesthetic ideology is the belief that art, or the powers that are exposed by art, forms a realm independent from the political-economic order, with a special, autonomous value system challenging and competing with that of bourgeois society. The big change in society and mentality which many modernists hoped for, postulated that the values of art – or, at least, *their* art – should replace the values of the prevalent economic world order. Hence the modernists cultivated an evidently rhetorical, and deliberately preposterous, confidence in the power of poetry.

Following the roots of this anti-monetarian tradition back through the 19th century, the historical connection to Christian religion becomes more obvious. The task is almost the same: to be the guard of Man against the threats of a society devoted to Mammon. For the Christian as well as for the Romantic artist, greed is to be fought with the support of the authority of another realm, a kingdom not of this world. But Baudelaire's famous prose poem about *The Stranger*, *L'Etranger*, who despises the gold "comme vous haïssez Dieu!", reminds us that modern poetry rather has taken over this Christian task, and then also turned it against the God of bourgeois society.[5] This agonistic succession may be illuminated by an interesting passage from August Strindberg's play *To Damaskus* from 1895. The protagonist, called The Unknown, and patently the author's *alter ego*, explains the purpose of his alchemical experiments to his female companion, the Lady:

> I am the one, who has done what no man has done before, I am the one who will precipitate the golden calf and knock down the tables of the moneychangers; the destiny of earth is in my melting pot, in eight days the richest of the richest shall be poor; gold, the false standard of value, is no longer in power, all are equally poor [...].[6]

The purpose of The Unknown is not sordid gain, but "to destroy the whole world order, to ruin, you see!" The Lady answers: "So that was the inner meaning of your last book, which then was not a poem!"

The dream to destabilize an unjust economic order by goldmaking, by, so to speak, undermining the gold standard, is recurrent in this anti-monetary tradition, from the first outbursts of Romanticism to the heyday of surrealism – and then, of

---

5 Charles Baudelaire, "L'étranger", in *Le Spleen de Paris (Textes de 1869)*, ed. Claude Roy (Paris: Le Livre de poche, 1964), p. 14.

6 August Strindberg, *Till Damaskus*, in *Samlade skrifter. Tjugonionde delen*, ed. John Landquist (Stockholm: Bonniers, 1987), p. 175: " Jag är den, som gjort det ingen gjort förr; jag är den, som skall störta den gyllene kalven och kullslå månglarenas växelbord; jag har jordens öde i min degel, och om åtta dagar är den rikaste av de rike fattig; den falska värdemätaren guldet har upphört härska, alla äro lika fattiga [...]."

course, particularly as a threatening metaphor. After all, the idea of getting rid of money, is rather childish. We must not forget: this is still rhetoric, still literature. The provocative metaphor is a drastic variety of the often used analogy between the art of alchemy and the art of poetry in Western literature. Before the well known *alchimie du verbe* by Arthur Rimbaud, we have, for instance, Goethe's *Faust*, with its alchemical analogies between the value of gold and the value of beauty. The conditions for these Romantic analogies are the same: that art and literature constitute their own reality and autonomous value system, radically different to but comparable with the value system of economy. There is, indeed, a conflict between them.

* * *

There are certain problems in trying to fix a historical starting point for this trope of mutually excluding, aesthetic/economic values. On the one hand, literature has always dealt with money, the power of money, with greed, wealth and poverty. Voltaire maintained that the poets had condemned luxury and loved it for two thousand years. You could claim that Christianity begins with Jesus throwing the moneylenders out of the temple. Western literature since then has been cultivating similar interests. Martin Luther said: "Money is the word of the devil, through which he creates everything in the world, just as God creates through the true word." [7] And so on. But there is something new under the sun.

In the last few decades, a number of important intellectuals have paid attention to the modernity of the concept of value. The general insight is that the question of aesthetic value is not one of the so-called perennial philosophical problems – and the same goes for economic value. Michel Foucault states in *Les Mots et les choses*, that value, even in the everyday way we think of it, is one of the important inventions of modern science.[8] In her influential book *Contingencies of Value* from 1988, Barbara Herrnstein Smith claims that "the double discourse of value" is a creation of aesthetic ideology and its rhetorical needs.[9] I have let myself be persuaded – albeit with some reservations – by a theory presented by Arthur Caygill in *Art of Judgment* and John Guillory in

---

7 Quoted in Marc Shell, "Language and Property. The Economics of Translation in Goethe's Faust", in *Money, Language, and Thought* (Baltimore & London: John Hopkins University Press, 1982), p. 84.

8 Michel Foucault, *Les Mots et les choses*, Engl. transl. *The Order of Things. An Archaeology of the Human Sciences* (New York: Vintage Books, 1994), chapter 6/V, "The Creation of Value".

9 Barbara Herrnstein Smith, *Contingencies of Value* (Cambridge, Mass. & London: Harvard University Press, 1988), p. 33.

Cultural Capital, that the twin concept of aesthetic and economic value was born in the writings of Adam Smith.[10]

In *The Theory of Moral Sentiments*, published in 1759, Adam Smith, following David Hume's principle of the utility of beauty, "derived the beauty of the social order [...] from a beauty he attributed directly to the commodity". Here, the distinction between art and commodity, taken for granted by many other writers on aesthetics, is replaced by a distinction "internal to the commodity itself" in Smith's theory. As Guillory explains, in Smith's view: "commodities are attractive [...] not simply because they can be used to satisfy needs, but because they possess an aesthetic dimension, because their 'fitness' to use can be admired. In this way Smith finds in the aesthetic disposition itself the motor of the economy".[11] So, in his consumer-oriented theory, where economy and aesthetics are inseparable from each other, Adam Smith sees the beauty of the object as a distinct economic value function, and as such an integral factor in the endlessly ongoing calculation of the market.

In the second of Adam Smith's famous books, *The Wealth of Nations* (1776), the idea of beauty as the locomotive of civilisation is abandoned. Another guiding principle, another invisible hand is found to guarantee the harmony of society – that power is the self-interest of Man. The theory of the value of beauty then becomes irrelevant to political economy.

There is an irony worth considering in the circumstances in which Adam Smith came to supply the enemies on both sides of the antagonistic double discourse of value-demarcation with ammunition. To the ideologists of aesthetics he delivered a veritable value of beauty to contemplate and elaborate – and when this value of beauty was brought together with the older notion of "intrinsic value", the Romantic belief in the autonomous aesthetic value system was established. Meanwhile, the men of economy and finance were blessed with a new science, Political Economy, in which the actions of Man in accordance with his self-interest were not condemned, but hailed as broadly humane and well-suited to the public good.

* * *

---

10 John Guillory, *Cultural Capital. The Problem of Literary Canon Formation* (Chicago & London: University of Chicago Press, 1993), presents and develops pp. 303-325 the achievements of Howard Caygill, *Art of Judgment* (Oxford & Cambridge, Mass.: Basil, Blackwell, 1989).

11 Guillory, *Cultural Capital*, pp. 310-312.

Mary Poovey has presented interesting observations on the increasing antagonism nourished by the double value discourse in the decades that followed after *The Wealth of Nations*. Already "by the 1790s, the gulf between aesthetics and political economy seemed unbridgeable", she says: "the man of business was now identified as an individual who lacked the 'aesthetic attitude'".[12] Half a century later, the conflict had escalated through a number of stages and was more intense than ever. Charles Dickens could celebrate the virtuous British housewife, for standing free from both waged slavery and the calculations of the much-despised utilitarians, the political economists – just like himself, the author![13]

As we all know, the belief in a special aesthetic value is one of the principal ideas of Romanticism. A much more unexplored and difficult historical problem arises, however, when we ask the question to what extent this aesthetic confession to an autonomous value, quite opposite to the value of money and materialism, has been fortified by a continuous confrontation with the doctrines of Political Economy, through the discourse of Adam Smith and his followers. I will now briefly comment on some aspects of these Romantic engagements with the economists.

Fania Oz-Salzberger writes in her excellent book *Translating the Enlightenment* on what was then called the "Smithianismus" in Germany, which began at the end of the 18th century. Kant mentioned Adam Smith as his "Liebling".[14] These remarks imply, that the sayings of Smith can be compared to the impact of – for instance – the Freudianism of the first half of the 20th century, which Harold Bloom has characterized as the major mythology of its time.[15] Such an established discourse is supposed to keep on generating different reactions among intellectuals and artists, not only among philosophers and political economists. But how strong was the Smithianismus – and therefore, also the Anti-Smithianismus – in its heyday? And how inspiring was it as a threat to the Romantics?

We know that Coleridge and a number of the English Romantic poets, among them his brother-in-law Robert Southey, were disturbed by the views of Adam Smith; as I have been working my way through his writings, I have found out that

---

12 Mary Poovey, "Aesthetics and Political Economy in the Eighteenth Century. The Place of Gender in the Social Constitution of Knowledge", in George Levine (ed.), *Aesthetics and Ideology* (New Brunswick: Rutgers University Press, 1994), pp. 90-91.

13 ibid., p. 98.

14 Fania Oz-Salzberger, *Translating the Enlightenment.Scottish Civic Discourse in Eighteenth-Century Germany* (Oxford: Clarendon Press, 1995), p. 61.

15 Harold Bloom, *The Breaking of the Vessels* (Chicago & London: University of Chicago Press, 1982), p. 62.

Coleridge not only read the major works of the political economists, but kept on condemning the moral and methodological shortcomings of this non-science, which mistook people for things.[16] Goethe seems to be an ambivalent reader of the writings of Adam Smith, whose importance ought not to be diminished. Obviously Faust does not go very well together with some of the doctrines of *The Wealth of Nations*. Hans Christopher Binswanger's book on Faust, focussing on its critique of modern economy, *Money and Magic*, presents a basic idea of how these contrasts work. He starts out from an important allusion in *Faust II* to a digression in *The Wealth of Nations*, where Adam Smith distances himself from his main doctrines and puts forward some shrewd arguments for the production of paper money as a method of increasing wealth. And that is precisely the bad principle of "alchemy" depicted and developed in the second part of *Faust*. While his general view is that "Goethe adopts a position diametrically opposed to that of the classical political economy", Binswanger concludes that "this digression by Adam Smith forms the basis of political economy as expressed in Faust".[17] For a receptive mind like Goethe's, there is a lot of food for thought in *The Wealth of Nations*, and in *The Theory of Moral Sentiments*, which is another quite remarkable book.

If we go to important Romantic ideologists like Thomas Carlyle and Adam Müller, it is obvious that direct engagement with the doctrines of Political Economy is of vital importance to them. Both mobilise their forces against the idea of self-interest as the engine of economic and social improvement, against the principle of competition as productive and, of course, against any belief in the autonomy of the Market or in Laissez faire.

In his conservative classic *Sartor Resartus*, written in the early years of the 1830s, Carlyle strongly rejects the utilitarian idea of self-interest as the road to common happiness. Against it he puts forward the moral of "Selbst-tötung" which he finds in Novalis, the Annihilation of Self, which he claims to be the foundation of the Social Idea. In a dystopian vision, the alter ego of Carlyle, Professor Teufelsdröckh, sees: "Liberals, Economists, Utilitarians [...] marching with its bier, and chanting loud paeans, towards the funeral pile" of society. The polemics of Carlyle are bombastic; in this miserable company the words "Laissez

---

16 John Morrow, *Coleridge's Political Thought. Property, Morality and the Limits of Traditional Discourse* (London: MacMillan, 1990), pp. 102-107; George Stigler, *The Economist as Preacher* (Oxford: Blackwell, 1982), chapter 3: "The Ethics of Competition. The Unfriendly Critics".

17 Hans Christoph Binswanger, *Money and Magic. A Critique of the Modern Economy in the Light of Goethe's "Faust"* (Chicago & London: University of Chicago Press, 1994), pp. 17, 10.

Faire" are "passionately proclaimed", even "the monster UTILITARIA" is evoked.[18]

I do not know if Carlyle ever read Adam Müller, but they share a deep affection for the writings of Novalis. Müller's *Die Elemente der Staatskunst* (1809) provides the most elaborate and, so to speak, complete Romantic alternative to the Smithonian economic theory in the first decades of the century. As Richard Gray has demonstrated in a rigorous article, the economic philosophy of Adam Müller is in almost every part a direct negation of Adam Smith.[19] Müller's concept of economic trust forms a theory of the wealth of nations – very unlike Smith's belief in the invisible hand – that rests on the spiritual human powers of the organic community, which preferably is a feudal social order. The writings of Müller have been much discredited by their importance to leading ideologists of the Third Reich. On the other hand, his conservative critique of classical Political Economy could also be associated with certain Humanist ambitions, not only among the anti-modern romanticists, but in today's beliefs in "the spiritualization of economic life" (Francis Fukuyama).[20]

Müller was influential among the Swedish romanticists, and so was the Smithianismus – in the latter case as a discourse to react against. Erik Gustaf Geijer, who was one of the main figures of the movement, emphasized in 1818 "the moral side of finance, which have not yet found its Adam Smith. The only preparatory studies to this higher political economy that I know of are the writings of the genius Adam Müller."[21] The most interesting of the Swedish romantic treatises on economy and money, *Hvad är Penningen*? ("What is Money?"), is written by the leading Romantic Carl Jonas Love Almqvist, who was certainly not conservative. Here one can easily sense an ambition to contribute to a different general theory of economy to the one which is provided by the utilitarian political economists.[22]

---

18 Thomas Carlyle, *Sartor Resartus. On Heroes and Hero Worship* (London: Everyman's library, 1959), pp. 174-177.

19 Richard T. Gray, "Hypersign, Hypermoney, Hypermarket: Adam Müller's Theory of Money and Romantic Semiotics", *New Literary History*, 31 (2000), pp. 295-314.

20 Francis Fukuyama, *Trust. The Social Virtues and the Creation of Prosperity* (London: Hamish Hamilton, 1995), chapter 31.

21 Erik Gustaf Geijer, "Feodalism och republikanism", in *Samlade skrifter. Andra delen* (Stockholm: Norstedts, 1924), p. 576: "här ligger finansernas moraliska sida, som ännu ej funnit sin *Adam Smith*. De enda förarbeten till denna högre nationalekonomi, som jag känner till, är den genialiske *Adam Müllers* skrifter."

22 See Anders Mortensen, "Att göra 'penningens genius till sin slaf'. Om Almqvists romantiska ekonomikritik", *Vetenskapssocieteten i Lund. Årsskrift 2004* (Lund 2004), pp. 48-76.

These Romantic writings on economy have for a long time been ignored, both by economists and scholars in Comparative Literature. They represent a once important attempt to challenge the Political Economy – an expression, which according to the Romantic view does not designate a neutral field of science, but rather a school of dangerous materialists and statisticians, who will keep on supplying the misers and the moneygrubbers with the most suitable ideology anyone could think of.

The great novel on that topic is of course Charles Dickens's *Hard Times*, the dystopian vision of a utilitarian Utopia which he dedicated to Thomas Carlyle. But that is another story.

Sheila Dickson

Finding Treasure in the Works of Achim von Arnim

Money, as we know, makes the world go round. It reaches into all spheres of inter-personal relationships, from the most intimate to the most public.[1] Looking at money, therefore, can tell us something about how efficiently many aspects of human life are functioning in a particular society. One route towards understanding the role of money in a certain time and place is to interpret its presentation in literary works, which are socio-historical documents but also an attempt to interpret what they describe.

Jochen Hörisch gives a historical overview of views of money in his study *Heads or Tails*. He argues, for example, that at the beginning of the 18th-century European intellectuals criticised greed and waste, not money per se. He cites as examples the German scholars Christian Thomasius, Johann Georg Walch, Johann Gottlieb Krüger, Johann August Unzer and Barthold Heinrich Brocke.[2] This line of thought was to continue in Germany throughout the 18th century, and the latter part of it can be characterised by a pragmatic view of money as the reward for hard work and by criticism of laziness and extravagance. Money was considered a means or a tool rather than a thing in itself; it had to be invested and could perform well or badly, depending on the individual in charge of it and the market into which it was invested. In *Die Metaphysik der Sitten* (1797) Immanuel Kant defined money as "(according to Adam Smith) that body, the disposal of which is both the means and the measure of the diligence with which individuals and peoples communicate with each other".[3] This protestant work ethic equates effort and reward: hard work and money.

The following is, firstly, a consideration of an individual writer as a representative of certain ways of thinking about money at the end of the 18th and beginning of the 19th century in Germany, or more specifically, Prussia. Achim

---

1 This point is made by Jochen Hörisch, *Heads or Tails. The Poetics of Money*, trans. Amy Horning Marschall (Detroit: Wayne State University Press, 2000), p. 49.

2 ibid., p. 44f.

3 "(nach Adam Smith) derjenige Körper, dessen Veräußerung das Mittel und zugleich der Maßstab des Fleißes ist, mit welchem Menschen und Völker unter einander Verkehr treiben", Immanuel Kant, *Werke in zwölf Bänden*, ed. Wilhelm Weischedel (Frankfurt a. M.: Suhrkamp, 1968), VIII: *Die Metaphysik der Sitten*, p. 403.

von Arnim (1781-1831), who published his first novel in 1802, has been allocated a place in 19th-century literary history and is commonly seen as a Romantic of the second generation whose writing already displays many characteristics of the Realist period. His academic and cultural education began in the 1790s in Berlin under the influence of the Berlin Late Enlightenment, however, and his earliest writings, from his school and university years, published as Volume 1 of the Weimar Arnim Edition,[4] demonstrate the practical, pragmatic bourgeois work ethic with which he grew up and, it will be argued, which defined his later social and moral philosophy. The second aim of this study is, therefore, to link this particular writer's thinking much more closely to the late 18th century than has previously been the case. Many of the references and allusions to money in his works can be cited as representative examples of the late 18th-century Enlightenment way of thinking whereby money is not bad or dangerous in itself; its role depends on how it is obtained and how it is used. It can be perceived and can function as a reward or a curse, but in itself it is necessary and natural. It is dynamic and as a result local economies boom and slump over time. In *Geschichte des Predigers Tanner* (1809) Arnim relates it to physical health and, more specifically, to the pulse of life itself:

> Money is inner health. It is nothing when we have it, but it is sorely missed. Money is health in human communication, which creates, in the calm exchange of the necessary giving and taking, the calm, healthy pulse of society.[5]

Money is also called "blood of the state" in Arnim's novel *Die Kronenwächter*.[6]

In order to contextualise these later views in terms of the writer's early development in the late 18th century some biographical information is necessary. Achim von Arnim was born in 1781 and his mother died shortly after his birth. His father was not interested in either of his sons (Arnim had an elder brother Carl Otto), and he sold the legal guardianship of them to the boys' maternal grandmother, Caroline von Labes, for 1,000 *Taler*. In spite of her name, Frau von

---

4 Ludwig Achim von Arnim, *Werke und Briefwechsel*, ed. Roswitha Burwick et. al. (Tübingen: Niemeyer, 2000ff.), vol. 1: *Schriften der Schüler- und Studentenzeit*, ed. Sheila Dickson (2004). All translations from the German are my own.

5 "Gesundheit ist das Geld im inneren Leben, sie ist an sich nichts, wenn wir sie haben aber schwer wird sie vermißt, das Geld ist die Gesundheit alles menschlichen Verkehrs das in ruhigem Verkehr des nötigen Empfangens und Zurückgebens den ruhigen gesunden Puls der Gesellschaft gibt." Achim von Arnim, *Werke in sechs Bänden*, ed. Roswitha Burwick et. al. (Frankfurt a. M.: Deutscher Klassiker Verlag, 1989-1994), vol. 3: *Sämtliche Erzählungen 1802-1817*, ed. Renate Moering (1990), p. 476.

6 "Blut des Staats". Von Arnim, *Werke in sechs Bänden*, op. cit., vol. 2: *Die Kronenwächter*, ed. Paul Michael Lützeler (1989), p. 170.

Labes belonged to the bourgeoisie, not the nobility. The noble 'von' in her married name was granted to that family in 1763 only after great efforts on the part of her husband, and by the Kaiser, Francis I, in Vienna, not Frederick the Great, then King of Prussia, the state in which the family lived; Arnim's grandfather was forbidden to use the title in Prussia under threat of a fine, and this was upheld several times. Arnim's upbringing was therefore bourgeois, not aristocratic, and Frau Labes was a strict guardian who was concerned to teach the value of money to her grandchildren. Before Achim and Carl Otto von Arnim were allowed to go on the obligatory grand tour in 1801 they had to sign a contract promising neither to gamble nor to buy anything without the consent of the other. In fact, they ran out of money in Scotland in 1803 and ended up so homesick and disillusioned that Arnim wrote to his uncle in 1804 that he was looking forward to returning home to Germany where other things than money counted.[7] As an adult his rather half-hearted attempts at making a career in the Prussian Civil and Diplomatic Services failed. He had constant money worries, not helped by the lifestyle and attitude of his elder brother or by his grandmother's will, which forced him by means of an entail to marry and tend his estates so as to provide his children rather than himself with independence and an income.[8]

Arnim started school in 1793 at the age of 12, attending the Joachimsthal *Gymnasium* in Berlin. Previously, and in parallel to this, he was taught by a series of private tutors. Headmaster of the Joachimsthal School at the time was Johann Heinrich Ludwig Meierotto, one of the leading pedagogues of the day, a founding member of the *Oberschulkollegium* (1787), a body set up to oversee state education, and, by all accounts, a highly gifted teacher. The programme he and his colleagues developed, in co-operation with the State Minister with responsibility for education, Karl Abraham von Zedlitz, was steeped in the

---

7 Von Arnim, *Werke und Briefwechsel*, op. cit., 31: *Briefwechsel 1802-1804*, ed. Heinz Härtl (2004). Letter to Hans von Schlitz, London 18th May 1804, p. 377.

8 For Achim von Arnim's relationship with his elder brother, see Sheila Dickson, Christof Wingertszahn, "'Selig sind deine Selbsttäuschungen': Carl Otto Ludwig von Arnim (1799-1861)", in *Romantische Identitätskonstruktionen: Nation, Geschichte und (Auto-)Biographie*, ed. Sheila Dickson and Walter Pape (Tübingen: Niemeyer, 2003), pp. 139-59. For details of Arnim's upbringing see Hildegard Baumgart, "Die große Mutter Caroline von Labes: Das Leben der Großmutter Arnims 1730-1810", in *'Frische Jugend, reich an Hoffen' Der junge Arnim. Zernikower Kolloquium der Internationalen Arnim-Gesellschaft*, ed. Roswitha Burwick and Heinz Härtl (Tübingen: Niemeyer, 2000), pp. 1-24; Helene M. Kastinger Riley, *Ludwig Achim von Arnims Jugend- und Reisejahre. Ein Beitrag zur Biographie mit unbekannten Briefzeugnissen* (Bonn: Bouvier, 1978).

philosophy of the Berlin Late Enlightenment and was truly enlightened and innovative. Education was to be targeted: each young man should follow a curriculum appropriate to his intended profession, and in so doing should subsequently use this knowledge to serve the state in that field.[9] The values propagated to all school pupils were those of hard work, a modest lifestyle, virtue and thrift.

In each academic year at the Gymnasium students were given a list of essay topics from which to choose. The titles set, often quotations from 18th-century and classical literature, give a clear picture of the moral views that were inculcated into the young pupils: "Oh how lucky is he whose wealth is free from curse and shame"; "Sleep, golden sleep is not enjoyed by the rich man"; "True happiness is not linked to any social class".[10] Furthermore, the pupil was invited to express pity for the poor and to acknowledge the efforts made by the Prussian state and by philanthropic individuals within it to improve their lot.[11] Arnim chose to write essays deploring the vice of laziness: "On the vice of laziness" and "Laziness punishes itself".[12]

Approval and praise was expressed for modesty and virtue. In the school year 1794-95, in the essay "Praise of the modest and simple lifestyle",[13] Arnim rejects the advantages of riches: they torture us; bring us worry and ill health. In another essay, on the importance of being truthful, he surmises that someone who has gone astray and tries in vain to quash the voice of his bad conscience through self-indulgence will wish he were poor and virtuous, rather than rich and full of vice.[14] In 1794-95 he wrote an essay criticizing expensive tastes in the provinces: "The extravagance that is spreading throughout the provinces."[15] This was a favourite topic ("A young man's complaints about the difficulties of resisting the

---

9 See von Arnim, *Schriften der Schüler- und Studentenzeit*, op. cit., pp. 442-44.

10 "O! Wie beglückt ist der, auf dessen Schätzen nicht Fluch noch Schande ruht"; "Der Schlaf, der goldne Schlaf ist nicht den Reichen eigen"; "Es ist das wahre Glück an keinen Stand gebunden", ibid., p. 120. These quotations were taken from the works of Friedrich von Hagedorn.

11 See, for example, the essay The state is attempting to alleviate unmerited hardship by building poorhouses and private individuals by founding the Mission (Der Staat durch Erbauung der Armenhäuser, und Privatpersonen durch Errichtung des Rettungs-instituts bemühen sich unverschuldeten Elend zu mildern), ibid., pp. 135-37.

12 "Von dem Laster der Faulheit"; "Faulheit bestraft sich selbst", ibid., pp. 33-35, 38.

13 "Lob der prachtlosen und einfachen Lebensart".

14 ibid., p. 71.

15 "Der in der Provinz sich verbreitende Luxus", ibid., p. 71.

spread of extravagance"[16] was another title set) and reflected a serious contemporary public debate, documented, for example by Friedrich Gedike in his series of letters "On Berlin. By a stranger" in the influential publication *Berlinische Monatsschrift*, in which he condemns the addiction to money and extravagance that make mothers sell their children to work in factories and spend all their money on fine clothes to make them look richer than they are. Such moral outrage led to anti-extravagance laws being passed.[17] The French were often given the blame for the newfound expensive tastes and Arnim expresses this sentiment clearly in his essay:

> For a long time French extravagance and fashionableness have been pushing out the simple and homely way of life of Germans in the cities. This extravagance and this way of life have equally changed the admirable traditions of the Germans. Before long they became ashamed of what was handmade, they exchanged simple neatness for shimmering finery. The emulation of such customs, traditions and way of life by city inhabitants has often plunged whole families into the misery of grinding poverty because they have devoted the diligence that they previously directed towards maintaining their riches to finery and society, and their income to the same things.[18]

Attempting to grow rich quick by playing the lottery was another widely condemned vice, as the following poem, also published in the *Berlinische Monatsschrift*, illustrates succinctly:

> Nature gave the East the plague.
> She is never wrong.

---

[16] "Klagen eines Jünglings über die Schwierigkeiten sich dem einreissenden Luxus zu widersetzen", ibid, p. 68.

[17] Friedrich Gedike, "Ueber Berlin. Briefe 'von einem Fremden'", *Berlinische Monatsschrift*, 18. Brief, July 1784, pp. 79-91, see in particular pp. 89-90, via http://www.ub.uni-bielefeld.de/diglib/aufkl/berlmon/. On the anti-extravagance laws ("Antiluxusgesetze") see Henri Brunschwig, *Gesellschaft und Romantik in Preußen im 18. Jahrhundert* (Frankfurt a.M., Berlin, Vienna: Ullstein, 1975), pp. 94-101.

[18] "Schon lange verdrängten Frankreichs Luxus und Moden die einfache und häußliche Lebensart der Deutschen in großen Städten. Dieser Luxus und diese neue Lebensart veränderte zugleich die guten Sitten der Deutschen. [...] Bald schämte man sich der Handarbeiten, man verwechselte einfache Reinlichkeit, mit dem schimmernden Putze [...] Durch eine solche Nachahmung der Sitten Gebräuche und Lebensart der Bewohner größerer Städte stürzen sich oft ganze Familien in das Elend des drükenden Mangels: indem sie den Fleiß, den sie sonst zur Aufrechterhaltung ihrer Glücksgüter anwandten, dem Putze und den Gesellschaften, und ihre Einkünfte denselben Gegenstanden widmen." Von Arnim, *Schriften der Schüler- und Studentenzeit*, op. cit., p. 73f.

To the West on the other hand
She gave the Lottery.[19]

The same newspaper reported the suicide of a servant woman in Berlin in 1785 who had lost all her money: "A dreadful victim of the passion of many a fool: to want to become rich without exerting oneself and without prudent thrift."[20]

In similar terms, the young Arnim denounced passivity based on fatalism in an essay for his Philosophy class, "Ueber Freyheit und Nothwendigkeit":

> Fatalism, to which the Turks also adhere, is tailor-made for any kind of lethargy. Those people who remain throughout their lives constantly in the familiar sphere of domestic work give themselves over to this very easily when they get into situations in which they mistrust their own feelings to any extent. They sell their last belongings in order to try their luck in the lottery or some other game of chance or wait, as the common proverb says, for everything to be handed to them on a plate.[21]

There is not always a clear dividing line between essays Arnim wrote as schoolwork and those written for his own pleasure. The above essay is written in the form of a letter and Arnim also wrote stylized letters to his father and uncle. In one of them, describing a journey to Hamburg, the fourteen-year-old passes the same kind of moral judgements he was obliged to make when writing for his schoolteachers. He criticises the inhabitants of Rheinsberg, who take their energies away from working the land and hope to earn an easier living through the court of Prince Henry (the earliest example of criticism of the nobility which would become a recurring theme in his work).

> Everything smells to some extent of court air and everyone tries all the harder to embalm himself with it. In the meantime the citizen withdraws his labour from the

---

19 "Die Pest gab die Natur dem Oriente./ Unbillig ist sie nie:/ Dafür gab sie dem Occidente/ Die Zahlenlotterie." "Lotto-Kabbala", *Berlinische Monatsschrift*, op. cit., (October 1793), pp. 360-69. The poem begins the article on p. 360.

20 "ein schreckendes Opfer der Leidenschaft manches Toren: ohne Anstrengung der Kräfte und ohne kluge Sparsamkeit reich werden zu wollen." "Selbstmord aus Lotteriesucht", *Berlinische Monatsschrift*, op. cit. (May 1785), p. 483.

21 "Der Fatalismus, welchem auch die Türken huldigen, ist der Trägheit überhaupt sehr angemessen. Leute, die während ihres Lebens stets in dem gewohnten Kreis häuslicher Arbeiten bleiben, überlassen sich sehr leicht demselben, wenn sie in Lagen kommen, in welchen sie in ihren eignen Rath einiges Mißtrauen setzen, verkaufen ihr letztes Eigenthum, um in der Lotterie oder andern Wagespielen ihr Glück zu suchen, oder warten, wie das gemeine Sprichwort sagt, ob ihnen eine bereitete Taube in den Mund fliegen werde." Von Arnim, *Schriften der Schüler- und Studentenzeit*, op. cit., p. 260.

> fields and tries to earn his daily bread more easily through the court. He gives himself over to extravagance.[22]

These examples from his juvenilia illustrate that the young Arnim was a conscientious student who took on board the main principles of the bourgeois morality he was taught. That this conformism was in no way a reflection of lack of imagination or creativity on his part can be seen in the lively and often scurrilous descriptions of events and individuals that intersperse and overshadow the sententious generalisations. In his final school year the essay topics set included "Money can get you everything" (which was to be challenged) and "Money is worth nothing".[23] Arnim chose the latter and reworked the theme of his earlier essay "Praise of the modest and simple lifestyle" into a lively fictional moral tale.[24] Dap is struggling under the heat in his velvet coat and rues his wealth. "'Vile money!' he cried, 'you rob me of any kind of freedom, any pleasure, if I had been poor I would have lived more modestly and would not now have to groan beneath the burden of fashion!'"[25] He gives his money to a friend and becomes a begging monk; however, on the evening before he takes his vows he meets a farmer who praises his own simple, hardworking life with a wife and children. Dap immediately sees the advantages of this existence for himself and so returns to retrieve his money instead of taking his final vows as a monk, but his friend has no memory of receiving any money, and because he has no money Dap cannot find a lawyer to take the matter to court. He concludes sadly: "Money is actually really good in some instances!"[26] (Namely in the cases where one is hard-working and modest.)

Another good example of how Arnim's acceptance of the moral values passed on to him at home and at school was coupled with an idiosyncratic, imaginative outlook on life is the fictional story about the shipwrecked Greek poet Simonides he wrote to address the essay title: "Expand your knowledge, for learning is useful and pleasurable"[27] based on the story by Phaedrus. Simonides brings

---

22 "alles riecht etwas nach Hofluft und jeder sucht noch mehr sich damit einzubalsamiren; unterdeß zieht der Bürger seinen Fleiß vom Ackerbau und sucht sein tägliches Brod auf eine leichtere Art durch den Hof zu verdienen er überläßt sich dem Luxus." ibid., p. 59.

23 "Für Geld hat man alles in der Welt"; "Geld ist nichts werth." ibid., p. 121.

24 ibid., pp. 147-49. Compare the original essay, ibid., p. 70f.

25 "Unseliges Geld, rief er aus, du raubst mir jede Freyheit, jede Freude, arm hätte ich mässiger genossen, und brauchte jetzt unter der Modenlast nicht zu seufzen!" ibid, p. 148.

26 "das Geld ist doch in gar manchen Fällen recht gut!" ibid., p. 149.

27 "Erweitert eure Erkenntniß, denn Wissenschaft nützt und ergötzt." ibid., pp. 142-47.

himself to safety with no thought for rescuing his material possessions. When asked by a young acquaintance where his treasures are, he points to himself. He then explains: "The treasure I possess is only a treasure to me, I can only tell you what it is, not show you what it looks like."[28] His treasure is a coin, a *Heckthaler*, from the goddess of childbirth, Lucina. He quotes her words:

> The power of this gift, said the kindly goddess, who could estimate its value! It can make you happy, and thousands through you. Turn it every day, and always to the right, for if it is turned daily to the right it will multiply itself by ten every day and by doing so you will begin the following day ten times happier. Oh! she sighed, I gave every mortal this gift when the light of the world first shines upon him, so that he can profiteer for the good of mankind. [...] I give it to everyone, everyone, but how few of them use it wisely.[29]

If one does what is right, one will be ten times happier with each day and can make others happy too. The moral of the tale of Simonides' treasure elegantly sums up the main lessons Arnim had to learn in his school years, namely the virtues of honesty, hard work and a modest lifestyle and, in addition, the need for a constant striving to expand one's knowledge and use this knowledge practically and usefully. Laziness, vice, especially dishonesty, self-indulgence and expensive tastes were held up as bad, and any attempt to enjoy riches not rightfully one's own or not earned by means of one's own efforts were shown to end inevitably in disaster. Where an individual experiences undeserved hardship, the other members of the society are there to help him, as long as he helps himself too. Riches are not a guarantee of happiness, neither are they evil per se, it depends on who acquires them and how, and to what use he puts them. The importance of material possessions is played down in Simonides' story, yet the symbol of the coin and the pecuniary implications of "to multiply" and "to profiteer" maintain a link between integrity and financial security. The existence of two sides to the *Heckthaler* coin is indicated through the polysemy of *Schatz* as precious or beloved person or thing as well as wealth, and Arnim continued to play on the two meanings of this word in later works. They represent two different

---

28 "Der Schatz, den ich besitze, ist mir nur Schatz, ich kann nur sagen was, nicht zeigen wie er ist", ibid., p. 145.

29 "Die Kraft dieses Geschenks, so sprach die gütige Göttin, wer könnte sie schätzen! Es kann dich, es kann tausende durch dich beglücken! Nur wende es täglich und stets zur rechten Seite; denn zur rechten Seite täglich gewendet, mehret es täglich sich zehnfach, und zehnfach glücklicher dadurch beginnst du die folgenden Tage. Ach! seufzte sie, jedem Sterblichen gab ich dies Geschenk, wenn ihn zuerst das Weltlicht umstrahlt, um damit zu wuchern zum Glück der Menschheit. [...] Jedem, Jedem ertheil' ich es, aber wie wenige brauchen es weise", ibid., p. 146.

discourses, economic and emotional, and in various narratives the former encompasses both earnings for honest toil and gifts or legacies; the latter is sometimes erotic, but also includes relationships with self, family and fellow men (*das Volk*). The ways in which the two inter-relate provide a key to this writer's social and moral philosophy, which requires money *and* love to make the world go round. According to Simonides, a person's main treasure is himself, always providing he uses the gods' gifts wisely. And that is something many of the characters in Arnim's later fictional works prove unable to do.

It is possible to interpret these later fictional works as advocating the same moral philosophical lessons of hard work, modesty and virtue as the key to progress, happiness and wealth for the individual and the state. In *Die drei liebreichen Schwestern und Golno der glückliche Färber*, a Novelle from a collection published in 1812, treasure, in the form of both love and money, is the reward for hard work and virtue. Although it is not earned – it falls into the main characters' laps – it can be seen as a supernatural reward in recognition of the innocence, goodness, honesty and industriousness of the individuals concerned. Lehne's treasure comes from a Madonna figure,[30] Golno acquires his by means of a miraculous lottery win: he believes he will win the lottery jackpot sum by buying a ticket, and does exactly this. This character's motivation in playing the lottery is above criticism as it is quite clearly different to that of ne'er-do-wells who throw money away hoping to become immediately, and undeservedly, rich. The money given to the characters in this story represents a good investment: both Lehne and Golno use the treasure with which they are entrusted wisely (with one exception, to which I will return), and the ending is happy, with the characters virtuous and financially secure because, in spite of Lehne's joke at the very beginning, the two meanings of *Schatz* really do coincide.[31] Although her treasure was bestowed upon her in a scene full of Catholic symbolism its function

---

30 She passes over the treasure with the words: "Nimm diesen Segen des Himmels und bewahre ihn für die rechte Stunde!" ("Take this blessing from heaven and keep it safe for the right moment.") (Achim von Arnim, *Sämtliche Erzählungen 1802-1817*, op. cit., p. 782.)

31 "'Who told you that you are my sweetheart (*Schatz*),' was the beautiful young Lene's quite matter-of-fact reply to the apprentice Fritz Golno. 'I have quite a different treasure (*Schatz*) and it is always in my thoughts.'" ("Wer hat ihm gesagt, daß er mein Schatz ist, antwortete das schöne Lehnchen ganz trocken dem Lehrburschen Fritz Golno, ich habe einen ganz andern Schatz, und der liegt mir immer in Gedanken.") Lehne responds to Golno's disbelief that she has any *Schatz* other than he by reformulating the either/or into a both/and: "I do have another sweetheart (*Schatz*) and so that you believe me, take a look in my work basket!'" ("Ich habe doch noch einen andern Schatz, und damit er es glaubt, seh er einmal in mein Arbeitskörbchen!") ibid., pp. 778f.

is to support a Protestant work ethic. Both episodes are based on folk-tale sources, namely the Grimms' version of *Das arme Mädchen*, mixed with elements from a similar story by Jean Paul in *Die unsichtbare Loge*, and Johann Peter Hebel's *Kannitverstan*[32] story from his *Schatzkästlein*[33] The content of the tales and the main motifs are, in this sense, identifiably Romantic, but as motor for the action in Arnim's narrative, their moral is based firmly in Enlightenment thought.

On a broader political and economic level, this story also gives us insight into the rise of Prussia, the ascension of Friedrich Wilhelm I, his policies and government and the machinations of members of his court. There is criticism of heavy-handedness and corruption, but the King's clumsy attempts at promoting trade and prosperity are more positive than the old feudal system, which prevented social and economic reward for honesty and entrepreneurial skill. On the other hand, a further comparison is made with the situation in Holland, where Golno literally hits the jackpot, and then is free to start up his business and grow wealthy through talent and hard work, unfettered by the rigid guild restrictions and centralised economic controls that still stifle growth in Prussia.[34] Arnim presents Prussia at this time, the early 18th century, as a great nation emerging as a result of individuals and the state at least attempting to follow the same path and support each other. The positive emphasis is laid firmly on the side of the small man (the representative of *das Volk*) who works hard and looks out for himself. This is shown to be the main treasure of any state.

The nature in which the treasure is acquired is, again quite literally, straight out of a fairy tale, yet becoming rich is an optimistic beginning, not a happy end. The way the treasure is bestowed on the virtuous and needy could be called a typically Romantic motif, but Arnim's characters must earn it in the sense that they must use it well and prove themselves worthy of it. The fantasy of receiving treasure as a heavenly gift, as a reward from heaven, rather than earning money by working for it, gives us insight into the naïve religious beliefs of the *Volk* in the early 18th century, and Arnim bases this story on such belief transforming reality: nevertheless, his ironic perspective of this bygone age, so different to his

---

32 "Can't understand." (This is misinterpreted as the person's name.)

33 ibid., pp. 1260f.

34 Arnim wrote to Joseph Görres in 1823 that Friedrich Wilhelm I took Holland as a model, but did no more than build a few houses in the Dutch style, ibid., p. 1263. See also pp. 1314f. on Karl August von Hardenberg's introduction of new tax laws as part of his programme of economic reforms. Bernd Fischer, "Interpretation als Geschichtsschreibung: Zur poetischen Imagination Achim von Arnims", *Etudes Germaniques* (1988), pp. 179-94, also highlights the contrast between liberal Holland and centralist Prussia in this story (pp. 188f.).

own, shimmers through the narrative, which is subtitled a story of life and customs "Sittengemälde" not a *Märchen* (Fairytale).[35]

The narrative establishes loose parallels, moreover, with Arnim's own family experience. His great-grandfather Daum was alive at this time and was a favourite of King Friedrich Wilhelm I, who often visited him with his entourage and played tricks and jokes (exactly such a meeting between the King and Golno is described in *Die drei liebreichen Schwestern*). Daum is characterised by his great-grandson in a collection of autobiographical notes as follows:

> Even if he was not very poor, he began with very little. [...] I am greatly indebted to the good man and know no ill of him, he was of more benefit to the factories in Prussia than all the subsequent factory collectives. Once, when out of respect I bought his picture at a second-hand market, I received fifty *Taler* unexpectedly.[36]

So, the treasure motif has autobiographical as well as fairy-tale origins. More important, however, is the way in which the folk superstition associated with the receipt of this money is coupled with the admiration expressed for the honesty and industriousness of Daum's character.

Other works by Arnim, with much less optimistic comment on inter-personal relations and historical structures than *Die drei liebreichen Schwestern*, illustrate the same fundamental beliefs, albeit in a negative way. Berthold in the novel *Die Kronenwächter* (1817) is given a similar gift to Lehne's and Golno's, but from a different source and which he puts to a different use. As a baby he is abandoned with an accompanying treasure – but also with a skull – and later, on finding Barbarossa's palace and having the opportunity to buy it, he is pointed in the direction of a further treasure in the form of a bag of money which constantly replenishes itself. Berthold's first treasure comes from his mother, his closest family member, and the second from a secret society, the Guardians of the Crown ("Die Kronenwächter"), who look after him as one of their own. Neither the mother figure nor the secret society that provides the treasure does so as an act of virtue or mercy; nor does Berthold use the treasure in this spirit. He is told that

---

35 On the role of irony in this story, see Christof Wingertszahn, *Ambiguität und Ambivalenz im erzählerischen Werk Achim von Arnims* (St. Ingbert: Röhrig, 1990), pp. 202, 210.

36 "wenn er auch nicht ganz arm gewesen, so fing er doch mit wenig an. [...] Dem guten Manne danke ich viel und weiß nichts Böses von ihm, er hat den Fabriken im Preussischen wesentlicher genutzt als alle späteren Fabrikcollegia. Als ich einmal [...] sein Bild vom Trödel aus Achtung einkaufte, erhielt ich unerwartet fünfzig Thaler gesendet." *Ludwig Achim von Arnim, Bettina von Arnim, Clemens Brentano, "Anekdoten, die wir erlebten und hörten."*, ed. Heinz Härtl (Göttingen: Wallenstein, 2003), p. 26.

his treasure is on loan; to earn it he should use it to gain knowledge and maturity.[37] Instead he subsequently fails as a businessman and a politician by sacrificing his responsibilities in both areas to maintain a dubious love triangle with Anna and her mother. The conspicuous lack of hard work, virtue and family loyalty leads to disaster for Berthold.

As mentioned above, in *Die Kronenwächter* money is called blood of the state by the Kaiser,[38] which sounds like a Hobbesian utilitarian view of society,[39] but which equally creates and nourishes the most intimate personal family bonds: Anton, the hero of Volume Two of the novel, is Berthold's blood brother on the basis of a transfusion carried out by Dr Faust for payment,[40] and Berthold subsequently sees Anton as his *Schatz.*[41] The most intimate family bond, that of blood, has been created, but love and money are linked in the most dubious terms in this version of the Faustian pact. The two characters' lives, and the lives of the businessman and the artist they symbolize, become inextricably intertwined, and Anton is equally unable to use his inherited treasure - the dagger and bag of endless money – virtuously and honestly. Once again the closest family unit breaks down and destructive personal motivation blinds the protagonist. Anton is in many ways a positive figure: vital, impulsive, full of energy and enthusiasm, but he is also violent and immoral and ultimately throws away his treasure in a gesture of contempt and revenge towards his wife Anna.[42]

---

37 "Do not forget that it is only loaned property and that I can ask for all of it back whenever I wish and when I want to lend it to someone else. The interest is not steep, as man is given the earth on the same condition, he takes nothing from it into the next world other than the insight and the faith he has gained there." ("vergiß nicht, daß es nur geliehenes Gut ist [...] und daß ich alles zurück fordern kann, wenn es mir gut dünkt und ich es einem andern verleihen will. Der Zins ist nicht hart, [...] ist doch dem Menschen unter gleicher Bedingnis die Erde geschenkt, er nimmt nichts von ihr in jene Welt, als die Einsicht und den Glauben, den er auf ihr gewonnen.") Von Arnim, *Die Kronenwächter*, op. cit., p. 48.

38 ibid., p. 170. He sees this in terms of military expansion and compares himself to Parzifal. Hörisch, op. cit., p. 281, uses this quotation as a noteworthy counterbalance to the "powerful religious tradition of the talk of 'blood money'".

39 The townspeople take the view that Berthold's money is useful no matter where it came from, cf. von Arnim, *Die Kronenwächter*, op. cit., p. 58.

40 ibid., pp. 113-17, 482-87. Faust claims that "Geld" not "Gott" ("money not God") is the creator of the world, ibid., p. 482.

41 ibid., p. 117.

42 ibid., p. 563. Anna is no less blinded by hatred and herself inadvertently gives the treasure away, ibid., p. 566.

There is sweeping criticism in the novel, set in the early 16th century, of the new merchant class, the nobility, the Kaiser and the Pope,[43] in other words of everyone who should take responsibility for the well being of those under their control, which was effectively the majority of the population. The Guardians of the Crown continue to fight the battle of feudalism in the face of rising mercantilism, represented by the Fugger dynasty. As such they might be expected to represent the clichéd idealization of the 'Golden' Middle Ages often associated with German Romanticism, but for Arnim they are eccentric and out-of-date and could not conceivably represent a political and social solution to the problems of either their own or Arnim's contemporary age.[44] In this novel the two meanings of *Schatz* remain at odds with each other as greed for money and power and exploitation of others to achieve selfish aims destroy goodwill, trust, co-operation, loyalty and affection in all the relationships depicted, from personal to political, from erotic to economic.

Many of Arnim's contemporaries were educated under the same regime of Late Enlightenment thought, and their understanding of socio-economic and personal relations moved on from their school days, in many cases developing diametrically opposite views in the early 19th century, in the Romantic period, when money as the basis of exchange in society was often presented in a negative way, as unpoetic and philistine, as a temptation of the devil, for example in Chamisso's *Peter Schlemihl* and in the tales of E.T.A. Hoffmann. There is an obvious link between this conception and the criticism of the misuse of money propagated at the end of the 18th century, but there is an important shift in emphasis as money itself is now 'bad'. Manfred Frank, referring to Marx, calls this a "money and goods fetisch"[45] and documents how the Romantic economist Adam Müller and others criticised a system in which everything is exchangeable and which therefore reduces the individual personality to its purely economic value.[46] Arnim's fictional works offer equally good examples of this attitude towards money. In *Die Kronenwächter* Berthold's mother warns her son that

---

43 See, for example, ibid., pp. 144-47.

44 Ernst Schürer, "Quellen und Fluss der Geschichte: Zur Interpretation von Arnims *Isabella von Ägypten*", in *Lebendige Form. Festschrift für Heinrich E. K. Henel*, ed. Jeffrey L. Sammons and Ernst Schürer (Munich: Wilhelm Fink, 1970), pp. 189-210, argues that Arnim's ideal was the "harmonische Zusammenspiel aller politischen, sozialen, religiösen und wirtschaftlichen Kräfte im Volke, wie es sich im 16. Jahrhundert nach seiner Ansicht zeigte" (p. 206), however the 16th-century world described in *Die Kronenwächter* is far from harmonious.

45 *Das kalte Herz. Texte der Romantik ausgewählt von Manfred Frank* (Frankfurt a.M., Leipzig: Insel, 1996), p. 318.

46 ibid., pp. 318-21, see also p. 345.

"their [the Guardians of the Crown's] gifts are like the devil's treasures: at night they shine like gold but by day they are lumps of coal."[47] Anton's son kills his half-brother Oswald, Berthold's son, and to test his innocence (in the sense of lack of evil intent) he is made to choose between an apple and a coin. (This interlude, like the treasure-finding episodes in *Die liebreichen Schwestern*, is based on literary sources.[48]) In *Die drei liebreichen Schwestern* there is an incident at the end of the story in which the unscrupulous machinations of members of the royal court place temptation in Golno's path in the form of alchemy, which turns the silver coins into gold and turns Golno's head with the possibilities of unlimited wealth this raises. This money is dangerous because it is neither acquired as a gift from a Christian or other benevolent supernatural source (a present from the 'gods', however this is understood), nor by hard work.[49] Once again, however, luck is on Golno's side as Lehne is there to bring him back to reason, although the fact that he nearly attacks her when she does so is a stark illustration of the corrupting effect money can have even on the most virtuous and hard-working individual.[50]

Money as an evil, daemonic force figures centrally in *Isabella von Ägypten*, probably the best known of Arnim's Novellen. There are many direct criticisms of the greed of the Emperor Charles V and, in more general terms, of the Jewish people. This is often cited as an illustration of Arnim's anti-Semitism.[51] Mercantilism and greed are criticised – as they were in the Enlightenment – but in this story they become a supernatural and daemonic force that turns humans into something inhuman.[52] The heroine Isabella creates a walking-talking treasure-hunter in the shape of the *Alraun* (mandrake man) Cornelius Nepos, a feat made possible due to her innocence. She loves him as a mother, he is her *Schatz* in purely emotional terms, Isabella, however, is in the power of the unscrupulous gypsy Braka who immediately exploits Cornelius' ability to locate financial treasures. Cornelius is the perfect example of the black sheep of the family whose egoism ruins his 'mother' Isabella's dream. He also personifies the folk belief in

---

47 "ihre [der Kronenwächter] Gaben sind wie des Teufels Schätze, in der Nacht glänzt es wie Gold, am Tage sind es Kohlen", von Arnim, *Die Kronenwächter*, op. cit., p. 90.

48 ibid., pp. 456-58. For Arnim's sources, see pp. 751f.

49 Fischer, op. cit., p. 190 argues that, as money that is created for its own sake in unlimited amounts, in the wrong hands it can lead to disaster.

50 Von Arnim, *Sämtliche Erzählungen 1802-1817*, op. cit., p. 832.

51 See, for example, Fischer, op. cit., p. 191 and p. 193, note 19.

52 This point is made by Schürer, op. cit., pp. 203f. The *Bärnhäuter* is torn between the two sides of his nature: alive and dead or "Mensch – Nichtmensch" (von Arnim, *Sämtliche Erzählungen 1802-1817*, op. cit., p. 728.

money as the root of all evil, which, interestingly, is a corruption of a biblical quotation condemning the love of money, not money itself, in other words, the one-sided view of *Schatz*.[53] The pseudo-family is further extended to include another folk-tale character, the *Bärnhäuter*, a revenant who, during his 'normal' lifetime, managed with some supernatural help to win a bride and a fortune and is visited on his wedding night by the spirit who tells him: "Fare well and look after your treasure".[54] Rather than interpreting *Schatz* as referring to both parts of the deal, however, he falls so deeply in love with his money that after his death he is doomed as punishment to spend eternity guarding his treasure.[55] In this story Isabella's treasure is her innocence (she is "deeply, innately innocent"[56]) and her ability to love (she is perhaps the first girl "who loves with the whole of her soul, without desire for the passion of her sex",[57] but her lover, the future Emperor Charles V, fails her by rejecting her unknowingly for a fake: a copy of her body in the form of a golem which has none of her soul and represents greed and avarice. Like Berthold and Anton in *Die Kronenwächter*, he rejects real treasure for something that looks attractive but is hollow and worthless. Finally, Charles chooses Cornelius over Isabella. He will regret this decision for the rest of his life, because, as he soon finds out, Cornelius' treasure is a curse. Moreover, as future ruler of the Holy Roman Empire, this personal decision will have far-reaching consequences for millions of people. Isabella, on the other hand, leads her people back to Egypt and finds real treasure in a mythical utopia of poverty. ("The splendour of the poverty that possesses everything because it can spurn everything."[58])

Money in the form of gold or precious stones was also symbolic in German Romanticism of a higher realm, of the eternal or the ideal with no materialistic connotations, for example in Ludwig Tieck's *Der Runenberg* in which the main character Christian does not want to spend the money he is given by a stranger: he is simply fascinated by it as treasure. Manfred Frank identifies a contrast between the hard work and money necessary to make the soil support life in our

---

53 Roland Hoermann, *Achim von Arnim* (Boston: Twayne, 1984), p. 98 comments on this passage as metaphoric. The biblical quotation is: "For the love of money is a root of all kinds of evil." (1 Timothy 6:10)

54 "Lebe wohl und bewahre Deinen Schatz".

55 Von Arnim, *Sämtliche Erzählungen 1802-1817*, op. cit., p. 656. The *Alraun* Cornelius places a further curse on him, ibid., p. 728.

56 "tief, innerlich unschuldig", ibid., p. 688.

57 "das mit ganzer Seele liebt, ohne Begierde zur Lust ihres Geschlechtes", ibid, p. 638.

58 "die Herrlichkeit der Armut, die alles besitzt, weil sie alles verschmähen kann.", ibid., p. 734.

world where everything is transient and the petrified, eternal beauty of the world of the *Bergkönigin*.[59] Frank explains Romantic writers' interest in money as due to its religious and aesthetic components, which excite the imagination and the senses.[60] The heavenly treasure in *Die drei liebreichen Schwestern* has clear religious associations as the first gift originates from the Madonna and because its appearance is linked with the religious festivals of Easter and Whitsun. It cannot be spent, it is almost a mascot, the sign of a 'chosen one', similar to Simonides' *Heckthaler* in Arnim's school essay. More important, however, for this author is love, as the other side of the *Schatz*-coin. The three sisters are "lieb*reich*"[61] and Golno is lucky and happy ("der glückliche Färber"[62]) because he becomes rich and prospers through this love – he gains a family and a beloved. Arnim also presents this view in *Des ersten Bergmanns ewige Jugend* (a story retold by several authors in this period and inserted by Arnim into his novel *Gräfin Dolores*) in which the young boy is not interested in gold except as an expression of love in the light from the Queen's eyes: "I do not like rubies or shimmering gold, the strong lad flatters her, I like the dark fiery glow of your wild countenance"[63] whereas his family are acquisitive and greedy: they build castles, call up an army and celebrate great feasts while he works: "He has to work hard while they live in unnecessary splendour."[64] The young miner leaves the mine not because he wants to share in the wealth created by his treasure, but because he is attracted to the "light and love" of organic life, as opposed to the coldness of petrified metal: "The Queen cannot hold him then, with her cold deathly arm, for warm light and love are welling up inside the boy."[65] At the feast he gives a young girl, whom he chooses as his future bride, a golden chain as a sign of his love and is subsequently left to drown by the jealous Queen. Arnim's version of the tale is about love and jealousy rather than about a man torn between two

---

59 Frank, op. cit., p. 283. This realm is highly ambiguous, of course, not clearly positive or desirable even for Christian himself.

60 ibid., pp. 322f., 387. Hörisch, op. cit., p. 27 compares coins to the Host. See also Jochen Hörisch, *Gott, Geld, Medien. Studien zur Medialität der Welt* (Frankfurt a.M.: Suhrkamp, 2004).

61 "Loving": literally "rich in love".

62 "Glücklich" means both "lucky" and "happy".

63 "Mag nicht Rubin, nicht Goldgeflimmer", / Der starke Knabe schmeichelnd spricht, / "Ich mag den dunklen Feuerschimmer / Von deinem wilden Angesicht." Von Arnim, *Werke in sechs Bänden*, op. cit., 1: *Hollins Liebeleben. Gräfin Dolores*, ed. Paul Michael Lützeler (1989), p. 617.

64 "Er muss in strenger Arbeit geben, Worin sie prunken ohne Not." ibid, p. 618.

65 "Da kann die Königin ihn nicht halten, / Mit irdisch kaltem Todesarm, / Denn in dem Knaben aufwärts wallten, / So Licht als Liebe herzlich warm." ibid.

realms of existence. The tragedy is that two different women personify the two meanings of treasure.

The elements of superstition, folk wisdom, including many religious beliefs, and the supernatural that one can identify in Arnim's writings are in many ways clearly Romantic, but the bottom line is not far removed from the rationalist principles of the Late Enlightenment, whereby innocence, virtue and hard work are the only viable way to acquire both love, in its widest sense, and riches, and thus to gain possession of the truly valuable treasure which unites the two meanings of *Schatz*. Any one-sided search for financial gain is reprehensible (in Enlightenment terms) *and* either philistine or evil (in Romantic terms). The utopian picture of Egypt in *Isabella von Ägypten*, where the gypsies are free from persecution and blessed by their poverty (Arnim's narrator quotes from the Bible about no rich man gaining entry into heaven[66]) could not be further from the optimistic description of industrial progress and success in *Die drei liebreichen Schwestern*, and this is clearly due, at least in part, to the fact that they describe very different historical periods, but both create the same link between doing what is right and being rewarded for it (not necessarily financially) that had been inculcated in Arnim as a young man.[67]

Arnim was not a systematic thinker and he never claimed to have a panacea for human affairs. His stories describe times of radical change and upheaval and this mirrored his own experience of reality.[68] In 1812 when *Die drei liebreichen Schwestern* and *Isabella von Ägypten* were published Prussia was still under Napoleonic rule and the political way forward was most unclear. Berthold's political ambitions in *Die Kronenwächter* – he tries to unite different antagonistic social groups – end in disaster as he is too inexperienced, however it is difficult to see how anyone could achieve marked success in the political confusion

66 Von Arnim, *Sämtliche Erzählungen 1802-1817*, op. cit., pp. 625f.

67 Bernd Haustein, *Romantischer Mythos und Romantikkritik in Prosadichtungen Achim von Arnims* (Göppingen: Kümmerle, 1974), pp. 53f., contrasts Lehne's work ethic with Isabella's retreat into a legendary, Romantic Egypt. For him only such "Überkindmenschen", Arnim's idealized female figures, are able to escape the evil influences in this world (p. 53). Haustein identifies money as a central theme in Arnim's works and interprets the motif as "der mythische Apfel der Versuchung [...], der Prüfstein der Unschuld und Symbol des Sündenfalls" (p. 51). My argument is based on the premise that it cannot be interpreted per se; what gives it any symbolic significance is the way in which it is used.

68 ibid., pp. 54f.

described,[69] and this was Arnim's own dilemma in the period in which he was writing. In works such as *Die Kronenwächter* and *Die Majorats-Herren* (1819) both the feudal society (based on the power of the unscrupulous nobility) and the bourgeois capitalist one (if based on the power of an unscrupulous business elite) misuse money and human resources. There is no idealised view of the past: in *Die Majorats-Herren* and *Die Kronenwächter* former ages are criticised as rotten and made to look grotesque.[70] But the present is also disappointingly uniform and superficial. Neither is clearly good or bad, right nor wrong: for Arnim, neither was even acceptable.[71] Nevertheless, in very different, inconsistent ways, his fictional works illustrate how personal moral values can prevail in any society. If these moral values were to function as a generally accepted principle the result would be a healthy circulation and exchange in both the economic and emotional spheres of life in which the two meanings of *Schatz* could co-exist in harmony,

---

69 This is also the case with Charles V in *Isabella von Ägypten*. The narrator is critical of his behaviour but comments "daß nur ein Heiliger auf dem Throne jene Zeit hätte bestehen können", von Arnim, *Sämtliche Erzählungen 1802-1817*, op. cit., p. 738.

70 This story contrasts the social structures of the past, represented by the *Hofdame* and her aged gentleman suitor, who appear as the last remaining fossils from a forgotten era, and those of the present, represented by the rapacious Jew Vasari, a shopkeeper who at the end of the story opens a Salmiak factory in the anscestoral home of the now defunct family of landed gentry, much as Berthold in *Die Kronenwächter* turns Barbarossa's palace into a textile factory, von Arnim, *Die Kronenwächter*, op. cit., pp. 56f. The narrator comments in *Die Majorats-Herren* that life before the French Revolution was much more colourful than afterwards, von Arnim, *Werke in sechs Bänden*, op. cit., p. 4: *Sämtliche Erzählungen 1818-1830*, ed. Renate Moering (1992), p. 107, however, this nostalgia illustrates Arnim's love of the extravagant rather than his political ideals.

71 Arnim wrote in the essay "Was soll geschehen im Glücke" that his goal would be to achieve "die Versöhnung des Geistes alter und neuer Zeit", von Arnim, *Werke in sechs Bänden*, op. cit., p. 6: *Schriften*, ed. Roswitha Burwick, Jürgen Knaack and Hermann F. Weiss (1992), p. 201. Many critics have identified Arnim's political views as moderate and as based on the desire to reconcile the past and present but without any real practical ideas for what should be aimed for and how it should be achieved. See, for example, Martin Neuhold, *Achim von Arnims Kunsttheorie und sein Roman 'Die Kronenwächter' im Kontext ihrer Epoche* (Tübingen: Niemeyer, 1994), p. 149: "Die Betrachtung der geschichtlichen Wirklichkeit in den 'Kronenwächtern' [...] ergibt [...] letztlich das zeitkritische Bild einer orientierungslosen Welt"; Hans Vilmar Geppert, *Achim von Arnims Romanfragment 'Die Kronenwächter'* (Tübingen: Niemeyer, 1979), p. 26: "Er sieht seine politischen Ideen und Hoffnungen gleichermaßen von der starrsinnigen Adelspartei verraten, wie von dem fast ausschließlich an wirtschaftlichen Interessen sich orientierenden Bürgertum." The emphasis of my interpretation is different in that I have argued that the personal as well as the political must be reconciled.

with both being granted equal importance, no matter what the historical background and the personal circumstances. After all, health, the circulation of blood, and the pulse are very individual elements which depend on many extraneous factors. This personal utopia reflects the basic optimism behind the philosophy of the Late Enlightenment in Berlin, enriched by many Romantic folk, supernatural and mythological beliefs. As such it is in many ways ambiguous and self-contradictory, and it makes Arnim both a unique and representative figure in his exploitation of the motif of money.

Kirill Postoutenko

Kapital and *Picaresque*: Towards the Typology of *Abstractio* in European culture*

I.

One of the best-known works of Russian literature – Nicholai Gogol's *Dead Souls* (1842) – starts with a string of paradoxes. The very first lines of this "poem" in prose reveal its actual genre (a novel); yet in those very lines one of the pillars of the novelistic plot – a lively protagonist – is torn to tatters. Indeed, just as Gogol's readers expect him to tell them something about his central character – Pavel Ivanovich Chichikov – the author promptly buries his protagonist in a pile of negative characterizations:

> To the door of an inn in the provincial town of N. there drew up a smart *britchka* – a light spring-carriage of the sort favoured by bachelors, retired lieutenant-colonels, staff-captains, land-owners possessed of about a hundred souls, and, in short, all persons who rank as gentlemen of the intermediate category. In the carriage was sitting such a gentleman -- a man who, though not handsome, was not bad-looking either, not fat but at the same time not too thin. Also, though not old, he was not too young.[1]

In fact, Chichikov is denied even that common level of distinctiveness that everyone else has: remarks pertaining to his age, stature or looks, which are all negative, rob Gogol's hero of individual properties as such. Christian Friedrich von Blankenburg – the first scholar to define the genre of novel in a systematic fashion – held that a work is a novel as long as its major character keeps coming

---

* This article was written with the support of the Academic Fellowship Program of the Open Society Foundation (USA). The author would also like to thank Irina Valkova for her helpful hints that triggered the work.

1 "В ворота губернского города NN въехала довольно красивая рессорная небольшая бричка, в какой ездят холостяки: отставные подполковники, штабс-капитаны, помещики, имеющие около сотни душ крестьян, – словом, все те, кого называют господами средней руки. В бричке сидел господин, не красавец, но и не дурной наружности, ни слишком толст, ни слишком тонок; нельзя сказать, чтобы стар, однако ж и не так чтобы слишком молод." Николай Васильевич Гоголь, *Мертвые души* in Н. В. Гоголь, *Полное собрание сочинений*, vol 6. Moscow, 1951, p. 7.

out of his/her shell.[2] But in *Dead Souls* the reverse happens: the place of a main character is taken by an abstract idea – as abstract as literature could imagine.

Yet the writer's eccentricity should not be overestimated. As far as the *artistic* generalization of human race is concerned, the author of *Dead Souls* might have been ahead of his time: the time of a modernist "man without qualities" (Musil) or an anti-utopian "D-503" (Zamiatin) has not yet arrived. Yet in non-figurative discourses (such as philosophy or mathematics) turning a blind eye on things' existential diversity for the purpose of their categorization became a routine operation many centuries before Gogol. The idea that the general geometrical shapes of things could be thought of separately from their specific substantial properties goes back to Aristotle's *Physics* and *Metaphysics* (334-324 BC): 'αφαιρεσιζ' means for Aristotle the subtraction of the mathematical principle, which governs the movement of objects, from the movement itself perceived by human senses in real life (*Phys. I, 2, 194 a 9-10*). Eight centuries later Boethius repackaged Aristotle's observation into succinct, user-friendly, long-lasting formulae:'αφαιρεσιζ – now called *abstractio* – was, for Boethius, the deduction of form from matter.[3] Indeed, the following excerpt from George Berkeley's treatise proves that 18th century abstraction did not differ much from its ancient Greek prototype:

> And as the mind frames to itself abstract ideas of qualities or modes, so does it, by the same precision of mental separation, attain abstract ideas of the more compound beings, which include several co-existing qualities. For example, the mind having observed that Peter, James and John, resemble each other, in certain common agreements of shape and other qualities, leaves out of the complex or compounded idea it has of Peter, James or any particular man, that which is peculiar to each, retaining what is common to all; and so makes an abstract idea wherein all the particulars equally partake, abstracting entirely from and cutting off all those circumstances and differences, which might determine it to any particular existence. And after this manner it is said we come by the abstract idea of man, or, if you please, humanity or human nature; wherein it is true, there is included colour, because there is no man but has some colour, but than it can be neither white, nor black, nor any particular colour: because there is no one particular colour wherein all men partake. So

---

2 Christian Friedrich von Blankenburg, *Versuch über den Roman* [1774], ed. Eberhard Lämmert (Stuttgart: Metzler, 1965), p. 121.

3 *Corpus scriptorum ecclesiasticorum latinorum* (Vienna: Verlag der Österreichischen Akademie der Wissenschaften, 1866ff.), vol. 1, p. 163.

> likewise there is included stature, but then it is neither tall stature nor low stature, nor yet middle stature, but something abstracted from all these. And so of the rest.[4]

The similarity between the "idea of man" in *A Treatise Concerning the Principles of Human Knowledge* and the idea of a hero in the first paragraph of *Dead Souls* is evident from the very language of abstracting (conjunctions *neither/ nor*). And yet this likeness pertains to only one element of αφαιρεσιζ – the purely intellectual discernment of a common shape in the bunch of sensually perceived objects scattered around the universe. Preoccupied with defining "political animals" in life and fiction, Berkeley and Gogol do not seem to care about the other antinomy of Aristotle's abstraction – the creation of an immovable mental image of physical movement. However, unlike the metaphysician, the novelist can hardly get away with a static interpretation of abstraction: no matter how "theoretical" Chichikov is, he must have a good ride in his light carriage before *Dead Souls* could be pronounced a novel. Hence it might be sensible to go beyond literal similes, important as they are, and look for those typological parallels to Gogol's abstraction that take into account the compulsory dynamics of his narrative.

Unsurprisingly, among discourses describing the essence of phenomena through (*and* despite) their substantial movements in time and space, monetary rhetoric occupies a prominent place almost since the invention of money.[5] Small wonder that in the works of Karl Marx – an economist with the greatest interest in philosophy after Adam Smith – one could easily spot a number of analogies to Gogol's version of *abstractio*. To be sure, some dialectic oppositions of the abstract and the concrete created by Marx resemble the traditional scholastic antinomies of universal names and singular things. Thus the generality of human work as such cancels out the immeasurable versatility of hands and machines creating values; measured in purely numerical units – such as hours or kilograms – all kinds of labour became one.

> As use-values, commodities are, above all, of different qualities, but as exchange-values they are merely different quantities, and consequently do not contain an atom of use-value. [...] But even the product of labour itself has undergone a change in our hands. [...] If we make abstraction from its use-value, we make abstraction at the same time from the material elements and shapes that make the product a use-value [...] Along with the useful qualities of the products themselves, we put out of sight both the useful character of the various kinds of labour embodied in them, and the concrete

---

4 George Berkeley, *A Treatise Concerning The Principles of Human Knowledge* [1710] (London, 1969), p. 21.

5 Cf. Raymond Bogaert, "Geld (Geldwirtschaft)", in *Reallexikon für Antike und Christentum* (Stuttgart: Hirsemann, 1941ff.), vol. IX (1975), p. 817.

> forms of that labour; there is nothing left but what is common to them all; all are reduced to one and the same sort of labour, human labour in the abstract.[6]

Other citations from Marx, however, hint at a more intricate relationship between the motionless speculative essence and its perpetually moving real-life representations. At first glance, money as a universal representation of material wealth, appears to be a typical abstraction of all kinds of products large and small, which continuously change hands as long as life on earth goes by. However, the radical reformer of political economy repeatedly hints that his major economical abstraction would only make sense if represented in real-life by its opposite – a tangible material object constantly changing hands in the process of valuation:

> Money in its final, completed character now appears in all directions as a contradiction, a contradiction which dissolves itself, drives towards its own dissolution. As the *general form of wealth,* the whole world of real riches stands opposite it. It is their pure abstraction – hence, fixated as such, a mere conceit. Where wealth as such seems to appear in an entirely material, tangible form, its existence is only in my head, it is a pure fantasy. [...] On the other side, as *material representative of general wealth,* it is realized only by being thrown back into circulation, to disappear in exchange for the singular, particular modes of wealth. [...] Its independence is a mere semblance; its independence of circulation exists only in view of circulation, exists as dependence on it.[7]

---

6 "Als Gebrauchswerte sind die Waren vor allem verschiedener Qualität, als Tauschwerte können sie nur verschiedener Quantität sein, enthalten also kein Atom Gebrauchswert. [...] Jedoch ist uns auch das Arbeitsprodukt bereits in der Hand verwandelt. [...] Abstrahieren wir von seinem Gebrauchswert, so abstrahieren wir auch von den körperlichen Bestandteilen und Formen, die es zum Gebrauchswert machen. [...] Mit dem nützlichen Charakter der Arbeitsprodukte verschwindet der nützliche Charakter der in ihnen dargestellten Arbeiten, es verschwinden also auch die verschiedenen konkreten, bestimmten Formen dieser Arbeiten, sie unterscheiden sich nicht länger, sondern sind allzusamt reduziert auf gleiche menschliche Arbeit, abstrakt, schlechthin menschliche Arbeit." Karl Marx, *Das Kapital* [1872], in Karl Marx, Friedrich Engels, *Gesamtausgabe* (MEGA) (Berlin: Akademie Verlag, 1976ff.), Abteilung II, vol. 6, pp. 71-72.

7 "Das Geld in seiner letzten, vollendeten Bestimmung erscheint nun nach allen Seiten als ein Widerspruch, der sich selbst auflöst; zu seiner eignen Auflösung treibt. Als allgemeine Form des Reichthums steht ihm die ganze Welt der wirklichen Reichthümer gegenüber. Es ist die reine Abstraktion derselben, – daher so festgehalten blose Einbildung. Wo der Reichthum in ganz materieller, handgreiflicher Form als solcher zu existieren scheint, hat es seine Existenz blos in meinem Kopf, ist ein reines Hirngespinst [...]. Seine Selbständigkeit ist nur Schein; seine Unabhängigkeit von der Circulation besteht nur in Rücksicht auf sie, als Abhängigkeit von ihr". Karl Marx,

The paradoxical symbiosis of abstract form and material reality, so defiantly paraded in Marx's posthumous notes, would indeed appear peculiar to Aristotle, Boethius and perhaps even Berkeley. (Given that the eternal idea of physical movement is already captured in its abstraction, why create a working model for this movement in real life?)

Equally doubtful would seem to Aristotelians the cognitive value of swinging back and forth between the abstract and the concrete. (Who needs to perform the same abstracting operations over and over again simply to affirm the existence of *universalia*?). Evidently, only in such dynamic *and* rational cosmologies as self-development of the absolute Spirit (Hegel) or self-exploitation of human society (Marx) would their meanings become apparent through the narrators' alternating appeals to perception and contemplation. For all his noticeable fondness of *abstractio* in *Phenomenology of Spirit*, in one of his pedagogical works Hegel made a point of giving the abstract and the concrete equal rights in philosophical discourse.[8] Carried out in a showier fashion, the same switching back and forth between the perceptible concreteness of money and its speculative abstractness allowed Marx to show a teleology of capitalist economics – the creation of surplus value. The cunning combination of metaphysical opening and novelistic plot gave the author of *Dead Souls* an opportunity to express the meaning of his "poem" in strikingly similar terms. Yet Gogol's fiction had nothing to do with Berkeley's philosophy of consciousness or Marx's philosophy of economics. By the time the future author of *Capital* was drafting his first article, European fiction was already in possession of its own time-honored dialectics of the abstract and concrete. Chichikov's carriage arrived to the provincial town of N just when the two traditions were about to become one. How close were they in reality, though?

II.

It is quite obvious that speculative metaphysics do not require any temporality other than the compulsory linearity of their own verbal representation. In other words, the only tense change one would normally (but not necessarily) see in a description of timeless entities would be the expression of philosophers' formal

---

Grundrisse der Kritik der politischen Ökonomie. Erster Teil [1858], in Marx, Engels, *Gesamtausgabe*, Abteilung II, vol. 11, p. 157.

8 Cf. Georg Wilhelm Friedrich Hegel, *Über den Vortrag der philosophischen Vorbereitungswissenschaften auf Gymnasien. Privatgutachten für Immanuel Niethammer* [1812], in G. W. F. Hegel, *Werke in 20 Bänden* (Frankfurt a.M.: Suhrkamp, 1970ff.), vol. 4, p. 413.

logic in terms of natural language. This grammatical succession from causes expressed in the past tense to the effects given in the present tense is noticeable in many interpretations of αφαιρεσιζ – from 6th century comments to Aristotle by Neoplatonic Simplicius to *A Treatise Concerning The Principles of Human Knowledge*.[9] As we remember, Berkeley was talking about the pure idea of human being which rendered null and void any differences between Australopithecus and a British subject. Accordingly, the temporal structure of his narrative was unrelated to the timing of any events in the life of "Peter, James and John". Rather, this structure coheres with Berkeley's reasoning in the process of abstracting. Indeed, its first stage – the isolation of a certain set of individuals – is expressed in the passage quoted by means of a past gerund (the mind [...] *having observed*), whereas for the next step – abstraction from the concrete properties of those individuals – a present verb is used (the mind [...] *leaves out*). The same grammatical composition unfolds in Marx's ascent from the concrete (professions) to the abstract (work): here again the loss of specificity by various occupations is described by means of the past active participle (die [...] bestimmten Formen dieser Arbeit] *sind* [...] *reduziert*), whereas the consequences of this loss that render abstraction possible are stated in the present (die [...] bestimmten Formen dieser Arbeit *unterscheiden sich nicht*). As long as the teleology of the world (or any of its components) is unrelated to temporal changes, *abstractio* would always be simple, unidirectional transition from present observation to future thought.

Conversely, the philosophical and other treatises that slant towards temporal images of reasonability (such as progress or degradation) have a much more complex and flexible logical structure than a simple ascension from facts to ideas. In its place one would usually find a constant swinging between the changing empirical reality and its growing abstract generalization: here belong, for instance, Schelling's attempts to create a universal mechanism of individual reflection in the ever-expanding cycles of self-observations and self-definitions.[10] In Marx's adroit flip-flopping between "money as a general form of wealth" and "money as a material representative of general wealth"[11] one could discern the same ceaseless collaboration of *sensus* and *ratio* that alone is capable of describing dynamic systems. And yet there is a whole world of difference

---

9 Cf. *Commentaria in Aristotelem Graeca, edita consiio et auctoritate Academia Litterarum Regiae Borussicae*, vol. 7: *Simplicii in Aristotelis de caelo commentaria*, ed. I. L. Heiberg (Berlin, 1894), p. 242.

10 Cf. Friedrich Wilhelm Joseph Schelling, *System des transzendentalen Idealismus* [1800] (Hamburg. Meiner, 2000), pp. 129-130.

11 See Footnote 7.

between *abstractio* in Schelling and Marx that alone makes *Capital* comparable to *Dead Souls*.

The unity of creative thinking and its description was a natural consequence of the belief in the isomorphism of Self and Being, shared by Schelling with other transcendental idealists of his time (Fichte, for instance, saw no principal difference between the world and human perception).[12] Marx's thought, on the other hand, was not constrained by this unity for two reasons. As a materialist, he firmly believed in the existence of objective reality independent from human perception: thus the evolution of matter – for example, human history as the sum of consecutive changes in production patterns on the way to classless society – was for Marx related to, but not identical with, the process of reflection (for example, human activity in the world). Under such circumstances the treatise on political economy was first and foremost a detached description of the objective dialectical process in which the author's introspective skills could only be practiced on the margins of the text or deep in its background. Marx's repeated references to money in pseudo- attestation ("money is a *jealous God of Israel a God of products*") could speak volumes of his intense love-hate relationship with Judaic mysticism, but the direct significance of this allegory for his economic analysis is limited.[13] As evocative as the latter allegory is, its complex dialectics of form and meaning could only be relevant to the extent to which the narrator of the *Outline of the Critique of Political Economy* pretended to march in step with money without losing sight of its overarching identity.

In the same way, the authorial voice in a novel could never be a simple iconic reflection of the writer's thoughts about the main hero. Unlike a philosopher, the author of a fictitious text could never subject the temporality of his text to the logical following of his argument without defying social and aesthetic foundations of verisimilitude. Indeed, in order to be understood, fiction cannot simply reveal to the reader the successiveness of its unwrapping in the writer's mind. More importantly, it has to imitate the generalized reading experience of temporality: both a lyrical poem, aimed to invoke the psychological time of

---

12 "Ja, von dem Gesichtspunkte einer transzendentalen Philosophie aus sieht man sogar ein, [...] daß die Welt nichts weiter sei, als das in seinen ursprünglichen Schranken angeschaute Ich." Johann Gottlieb Fichte, *Grundlage des Naturrechts nach Prinzipien der Wissenschaftslehre* [1796] (Hamburg: Meiner, 1991), p. 18.

13 Kirill Postoutenko, "Не-отчуждение у Достоевского (политико-экономический ракурс)" [Non-alienation in Dostoevskii: Political and Economical Aspects], in *Wiener Slawistischer Almanach*, Sonderband 54 (2001), p. 138.

individual instant emotion and an epic, set to reconstruct the cumulative social time of the whole generation are based on this all-round mimesis.[14]

Not only would the abstraction in a strict philosophical sense, but also its more liberal aesthetic version – synecdoche – make aesthetic sense only in one case – if the transition from the concrete whole to its abstract part did not predate but follow the progressive neutralization of the hero's differences in the course of the plot. In other words, the "idea of a personage" in a novel could not be conveyed to the reader except through its regular (dialectical) self-negation. To the extent that the protagonist in the flesh shows up again and again to perform old textual functions or assume new ones, whether this be mediation or meditation, he is turning into an abstract principle of the novel, slowly but steadily wresting the teleology of the narrative away from the plot and even the author himself.

Most of the novels written in the genre of *Dead Souls* – the picaresque novel – bear the marks of this struggle.[15] As in Marx's *Outline of the Critique of Political Economy*, the moral evaluation of the central image can be quite separate from its functional description. So as early as the attempts at *picaresque* – the anonymous *Lazarillo de Tormes* (1554) and Mateo Alemán's *Life of the Rogue [Picaro] Guzman de Alfaráche* (1604) – the long-winded confessions of the first-person narrators that piece novels together, are offset by their own self-contradictions and rancour, brought to light by dissenting authors.[16] However, in the long run the alleged moral and rhetorical weakness of the hero turned out to be his force. Gogol's eloquent plea to set free "the virtuous person" who compliantly dragged all plots of all novels until "ridden to death" by abusive writers, and "yoke a scoundrel" in his stead, was certainly superfluous: the dreamlike protagonists of the pastoral novels and tales of chivalry gave way to down-to-earth survivors a

---

14 Paul Ricœur, *Temps et récit. Vol. II.: La configuration dans le récit de fiction* (Paris: Le Seuil, 1984), pp. 143-150.

15 For the most recent survey on *Dead Souls* as a picaresque novel see: Ronald D. Leblanc, "Gogol's Chichikov: Russian Picaro or Real Vyzhigin?", in *Canadian-American Slavonic Studies* 23, no. 4 (1983), pp. 410-411.

16 Edward H. Friedman, *The Antiheroine's Voice. Narrative Discourse and Transformations of the Picaresque* (Columbia: University of Missouri Press, 1987), pp. 25-33; Matthias Bauer, *Der Schelmenroman* (Stuttgart: Metzler, 1994), p. 126; Alexander A. Parker, *Literature and the Delinquent. The Picaresque Novel in Spain and Europe 1599-1753* (Edinburgh: Edinburgh University Press, 1967), p. 20; Antonio Gómes-Moriana, "Intertextualidad, interdiscursividad y parodia (sobre los origins de la forma narrativa en le novella picaresca)" in *Dispositio*, vol. VIII, no. 22-23 (1976), pp. 132, 134.

long time ago.[17] And yet his emphasis on the negative morality of his anti-hero draws attention to one of the key mechanisms of picaresque fiction. The immoral, insignificant, indistinct social climber moved the narration forward and accumulated semantic value in proportion to the frequency and diversity of his interactions with other personages: the early *picaro* was largely tolerated only insofar as his frenetic social activity was unfolding the whole panorama of social types from avaricious priests to reclusive beauties.[18] That the lowly protagonist was expected to change his language, occupation and manners with every new master, was long considered no more than a passable survival strategy, smartly concocted out of self-defense in the tradition of the Old Testament and the

---

17 "А добродетельный человек все-таки не взят в герои. [...] Потому что пора наконец дать отдых бедному добродетельному человеку; потому что праздно вращается на устах слово: добродетельный человек; потому что обратили в рабочую лошадь добродетельного человека, и нет писателя, который бы не ездил на нем, понукая и кнутом и всем, чем попало; потому что изморили добродетельного человека до того, что нет на нем и тени добродетели, и остались только ребра да кожа вместо тела. [...] Нет, пора наконец припрячь и подлеца. Итак, припряжем подлеца!" Гоголь, *Мертвые души*, p. 223. On picaresque hero as an alternative to hidalgos and swains see Bauer, *Der Schelmenroman*, p. 93; D. J. Dooley, "Some Uses and Mutations of the Picaresque" in *Dalhousie review* vol. 35 (1958), p. 363, Kathrine Sørensen Ravn Jørgensen, "Pour une nouvelle approche du roman picaresque" in *Revue Romane* 21, no. 1 (1986), p. 82; Gerhart Hoffmeister "Zur Problematik der pikarischen Romanform" in Gerhart Hoffmeister (ed.), *Die deutsche Schelmenroman im europäischen Kontext: Rezeption, Interpretation, Bibliographie* (Amsterdam: Rodopi, 1987), p. 3; Heide E. Faletti, "The Picaresque Fortunes of the Erotic", in Douglas Radcliff-Umstead (ed.), *Human Sexuality in the Middle Ages and Renaissance* (Pittsburgh: Center for Medieval and Renaissance Studies, 1978), p. 167; Robert S. Stone, *Picaresque Continuities. Transformations of Genre From the Golden Age to the Goethezeit* (New Orleans: University Press of the South, 1998), p. 16; Frederick Monteser, *The Picaresque Element in Western Literature* (University: Univ. of Alabama Press, 1975), p. 3; Jean Ducrocq, Suzy Halimi, Maurice Lévy, *Roman et société au XVIIIe siécle* (Paris: Presses Universitaires de France, 1978), p. 122.

18 Cécile Cavillac, "Roman picaresque et théorie du roman", in Jean Bessière (ed.), *Fiction: Narratologie. Texte. Genre* (Paris, New York, Bern, Frankfurt a.M.: Peter Lang, 1989), p. 168; Jean Marie Valentin, "Kulturtransfererscheinungen im Bereich der Literaturgeschichte am Beispiel des europäischen und deutschen Schelmenromans", in Gisela Quast (ed.), *Einheit in der Vielfalt: Festschrift für Peter Lang zum 60. Geburtstag* (Bern, Frankfurt a.M., New York, Paris: Peter Lang, 1989), p. 548. For the specific "monetary" overtones of this abstraction see: Bernhard Malkmus "The Mode of the Picaresque Economies of Circulation" (unpublished talk at the conference *Money and Culture*, National University of Ireland, University College Cork, May 6-8, 2005).

servant mentality of the feudal society. (Thus Lazarillo de Tormes, whose skull was all of a sudden stoned by his first master, a blind beggar, at the beginning of his apprenticeship, retorted later by sending his unsuspecting torturer against a brick wall).[19] Chichikov himself demonstrates remarkable aptness to chameleonic imitation of his counter-agents: nearly everything we see of his personality in one chapter becomes obsolete in another. With the well-mannered dreamer Manilov Chichikov behaves like a well-mannered dreamer, coming to copycat his mellow guest in every sentence of a long dialogue ("Well, allow me, and how did you like the police inspector? Isn't he a nice person? / "A very nice [person] indeed, and how smart, how well-read a person!"). However, with the compulsive liar and rude Nozdrev a gentleman turns into a pushy wheeler-dealer ("No, now you are lying! / No, buddy, that's you who are lying").[20] To be sure, the hero's abnormal flexibility is rooted at least in part in conventions of the picaresque novel dictated by its now obsolete social preconditions – and yet its function becomes even more important now than then.

The increasingly secular culture of the late 17th and early 18th century France and England saw the victory of the picaresque first-person narrative over its shadowy super-ego: for instance, in their translations of *Life of the Rogue [Picaro] Guzman de Alfaráche*, Alain René Lesage and Gabriel de Bremond streamlined narratives so that the small worldly successes of enterprising picaros were more visible and uplifting to the reader.[21] The moral teleology of the picaresque became no more than an intermediary step in the acquisitive practice

---

19 Klaus Poenicke, "Fortune's Wheel and Revolution: On the Picaresque View of History", in Winfried Fluck, Jürgen Peper, Willi Paul Adams (eds.), *Forms and Functions of History in American Literature. Essays in Honor of Ursula Brumm.* (Berlin: Erich Schmidt Verlag, 1981), pp. 121-123; Maurice Molho, "Picarisme des origins ou la dialectique du maître et de l'esclave", in *Caliban* XX (1983), pp. 6-7; Harry Sieber, "Literary Continuity, Social Order, and the Invention of the Picaresque", in Marina S. Brownlee and Hans Ulrich Gumbrecht (eds.), *Cultural Authority in Golden Age Spain* (Baltimore: The Johns Hopkins University Press, 1995), p. 154.

20 "Ну позвольте, а как вам показался полицмейстер? Не правда ли, что очень приятный человек?" – "Чрезвычайно приятный, и какой умный, какой начитанный человек! [...]"; "Нет, врешь, ты это не можешь сказать!" – "Нет, брат, сам ты врешь!" Гоголь, *Мертвые души*, pp. 26, 85). On similar traits in Lazarillo de Tormes see: Alexander Blackburn, *The Myth of the Picaro: Continuity and Transformation of the Picaresque Novel, 1554-1954* (Chapel Hill: Univ. of North Carolina Press, 1979), p. 63.

21 See Parker, *Literature and the Delinquent*, pp. 115, 137-138; Ellen Turner Gutiérrez, *The reception of the picaresque in the French, English, and German traditions* (New York: Peter Lang, 1995), p. 26.

of the new, bourgeois *picaro*: in Daniel Defoe's *Moll Flanders* the main heroine, an enterprising courtesan, uses the admission of guilt – merely to get out of prison and get back on the road full of unsuspecting admirers.[22] The celebrated mercantilism of in *Moll Flanders* sheds a new light on Chichikov's light carriage and its meandering route around the town of N. Each of his estate visits starts with his face change, and yet none of those changes leads to the discovery of the hero's real, substantial, tangible Self. On the contrary, the whole affair seems to rest on the irrelevance of the protagonist's masks to his real appearance (which is never revealed to the reader) and character (which remains unknown to other heroes and is only revealed to the reader in an old-fashioned intrusion of the author at the very end). It is thanks to this moralistic outburst quoted above that Chichikov's only faceless self and the multitude of his selfless faces become two sides of the same coin: the first, elusive and immaterial, grows in wealth and prestige only because the second, always on the move, makes friends with fiends and keeps smiling at strangers. The meaning of abstraction – "not handsome, was not bad-looking either, not fat but at the same time not too thin" turns out to be a variable dependent on the number of Chichikov's interactions with other, less mobile and flexible heroes: *abstractio* cancels out the difference between the causality of the plot and the logic of self-enrichment.

Like the grandiose edifice of *Dead Souls*, Marx's deconstruction of monetary economy has never been brought to complete fruition. However, taken as bits of a larger narrative, *Outline of the Critique of Political Economy* and *Capital* hints at the similar isomorphism of textual structure and textual meaning. Not only do the dialectics of the abstract and the concrete become the major driving force of both narratives but also their major paradox – the unexplainable growth of abstract (surplus) value in the capitalist economics – is explained by the breakdown of this value in time into the multitude of its concrete manifestations ("But the quantity of money in circulation is, as we have seen, determined not only by the sum of commodity-prices to be realized, but also by the velocity with which money circulates, i.e., the speed with which this realization of prices is accomplished during a given period").[23] Yet it would be a wasted effort to end at the point

---

[22] See Parker, *Literature and the Delinquent*, p. 104.

[23] "Die Quantität des zirkulierenden Geldes ist aber, wie wir sahen, nicht nur durch die Gesamtsumme der zu realisierenden Warenpreise bestimmt, sondern zugleich durch die Geschwindigkeit, womit das Geld umläuft oder in einem gegebenen Zeitabschnitt das Geschäft dieser Realisation vollbringt." Marx, *Grundrisse der Kritik der politischen Ökonomie*, p. 152.

when Chichikov is almost proved to play the role of money in Gogol's poem in prose, and money seems to poses as *picaro* in the Marx's treatise: who needs analogies that lead nowhere? Whether this "where" is to be sought in a history of literary forms or in a history of philosophical abstraction is too early to say. But we should probably start looking for the answer.

Armin Schäfer

Mad Money: Melville's Doubloon*

Money plays a particular role in Herman Melville's novel *Moby-Dick*. On the one hand Captain Ahab is deeply involved in economic interests. While his ship *Pequod* was itself no part of the marketplace, it nevertheless debarked for whaling and profit. Whaling, as Charles Olson has suggested, was the biggest industry in America in the first half of the 19th century.[1] (After petrol was discovered in 1859 in Pennsylvania, replacing train oil as an illuminant, whaling started to decline.) The common practice was "that in the whaling business they paid no wages; but all hands, including the captain, received certain shares of the profit called lays, and that these lays were proportioned to the degree of importance pertaining to the respective duties of the ship's company" (p. 75).[2] On the other hand, Ahab is characterized as a madman pretending an economic purpose for the *Pequod's* voyage in order to act out his "monomaniac revenge" (p. 187) on Moby Dick.

These two aspects, the economic purpose and Ahab's madness, cannot be separated. No private madness of Ahab could operate in opposition to a reasonable public economy of whaling. Rather, the novel systematically interrelates psychopathology and modern capitalism.[3]

---

* This paper is the English version of my talk given at the conference *Herman Melville: Moby Dick or The Whale*, organised by Bernhard Siegert, Bauhaus University Weimar, 19 April 2006. I wish to thank Michael Shields, Galway, who helped me so much to re-write this paper in English.

1 Cf. Charles Olson, "Call Me Ishmael", in: *Collected Prose*, ed. by Donald Allen and Benjamin Friedlander, with an introduction by Robert Creeley (Berkeley, Los Angeles, Cal., London: University of California Press, 1997), pp. 1-106.

2 Herman Melville, *The Writings of Herman Melville. The Northwestern-Newberry Edition. Vol. 6: Moby-Dick or The Whale*, ed. by Harrison Hayford, Hershel Parker and G. Thomas Tanselle (Evanston, Chicago, Ill.: Northwestern University Press, The New Library, 1988). The page numbers for all quotations are given in brackets and refer to the Northwestern-Newberry Edition.

3 Since Olson's groundbreaking study *Call Me Ishmael*, this hypothesis has often been advanced. Cf. Michael Paul Rogin, *Subversive Genealogy: The Politics and Art of Herman Melville* (New York: Alfred A. Knopf, 1983); Petra and Uwe Nettelbeck, "More Light,/ And the Gloom Of That Light./ More Gloom,/ And The Light Of That Gloom.", *Die Republik* 82-85 (1988), pp. 29-192; Pierre Lefebvre, "Die Arbeit des

> Ahab had purposely sailed upon the present voyage with the one only and all-engrossing object of hunting the White Whale. Had any one of his old acquaintances on shore but half dreamed of what was lurking in him then, how soon would their aghast and righteous souls have wrenched the ship from such a fiendish man! They were bent on profitable cruises, profit to be counted down in dollars from the mint. He was intent on an audacious, immitigable and supernatural revenge." (p. 186)

In the following, it shall argued that 1) monomania is a specific form of madness that does not derogate reason, but rather enhances the performance of reason and enhances the performance of the maniac as well, that 2) a particular concept of money, the gold coin, belongs to a class of signs that produce that which they represent, carrying out "a semiosis in which signs are seen to create the very objects they are taken to depicting, naming, and representing",[4] and that 3) the interpretation of such signs endlessly proliferates.

At the start of the chapter "The Doubloon", the narrator repeats something he has already reported: "Ere now it has been related how Ahab was wont to pace his quarterdeck". (p. 430) The present perfect tense indicates that the narration began in the past but is still ongoing; Ahab is still pacing the quarterdeck. And the temporal phrases "Ere now" and "But one morning" (ibid.) give the story an immediacy that relieves the simple past of its function of referring to what is past, making it into a more subjective tense. Time passing within the narration begins to become the time it takes to narrate events. In the end, the narration switches to the present tense, becoming a full-blown theatre script as it moves from *telling* to *showing*, a recitation of direct speech: narrated time and time of narration become one in a dramatized sequence of present-tense scenes. Whereas large portions of Ahab's soliloquy after the scene on the quarterdeck can be construed as blank verse,[5] it is not possible to talk of a coherent linguistic patterning of this kind in "The Doubloon". Here, what is emphasized is the immediacy of speech acts – realized, for example, by the increased frequency of deictic expressions – and the self-referential nature of the act of speaking, as well as a 'quoted' quality about what is said, when exceptional turns of phrase stand out like aphorisms. Although direct speech also has a performative dimension within narrative, it presupposes a passive observer within the narration, someone who is separated from the speaker as though by a 'fourth wall' so that the fiction of a theatre scene can develop. It is

---

Wals. Red Mob &/or: Das Kapital", *Schreibheft. Zeitschrift für Literatur* 37 (1991), pp. 4-14.

4 Brian Rotman, *Signifying Nothing: The Semiotics of Zero* (New York: St. Martin's Press, 1987), p. 54.

5 Cf. Melville, *Moby-Dick*, op. cit., p. 167. "I leave a white and turbid wake / Pale waters, paler cheeks, where'er I sail. / The envious billows sidelong swell to whelm / My track; let them, but first I pass." etc.

the intra-narrational listeners that enable Ahab's speech to become a performance that sets a sequence of scenes in motion, and it is only by means of this relay of scenes that the narration is successively updated to the present.

This peculiar structuring of time during narration is closely linked to what is being narrated. The narrator[6] has already repeatedly called Ahab a monomaniac: Although "it is not probable that this monomania took its instant rise at the precise time of his body dismemberment" (p. 184), on the homeward voyage, after the encounter with Moby Dick, that "the final monomania seized him, seems all but certain from the fact that, at intervals during the passage, he was a raving lunatic" (p. 185). While Ahab is "the monomaniac old man" (p. 200; cf. pp. 237, 550), the white whale is "the material counterpart of her monomaniac commander's soul" (p. 199). Moby Dick is "his grand, monomaniac object" (p. 292) or "the monomaniac incarnation of all those malicious agencies" (p. 184) that are encapsulated in Ahab. Nevertheless, in Ahab's "broad madness, not one of his great natural intellects had perished. [...] If such a furious trope may stand, his special lunacy stormed his general sanity, and carried it, and all its concentrated cannon upon its own mad mark; so far that from having lost his strength, Ahab, to that one end, did now possess a thousand fold more potency than ever he had sanely brought to bear upon any reasonable object." (p. 185) The narrator regards his diagnosis as confirmed by the captain's mechanical pacing: it is a symptom of the illness, and particular signals are treated as symptomatic. Ahab's footsteps leave traces on the board, "upon planks so familiar to his tread, that they were all over dented, like geological stones, with the peculiar mark of his walk", his ceaselessly circulating thoughts leave footprints on his "ribbed and dented brow". (p. 160) Ahab's thoughts are "so completely possessing him, indeed, that it all but seemed the inward mould of every outer movement". (ibid.)

In the chapter entitled "The Doubloon", the eponymous object yields a connection between money and madness. The French psychiatrist Pinel observed "alienated inmates at the Salpêtrière who 'at no point showed any damage to their understanding, and who were dominated by a sort of instinct of frenzy, as though the affective faculties alone had been damaged'."[7] According to Pinel's disciple, Jean-Etienne-Dominique Esquirol, monomania is a specific form of mania. While mania is characterized by a general delirium that saps all the mental faculties of

---

6 Although there is an "I", a first person narrator, in the book, he tells us things he cannot possibly know. Here, the term "narrator" is used as an abbreviation for a more complex instance; cf. Gerard Génette, *Figures III* (Paris: Seuil, 1972).

7 Michel Foucault, *History of Madness*, ed. by Jean Khalfa, transl. by Jonathan Murphy and Jean Khalfa (London, New York: Routledge, 2006), p. 524. Foucault quotes Philippe Pinel, *Traité médico-philosophique sur l'aliénation ou La manie* (Paris: Richard, Caille et Ravier, 1801), p. 214.

the patient, monomania directs the delirium to one particular object, leaving the patient's remaining mental faculties unaffected. In cases of mania, Esquirol explains, intellectual and moral faculties are entirely perverted, all actions are in disarray; but in cases of monomania the confused state of the patient's actions is, like his state of mind, only partial. While the mental confusion in cases of mania often results in violent outbursts of passion, in cases of monomania it is violent passion that causes the mental confusion. Putting it in a simplified form, monomania is a combination of madness and reason and need not even result in delirium – it can find expression, as Esquirol says, in "instinctive, automatic actions which have not been preceded by reflection".

A general feature of the illness is a propensity for "false association of ideas". What causes the sickness is, on the one hand, the subordination of ideas to one dominant but false principle and, on the other, the manner in which ideas are linked, since monomania creates similarities and causal links where there are none. In other words, the main symptom of the illness is a specific way of generating meanings. Not that it is possible to distinguish the illness from its symptoms: while we can distinguish, for example, an illness like pneumonia from its symptom – fever – which is not the illness itself, in the case of monomania the illness and its symptom are inextricably bonded. The symptom is not the result of its cause, the illness, but includes its own cause within itself, as if an exchange between cause and effect were taking place. Monomania is not expressed by one or more natural signs that permit a reliable, causally motivated and transparent association between the symptom (or signifier) and the sickness (or signified), but by arbitrary signs for which an associative link is manufactured. So monomania imposes a secondary layer of false associations between previously existing ideas; it strips signs of their 'natural' identity and then equips them with an artificial association, thereby blurring the distinction between 'natural' and 'arbitrary' signs; and it is itself a faculty for generating meanings that reject both the signifying power of nature and the forces of convention.[8]

---

8 Jean-Etienne[-Dominique] Esquirol, *Des maladies mentales considérées sur les rapports médical, hygiénique et médico-legal. Tome premier* (Bruxelles: J. B. Tircher, 1838), p. 332: "La monomanie et la lypémanie [i.e. mélancolie avec délire] sont des affections cérébrales chroniques, sans fièvre, caractérisées par une lésion partielle de l'intelligence, des affections ou de la volonté. Tantôt le désordre intellectuel est concentré sur un seul object ou sur une série d'objects circonscrits, les malades partent d'un principe faux, dont ils suivent sans dévier les raisonnements logiques, et les actes de leur volonté; hors de ce délire partiel, ils sentent, raisonnent, agissent comme tout le monde; des illusions, des hallucinations, des associations vicieuses d'idées, des convictions fausses, eronnées, bizarres, sont la base de ce délire que je voudrais appeler *monomanie intellectuelle*. Tantôt les monomaniaques ne déraisonnent pas,

In "The Doubloon", Ahab's monomania finds new expression in the way he gazes upon the doubloon. He has fashioned a sign of his monomania from a piece of gold, 'recoining' its markings without removing them and without ignoring the coin's conventional monetary value:

> "All ye mast-headers have before now heard me give orders about a white whale. Look ye! d'ye see this Spanish ounce of gold?" – holding up a broad bright coin to the sun – "it is a sixteen dollar piece, men – a doubloon. D'ye see it. Mr, Starbuck, hand me your top-maul."
> While the mate was getting the hammer, Ahab, without speaking, was slowly rubbing the good piece against the skirts of his jacket, as if to heighten its lustre, and without using any words was meanwhile lowly humming to himself, producing a sound so strangely muffled and inarticulate that it seemed the mechanical humming of the wheels of his vitality in him.
> Receiving the top-maul from Starbuck, he advanced towards the mainmast with the hammer uplifted in one hand. Exhibiting the gold with the other, and with a high raised voice exclaiming: "Whosoever of ye raises me with a white-headed whale with a wrinkled brow and crooked jaw: whosoever of ye raises me that white-headed whale, with tree holes punctured in his starboard fluke – look ye, whosoever of ye raises me that same white whale, he shall have his gold ounce, my boys!"
> "Huzza! Huzza!" cried the seamen, as with swinging tarpaulins they hailed the act of nailing the gold to the mast. (pp. 161ff.)

Neither the signifier (the doubloon) nor its signified is lost in its refashioning. However, additional meanings or semantic attributions that are stable (though they may be unclear) can subsequently become part of the sign. The realisation of Ahab's monomania comes when he interprets the doubloon. The narration focuses on Ahab as he is looking at the doubloon once more and sees it as if for the first time: "But one morning, turning to pass the doubloon, he seemed to be newly attracted by the strange figures and inscription stamped on it, as though now for the first time beginning to interpret for himself in some monomaniac way whatever significance might lurk in them." (p. 430) Ahab goes on to read the image stamped on the doubloon as signifying himself. Once he has interpreted the

---

mais leurs affections, leur caractère sont pervertis; par des motifs plausibles, par des explications très-bien raisonnées, ils justifient l'état actuel de leurs sentiments et excusent la bizarrerie, l'inconvenance de leur conduite: c'est ce que les auteurs ont appelé *manie raisonnante*, mais je voudrais nommer *monomanie affective*. Tantôt la volonté est lésée: le malade, hors de voies ordinaires, est entraîné à des actes que la raison ou le sentiment ne déterminent pas, que la conscience réprouve, que la volonté n'a plus la force de réprimer; les actions sont involontaires, instinctives, irrésistibles, c'est la *monomanie sans délire*, ou la *monomanie instinctive*. Tels sont les phénomènes généraux que présente le délire partiel ou la monomanie; mais, suivant que le délire est expansif ou concentré, gai ou triste, il existe des différences qu'il faut signaler."

doubloon in this way he discovers its ability to take on arbitrary meanings. The interpretation showers the doubloon with comparisons: the shiny gold coin is like a mirror whose reflection also unleashes similarities in which the beholder becomes engrossed. The image reflected off the metal becomes a symbolic process, just as the verb 'to mirror back' means the metal's optical reflection but also a general 'projection process'. The very form of the coin corresponds to the things that it reflects, and the doubloon endows everything with which it is compared with an additional meaning. In the mirror image cast by the doubloon, similarities begin to oscillate before bouncing back in formal and physical echoes: its metal shines like the stars depicted as signs upon its disc, and the stars' signs shine in turn, since they are made of the same material.

The doubloon, which Ahab has nailed to the mast and promised to the first man who sights the white whale, signifies, among other things, an unclear mode of signifying. Our difficulty in determining what the doubloon *is* largely arises from the fact that it only has meaning in the moment of its interpretation. This leads the narrator to an enquiry into the relationship between meaning and value, when Ahab starts to interpret the stamped figures and inscription: "And some certain significance lurks in all things, else all things are little worth, and the round world itself but an empty cipher, except to sell by the cartload, as they do hills about Boston, to fill up some morass in the Milky Way." (p. 430) The value of the world, according to this formulation, is founded upon the fact that meaning gives value to all things, or the world itself would be a meaningless sign, "an empty cipher". The reasoning induces vertigo: the derivation of 'value' from 'meaning' slots into a spiral of values, meanings and natural signs, but cancels itself out because value is based merely on meaning rather than on a natural sign: how can a system of values have any basis once it is separated from nature?

The doubloon in *Moby Dick* is a real object as well as a sign endowed with meaning,[9] although the sign is undefined and meant to stand in for others and their operation. On the one hand it is a money coin, a means of payment. It evokes the connection between whaling and economic life, even if it has been temporarily withdrawn from circulation on board the *Pequod*, since it is impossible to buy anything on board. But even if the function of money has been suspended to some degree, the sailors' lives are still dominated by financial realities. Stubb articulates this in no uncertain terms to Pip in the chapter "The Castaway" after the latter falls into the sea: "Stick to the boat, Pip, or by the Lord,

9 Marc Shell has called the doubloon "a coin shown to be not merely an economic token with exchange value but also an esthetic symbol to be infinitely interpreted". Cf. Marc Shell, *The Economy of Literature* (Baltimore, MD, London: The Johns Hopkins University Press, 1978), p. 83.

I won't pick you up if you jump; mind that. We can't afford to lose whales by the likes of you; a whale would sell for thirty times what you would, Pip, in Alabama." (p. 413) On the other hand, the doubloon directs our attention towards an underlying semiotic problem inherent in money and what it represents, a problem that was fundamentally transformed and complicated by the introduction of paper money.[10]

Early theories of money had been based on the signifiers of value or even on the material of which the coin was made, rather than on the money's form. In these terms, wealth is a pile of coins. During the first half of the 19th century, America was the theatre of a bitter dispute about the proper relationship between the dollar and stocks of precious metals. The suspicion was that the power of paper money to represent value was, at best, weak, and that it furthermore undermined the representative power of gold, the functions of which (as a standard of value, a unit of currency and payment) would have to be reassessed. And in turn, it had become obvious that gold and silver had no permanent value. Their value fluctuated and fell because new discoveries expanded supply faster than demand – in 1849, the California Gold Rush had begun.

The idea that money's value was founded upon its link with precious metals was contradicted by the idea that money was a pure sign whose value consisted solely of the fact that it could be used for payment. Money made of precious metal still has a standard of value and still functions as a unit of currency and payment, but only plays a role as "pseudo-gold": "the coin becomes increasingly ideal as a result of a practice, its golden or silver substance being reduced to a mere pseudo-existence".[11]

As far back as Lucian, it has been a cliché that the value of gold is not apparent:

> *Charon*. Oh, so that is *gold*, that glittering yellow stuff, with just a tinge of red in it. I have often heard of gold, but never saw it before.
> *Hermes*. Yes, that is the stuff there is so much talking and squabbling about.
> *Ch*. Well now, I see no advantages about it, unless it is an advantage that it is heavy to carry.
> *Her*. Ah, you do not know what it has to answer for; the wars and plots and robberies, the perjuries and murders; for this men will endure slavery and imprisonment; for this

---

10 Cf. Marc Shell, "The Gold Bug", *Genre* 13:1 (1980), pp. 11-30, here: p. 15; Joseph Vogl, *Kalkül und Leidenschaft: Poetik des ökonomischen Menschen* (Munich: sequenzia, 2002), pp. 272-279.

11 Karl Marx, *Outline of the Critique of Political Economy (Rough Draft of 1857-58) [Second Instalment]*, transl. Victor Schnittke, in Karl Marx, Frederick Engels, *Collected Works. Vol. 29. Karl Marx: 1857–1861* (London: Lawrence & Wishart, 1987), p. 344.

> they traffic and sail the seas.
> *Ch.* For this stuff? Why, it is not much different from copper. I know copper, of course, because I get a penny from each passenger.
> *Her.* Yes, but copper is plentiful, and therefore not much esteemed by men. Gold is found only in small quantities, and the miners have to go to a considerable depth for it. For the rest, it comes out of the earth, just the same as lead and other metals.
> *Ch.* What fools men must be, to be enamoured of an object of this sallow complexion; and of such a weight![12]

One of the questions that paper money raises is: of all the things that could be used as money, why did gold have a monopoly for so long? Marx, who developed his concept in terms of production and consumption, but not in terms of money, hinted at the following explanation:

> The material used to express this symbol is a matter of some consequence, however varied it has been historically. As society develops it also evolves – along with the symbol – the material that more and more corresponds to the symbol, though it later strives to free itself from that material again; a symbol, if not arbitrary, requires certain conditions as regards the material in which it is presented. Thus, e.g. the signs for words possess a history; alphabetic script, etc.[13]

Although it is not necessary that money take the shape of coin, the genesis of the peculiar form of money can be explained. Gold served "as a *universal measure of value*. And only by virtue of this function does gold, the equivalent commodity *par excellence*, become money."[14] Money is indifferent to the material of which it consists. It seems that even the most useful object would have to renounce its usefulness in order to function as money. The potential usefulness of gold and silver cannot be realised while they are in circulation as money. Gold "is capable of being so replaced only in so far as it functions exclusively as coin, or as the circulating medium, and as nothing else."[15] Money's "functional existence absorbs, so to say, its material existence" (p. 139)

---

12 Lucian, "Charon", in: *The Works of Lucian of Samosata*, trans. H. W. Fowler and F. G. Fowler (Oxford: Clarendon Press, 1905), pp. 174ff.

13 Karl Marx, *Outline of the Critique of Political Economy (Rough Draft of 1857-58) [First Instalment]*, trans. Ernst Wangermann, in: Karl Marx, Frederick Engels, *Collected Works. Vol. 28. Karl Marx: 1857-1861* (London: Lawrence & Wishart, 1986), p. 344.

14 Karl Marx, *Capital. A Critique of Political Economy. Volume I. Book One: The Process of Production of Capital*, trans. from the third German edition by Samuel Moore and Edward Aveling, ed. Frederick Engels, in: Karl Marx, Frederick Engels, *Collected Works. Vol. 35* (London: Lawrence & Wishart, 1996), p. 104.

15 ibid., p. 139.

up to the point where "it serves only as a symbol of itself, and is therefore capable of being replaced by a token"[16]. The transition from gold to paper had been stimulated, as Marx analyses, by the *concept* of gold coins that were serving as money. When circulating, the gold coin loses real value, because it gets worn out, so that real and nominal values diverge increasingly: "The fact that the currency of coins itself effects a separation between their nominal and their real weight, creating a distinction between them as mere pieces of metal on the one hand, and as coins with a definite function on the other – this fact implies the latent possibility of replacing metallic coins by tokens of some other material, by symbols serving the same purposes as coins."[17] Circulation turns the gold coin into a symbol of itself. Marx noted "the natural tendency of circulation to convert coins into a mere semblance of what they profess to be, into a symbol of the weight of metal they are officially supposed to contain".[18]

This purely symbolic character of economic values is the ideal state towards which money evolves in the course of its development. As money and circulating currency, gold can be replaced by 'representatives' such as metal tokens. Once gold has been completely assimilated (as currency) into a symbolic system it becomes possible, according to Marx, to make an absolute distinction between the nominal and physical content of the coin. The representative will become a "gold token"[19], which, although it is not made of gold, can represent it, because once gold has been in permanent circulation it is possible to ignore its actual properties. "Silver and copper tokens take the place of gold in those regions of the circulation where coins pass from hand to hand most rapidly, and are subject to the maximum amount of wear and tear."[20] In the course of its development, money changed from substance to fetish, from fetish to symbol, from symbol to pure sign, undergoing a transition from undefined substratum to semiotic relation, until in the end paper signs can represent gold. "The function of gold as coin becomes completely independent of the metallic value of that gold. Therefore things that are relatively without value, such as paper notes, can serve as coins in that place. This purely symbolic character is to a certain extent masked in metal tokens. In paper it stands out plainly."[21] These paper signs correspond to a new financial modus operandi: whereas gold appeared as an iconic sign because the

---

16 ibid.

17 ibid., p. 136.

18 ibid.

19 Marx, *Outline of the Critique of Political Economy [Second Instalment]*, op. cit., p. 349.

20 Marx, *Capital. Vol. 1*, op. cit., p. 136.

21 ibid., p. 137.

material was regarded as valuable, paper money operates self-referentially – even when it is alleged to be backed by corresponding amounts of precious metal – and thus itself becomes a medium. Circulation is not external to the sign. The sign of money is not something that exists in itself so that it may then, in addition, be passed on, but instead it only exists because it has been thrown into circulation. Therefore it is senseless to look for the ultimate foundation of money, even if it were guaranteed by material assets or by the state. It is, ironically, only guaranteed by sheer shortage of money.

In the end the doubloon designates something tied into historical processes, as well as aesthetics – an object in which economic aspects coincide with aspects of sign theory. Even if the material value of a coin need not in itself be valuable (i.e. scarce, useful and desirable) for it to fulfil its functions, it makes a coin more desirable if it can be aesthetically enjoyed. There are signs stamped on the doubloon that designate something more than its value:

> [O]n its round corner it bore the letters, REPUBLICA DEL ECUADOR: QUITO. So this bright coin came from a country planted in the middle of the world, and beneath the great equator, and named after it [...]. Zoned by those letters you saw the likeness of three Andes summits: from one a flame; a tower on another; on the third a crowing cock; while arching over all was a segment of the partitioned zodiac, the signs all marked with their usual cabalistics, and the keystone sun entering the equinoctial point at Libra. (p. 431)

Once nailed to the mast, the doubloon draws attention to these signs – unlike a coin in normal circulation whose appearance often goes barely noticed. The doubloon's inscription and image attract the glance: whereas in the framework of a symbolic system it is necessary to forget that the symbols are made from the same material as the coin, looking at this exposed coin we remember the materiality of the symbol. Like paper money, the doubloon is promised into the future. As opposed to paper money, the doubloon does not anticipate its cashing into gold, but it is gold. It is not promised for success (i.e. the killing of Moby Dick), but promised only for the promise of success (i.e. the sighting of Moby Dick).

In "The Doubloon", a series of updates is given, each of which keeps events in the present. By being observed, each speech is transformed into a theatrical entrance that is broken off as soon as the act of observing impinges upon it. In "The Quarterdeck", Ahab's speech is a fully dramatised appearance on the stage of the quarterdeck; in "The Doubloon" a shift occurs, replacing the communal act of ritualised experience with a sequence of involuntary scenes, secretive asides and unconnected interpretations. This shift in the novel from formalised language, integrated self-portrayal and the creation through ritual of a common purpose, to observation and a communicative relaying of events, is centred on the doubloon.

The competing interpretations of the doubloon do not simply follow one another but are placed in relation to each other. Each speech is only an interpretation of the doubloon in so far as it in turn is interpreted, and every interpretation is integrated into the following interpretation, which will, again, uncover a new way of reading its predecessor and proliferating meaning. Ahab's and Starbuck's interpretations communicate with one another. Starbuck not only contradicts Ahab's interpretation, but updates and interprets it. Unlike Ahab he does not regard the doubloon as a sign of Lucifer but as an almost lacklustre, earthly symbol of the Trinity, upon which the devil (in the person of Ahab) has left his traces. And he understands Ahab's self-interpretation as a *mene tekel* and a prophecy of the apocalypse, as in the Book of Daniel. The Book of Daniel is preoccupied with signs – those that are known to be hidden and those that cannot be understood. Daniel, who is called Belteshazzar at Nebuchadnezzar's court, gives an interpretation of the latter's dream even though the king does not reveal what he has dreamt.

> The king answered and said to Daniel, whose name was Belteshazzar, Art thou able to make known unto me the dream which I have seen, and the interpretation thereof? Daniel answered in the presence of the king, and said, The secret which the king hath demanded cannot the wise men, the astrologers, the magicians, the soothsayers, shew unto the king; But there is a God in heaven that reveleath secrets, and maketh known to king Nebuchadnezzar what shall be in the latter days.[22]

Daniel also interprets the words which King Belshazzar, Nebuchadnezzar's son and successor, finds written on the wall: "And this is the writing that was written, MENE, MENE TEKEL, UPHARSIN. This is the interpretation of the thing: MENE; God hath numbered thy kingdom, and finished it. TEKEL; Thou art weighed in the balances, and art found wanting. PERES; Thy kingdom is divided, and given to the Medes and Persians."[23] On the one hand the prophetic interpretation defers indefinitely any fulfilment of the sign's message. On the other it explains that the sign's meaning and its fulfilment have been there forever. Similarly, Starbuck's and Ahab's interpretations of the doubloon assume a transcendental *signifié* – God, Ahab – but defer establishing any firm meaning until later. In other words, in interpretations of this kind, the doubloon does not stand for something else, but guarantees a kind of meaningfulness that can be realised in different interpretations. In the end, the sequence of interpretations adverts to the historicity of interpretative acts.

---

22 "The Book of Daniel", *The Holy Bible, Containing the Old and New Testament*, Oxford, New York, London, Toronto (Oxford: University Press, n.d.), 2, pp. 27ff.

23 "The Book of Daniel", *The Holy Bible*, op. cit, 5, pp. 25-28.

Stubb, who has followed the previous interpretations, does not succeed in producing an overall interpretation, nor is he willing to reduce the doubloon to its monetary value. For him the doubloon becomes a compendium of signs that can be decoded with the help of reference works. But meanings are reduced to synonyms and tautologies by this kind of decoding; moreover, the successive interpretations keep the meaning opaque rather than leading to resolution or transparency. The doubloon remains undecipherable, and the enactment of the interpretative process becomes an unintended farce. Once interpretation becomes comedy, the ground rules are eventually reversed. When Flask regards the doubloon as money and calculates its monetary exchange value rather than interpreting it, Stubb comments: "Shall I that call wise or foolish, now; if it be really wise it has a foolish look to it; yet, if it be really foolish, then has it a sort of wiseish look to it." (p. 433) Stubbs' bon mot is formulated in imitation of Shakespeare's proverbs; his entire speech is modelled on Shakespeare's plays. Since Charles Olson, a considerable body of research on Melville's reception of Shakespeare has developed,[24] but the point here is simple: Stubb's switch from an interpretation of the doubloon to an observation of the interpreters is continued in the entry of Pip, which is largely modelled on the fool in *King Lear*.[25] Pip's madness is apparent in his speech from the fact that looking and talking go their separate ways. For apparently Pip does not talk of what he is looking at; when he does talk of looking, his speech trails off into nothing, and he conjugates the verb 'to look'. At the same time, however, Pip speaks of what his predecessors have been doing: by switching from looking to speaking, they have been creating meanings that do not exist. While the interpreters have taken turns at (more or less) finding themselves in the doubloon, Pip begins to transform himself while speaking. The others' interpretations say what the doubloon is; Pip, in contrast, launches into indirect speech to report what he has seen or heard. In the end it is Pip who once more separates narrated time from the narration time: "My father, in old Tolland county, cut down a pine tree once." (p. 435)

"The Doubloon" invites interpretations while displaying the principles underlying these interpretations. Its meaning is not exhausted in what is said, nor is it clear how this tension is to be resolved. Right from the start the narration demolishes hope of there being one central argumentative thread: either one calculates the exchange value of the coin rather than interpreting it, or one re-interprets things unrealised in language – for example Queequeg's or Fedallah's entries. Or interpretations that take the coin's representative character seriously

24 Cf. Olson, "Call Me Ishmael", op. cit.; cf. "Melville's Notes (1848-51) in a Shakespeare Volume", Melville, *Moby-Dick*, op. cit., pp. 955-970.

25 Cf. Olson, "Call Me Ishmael", op. cit. ("Captain Ahab and his fool").

are broken off, for example by Ahab's "So be it, then" (p. 432) or Starbuck's shuddering: "I will quit it, lest Truth shake me falsely." (ibid.)

The doubloon plays a central role in two chapters, both of which present dramatised scenes. While "The Quarterdeck" turns the coin into a sign for Ahab's monomania, his monomania is brought up to the present in "The Doubloon" via a short-circuit of its own signs. Just as monomania produces false associations in some ideas, and artificial signs to go with them, so too the semiotic configuration of the doubloon generates a chain of resemblances. Admittedly, Ahab projects fresh meaning into the monetary sign (the doubloon) upon which the monomaniac sign comes to rest. But the relation between the monetary sign and the monomaniac sign is not exclusively to be understood by focusing on Ahab. The narrator takes for granted a logical reversal, assuming that it is the coin itself that gives rise to Ahab's monomania. It is precisely because it is impossible to say what the doubloon means that it invites open-ended interpretative installments. The coin's markings allow an aesthetic heightening of its monetary value and are the starting point for these interpretations, since they conceal (so the interpreters assume) an unspoken meaning, which finds expression precisely in money's visually aesthetic aspects. The interpretations regard the presence of a sign as a promise that there will be meaning. Or they see in it symbolic preconditions for action. Or they decode the signs and inscribe a tautological meaning.

The chapter's layout as a sequence of scenes, the entrances and exits of characters, and the visibility of the doubloon and of the sign, lead one to ask how looking becomes speaking; in the context of the connections to Shakespeare "The Doubloon" draws attention to a specific way of manufacturing illusions. In Shakespeare the problem is how to transform something non-existent into something effective through speech.[26] In *King Lear*, Edgar acts the part of a madman who convinces Gloucester, whose eyes have been put out, that they are climbing up a (non-existent) mountain; although he is blind, once he has made the imaginary climb to the top of the cliffs of Dover and leapt into the abyss, Gloucester "sees" once more. The fool's speech works because it depicts nothing, but creates an illusion that is completely uncoupled from anything visible. Pip's speech comprises elements of this act of "speaking": here, speech does not take as its subject the doubloon which is seen, but begins instead to narrate. Although Ahab's madness is directed upon the economy, *Moby-Dick* is not about whaling, the motor of industry, versus Ahab's private madness, so much as about an all-inclusive madness, the symbolic order of capital.

---

26 Cf. Charles Olson, "*Lear* and *Moby-Dick*", *Twice a Year* 1 (1938), pp. 165-189; Olson, "Call Me Ishmael", op. cit. ("Captain Ahab and his fool").

Fiona Cox

Pygmalion and the Prostitute: Processes of Exchange in *Les Misérables*

Exchange – transactions, commerce, buying and selling – is the fundamental dynamic of *Les Misérables*. Hugo's exposition of the world inhabited by the poor in nineteenth century France entails an analysis of the endless negotiations in which its subjects must engage in order to ensure the survival of both body and soul. Hugo encloses the whole epic within these two exigencies: at the start of the book Bishop Myriel buys with two silver candlesticks the soul of Jean Valjean, the book's protagonist,[1] and towards the end of the work Hugo shows how the cycle of misery is set to continue, as the villainous Thénardier emigrates to America in order to make his fortune in the slave trade, the market of human flesh. Between these two extremes everything is sold and innumerable contracts are made. Children are bought and sold, most notably Cosette; the gentle scholar Mabeuf is forced to sell his books, one by one, in order to buy food (and the disappearance of his library entails the diminishing of his identity); the young mother, Fantine, is forced to strip herself of all that she has in order to protect and provide for her daughter, Cosette[2] – she sells first her hair, then her teeth and finally her body, as she is driven into prostitution.

Prostitution is one of the dominant themes of *Les Misérables*. The first of the five volumes that make up the work is named after Fantine, and Hugo gives a detailed account of her fall immediately after the episode in which Bishop Myriel buys Jean Valjean's soul. In his 'Préface' Hugo rails against the human embodiments of misery forged by society, one of which is the prostitute: "So long as there shall exist, by reason of law and custom, a social condemnation, which, in the face of civilisation, artificially creates hells on earth, and complicates a destiny that is divine, with human fatality; so long as the three problems of the

1 For a full discussion of this episode see Fiona Cox, "Money and Identity in *Les Misérables*", in Sarah Capitanio, Lisa Downing, Paul Rowe and Nicholas White (eds.), *Currencies – Fiscal Fortunes and Cultural Capital in Nineteenth Century France* (Bern: Peter Lang, 2005), pp. 121-132.

2 In an excellent account Kathryn Grossman points out that "[a]s in a hideous striptease, she [Fantine] inverts the conventional view of prostitution by selling first her hair, then her teeth, and finally her virtue." Kathryn Grossman, *Figuring Transcendence in Les Misérables – Hugo's Romantic Sublime* (Carbondale and Edwardsville: Southern Illinois University Press, 1994), p. 35.

age – the degradation of man by poverty, the ruin of woman by starvation, and the dwarfing of childhood by physical and spiritual night – are not solved; [...] books like this cannot be useless."[3] Prostitution is not only the most visible form of suffering amongst the female *misérables* but Hugo's treatment of the theme highlights society's lack of regard for the individual and his/ her humanity generally. A work whose protagonist is designed to function as Everyman necessarily focusses upon the ways in which one identity is substituted for another, in which human beings segue from one name to another and from one role to another. This chapter will examine the way in which Hugo engages with the myth of Pygmalion to depict society as both creator and abuser of Fantine and will show how his subversion of Ovid's *Metamorphoses* is intimately linked to his vision of a world that is driven by exchange and profiteering.

When we first meet Fantine she appears as someone with no attachments and no family history – she is simply known as Fantine. This not only establishes a parallel with Jean Valjean, whose family are lost to him while he is in prison and who adopts various new names in the course of the book, but it also emphasises her vulnerability. "Un nom est un moi" ("A name is a self") observes Valjean, and with no solid identity of her own Fantine is all the more susceptible to being forced into prostitution, into assuming the many different identities her clients demand. Anne Übersfeld examines the way in which Hugo quite deliberately eradicates Fantine's real name in order to present a being whose name announces her feyness and fragility, "une fantine", a word that means sprite or fairy.[4] Übersfeld cites Hugo at some length in order to analyse the origins of Fantine's anonymity:

---

3 Victor Hugo, *Les Misérables*. Introduced and edited by Roger Clark (Ware: Wordsworth Editions, 2002). All citations from the English edition will be from this edition.
"Tant qu'il existera, par le fait des lois et des mœurs, une damnation sociale créant artificiellement, en pleine civilisation, des enfers, et compliquant d'une fatalité humaine la destinée qui est divine; tant que les trois problèmes du siècle, la dégradation de l'homme par le prolétariat, la déchéance de la femme par la faim, l'atrophie de l'enfant par la nuit, ne seront pas résolus [...] des livres de la nature de celui-ci pourront ne pas être inutiles." Victor Hugo, *Les Misérables* (Paris: Laffont 'Bouquins', 1985). All references to the French text will be to this edition.

4 "Or, sans doute n'est-ce pas un hasard si ceux dont la trace familiale est la plus aléatoire est la plus profondément perdue sont ceux dont le nom est le plus aléatoire." Anne Übersfeld, "Nommer la misère". First published in *Revue des sciences humaines*, XXXIX no. 156 (octobre-décembre 1974), pp. 581-596. Reprinted in Guy Rosa (ed.), *Les Misérables – Parcours critique* (Paris: Klinksieck, 1995), pp. 114-126, here: p. 115.

> Fantine was one of those beings which are brought forth from the heart of the people. Sprung from the most unfathomable depths of social darkness, se bore on her brow the mark of the anonymous and unknown. She was born at M – on M—. Who were her parents? None could tell, she had never known either father or mother. She was called Fantine – why so? because she had never been known by any other name. At the time of her birth, the Directory was still in existence. She could have no family name, for she had no family; she could have no baptismal name, for then there was no church. She was named after the pleasure of the first passer-by who found her, a mere infant, straying barefoot in the streets. (p. 83)[5]

"Anonymat délibéré" concludes Übersfeld, before arguing convincingly that Fantine's real name was Marguerite Louet. The name Marguerite reminds us of the pearls to which Fantine's teeth are likened before she has to sell them, while the surname Louet is suggestive of the word 'louer', 'to hire out, to rent' and foreshadows Fantine's destiny as a prostitute. On this reading a note of doom is sounded in one of the earliest descriptions we have of her: "Fantine was beautiful and remained pure as long as she could. She was a pretty blonde with fine teeth. She had gold and pearls for her dowry; but the gold was on her head and the pearls in her mouth." (p. 84)[6] By effacing Fantine's family history Hugo is able to show how she becomes vulnerable to society's basest desires, how her identity is moulded by the extreme circumstances into which she is driven. Paradoxically we are shown the Pygmalion myth in reverse.

That Hugo plans to engage extensively with this myth is clear from his frequent evocation of ancient Rome at the start of Fantine's story. This is facilitated by the fact that she is romantically linked to a student, and so frequently finds herself in the Latin quarter of Paris: "Fantine, in those labyrinths of the hill of the Pantheon, where so many ties are knotted and unloosed, long fled from Tholomyès, but in such a way as always to meet him again. There is a way of avoiding a person which resembles a search. In short, the eclogue took

5 "Fantine était un de ces êtres comme il en éclot, pour ainsi dire, au fond du peuple. Sortie des plus insondables épaisseurs de l'ombre sociale, elle avait au front le signe de l'anonyme et de l'inconnu. Elle était née à Montreuil-sur-Mer. De quels parents? Qui pourrait le dire? On ne lui avait jamais connu d'autre nom. A l'époque de sa naissance le Directoire existait encore. Point de nom de famille, elle n'avait pas de famille; point de nom de baptême, l'église n'était plus là. Elle s'appela comme il plut au permier passant qui la rencontra toute petite, allant pieds nus dans la rue." (pp. 98-99)

6 "Fantine était belle et resta pure le plus longtemps qu'elle put. C'était une jolie blonde avec de belles dents. Elle avait de l'or et des perles pour dot, mais son or était sur sa tête et ses perles étaient dans sa bouche." (p. 99)

place." (p. 84)[7] The charming pastoral idyll, suggested by the word "églogue", will soon darken and become a far more threatening and sinister scenario. Tholomyès' wealth allows him to avoid any kind of responsibility. In a ghastly foreshadowing of Fantine's fall Hugo describes how this *bon viveur* is able to repair both his moral and physical shortcomings with money:

> Tholomyès was a good liver, thirty years old, and ill preserved. He was wrinkled, his teeth were broken, and he was beginning to show signs of baldness, of which he said, gaily: "*The head at thirty, the knees at forty.*" His digestion was not good and he had a weeping eye. (p. 84)[8]

Hugo is fond of establishing cycles of opposing fortunes between his characters – most notably as Napoleon's star wanes Jean Valjean's fortune is on the rise. Where Tholomyès is able to compensate for his natural physical decline with an irony made affordable through wealth, Fantine has to drive her body into a parallel decline in order to raise money to save her child. By his progressive charting of the various stages of Fantine's fall Hugo shows that her descent is both inexorable and inevitable, as she sells off various parts of her body. She begins by selling her hair in order to clothe her child:

> Her beautiful fair hair fell below her waist. "What beautiful hair!" exclaimed the barber.
> "How much will you give me for it?" said she.
> "Ten francs."
> "Cut it off."
> She bought a knit skirt and sent it to the Thénardiers. [...]
> Fantine thought: "My child is no longer cold, I have clothed her with my hair." (p. 123)[9]

---

7 "Fantine, dans ces dédales de la colline du Panthéon, où tant d'aventures se nouent et se dénouent, avait fui longtemps Tholomyès, mais de façon à le rencontrer toujours. Il y a une manière d'éviter qui ressemble à chercher. Bref, l'églogue eut lieu." (p. 99)

8 "Tholomyès était un viveur de trente ans, mal conservé. Il était ridé et édenté; et il ébauchait une calvitie dont il disait lui-même sans tristesse: *crâne à trente ans, genou à quarante.* Il digérait médiocrement, et il lui était venu un larmoiement à un œil. Mais à mesure que sa jeunesse s'éteignait, il allumait sa gaîté; il remplaçait ses dents par des lazzis, ses cheveux par la joie, sa santé par l'ironie, et son œil qui pleurait riait sans cesse." (p. 99)

9 "Ses admirables cheveux blonds lui tombèrent jusqu'aux reins.
Les beaux cheveux! s'écria le barbier.
Combien m'en donneriez-vous? dit-elle.
Dix francs.
Coupez-les.

She then has to sell her teeth in order to buy her child's medicine:

> Then she looked at Fantine who sadly turned her shorn head.
> Fantine had grown ten years older since evening.
> "Bless us!" said Marguerite, "what is the matter with you, Fantine?"
> "Nothing," said Fantine. "Quite the contrary. My child will not die with that frightful sickness for lack of aid. I am satisfied."
> So saying, she showed the old woman two Napoleons that glistened on the table.
> "Oh! good God!" said Marguerite. "Why there is a fortune! where did you get these louis d'or?"
> "I got them," answered Fantine.
> At the same time she smiled. The candle lit up her face. It was a sickening smile, for the corners of her mouth were stained with blood, and a dark cavity revealed itself there.
> The two teeth were gone.
> She sent the forty francs to Montfermeil. (p. 125)[10]

Finally she becomes a prostitute, offering herself to the men on the street, so that her child will not be turned out onto the street:

> About the same time, Thénardier wrote to her that really he had waited with too much generosity, and that he must have a hundred francs immediately, or else little Cosette, just convalescing after her severe sickness, would be turned out of doors into the cold and upon the highway, and that she would become what she could, and would perish if she must. "A hundred francs," thought Fantine. "But where is there a place where one can earn a hundred sous a day?"
> "Come!", said she, "I will sell what is left."
> The unfortunate creature became a woman of the town. (p. 126)[11]

Elle acheta une jupe de tricot et l'envoya aux Thénardier. [...]
Fantine pensa. – Mon enfant n'a plus froid. Je l'ai habillée de mes cheveux." (p. 146)

10 "Puis elle regarda Fantine qui tournait vers elle sa tête sans cheveux.
Fantine depuis la veille avait vieilli de dix ans.
- Jésus! fit Marguerite, qu'est-ce que vous avez, Fantine?
- Je n'ai rien, répondit Fantine. Au contraire. Mon enfant ne mourra pas de cette affreuse maladie, faute de secours. Je suis contente. [...]
En parlant ainsi elle sourit. La chandelle éclairait son visage. C'était un sourire sanglant. Une salive rougeâtre lui souillait le coin des lèvres, et elle avait un trou noir dans la bouche.
Les deux dents étaient arrachées.
Elle envoya les quarante francs à Montfermeil." (p. 148)

11 "Vers le même temps, le Thénardier lui écrivit que décidément il avait attendu avec beaucoup trop de patience, et qu'il lui fallait cent francs, tout de suite; sinon qu'il mettrait à la porte la petite Cosette, toute convalescente de sa grande maladie, par le froid, par les chemins, et qu'elle deviendrait ce qu'elle pourrait, et qu'elle crèverait, si

Fantine's transformation is all the more striking precisely because her first appearance in the book is as this "fantin" this unearthly nymph, the description of whom owes much to Ovid's *Metamorphoses.* When we first meet her it is under yet another nickname; she is known as "la Blonde" because of her glorious hair (p. 97) By superimposing his presentation of Paris on the mythical world of the ancients Hugo demonstrates that Fantine, through her innate beauty and grace, belonged naturally to the race of Daphne or Galatea:

> Fantine was beautiful, without being too conscious of it. Those rare dreamers, the mystrious priests of the beautiful, who silently compare all things with perfection, would have had a dim vision in this little work-woman, through the transparency of Parisian grace, of the ancient sacred Euphony. This daughter of obscurity had race. She possessed both types of beauty – style and rhythm. Style is the force of the ideal, rhythm is its movement. (p. 86)[12]

The end of her story shadows the presentation of her here. Hugo reminds us that she is a "fille de l'ombre". On one level he is simply referring to her unknown origins, but the phrase is also suggestive of the darkness that lies ahead of her and reminds us that she ends up as a "fille publique". This note of foreboding echoes Hugo's warning uttered in his Préface, that it is through society's articial creation of hell that women such as Fantine are driven into prostitution. Nature designed Fantine as a nymph; society transformed her into a prostitute.

This theme of transformation, of metamorphosis, is emphasised by Hugo's evocation of the myth of Pygmalion.[13] The myth is one of those treated by Ovid in the *Metamorphoses* and tells the story of the sculptor, Pygmalion, who created a statue of a nymph, Galatea, that was so beautiful and realistic that his love for her warmed the marble and brought her to life. As Hugo unfolds the description of Fantine his language borrows more and more heavily from the world of

---

elle voulait. – Cent francs, songea Fantine. Mais où y a-t-il un état à gagner cent sous par jour?
Allons! dit-elle, vendons le reste.
L'infortunée se fit fille pudique." (p. 149)

12 "Fantine était belle sans trop le savoir. Les rares songeurs, prêtres mystérieux du beau, qui confrontent silencieusement toute chose à la perfection, eussent entrevu en cette petite ouvrière, à travers la transparence de la grâce parisienne, l'antique euphonie sacrée. Cette fille de l'ombre avait de la race. Elle était belle sous les deux espèces qui sont le style et le rhythme. Le style est la forme de l'idéal; le rhythme en est le mouvement." (p. 102)

13 This myth was particularly popular in nineteenth century France. The most notable treatments of the Pygmalion myth were written by Balzac, *Le Chef d'œuvre* and Zola, *L'Œuvre.*

sculpture, to the point where he identifies in the form of Fantine mouldings reminiscent of the sculptor, Coustou:

> A brilliant face, delicate profile, eyes of a deep blue, heavy eyelashes, small, arching feet, the wrists and ankles neatly encased, the white skin showing here and there the azure arborescence of the veins; a cheek small and fresh, a neck robust as that of Aegean Juno, the nape firm and supple, shoulders modelled as if by Coustou, with a voluptuous dimple in the centre, just visible through the muslin; a gaity tempered with reverie, sculptured and exquisite – such was Fantine, and you divined beneath this dress and these ribbons a statue, and in this statue a soul. (p. 86)[14]

The passage depicts a being on the brink of metamorphosis, halfway between statue and flesh. For Hugo it is Fantine's innate purety that makes her statuesque and her *joie de vivre* that animates her loveliness. That we are expected to see in her story an adaptation of the Pygmalion myth is made clear earlier in the chapter when Hugo actually likens her to Galatée:

> As to Fantine, she was joy itself. Her splendid teeth had evidently been endowed by God with one function – that of laughing. She carried in her hand rather than on her head, her little hat of sewed straw, with long, white strings. Her thick, blonde tresses, inclined to wave, and easily escaping from their confinement, obliging her to fasten them continually, seemed designed for the flight of Galatea under the willows. Her rosy lips babbled with enchantment. The corners of her mouth, turned up voluptuously like the antique masks of Erigone, seemed to encourage audacity; but her long, shadowy eyelashes were cast discreetly down towards the lower part of her face as if to check its festive tendencies. (p. 86)[15]

---

14 "Eclatante de face, délicate de profil, les yeux d'un bleu profond, les paupières grasses, les pieds cambrés et petits, les poignets et les chevilles admirablement emboîtés, la peau blanche laissant voir çà et là les arborescences azurées des veines, la joie puérile et fraîche, le cou robuste des Junons éginétiques, la nuque forte et souple, les épaules modelées comme par Coustou, ayant au centre une voluptueuse fossette visible à travers la mousseline; une gaîté glacée de rêverie; sculpturale et exquise; telle était Fantine; et l'on devinait sous ces chiffons et ces rubans une statue; et dans cette statue une âme." (p. 102)

15 "Quant à Fantine, c'était la joie. Ses dents splendides avaient évidemment reçu de Dieu une fonction, le rire. Elle portait à sa main plus volontiers que sur sa tête son petit chapeau de paille cousue aux longues brides blanches. Ses épais cheveux blonds, enclins à flotter et facilement dénoués et qu'il fallait rattacher sans cesse, semblaient faits pour la fuite de Galatée sous les saules. Ses lèvres roses babillaient avec enchantement. Les coins de sa bouche, voluptueusement relevés comme aux mascarons antiques d'Erigone, avaient l'air d'encourager les audaces; mais ses longs cils pleins d'ombre s'abaissaient discrètement sur ce brouhaha du bas du visage comme pour mettre le holà." (p. 101)

Once more there is a tension in this passage between the fluidity of Fantine's natural grace and the rigidity of stone suggested by the "antique masks of Erigone." By representing Galatea as a nymph at flight through the trees Hugo also evokes the myth of Daphne fleeing Apollo and finding sanctuary by being transformed into a laurel tree. One of the most famous responses to the myth of Daphne is Bernini's statue in the Galleria Borghese which is exquisitely poised between living being and statue, stasis and flight. Moreover this evocation introduces a sense of menace into the description that is further developed by the mention of the shadow haunting Fantine's modest downward gaze. Hugo's description here alerts us to the more sinister elements shading the Ovidian account of the story of Pygmalion:

> Meanwhile, with wondrous art he successfully carves a figure out of snowy ivory, giving it a beauty more perfect than that of any woman ever born. And with his own work he falls in love. The face is that of a real maiden, whom you would think living and desirous of being moved if modesty did not prevent. [...] Often he lifts his hands to the work to try whether it be flesh or ivory. [...] Pygmalion, having brought his gift to the altar, stood and falteringly prayed: "If ye, O gods, can give all things, I pray to have as wife – he did not dare add "my ivory maid", but said, "one like my ivory maid." [...] When he returned he sought the image of his maid, and bending over the couch he kissed her. She seemed warm to his touch. Again he kissed her, and with his hands also he touched her breast. The ivory grew soft to his touch and, its hardness vanishing, gave and yielded beneath his fingers, as Hymettian wax grows soft under the sun and, moulded by the thumb, is easily shaped to many forms and becomes usable through use itself. The lover stands amazed, rejoices still in doubt, fears he is mistaken, and tries his hopes again and yet again with his hand. Yes, it was real flesh! The veins were pulsing beneath his testing finger. Then did the Paphian hero pour out copious thanks to Venus, and again pressed with his lips real lips at last. The maiden felt the kisses, blushed and, lifting her timid eyes up to the light, she saw the sky and her lover at the same time.[16]

The Pygmalion myth is commonly adopted as a means of thinking about the mimetic and transformative powers of art.[17] It is also, however, a myth that meditates upon the force of desire and the fantasising gaze. The above passage blends the innocence of the ivory maid with the libidinous urges of her creator that bring her to life. The blush suffusing her face, even as she is being born, indicates the corruption of her purity – and the fact that she beholds the daylight

16 Ovid, *Metamorphoses* X, 247-251, 254-55, 280-294, ed. and trans. by Frank Justus Miller (Cambridge Massachussetts and London: Harvard University Press, Loeb Edition, 1984). All references will be to this edition.

17 Leonard Barkan, *The Gods made Flesh – Metamorphosis and the Pursuit of Paganism* (New Haven and London: Yale University Press, 1986), pp. 284-85.

and the signs of her lover's lust at one and the same time indicates that she is born purely as a vehicle to satisfy his desires. Ovid emphasises this by pointing out that Pygmalion would have been content with a living woman standing in for his work of art, "one like my ivory maid", but is delighted by the animation of his own creation. In this case a prostitute is unnecessary as, by a miracle, the embodiment of all his wishes is brought to life. There is no need to brush aside any other identity in order to force his partner to conform absolutely to his needs. But that Pygmalion is a treatment of prostitution is indicated by the fact that Ovid's stories in the *Metamorphoses* are thematically linked; the story immediately following Pygmalion and Galatea is the tale of Pygmalion's great granddaughter, Myrrha, who falls in love with her father, while the story immediately preceding it is that of the "foul" Propoetides who "are said to have been the first to prostitute their bodies and their fame; and as their shame vanished and the blood of their face hardened, they were turned but with small change to hard stones."

The juxtaposition of the myths of the Propoetides and Myrrha heighten the unwholesome tone of the Pygmalion episode. Where Galatea modestly responds to the passion of her creator, Myrrha falls passionately in love with her father (her creator) and seduces him, allowing Ovid to contemplate the nature of incestuous desire. And immediately before the statue of Galatea is transformed into a living woman who can fulfil all of Pygmalion's desires, the first prostitutes of the world are transformed into statues as punishment for their shamelessness. The triumph of this miraculous transformation of the work of art is therefore undermined by these overtones of perverted sexuality,[18] and these overtones remind us also that a common strategy on the part of the prostitute or the unwilling sexual partner is to disengage mind from body, to become as stone. Carol Ann Duffy examines this in her poem *Pygmalion's Bride* which retells the myth from Galatea's perspective:

> Cold, I was, like snow, like ivory.
> I thought *He will not touch me*,
> but he did.

---

[18] ibid., p. 78: "Finally, though, it must be said that Ovid does not leave everything in such an affirmative condition as we have been suggesting. Pygmalion's story leads directly to the tale of Myrrha, the great-granddaughter of Pygmalion and his statue. Myrrha falls in love with *her* creator, and that experience leads to an undoing of all the certainties celebrated by the story of Pygmalion. Still, the Pygmalion story stands not only as a statement about art and not only as a vindication of human transformation but also an affirmation of metamorphosis as a force leading individuals to find and define their own nature."

He kissed my stone-cool lips.
I lay still
as though I'd died.
He stayed.
He thumbed my marbled eyes.[19]

Paradoxically, therefore, Hugo's reliance on statue imagery to evoke Fantine's youthful and unblemished beauty is suggestive of her transformation into a prostitute. The innocence that enhances her appeal is precisely the quality that makes her so vulnerable. When we first meet her it is as one of a group of four girls who are the consorts of a group of four young men. Of the four girls she is the only one to remain faithful to her lover: "She was the only one of the four to be petted by but one." (p. 83)[20] Her constancy is not matched by that of her lover who mistakenly kisses one of her friends instead of Fantine, indicating already that others can stand in for Fantine, just as she will end up standing in for other women when she prostitutes herself: "'Everything is beautiful; the flies hum in the sunbeams. The humming birds whizz in the sunshine. Kiss me, Fantine!' And, by mistake, he kissed Favourite." (p. 94)[21] Fantine's guilelessness is further indicated by the fact that, when the four men announce that they have a surprise for them, she is the only one of the four not to ask for anything in exchange for her affections:

"Do not be long!" cried Fantine.
"What are they going to bring us?" said Zéphine.
"Surely something pretty," said Dahlia.
"I hope it will be gold," resumed Favourite. (p. 96) [22]

Unhappily the surprise is all four men are abandoning their lovers in order to concentrate on their careers and their social standing. In their jointly written letter they explain that: "The Toulouse diligence snatches us from the abyss, and you are this abyss, our beautiful darlings!" (p. 97)[23] Shortly after their departure Fantine discovers that she is pregnant by Tholomyès, and is thereby cast into

---

19 Carol Ann Duffy, *The World's Wife* (London: Picador, 1999), p. 51.

20 "Elle était la seule des quatre qui ne fût tutoyée que par un seul." (p. 98)

21 "'Tout est beau. Les mouches bourdonnent dans les rayons. Le soleil a éternué le colibri. Embrasse-moi, Fantine!' Il se trompa, et embrassa Favourite." (p. 111)

22 "Ne soyez pas longtemps! cria Fantine.
Que vont-ils nous rapporter? dit Zéphine.
Pour sûr, ce sera joli, dit Dahlia.
Moi, reprit Favourite, je veux que ce soit en or." (p. 113)

23 "La diligence de Toulouse nous arrache à l'abîme, et l'abîme c'est vous, ô nos belles petites!" (p. 115)

precisely the abyss that Tholomyès himself avoids. In her fall, however, Fantine is returning to her origins. She flowered from the basest and most degraded of backgrounds: "Fantine was one of those beings which are brought forth from the heart of the people. Sprung from the most unfathomable depths of social darkness, she bore on her brow the mark of the anonymous and unknown." (p. 83)[24] Later in the book Hugo develops the imagery with regard to the city urchin:

> Whoever ye are who call yourselves Prejudice, Abuse, Ignominy, Oppression, Iniquity, Despotism, Injustice, Fanaticism, Tyranny, beware of the gaping *gamin*.
> This little fellow will grow.
> Of what clay is he made? Of the first mud of the street. A handful of common soil, a breath and, behold, Adam! (p. 391)[25]

Once more Hugo underlines the callous indifference shown by society towards the individual. Just as Fantine is named by the whim of the first passer-by, the urchin is formed from the first lump of clay that happens to be to hand. The passage not only perpetuates the sculpture imagery by focussing on the raw materials needed to form a human being, but places society in the position of creator, the being that gives breath to its subjects. As much as the urchin Fantine is shaped by her background. Hugo gives us a detailed account of her gradual decline into prostitution, constantly reminding us that it is society that has manipulated her into degradation and disintegration, a position that is a far cry from her statuesque loveliness. Fantine loses her marmoreal beauty and becomes progressively more corporeal, more earthy. The metaphors that Hugo employs show the veneer of wealth dissolving:

> It was Fantine. Hard to recognise, yet, on looking attentively, you saw that she still retained her beauty. A sad line, such as is formed by irony, had marked her right cheek. As to her toilette – that airy toilette of muslin and ribbons which seemed as if made of gaiety, folly and music, full of baubles and perfumed with lilacs – that had vanished like the beautiful, sparkling hoarfrost, which we take for diamonds in the sun; they melt, and leave the branch dreary and black. (p. 100)[26]

---

24 "Fantine était un de ces êtres comme il en éclôt, pour ainsi dire, au fond du peuple. Sortie des plus insondables épaisseurs de l'ombre sociale, elle avait au front le signe de l'anonyme et de l'inconnu." (p. 98)

25 "Qui que vous soyez qui vous nommez Préjugé, Abus, Ignorance, Oppression, Iniquité, Despotisme, Injustice, Fantisme, Tyrannie, prenez garde au gamin béant.
Ce petit grandira.
De quelle argile est-il fait? De la première fange venue. Une poignée de boue, un souffle, voilà Adam." (p. 460)

26 "C'était Fantine. Difficile à reconnaître. Pourtant à l'examiner attentivement, elle avait toujours sa beauté. Un pli triste, qui ressemblait à un commencement d'ironie, ridait sa

Fantine's appearance has been damaged by the manual labour that she has to take on in order to look after her child. Hugo emphasises the changes in her by focussing on the same body parts that he has already glorified – the golden hair, the pearly teeth. Even before she is forced to sell hair and teeth they are already losing their lustre as she is unable to animate them with her carefree *joie de vivre*; and her delicate, floating clothes have been replaced with clumsy, practical and ugly clothing:

> she had the appearance of a working woman who is seeking to return to the life of a peasant. She was young, – and pretty? It was possible, but in that garb beauty could not be displayed. Her hair, one blonde mesh of which had fallen, seemed very thick, but it was severely fastened up beneath an ugly, close, narrow nun's head-dress, tied under the chin. Laughing shows fine teeth when one has them, but she did not laugh. Her eyes seemed not to have been tearless for a long time. She was pale, and looked very weary, and somewhat sick. She gazed upon her child, sleeping in her arms, with that peculiar look which only a mother possesses who nurses her own child. Her form was clumsily masked by a large, blue handkerchief folded across her bosom. Her hands were tanned and spotted with freckles, the forefinger hardened and pricked with the needle; she wore a coarse brown delaine mantle, a calico dress, and large, heavy shoes. It was Fantine. (p. 100)[27]

The ephemerally delicate overtones of the nickname Fantine become more and more obscene as her appearance changes, a process which indicates yet again how much of Fantine's downfall was written into her history from the very beginning. As in Ovid's *Metamorphoses* her fall into degradation is accompanied by a progressive decline in appearance. Fantine's honour is ransomed to her child; she is forced to sell her very self to society's lusts and desires, and the fact that she has no rights to a full human existence is indicated by the transformation even in the quality of light she is allowed to enjoy. For the poor the very light of the sun is rationed:

---

joue droite. Quant à sa toilette, cette aérienne toilette de mousseline et de rubans qui semblait faite avec de la gaîté, de la folie et de la musique, pleine de grelots et parfumée de lilas, elle s'était évanouie comme ces beaux givres éclatants qu'on prend pour des diamants au soleil." (p. 119)

27 "Elle avait la mise d'une ouvrière qui tend à redevenir paysanne. Elle était jeune. Etait-elle belle? peut-être; mais avec cette mise il n'y paraissait pas. Ses cheveux, d'où il s'échappait une mèche blonde, semblaient fort épais, mais disparaissaient sévèrement sous une coiffe de béguine, laide, serrée, étroite et nouée au menton. Le rire montre les belles dents quand on en a ; mais elle ne riait point. [...] Elle avait les mains hâlées et toutes piquées de taches de rousseur, l'index durci et déchiqueté par l'aiguille, une marlebrune de laine bourrue, une robe de toile et de gros souliers. C'était Fantine." (p. 119)

> She had been discharged towards the end of winter; summer passed away. But winter returned. Short days, less work. In winter there is no hear, no light, no noon, evening touches morning, there is fog, and mist, the window is frosted, and you cannot see clearly. The sky is but the mouth of a cave. The sun has the appearance of a pauper. Frightful season! Winter changes into stone the water of heaven and the heart of man. (p. 123)[28]

Fantine's flesh becomes increasingly frail the more she has to respond to the stony-heartedness of humanity. The paucity of light and the cruelty of society fast-forward her through life so that it is no longer the graceful statue staring out from behind her features, but the corpse. Hugo describes Fantine towards the end of her life when she has succumbed to the inevitable and turned herself into a prostitute; his description both depicts a creature from beyond the grave, and föcusses upon the detail of her ravaged appearance, so as to highlight the contrast between this pitiful being and the woman we first met whose exquisitely formed features so resembled classical sculpture:

> A few months earlier, when Fantine had lost the last of her modesty, her last shame and her last happiness she was the shadow of herself; now she was the spectre of herself. Physical suffering had completed the work of moral suffering. This creature of twenty five years had a wrinkled forehead, flabby cheeks, pinched nostrils, shrivelled gums, a leaden complexion, a bony neck, protruding collar-bones, skinny limbs, an earthy skin, and her fair hair was mixed with grey. Alas! How sickness extemporizes old age. (p. 170)[29]

Already in this description she has begun the process of disintegration that will see her return to the earth, to the clay from which she was originally formed. Her skin has taken on a greyish hue, has become earthy.[30] The moment of death is

---

28 "Elle avait été congédiée vers la fin de l'hiver; l'été se passa, mais l'hiver revint. Jours courts, moins de travail. L'hiver, point de chaleur, point de lumière, point de midi, le soir touche au matin, brouillard, crépuscule, la fenêtre est grise, on n'y voit pas clair. Le ciel est un soupirail. Toute la journée est une cave. Le soleil a l'air d'un pauvre. L'affreuse saison ! L'hiver change en pierre l'eau du ciel, et le cœur de l'homme." (p. 145)

29 "Quelques mois auparavant, à ce moment où Fantine venait de perdre sa dernière pudeur, sa dernière honte et sa dernière joie, elle était l'ombre d'elle-même; maintenant elle en était le spectre. Le mal physique avait complété l'œuvre du mal moral. Cette créature de vingt-cinq ans avait le front ridé, les joues flasques, les narines pincées, les dents déchaussées, le teint plombé, le cou osseux, les clavicules saillantes, les membres chétifs, la peau terreuse, et ses cheveux blonds poussaient mêlés de cheveux gris. Hélas! comme la maladie improvise la vieillesse." (p. 199)

30 A.S. Byatt depicts a comparable moment in Zola's *L'Oeuvre* where his treatment of the Pygmalion myth involves equating the protagonist's lover Christine with his

quite simply a natural progression of this process. In the way in which society disposes of her body also there is no distinction to be drawn between the way in which she was treated in life and the dignity accorded to her in death. She was given no rank or status through a family name in life; in death she is cast into the anonymity of a pauper's grave. In life she was forced to share her bed with anyone who chose her; in death she is equally subject to the laws of chance with regard to bedfellows:

> And so Fantine was buried in the common grave of the cemetery, which is for everybody and for all, and in which the poor are lost. Happily, God knows where to find the soul. Fantine was laid away in the darkness with bodies which had no name; she suffered the promiscuity of dust. She was thrown into the public pit. Her tomb was like her bed. (p. 203)[31]

Hugo charts the metamorphosis of Fantine from graceful nymph to grotesque, diseased prostitute to clay and bone. Unlike the transformations that Ovid records which are predominantly governed by the favours or displeasures of the gods Fantine's fall was created by society's attitudes towards its most vulnerable members; Hugo's subversion of the myth of Pygmalion is a direct commentary on the interplay between money and culture in nineteenth century France. Fantine is forced to sell herself off piece by piece. Indeed she is explicitly ordered to do so by her landlord:

> Fantine offered herself as a servant in the neighbourhood; she went from one house to another. Nobody wanted her. She could not leave the city. The second-hand dealer to whom she was in debt for her furniture, and such furniture! Had said to her: "If you go away, I will have you arrested as a thief." The landlord, whom she owed for rent, had said to her: "You are young and pretty, you can pay." (p. 122)[32]

---

sculpture of the Woman Bathing. This sculpture eventually disintegrates and collapses: "In French the mind flickers between seeing her as the female and as the 'it' of the art object she was, and the clay to which she is returning. The passage might be said to combine the female image as created life, as erotic object, and as lifelessness and death in one movement of dissolving clay." *Portraits in Fiction* (London: Vintage, 2002), p. 36.

31 "Fantine fut donc enterrée dans le coin gratis du cimetière qui est à tous et à personne, et où l'on perd les pauvres. Heureusement Dieu sait où retrouver l'âme. On coucha Fantine dans les ténèbres parmi les premiers os venus ; elle subit la promiscuité des cendres. Elle fut jetée à la fosse publique. Sa tombe ressembla à son lit." (p. 237)

32 "Fantine s'offrit comme servante dans le pays; elle alla d'une maison à l'autre. Personne ne voulut d'elle. Elle n'avait pu quitter la ville. Le marchand fripier auquel elle devait ses meubles, quels meubles! lui avait dit : Si vous vous en allez, je vous

Hugo meticulously imagines the fear and despair experienced by Fantine as she slides inexorably into degradation. He restores the humanity denied to her by a society that did not even dignify her with a proper name, and at the same time presents her story as one of the many thousands that could have been told. In the middle of her story Hugo reminds us of his admonitory Préface in which he calls society to account for its treatment of those whom it has driven into prostitution:

> What is this story of Fantine? It is society buying a slave.
> From whom? From misery.
> From hunger, from cold, from loneliness, from abandonment, from privation. Melancholy barter. A soul for a bit of bread. Misery makes the offer, society accepts. The holy law of Jesus Christ governs our civilisation, but it does not yet permeate it; it is said that slavery has disappeared from European civilisation. This is a mistake. It still exists, but it weighs now only upon woman, and it is called prostitution. (p. 126)[33]

Hugo has already shown society to be a thief in its treatment of Jean Valjean in the galleys and as a former convict.[34] He presents Fantine's prostitution as part of a spiral of exchange in which she was always doomed to lose; the more of herself she sold, the less there was to sell and the more urgently she needed the money. By depicting her plight as a form of slavery he also links her to Thénardier's ambition at the end of the book to set up in the slave trade in America. Where Thénardier's project is an explicit marketing of human flesh, the exploitation of resourceless women in nineteenth century France is a hidden form of slavery.

The detailed account of Fantine's fall gives her a face and forces society to gaze unflinchingly at the changes it has wrought, to examine its role as an anti-Pygmalion, a force that unmakes the statue and that reduces Fantine to clay and bone before throwing her back in the earth. Hugo creates universal history out of the story of one human history:

---

ferai arrêter comme voleuse. Le propriétaire auquel elle devait son loyer lui avait dit : Vous êtes jeune et joli, vous pouvez payer." (p. 144)

33 "Qu'est-ce que c'est que cette histoire de Fantine? C'est la société achetant une esclave.
A qui ? A la misère.
A la faim, au froid, à l'isolement, à l'abandon, au dénûment. Marché douloureux. Une âme pour un morceau de pain. La misère offre, la société accepte.La sainte loi de Jésus-Christ gouverne notre civilisation, mais elle ne la pénètre pas encore. On dit que l'esclavage a disparu de la civilisation européenne. C'est une erreur. Il existe toujours, mais il ne pèse plus que sur la femme, et il s'appelle prostitution." (p. 149)

34 "Là encore il se considéra comme volé.
La société, l'état, en lui diminuant sa masse, l'avait volé en grand. Maintenant c'était le tour de l'individu qui le volait en petit." (p. 79)

> History neglects almost all these peculiarities, nor can it do otherwise; it is under the dominion of infinity. Nevertheless, these details, which are wrongly called little – there are neither little facts in humanity nor little leaves in vegetation – are useful. The physiognomy of the years makes up the face of the century. (p. 82)[35]

In its treatment of Fantine nineteenth century French society can see a mirror of its values and practices. The invocation of an ancient epic within a modern text is always an invitation to examine the identity of the society from which the modern text springs, revealed by the anxieties and preoccupation with which it invests the original. At the beginning of his *Metamorphoses* Ovid prays for the ability to create a *carmen perpetuum,* an unbroken song that will link the origins of the world to his own time. By inscribing Ovid's epic into *Les Misérables* Hugo is ensuring the perpetuation of Ovid's work and endorsing Ovid's ambition, but he is also demanding that we meditate on what happens when the myth of Pygmalion is subverted by the harsh economics of nineteenth century France. The sinister dangers that were always inherent in the myth overwhelm the narrative and cannot be stopped until the statuesque beauty of Galatea has been transformed into Fantine's grotesque and broken corpse.

---

35 "L'histoire néglige presque toutes ces particularités, et ne peut faire autrement; l'infini l'envahirait. Pourtant ces détails, qu'on appelle à tort petits – il n'y a ni petits faits dans l'humanité ni petites feuilles dans la végétation – sont utiles. C'est de la physionomie des années que se compose la figure des siècles. (p. 97)

Niamh Sweeney

Strategies of Potential: The Idea of Gaming in Baudelaire's Aesthetic of Modern Life

In his early art and literary criticism, Baudelaire displays a sanguine expectation, if a sometimes canny watchfulness, of the potential of the bourgeois public as a consumer of art. The contentious dedication of the *Salon de 1846* to this newly moneyed class, although arguably not devoid of irony, is a case in point: "You are the majority", he tells them, "thus you are the force."[1] For, to address the economically empowered *majorité* is a strategic endeavour to harness and mobilise a potential force to successfully enact the crucial change in aesthetic practice that is called for in the final chapter of the *Salon*. This exhortation to embrace the heroism of modern life is, I would contend, directed not only to the receptive artist, as has often been argued, but is especially addressed to the same bourgeois Salon visitor of the *dédicace*, because its success hinges on their economic collaboration in its realisation.[2] Indeed the main target of the critic's

---

1 "Vous êtes la majorité [...] donc vous êtes la force", Charles Baudelaire, *Oeuvres complètes*, ed. Claude Pichois, Bibliothèque de la Pléiade, 2 vols. (Paris: Gallimard, 1975-1976), II, p. 415. Further references to Baudelaire's collected works will occur with the abbreviations 'Baudelaire I' (vol. I) or 'Baudelaire II' (vol. II).
The question of the sincerity of the *dédicace*, "Aux Bourgeois", of the *Salon de 1846*, has long been a point of contention in the various examinations of Baudelaire's art criticism. Dolf Oehler argues that an ironical reading is justified on the basis of Baudelaire's antipathy for the bourgeois parliamentarians of the July monarchy, a *majorité* only in name, founded on the suffrage of a mere 3% of the male population. See Dolf Oehler, "Le Caractère double de l'héroïsme et du beau modernes", *Études Baudelairiennes,* viii (1976), pp. 137-216. J.A. Hiddleston, on the other hand, considers the dedication to be a coded in-joke amongst artistic friends at the expense of the predominantly bourgeois visitors to the Salon (J.A Hiddleston, "In search of an Aesthetic", *Baudelaire and the Art of Memory* (Oxford, New York: Clarendon Press) pp. 1-49, 252-288. Such analyses, however, tend to overlook the possibility that, in the act of addressing the sizeable, art-buying bourgeois public, Baudelaire is cognisant of their potential impact on his designs for a revolution in artistic practice. The critic's dédicace displays a recognition of the complexity and plurality of the readership he addresses – they are "les uns savants" and "les autres riches" – or, possibly, the political *as distinct from the* economic.

2 "[L]a plupart des artistes qui ont abordé les sujets modernes se sont contentés des sujets publics et officiels, de nos victoires et de notre héroïsme politique. Encore les font-ils en rechignant, et parcqu'ils sont commandés par le gouvernement qui les paye.

opprobrium in 1846 are rather the "guardians of tradition", the academic "accapareurs"[3] (monopolisers) who have essentially failed to provide coherent leadership, resulting in a generation of artists as "ouvriers émancipés" (emancipated workers),[4] as Baudelaire terms them, appropriating a political metaphor for an aesthetic purpose. The critic's grievances can be mainly pinned down to the academy's refusal to abandon their essentially redundant relationship with the past, its failure to recognise and encourage original talent, instead preserving honours and privilege only for the truly mediocre: that rag-bag of journey-men artists he so witheringly pursues in the final chapters of the Salon – the *éclectiques*, the *douteurs*, the *singes du sentiment* – those who doggedly repeat the stock vocabulary of the classical and indeed romantic repertoire.[5] Instead, with the zeal of a proselytist, Baudelaire attempts to rally the support of his Salon-going readership, laying out their rights and obligations in the first chapters in terms of an aesthetic contract: their industry has brought wealth and financed the building of museums[6] and now they are not only entitled but compelled to take sustenance from art.[7] Thus, as becomes clear in the first chapter following the *dédicace*, "À Quoi bon la critique" (What use is criticism?), the critic's self-prescribed function as a mediator is to provide a lesson in ideal viewing: the "initiation particulière"[8] through which the viewer might access the sublime.[9] That lesson is neatly condensed in the caveat that a pure understanding

---

Cependant il y a des sujets privés, qui sont bien autrement héroïques." Baudelaire II, p. 495 "The majority of artists who have tackled modern subjects have had to make do with the representation of public and official subjects, of our victories and political heroism. They continue to do this with great reluctance, because they have been commissioned by the government who pays them. Yet, there are subjects of a private nature, which are heroic in an altogether different way." What Baudelaire seems to imply is that because state patronage has heretofore inevitably guaranteed the predominance of official and political subjects in the representation of modern life – its public heroism – then the proposal for an "altogether different" art of private heroism will necessarily be financed by similarly private means.

3 Baudelaire II, p. 415.

4 ibid.

5 Baudelaire II, pp. 472-479.

6 "Bourgeois, vous avez – roi, législateur ou négociant, – institué des collections, des musées, des galleries", Baudelaire II, p. 416. "Bourgeois, you have – be you king, lawmaker or merchant – established collections, museums, galleries".

7 "Vous pouvez vivre trois jours sans pain; – sans poésie, jamais", Baudelaire II, p. 415. "You can survive three days without bread. Without poetry, never".

8 "private initiation", Baudelaire II, p. 415.

9 "[U]n beau tableau étant la nature réfléchie par un artiste, [la meilleure critique est] celle qui sera ce tableau réfléchi par un esprit intelligent et sensible", Baudelaire II, p.

of art may be achieved only through "le sentiment"[10] because, as he sees it, it is analogously via "le sentiment", rather than the procedural adherence to the academic canon, that great art in the vein of Delacroix, is produced.[11] So the objective to overhaul artistic practice consists in a necessary co-ordination of efforts and interests, where artist/producer and viewer/consumer are set up in symbiotic relation via the indispensable intervention of the critic.[12]

The aim of this initial, admittedly abbreviated, review of some of the major motifs of the *Salon de 1846*, is to emphasise the necessity of contextualising Baudelaire's criticism in terms of changing economic power relations and interests, which, even in pre-revolutionary Paris, prompted changes in the concept of a state-sponsored Salon and the processes by which art is produced and sold. Although, Baudelaire's critical work is frequently singled out for its innovative, albeit qualified, advocacy of modern life, the question of the artist's calculation and negotiation in the face of modern economic realities has rarely been considered in depth.[13] It is helpful in the first instance to consider his concerns within the context of an older, albeit marginal, tradition of art criticism which sought to seriously consider the potential of the public as a new authority in the art appreciation. Indeed, the emergence of the bourgeois public as a principal arbiter in the matters of art, and ultimately its chief consumer, as well as that of the art-critic as its advocate, can be largely traced back to the very beginnings of the Salon system in France in the mid-17th century. As early as 1719, Du Bos, in *Réflexions critiques sur la poésie et la peinture (Critical Reflections on Poetry and Painting)*, had already pinpointed "le sentiment" as the main criterion for the reception of art: the aptitude to judge did not presuppose an initiation into the

---

418. "As a beautiful painting is nature contemplated by an artist, [so the best critique is] one which will be that painting contemplated in turn by an intelligent and responsive mind."

10 "C'est par le sentiment seul que vous devez comprendre l'art", Baudelaire II, p. 416. "It is through sentiment alone that you must understand art".

11 Baudelaire II, p. 440.

12 "Le critique doit accomplir son devoir avec passion; car pour être critique on n'en est pas moins homme, et la passion rapproche les tempéraments analogues", Baudelaire II, p. 419. "The critic must accomplish his duty with passion, as one is no less a man for being a critic, and it is passion which brings together those of like temperaments".

13 See particularly, Walter Benjamin, *Charles Baudelaire: A Lyric Poet in the Era of High Capitalism*, trans. Harry Zohn (London, New York: Verso, 1997), pp. 33-34. For a discussion on the correlation between Baudelaire's poetry and the commercial, as well as the socio-political, contexts, see Eugene W. Holland, *Baudelaire and Schizoanalysis: The Sociopoetics of Modernism* (Cambridge: Cambridge University Press, 1993), pp. 2-49, 137-173, 177-219.

technicalities of art-making process, thereby suggesting that *anyone* is fit to assess its merits.[14] Furthermore, the contemporaneous emergence of the concept of the citizenry and its rights, integrated the notion of public custodianship of, and right of access to, works of art, as propounded by Louis de Jaucourt and Sulzer.[15] Oskar Bätschmann has deftly described such far-reaching consequences of this effective induction of the public which was accommodated and indeed promoted by the Salon, as a virtual inevitability of its format: in affording an unprecedented setting in which numerous contemporary artists might be displayed collectively for public enjoyment/scrutiny, they were obliged for the first time, as Bätschmann writes, "to define, legitimate and finance their work in public competition with each other"[16], rather than merely in accordance with established tenets or the particular exigencies of a court or church patron within a relatively closed system where work is commissioned and prices agreed in advance.

Patricia Mainardi in *The End of the Salon* has similarly traced the stresses accompanying the adaptation of cultural practice to the principles of free-market economics which leads to the eventual collapse of the state-sponsored Salon in 1883. Mainardi contends that proposals for a two-tiered Salon system spanned the life-time of the Salon, where elite interests consistently favour an "exclusive Salon dominated by the Academy and based on tradition and privilege" above the increasingly prevalent 'free-market' exhibition through which artists hoped to gain fame and fortune".[17] Although the vitiation of Academic authority and of the sway of royal, church and later state patronage, is not an immediate and wholesale consequence of the encroachment of commercial interests into the domain of art, nonetheless, the possibilities which the private exhibition affords are vital to the many artists, who may not have benefited from the fruits of state support, and who required a forum through which their works might be marketed and sold. Long before the Impressionists cornered the market in the private exhibition, Courbet set up his *Pavillon du Réalisme* in protest to his exclusion from the Exposition Universelle in 1855, charging an admission fee and offering potential clients the possibility of acquiring copies of his works in any format;

---

14 "Mais tous les hommes peuvent juger des vers & des tableaux, parceque tous les hommes sont sensibles", Du Bos, *Réflexions critiques sur la poésie et la peinture*, 1719 (1733), vol. 2, sect. 24, pp. 354-365, here: p. 360, cited in Oskar Bätschmann, *The Artist in the Modern World: The Conflict Between Market and Self-expression*, trans. Eileen Martin (Cologne: Du Mont Buchverlag, 1997), pp. 53, 252, n. 171. "But all men can judge verse and painting, because all men are possessed of sensibility."

15 Bätschmann, *The Artist in the Modern World,* p. 16.

16 ibid., p. 9.

17 Patricia Mainardi, *The End of the Salon: Art and the State in the Early Third Republic* (Cambridge: Cambridge University Press, 1993), p. 2.

earlier still, David exhibited *Les Sabines* outside the main Salon of 1814.[18] For both David and Courbet, the private exhibition presented greater possibilities for financial security, thus affording greater freedoms to pursue awards and honours through large-format state commissions, which continued to be greatly coveted by such artists, but were comparatively only an occasional opportunity. Yet the idea of a mutually rewarding collaboration between the artist and society is in reality fraught with tensions and uncertainties: the commodification of artistic practice through which, as Mainardi says, the artwork becomes an object of "private interest or speculation" inevitably generates questions regarding artistic legitimacy and aesthetic value.[19] In 'L'Enchère de l'oeuvre d'art ' ('The bid of the work of art'), Baudrillard identifies what he calls the 'transmutation' of aesthetic value as an outcome of the art-auction, not just in monetary but also in symbolic terms, contending that power relations are dictated as much by the control of the processes of signification as of production.[20] This quandary concerning the means and the authority by which aesthetic value was to be calibrated and legitimised, when the terms of the capitalist market place are potentially random and variable, largely originates in the 19th-century crisis of legitimacy which was significantly underway before Baudelaire made his initial foray into art criticism.

Yet Baudelaire's criticism acutely registers the haphazard conditions of the market and its seemingly arbitrary designation of worth; the unstable sign under which the artist is forced to labour. In the *Salon de 1859*, soured perhaps by his regretted involvement in the revolution of 1848 and the hostile reception of *Les Fleurs du Mal*, the tone is substantially more embittered than that of 1846, and the critic is unambiguously vehement in his denunciation of the Bourgeoisie, their "mediocrity" and their "mauvais gout" (bad taste), the focal point of his polemic.[21] His earlier optimistic exhortation to embrace the aesthetic of modern life seemingly gone unheeded, the critic visualized an all-pervasive market, dictated purely by the whim of the economically empowered, whose tastes reign unchecked and which does not necessarily reward the deserving: "At the very time when a delightful painting by Delacroix found it difficult to find a buyer for a thousand francs, Meissonier's barely noticeable figures were being sold for ten

18 Bätschmann, *The Artist in the Modern World,* pp. 44-52, 124-126.

19 Mainardi, *The End of the Salon*, p. 33.

20 Jean Baudrillard, "L'Enchère de l'oeuvre d'art", in *Pour une critique de l'économie politique du signe* (Paris: Gallimard, 1976), p. 137.

21 Baudelaire II, pp. 608-613.

times and twenty times as much."[22] This later disillusion is at odds with the objectives for a more holistic relationship between artist and consumer in his earlier criticism, where already in the *Salon de 1845,* anticipating the concerns of 1846, Baudelaire proffers the stark reminder to the artist that "The bourgeois [...] is worthy of respect, for it is necessary to appeal to those from whom one wishes to make a living".[23] In 1846, the critic is still capable of envisaging, if not quite an autonomous market of ideas, then certainly an ideal hierarchy of aesthetic over economic interests with the latter in service to the former, so long as any discrepancy between the artistic mission and commercial preferences might be squared. This constitutes an endeavour which anchors his objective as a critic: "taste" in 1846, it is suggested, may be tweaked, the bourgeoisie flattered, tickled, even pressurized into compliance once the critic performs his duty adequately. The artist, for his part, is obliged to confront the market with level-headed pragmatism: in the remarkable co-text of the *Salon de 1846*, *Conseils aux jeunes littérateurs* (*Advice to young writers*), also published that year, Baudelaire's counsel to aspiring writers is to immediately disabuse themselves of the notion that success or its absence is matter of good fortune, "le bonheur" or bad luck, "le guignon". "I believe rather that one success is, whether in arithmetic or geometric proportion according to the strength of the writer, simply the outcome of previous successes."[24] Chance then is a question of perception, and bears no relation to economic reality; the seeming over-night success is simply the outcome of incremental achievements. What is understood as chance is rather a confluence of external dynamics in which the artist elects to manœuvre and toil: "I am allowing for the thousand circumstances which envelop human will and which themselves have their own valid causes."[25] More surprising again, than this prescient contemplation of chance, is the apparently linear correlation of artistic labour with monetary success, an equation which smacks of Saint-Simonian notions of progress and of the artist as entrepreneur. Indeed the enjoinder issued in the same breath to "double, triple, and quadruple" their efforts, "for the bourgeois will be

---

22 "à la même époque où un ravissant tableau de Delacroix trouvait difficilement acheteur à mille francs, des figures imperceptibles de Meissonier se faisaient payer dix fois et vingt fois plus." Baudelaire II, p. 612.

23 "le bourgeois [...] est fort respectable; car il faut plaire à ceux aux frais de qui l'on veut vivre." Baudelaire II, p. 352.

24 "je crois plutôt qu'un succès est, dans une proportion arithmétique ou géométrique, suivant la force de l'écrivain, le résultat des succès antérieurs". Baudelaire II, p. 13.

25 "Je fais la part des mille circonstances qui enveloppent la volonté humaine et qui ont elles-mêmes leurs causes légitimes." Baudelaire II, p. 14.

with you",[26] would seem to reinforce such a conviction. Yet this seeming equation of artist with labourer, expending force through time for commensurate financial reward, is then blatantly belied by his musing that artistic labour does not, of necessity, yield a proportionate return. Seemingly switching tack he writes: "The literary architect whose name alone is no promise of reward must sell at all costs", those who demur that such effort is financial folly, are swiftly chastised: "even while poorly paid, honour might have been theirs for the taking; however, not only have they been poorly paid, they have moreover brought dishonour upon themselves."[27] In short, the profit motive does not a work of art create, so the artist must put a premium on the creation of aesthetic before financial capital. Although the critic's counsel seems counterintuitive, even paradoxical, in fact it bears witness to the early stirrings of rather an anti-progressive world-view, which receives its most systematic consideration in his appraisal of the 1855 International Exhibition.

For adherents of Saint-Simonianism, the *beaux arts*, like industry, are yoked to the project of progress, rather than being its paramount objective; and the artist assumes the role of the prophet forging a future for universal betterment, whence the derivation of the notion of the artistic avant-garde, an application of an originally militaristic term to couch the function of the artist who works in step with progress.[28] In the *Salon de 1846*, Baudelaire famously describes Delacroix, in quasi-oxymoronic terms, as "the last expression of progress in art",[29] and later in the 1859 *Salon*, as an artist who "raised himself up very high *in spite of* his century."[30] In both the *Salons* of 1846 and 1859, the figure of Delacroix is employed as an emblem of an oppositional aesthetic, and an essential function in the critic's work as he undertakes to herald the new. Yet the application of the term avant-garde to the arts sits uneasily with the critic: as he writes in the *Journaux Intimes* – a remarkable testament to his own emasculation and prodigality – "These ways with military metaphors are evidence of minds which are capable only of herd-like thinking."[31] Delacroix rather works *despite* his own

---

26 "car le bourgeois sera avec vous." Baudelaire II, p. 14.

27 "l'architecte littéraire dont le nom seul n'est pas une chance de bénéfice, doit vendre à tout prix [...] mal payé, ils eussent pu y trouver de l'honneur; mal payés, ils se sont déshonorés". Baudelaire II, p. 15.

28 For an especially cogent discussion of Saint-Simonian concepts of the avant-garde, see Bätschmann, *The Artist in the Modern World*, pp. 73-74.

29 "la dernière expression du progrès dans l'art", Baudelaire II, p. 441.

30 "s'est élevé très haut *malgré* son siècle" Baudelaire II, p. 634.

31 "Ces habitudes de métaphores militaires dénotent des esprits [...] qui ne peuvent penser qu'en société." Baudelaire I, p. 691.

time, effectively assuming the quality of the prophetic, but at variance with linear-progressive time. He is the *telos* towards which a particular phase of time has been progressing – he is a superlative example of a potential decreed by a superior will and fulfilled in identity with the order of things. This idea is made particularly explicit in Baudelaire's consideration of the *Exposition Universelle de 1855*, where the idea of Western civilisation's impending decline, the inevitable "déplacement de la vitalité" (displacement of the life-force) as he characterises it, subtends his critique of the arts.[32] The effective juxtaposition of art with industry, which the Exposition realised in form, spurs the critic to fulminate against the conceit of progress, yet again re-appropriating the term for his contrary agenda. About Ingres, for instance, he writes: "As he has not progressed, so he will not age."[33] Having earlier declared that it is providence, rather than human will, which presides over the affairs of art:[34] the stolid absence of variation in Ingres's œuvre is evidence of potential decreed by providence but not properly fulfilled, and rather an abuse of human will. Delacroix's œuvre is conversely in deference with cyclical or fatal time and has accordingly matured, effectively closing off the period of romanticism and clearing the way for the art, and artist, of modern life. This is the actualisation of the phase of decline decreed by a superior will, rather than the outcome of the human hand of progress.

While the promise of a vital future for art may be superfluous to Baudelaire's aesthetic of modern life, nonetheless an awareness of the terms of the market place is not quite so dispensable. To return briefly to *Conseils aux jeunes littérateurs*, Baudelaire's directive to work so as to secure reputation rather than financial gain is coupled with a signalling of the necessity to study and anticipate the dynamics of the modern quotidian: "All manifestations of human will vary at every moment their reciprocal play [...] this ineffable something, know it, analyse the play of neighbouring wills so as to displace the circumference."[35] Thus, the artist wishing to have some purchase on the future must attune to the "game", and devise tactics of adaptation and manipulation within it. This discerning approach to the nature of modern existence is of course subtended by the conditions of capitalist economics. The double-bind in which the artist produces the work of art – where consistent output must be realised with no guarantee of recompense and where a speculative approach to realities of the

---

32 Baudelaire II, p. 575.

33 "Comme il n'a pas progressé, il ne vieillira pas." Baudelaire II, p. 589.

34 Baudelaire II, p. 586.

35 "Toutes les volontés humaines [...] varient à chaque instant leur jeu réciproque [...] ce quelque chose, connaissez-le, étudiez le jeu des volontés voisines pour déplacer la circonférence." Baudelaire II, p. 14.

market is advised – is simply an instance of the yoke of capitalism already writ large in the city. The irreducible but mutually dependent facets of capitalism – the promulgation of progress through which capital is produced, coupled with the speculative function which displaces it – have already been assimilated by the critic as contextual realities to which the artist adjusts, like Benjamin's worker's gesture adapts to the machine. But it is the characterisation of "reality" as a game which opens the possibility for manipulation and intervention by the artist. The irony was not lost on many of his contemporaries that, when the gaming-houses of the Palais Royal were more strictly regulated after 1837, gambling became normalised through speculation at the Bourse.[36] Similarly the gaming principle subsists in the commonplace characterisation of the urban quotidian in terms of chance and risk. As T.J. Clark puts it however, contingency is a matter of "representation" rather than of "empirical life-chances."[37] It might be ventured then that Baudelaire's representation of the possibilities opened up to the artist through the embrace of chance, appears to occur on two levels: initially the artist is encouraged to be as a "joueur" in formulating an externalised strategy towards the market, to calculate and even forestall its shifts and transfers. Then, as delineated in *Le Peintre de la vie moderne* particularly, as will be shown, the strategy undergoes an internalisation which afterwards reproduces itself through the work of art. An example of the initial stance occurs in the essay *Peintres et Aqua-Fortistes* published in 1862, where, in reference to Meyron's destruction of his work for the abortive *Paris* album, Baudelaire delights in the market's contingencies, and the potential for manipulation ostensibly available to the artist: "M. Meyron recently destroyed the plates from his album, *Paris*. And almost immediately thereafter, twice in quick succession, the Meyron collection was sold at public auction for four and five times its original value."[38] It is perhaps an instance of the duality of satanic laughter that allows the artist, once reputation is acquired, to attempt to reverse to his advantage the economic conditions which too often frustrate his potential for gain, to become *bourreau* (executioner) rather than *victime* (victim). A similar technique is savoured in the earlier 1845 essay: *Comment on paie ses dettes qu'on a du génie* (*How to pay off one's debts when*

[36] "For if playing the market is just like our roulette, Why proscribe the latter and the former abet?", Louis Bourlier, *Stances à l'occasion de la loi qui supprime la ferme des jeux; Addressées à la Chambre* (Paris, 1837), p. 5, cited in Walter Benjamin, *The Arcades Project* (Harvard: Harvard University Press, 2002), p. 503.

[37] T.J. Clark, *Farewell to an Idea: Episodes from a History of Modernism* (New Haven, London: Yale University Press, 1999), p. 11.

[38] "M. Meyron a récemment détruit les planches de son album *Paris*. Et tout de suite, à peu de distance, deux fois de suite, la collection Meyron se vendait en vente publique quatre fois et cinq fois plus cher que sa valeur primitive." Baudelaire II, pp. 740-741.

one is a genius), where the critic shamelessly recounts an anecdote, apparently conveyed in confidence, which tells of an author of great renown – Baudelaire all but proclaims that it is Balzac – who commissions articles by younger writers to fulfil a deadline for a sum of money which will amply pay off a debt; the first article, we are told, is published under a different name, thereby safeguarding his reputation, while remuneration is forthcoming without any unnecessary exertion on the part of the writer. Baudelaire's concluding rationale for relaying the anecdote is ostensibly to show that "[the] great poet knew how to resolve the matter of a bill of exchange as effortlessly as the most complex and mysterious of novels"[39] in short, that the capacity for opportunism is of a piece with true genius. Moreover, in the preamble to the anecdote, Baudelaire, unabashed, declares that it is precisely because the story is told to him in confidence that he wishes to divulge it. That which delights the narrator is the range of possibilities opened up through this effective *mise en jeu* of a counter-productive gaming strategy – the potential to instigate a sequence of events which disrupt linear-progressive time. Of the many ostensibly paradoxical stances taken on by Baudelaire as both a critic and a poet, this is ironically one of the more consistent, in evidence too in his later writings. It might even be ventured that role of the "joueur" is central to any consideration of his aesthetic perspective.

In many of the poems from *Spleen de Paris* collection, published in 1859, there is, for example, an analogous concern with risk-taking as an end in itself. The narrator of *La Fausse Monnaie* (*The Counterfeit Coin*) speculates on the range of potential outcomes for the life of the beggar to whom his companion gives a counterfeit gold coin, conjecturing whether its circulation will lead him to wealth or imprisonment.[40] Again in *Le Mauvais Vitrier* (*The Bad Glazier*), the narrator characterizes the compulsion to precipitate a series of incidents as "une force irresistible", an absurd and even perilous condition, evident in the most idle of souls who, in the face of possible damnation, wish to realise an infinite joy in a second.[41] This subject engages in the game of risk simply "to see, to know, to tempt fate."[42] It is an impulse akin to the "goût de l'infini"[43] displayed by the haschish smoker, who similarly yearns to create "in himself a kind of divinity"[44]. But whereas haschish leads to emasculation, he says, proffering "imagination"

---

39 "grand poëte savait dénouer une lettre de change aussi facilement que le roman le plus mystérieux et le plus intrigué." Baudelaire II, p. 8.

40 Baudelaire I, p. 323.

41 Baudelaire I, p. 287.

42 "[...] pour voir, pour savoir, pour tenter la destinée." Baudelaire I, p. 285.

43 Baudelaire I, pp. 401-404.

44 "en lui une sorte de divinité", Baudelaire I, pp. 388.

certainly but "without the ability to exploit it,"[45] the trajectory of gambling reverses passivity into action allowing the subject to capitalise on the present and maximise a temporal profit within it so as to attain to either the divine or damnation – *peu importe* – for the accession to either state would constitute a means of resistance against the increasing currency of secular, progressive time.

The gaming motif which merges that sudden dynamism with calculation and anticipation – which Derrida designates in his reading of *La Fausse Monnaie* by the Aristotelian notion of *tycké* as the seeming chance event which is anticipated[46] – is played out in the prose poems as a *mise en abyme* of an overriding aesthetic strategy. This pertains not only to a wariness and manipulation of external forces but also to an ideal particularisation of the messianic mission of the artist of modern life through the very process of creating the work of art, an idea which receives its most coherent consideration in *Le Peintre de la vie moderne*. For Baudelaire, this superlative symbiosis is inferred from, and emblematised by, the artistic strategy of Constantin Guys, the designated painter of modern life. Firstly, not only is the rapid sketch, the method which M. G. chooses to employ, economically expedient, but it is also an apposite form for the rendering of the aesthetic of modern life:

> For the sketching of contemporary manners, the representation of bourgeois life and the spectacles of fashion, the most expeditious and least costly means are clearly the most preferable. The more an artist seeks to make it beautiful, the more precious his work will be; but in the inconsequential, in the daily metamorphosis of visible things, the rapid movement of life demands of the artist an analogous velocity of execution.[47]

More significant still, however, is Baudelaire's description of this artistic process in action: although the painter of modern life bathes in the crowd ostensibly as a detached *homme du monde* or *flâneur*, in reality he is urged by an overwhelming dynamism, like the damned souls in *Le Mauvais vitrier*: "M.G [...] is governed by an insatiable passion, one which compels him to see and to feel."[48] Again, the likening of the artist's motivation to action with that of the convalescent looking out from the interior of a café, urged out of inertia by the contemplation of the

---

45 "imagination [...] sans la faculté d'en profiter." Baudelaire I, p. 440.

46 Jacques Derrida, *Donner le temps* (Paris: Galilée, 1991), pp. 157-159.

47 "Pour le croquis de mœurs, la représentation de la vie bourgeoise et les spectacles de la mode, le moyen le plus expéditif et le moins coûteux est évidement le meilleur. Plus l'artiste y mettra de beauté, plus l'œuvre sera précieuse; mais il y a dans la vie triviale, dans la métamorphose journalière des choses extérieures, un mouvement rapide qui commande à l'artiste une égale vélocité d'exécution." Baudelaire II, p. 686.

48 "M. G. [...] est dominé par une passion insatiable, celle de voir et de sentir." Baudelaire II, p. 691.

crowd, is similarly redolent of the dynamism of *le jeu*: "He hurries towards the crowd in pursuit of some unknown whose aspect barely glimpsed has, in a twinkling, fascinated him. Curiosity has become a fatal, irresistible passion."[49] Thus this irresistible impulse whereby the artist "seeks that certain something which we might call modernity",[50] is evidence of a speculative, gaming gesture which is reinforced by the idea that the artist reads the signs of *modernité* and, like Aristotle in the market-place, knows how to anticipate a good thing: "If a style, the cut of a garment has been slightly altered [...] his eagle's eye has already anticipated it."[51] It is however the faculty for intervention, the canniness to exploit, which singles out the artiste-joueur. In terms virtually mirroring his signalling of the failings of the haschish smoker to capitalise on his accession to the sublime, Baudelaire writes: "Few men are endowed with the ability to see, fewer still possess the power to convey."[52] The artist's capacity for the *mise en jeu* however consists in an inversion of the disordering trajectory of gaming which seeks to disrupt in the external; instead, a decisive internalisation and ordering is undertaken: "All this haphazardly permeates him; and within minutes, the accompanying poem will be virtually composed".[53] This "barbarism and inevitable synthesis"[54], in which artistic determination and *ivresse (intoxication)* collide, is an idealised subjectivisation of the gaming-strategy's effects; a supreme endeavour to transcribe and submit them to form, to plot them out on the canvas:

> M. G. begins with slight traces in pencil, which only barely pinpoint the position which objects should occupy in space [...] At the final moment, the contour of the

---

49 "Il se précipite à travers cette foule à la recherche d'un inconnu dont la physionomie entrevue l'a, en un clin d'œil, fasciné. La curiosité est devenue une passion fatale, irrésistible." Baudelaire II, p. 690.

50 "cherche ce quelque chose qu'on nous permettra d'appeler la modernité". Baudelaire II, p. 694.

51 "Si une mode, une coupe de vêtement a été légèrement transformée [...] son oeil d'aigle l'a déjà deviné." Baudelaire II, p. 693.

52 "Peu d'hommes sont doués de la faculté de voir; il y en a moins encore qui possèdent la puissance d'exprimer." Baudelaire II, p. 693. 'Few men are endowed with the ability to see, fewer still possess the power to convey".

53 "tout cela entre pêle-mêle en lui; et dans quelques minutes, le poème qui en résulte sera virtuellement composé". Baudelaire II, p. 693.

54 "barbarie, inévitable synthétique", Baudelaire II, p. 697.

> objects is definitively outlined in ink [...] You will call this a sketch if you wish, it is however a perfect sketch.[55]

In T. J. Clark's estimation, proposed in his incisive "final analysis" of the modern project, *Farewell to an Idea,* it is the persistent preoccupation with contingency "as a fate to be suffered, and partly to be taken advantage of", that characterised the art of modernism; its contradictory objectives of unity and dispersal, or more specifically, of unity *within* dispersal, betrayed a troubled optimism that "out of the flux of visual particles would come the body again."[56] Although Guys's reputation was hardly secured by Baudelaire's seeming endorsement in *Le Peintre de la vie moderne,* the latter's prescience is by no means tainted for that, in so far as his portrayal of Guys's methodology is a primary template for an art of contingency where form attempts to take leave of substance all the while holding fast to the possibility of its retrieval: Guys, or rather the generic painter of modern life, begins with seemingly random dabs on the page, from which, Fuseli-like, form is summoned but only just maintained, at once signalling and suspending the possibility of future unity, freeze-framing the trajectory of the *jeu,* and transfiguring all that is potential into an art-form.

55 "M. G. commence par de légères indications au crayon, qui ne marquent guère que la place que les objets doivent tenir dans l'espace [...] Au dernier moment, le contour des objets est définitivement cerné par l'encre [...] Vous nommerez cela une ébauche si vous voulez, mais une ébauche parfaite." Baudelaire II, p. 699.

56 T.J Clark, *Farewell to an Idea,* p. 11.

Dick Collins

The Price of Mrs Lovett's Pies
Blood and Cash in the Penny Dreadful

Money and the High Gothic

A familiar, simplistic thought is no bad way to start an article. Saint Paul tells us that "the love of money is the root of all evil" (I Timothy 6:10). If that is true, then should we not expect a plethora of money-references in those paeans to evil, the Gothic novels that appeared between 1765 and 1820?

Apparently not. The word *money* does not appear in *The Castle of Otranto*;[1] neither does the word *coin*, nor *gold*, nor *silver*. The last two words, though they seem the more surprising, explain the absence of money: Otranto is a dark, dank, dismal place, and to add the beauteous sheen of gold and silver would destroy its atmosphere. In the same way Manfred, Prince of Otranto, holds his power, which is absolute, through his birth, and so through his feudal status, and thence through the terror this enables him to exert. If he were to be involved even tangentially with the world of commerce and money, what the Victorians sneeringly dismissed as 'trade'; if his power were based on his ability to buy his vassals services – in short, if relations between characters were governed by £.s.d. rather than the thumbscrew, then Manfred would not be Manfred, and *Otranto* would simply not be Gothic. The whole book would be thrown off-balance, with an entirely new, usurping dynamic present, and new characters and subplots would be needed to balance the tale and put it back on its course, and bring it to a satisfying ending.

The prime mover of the Gothic novel is pure feudal, aristocratic power, exercised because of who one is, and who one's ancestors were. Typically the heroine's family was formerly a part of this higher world, but she has "gone down in the world", and is persecuted or detained by one whose power is greater, because his status is higher. Thus she becomes a victim because of who she is, and who her ancestors were. The plot is resolved, time after time, when she discovers she is the true, cheated heir to even greater power than that of the villain, and so becomes immune to him: social status is the commonest, as well as the most powerful, character in the Gothic novel.

---

1 Horace Walpole, *The Castle of Otranto* (privately printed, 1764); 2nd edition 1765. For later comparison, it is approx. 38,000 words long.

A Gothic villain needs a gloomy castle and a satanic personality; to have him a businessman empowered by the contents of his wallet would not be Gothic at all; and, for the heroine, to be rich rather than virtuous would not be Romantic at all.

Clara Reeves wrote *The Old English Baron; or, The Champion of Virtue*,[2] as she saw it, to correct the more outrageous aspects of *Otranto*; one of her more realistic touches is to mention money four times, in roughly 55,000 words. But the word does not appear at all in Eleanor Sleath's *The Orphan of the Rhine*.[3] Again, it is not hard to find an explanation. The ubiquitous motif of the cheated heiress tells us that the Gothic is above all a literature of social aspiration. In M.G. Lewis's *The Monk* it appears nine times – seven times in Book One (in 38,173 words), twice in Book Two (47,426 words), and not at all in Book Three (51,756 words);[4] in Eliza Parsons's *The Castle of Wolfenbach*[5] it is used twenty-one times (in roughly 90,000 words). The difference is in the books: where *Wolfenbach* is a typical "lost-heir" romance, *The Monk* is a version of *Faust*, wherein Ambrosio is tempted and damned. Nevertheless, the rules hold true for both, the view of money is the same. None of the occurrences in *The Monk* come from the mouth of a leading character: a comic *duenna* speaks them, and a gypsy hears her and moves in on her. It is thus permissible to mention money when portraying the working classes. This may be why Parsons has such a high cash-count – she had genuine experience of poverty, and when her heroine "drops" in the world she depicts it more realistically than do the rich-born Walpole and Lewis. Sleath, though she led a troubled enough life, follows Walpole, and does not soil her heroine with the stuff.

For Sleath, Parsons, Sarah Wilkinson and the other women novelists of "lower" birth, the act of writing and publication is an act of social aspiration. Ann Radcliffe, a daughter of the professional *bourgeoisie*, finds a good middle way. We can see that money would never fit with her taste for the Sublime, but, paradoxically, it has its uses for showing her heroine's goodness of heart. In her *Mysteries of Udolpho*[6] the word money occurs twenty-six times (in 291,604 words); but most of these are when Emily is helping out a virtuous shepherdess – all the rage at the time, thanks to Marie Antoinette. Radcliffe's true opinion of money is shown in a vinegarish judgement:

---

2 Clara Reeve, *The Old English Baron. A Gothic Story* (London: Edward & Charles Dilly, 1777). Repr. 1778 as *The Champion of Virtue*.

3 Eleanor Sleath, *The Orphan of the Rhine* (London: William Lane, 1798).

4 Matthew Gregory Lewis, *The Monk* (London: J. Bell, 1796).

5 Eliza Parsons, *The Castle of Wolfenbach* (London: William Lane, 1793).

6 Ann Radcliffe, *The Mysteries of Udolpho* (London: G.G. & J. Robinson, 1794).

> In this occupation [gambling] he had passed the night with Cavigni and a party of young men, who had more money than rank, and more vice than either.[7]

For the true Gothic heroine lucre is always filthy, except when expended on shepherdesses. Money becomes virtuous - or, at least, loses its taint - when dispensed as alms.

The word *buy* and its related terms occur even less frequently; and when they do, they either apply most often to the moral sphere – buying or selling people's faith – or they are done by lower people such as shepherdesses, gypsies or Jews (both *sic,* I'm afraid). A typical usage, from *The Monk,* with the Devil speaking:

> "Was Purgatory meant for guilt like yours? Hope you that your offences shall be bought off by prayers of superstitious dotards and droning Monks? Ambrosio, be wise!"[8]

And from *Udolpho*:

> "You hear, that Montoni is a villain," exclaimed Morano with vehemence, — "a villain who would have sold you to my love! — Who —"
> "And is he less, who would have bought me?" said Emily, fixing on the Count an eye of calm contempt. "Leave the room, sir, instantly."[9]

To sum up: money and commerce in the Gothic are signs of a lower order of life; they are inimical to the Gothic heroine. They might name it *in extremis*, and they might pass it down to the lower orders, but they *never, ever* use it.

The String of Pearls

If we go forward fifty years from *Udolpho*, we see a complete change. The High Gothic was replaced by the Low, the Penny Blood or Dreadful, its bastard child through the chap-book, the magazine story and the *Newgate Calendar*. If in the Gothic money was peripheral, in the Dreadful it is of the essence, essential almost in the Scholastic sense: its ubiquity is such that simple word-counts of 'money' and its relative terms are meaningless. The very name of the genre speaks of it, and money is a constant and powerful theme. The pattern of predator-prey is the same as in the High Gothic, but the Dreadful villains, such as Sweeney Todd and *Varney the Vampyre*, are driven to their crimes by the lust for riches; the victims,

---

7 ibid., vol. 2, Chap. IV.

8 Lewis, *The Monk*, vol. 3, Chap. V.

9 Radcliffe, *The Mysteries of Udolpho*, vol. 2, Chap. 6.

such as *Fatherless Fanny*[10] and *Ela, the Outcast,*[11] are powerless because they are poor. The result is a fixation with cash that would shock even Eliza Parsons.

We can take as an illustration *The String of Pearls,*[12] the magazine serial in which Todd made his first appearance. The very first piece of dialogue establishes the disparity between villain and victim in terms of wages and conditions:

> "You will remember," said Sweeney Todd, and he gave his countenance a most horrible twist as he spoke, "you will remember, Tobias Ragg, that you are now my apprentice, that you have of me bed, board, washing, and lodging, with the exception that you don't sleep here, that you take your meals at home, and that your mother, Mrs. Ragg, does your washing, which she may very well do, being a laundress in the Temple, and making no end of money: as for lodging, you lodge here, you know, very comfortably in the shop all day. Now, are you not a happy dog?"
> "Yes, sir," said the boy timidly.[13]

Todd cuts Lt. Thornhill's throat for a string of pearls he is carrying. His attempts to sell the pearls occupy five whole chapters – more than one-eighth of the book – and a good part of several others. He goes to a lapidary in Moorfields, late at night:

> "The pearls are worth £12,000, and I will let you have them for ten. What do you think of that for an offer?"
> "What odd noise was that?"
> "Oh, it was only I who laughed. Come, what do you say, at once; are we to do business or are we not?"
> "Hark ye, me friend, since you do know the value of your pearls, and this is to be a downright business transaction, I think I can find a customer who will give £11,000 for them, and if so, I have no objection to give you £8,000."
> "Give me the £8,000," said Sweeney Todd, "and let me go. I hate bargaining."[14]

But, in a flash-back to the true Gothic feeling, the lapidary cannot see how a ugly, common, bizarre-looking fellow such as Todd came by the pearls honestly: he

---

10 T. P. Prest, *Fatherless Fanny* (London: Edward Lloyd, 1841). A piracy of another book of the same title, author unknown, but attributed to Clara Reeve.

11 T. P. Prest, *Ela, the Outcast* (London: Edward Lloyd, 1839). A partial piracy of Hannah Maria Jones, *The Gypsey Girl; or, The Heir of Hazell Dell* (London: London Printing and Publishing Co., circa. 1824).

12 Anonymous, *The String of Pearls: A Romance*, ed. Dick Collins (Ware: Wordsworth Press, 2005). I am limiting my discussion of the Penny Dreadfuls to those which are currently in print or available.

13 ibid., p. 3.

14 ibid., p. 49.

raises the hue-and-cry, and Todd barely escapes. The next time he tries he dresses in fine clothes, and goes to the biggest dealer in jewellery in London, John Mundell, "a Dutchman by extraction." He allows Mundell to believe that he is acting on behalf of the Queen, and finally gets £7,500 for Thornhill's pearls. Note that it is not simply the Royal connection that makes Mundell part with his money: it is the appearance of wealth that Todd puts on that convinces Mundell he is a Duke. This royal haul is enough to persuade Todd to retire from his business. But as it happens he has not seen the last of the string of pearls: Mundell has a cousin, a Mr. Wrankley, a tobacconist of 92 Fleet Street, and Mundell uses Wrankley as a go-between to sell the pearls on. Naturally, if he is acting in such a capacity, Wrankley must be well-shaven, and he goes to Todd's shop – the same mistake Thornhill made. He mentions the pearls to Todd, who cuts his throat and takes them back. With the proceeds he will retire.

This is a small part of the book, but it is typical of the whole. Todd is entirely motivated by his desire to make money, so much so that, as everyone knows, he even sells off the bodies of his victims – at least, the edible parts. His delectable confederate Mrs Lovett makes them into pies, which she sells for three-pence each. If the meat in the pie accounts for a half of the cost of producing it (which taking into account the pastry, the gravy and the labour seems a reasonable estimate) and we allow Mrs Lovett a reasonable profit on her outlay, then each portion of human flesh can be valued at one penny – a point to which we shall return.

Mrs Lovett is persuaded that Todd will give her £20,000 as a final pay-off, so that she can retire to Paris. She agrees to this offer, and goes into the shop to serve a customer; Todd promptly puts poison in her brandy. The poison has been bought at a little chemist's shop on the Strand, and the transaction is described in some detail. Compare the only similar episode in *Wolfenbach,* where commerce is mentioned only in glancing past it:

> The next day was appropriated to shopping and excursions round the town; and indeed, except sleeping hours, they passed their time solely together; Mrs Courtney having shut her doors to all company till they were settled in their new abode for the same reason the Marquis deferred sending all his letters of recommendation or waiting on the French Ambassador.[15]

Mrs Lovett's compliance is gained with money, and her compliance kills her; and such compliance, so gained, is another major feature of *The String of Pearls*. Tobias Ragg searches Todd's shop while he is visiting Mundell, and finds thousands of pounds in cash, as well as hundreds of stolen objects. Driven to

---

15 Parsons, *The Castle of Wolfenbach*, chap. 10.

distraction by this proof of murder – the cash and the property standing for people – he flees the place; Todd catches him, and places him in Mr. Fogg's mad-house in Peckham Rye. Now Fogg is naturally driven by money too; and so are his customers, but his inmates are betrayed by it. We are given two long, independent stories of such victims, briefer versions of the "novel-within-the-novel" convention of the High Gothic: in both cases they are persecuted by their relatives in order to stop them inheriting. Here, of course, we are straight back to the Gothic: but what both heiresses stand to inherit is *money*, not land or feudal power, and the means adopted to cheat them are correspondingly base and cruel. (The parents of one child, for example, soak her bed-sheets with water, in the hope that she'll die of a fever). Mr. Fogg's mad-house is the direct descendant of Udolpho and the dungeons of the Inquisition, but it is run as a private business. A foolish, octogenarian doctor is paid £10 a time to certify sane people insane, and those who use Mr. Fogg's services also pay in cash. When the money runs out, as it is calculated to do, the patients mysteriously die, and Dr. Popplejoy certifies they died of natural causes: again, for a fee in cash. We might think that the cold, grasping motives of Fogg make his mad-house a more terrible place than castle or dungeon, a striking confirmation of the Gothic assumption that money is a low and heartless thing.

Varney the Vampyre: A Romance of Compound Interest

If we turn to *Varney, the Vampyre,*[16] we find the Bannerworth family in reduced circumstances after their father's death:

> He had, but a few hours before he was found lying dead, made the following singular speech to Henry,—
> "Do not regret, Henry, that the old house which has been in our family so long is about to be parted with. Be assured that, if it is but for the first time in my life, I have good and substantial reasons now for what I am about to do. We shall be able to go to some other country, and there live like princes of the land."
> Where the means were to come from to live like a prince, unless Mr. Bannerworth had some of the German princes in his eye, no one knew but himself, and his sudden death buried with him that most important secret.
> There were some words written on the leaf of his pocket-book, but they were of by far too indistinct and ambiguous a nature to lead to anything. They were these: —
> "The money is —"
> And then there was a long scrawl of the pencil, which seemed to have been occasioned

16 Anon., *Varney, the Vampyre; or, the Feast of Blood. A Romance of Exciting Interest* (London: Edward Lloyd, 1845-47). Facsimile edition Dover, 1970.

> by his sudden decease.
> Of course nothing could be made of these words, except in the way of a contradiction, as the family lawyer said, rather more facetiously than a man of law usually speaks, for if he had written "The money is not," he would have been somewhere remarkably near the truth.[17]

Mysterious indeed!

When troubles come for the Bannerworths, they come not single spies: their sister Flora has been attacked by a vampire. The next day they have a visit from their new neighbour, Sir Frances Varney, a singularly ugly man who has bought the nearby Hall. Varney has worked out that old Mr. Bannerworths' treasure is hidden nearby, and he is trying to scare the Bannerworths into selling their property to him, so that he can get hold of the treasure: the 'vampire' disguise is a trick, a fiendish device of his own. In the end he tries it once too often – he is shot dead and his body is left in a field. But now something wondrous happens: the body is touched by the rays of the rising moon – Varney revives! It turns out that, unknown even to himself, he really *was* a vampire all the time! This bizarre twist allows the story to continue episodically for another seven hundred pages, and for at least a century after the deaths of all the Bannerworths (all from natural causes, by the way). Again, the motive for this twist is money: but it is not a motive *only within the story*. We shall come back to *Varney*.

G.W.M. Reynolds and the Chartering Classes

While both Todd and Varney are moved into action by money, George W. M. Reynolds[18] is obsessed by it from another angle. A socialist and Chartist, Reynolds used his stories to point out the extreme cruelty with which society treats its poor. A typical interpolation into his *Mysteries of London* is worth quoting at length:

> In England men and women die of starvation in the streets.
> In England women murder their children to save them from a lingering death by famine.
> In England the poor commit crimes to obtain an asylum in a gaol.
> In England aged females die by their own hands, in order to avoid the workhouse.
> There is one cause of all these miseries and horrors — one fatal scourge invented by the rich to torture the poor — one infernal principle of mischief and of woe, which has

17 ibid., p. 26.

18 Born 31 July 1814, Sandwich, Kent; died Bloomsbury, London, 17 June 1879.

taken root in the land — one element of a cruelty so keen and so refined, that it outdoes the agonies endured in the Inquisition of the olden time.
And this fertile source of misery, and murder, and suicide, and crime, is —

THE TREATMENT OF THE WORKHOUSE.

Alas! when the bees have made the honey, the apiarist comes and takes all away, begrudging the industrious insects even a morsel of the wax! Let us examine for a moment the social scale of these realms:

•\The Sovereign.
• • \The Aristocracy.
• • •\The Clergy.
• • • • \Middle Classes.
• • • • •\The Industrious Classes.

The lowest step in the ladder is occupied by that class which is the most numerous, the most useful, and which ought to be the most influential.
The average annual incomes of the individuals of each class are as follows: —

The Sovereign .... £500,000.
The member of the Aristocracy .... £30,000.
The Priest... £7,500.
The member of the middle classes ....£300.
The member of the industrious classes ......£20.

Is this reasonable? is this just? is this even consistent with common sense?
It was New Year's Day, 1839.
The rich man sate down to a table crowded with every luxury: the pauper in the workhouse had not enough to eat. The contrast may thus be represented : —

Turtle, venison, turkey, hare, pheasant, perigord pie, plum-pudding, mince-pies, jellies, blancmanger, trifle, preserves, cakes, fruits of all kinds, wines of every description.	4 oz. bacon. 1/2 lb. potatoes. 1 1/2 pint gruel. 1/2 lb. bread.

And this was New Year's Day, 1839!
But to proceed.[19]

---

19 G.W.M. Reynolds, *The Mysteries of London*, ed. Trefor Thomas (Keele: Keele University Press, 1996), pp. 92-93.

And, mopping his brow, he goes back to his story, for a while.

Reynolds had spent some time in France, where he claimed to have met the ageing Beau Brummel, and to have started a newspaper for ex-patriate English speakers. He was the first to give W. M. Thackeray paid employment. He was a huge admirer of Hugo and of Eugène Sue, on whose *Mystères de Paris* his *Mysteries of London* were based. The plot, however, is very reminiscent of Sade's novels, *Justine* and *Juliette*; and Reynolds' occasional outbursts of number-obsession mirror those of Sade himself. There is no character like Saint Fond, the financier of *Juliette*; the author himself takes the role. He has something of Sade's cruelty, and a distinct taste for scenes where naked women are flogged by enthusiastic nuns. These events are celebrated in the illustrations to his books, which often have an erotic, or salacious, feel to them. It is rare for Reynolds to publish a print without at least one bosom in it; his record, in *Wagner the Wehr-wolf*, is, I think, twelve, a bumper feature that also has a Mother Superior, an altar and two whips. Clearly, for Reynolds, money isn't everything.

The Mysteries of London also deals extensively with grave-robbing, another means of selling bodies. The average price for a fresh corpse was £10; if we take the edible parts – roughly the muscles – as being a fifth of the whole, that makes £2 per body. Thus, if she sold them at threepence each, and the meat made up half the overhead cost, with a profit of one penny, we can estimate that Mrs Lovett would have made £4 4s profit out of each body: perhaps the most chilling and horrific reduction of the human being in literature.

The Daughters of the Poor and Gentlemen of the Road

The Penny Dreadful tends to dwell on, and admire, the perpetrators of crime; but, in true Victorian style, it reserves more than a tear for its victims. These are, of course, women: we are dealing here with a literature of fantasy and identification, and not only will women (girls) identify with the heroines, but other readers will see themselves as their rescuers, if not as their oppressors. Girls become victims when they do not have the money to survive a Gothic life. The titles of this Dreadful sub-division abound: *Ada, the Betrayed; or, the Murder at the Old Smithy. A Romance of Passion*; *Agnes the Unknown; or, the Mendicant's Secret. By the author of "Ela, the outcast," etc.*; *Evelina, the Pauper's Child: or Poverty, Crime, and Sorrow. A Romance*; *Adeline; or, the Grave of the Forsaken. A domestic romance. By the author of "The Miller's Maid"* and so on forever. Some are based loosely on true events: *Susan Hoply; or, the Trials and Vicissitudes of a Servant Girl. A tale of deep interest. By the author of "Kathleen"*; *Mary Clifford;*

or, the Foundling apprentice girl. A tale. Here the theme of the Cheated Heiress is introduced to form the plot, which is a very different matter from the facts.

As well as taking from ordinary melodrama, the Oppressed Maiden strand derives much from the *Newgate Calendars*, one of the most popular publications of all time. They are very frank about the link between money and crime, and frank too about how some people earn it:

> There is no state in human nature so wretched as that of the prostitute. Seduced, abandoned to fate, the unhappy female falls a prey to want; or she must purchase existence at a price degrading, in the last degree, to the mind of sensibility. Subject to the lust and debauchery of every thoughtless blockhead, she becomes hardened in shame. Hence modesty is put to the blush by the obscenity of those, once pure as our own darling daughters.[20]

Clearly the writer believes prostitutes don't have mothers; or, in cases where they do, these mothers don't read the *Newgate Calendar*.

The female lead in the Penny Dreadful is not always of the fainting, "dead-and-never-called-me-mother" variety. Given the popularity of highwayman stories, it was inevitable that girls would soon feature in that role. Again the titles are legion: *Blanche Langdale, the Outlaw's Bride. A Romance of Sherwood Forest. By the author of "The Jew and the Foundling"; Ernnestine de Lacy: or, the Robber's Foundling. An Old English Romance.* But the important point is, there is little difference, in the end, between the 'masculine' and the 'feminine' highwayperson; both have more or less the same adventures; both employ constantly a rhetoric of freedom, with the gallows in the future, and all have a regard for money that soaks each work. The money and the freedom are, despite the heroic ethos, equivalents: one earns one's money free of the restraints of the law, and then lives freely because one has the money to do so. Thus the Abandoned Daughter type of Dreadful is seen as the negative, the reverse of the Highwayman story: if you have no money, or have not the courage to steal it, this is what will happen to you. We have gone almost 180° from the poor but virtuous heroine of *Udolpho* and *Wolfenbach*.

The Readership of the Dreadful

What has happened between 1797 and 1847, between the High Gothic and the Penny Dreadful, such that money is nearly absent from the former and then takes such a huge part in the latter?

---

20 "Sarah Priddon, alias Sally Salisbury", in Andrew Knapp and William Baldwin, *The Newgate Calendar* (London: J. Robins & Co., 1825) p. 415.

Louis James makes the excellent point that in the Dreadful plagiarisms of "proper" literature – such as *Oliver Twiss, Dombey and Daughter,* and the many piracies of *The Pickwick Papers* – the shift of interest for the reader drops drastically in the social scale.[21] Where Dickens is interested primarily in the middle classes, and Walpole only in the aristocracy, the Dreadfuls shift their attention to the working class characters such as the Wellers and Fagin's thieves. Thus Thomas Prest writes a parody of *Pickwick*, called *The Cadgers Club*, set in the Rookery of St. Giles. This observation can be applied throughout the ethos of the Dreadfuls. The language "falls" from high-literary Eighteenth Century to Victorian demotic; the setting goes from castle to cottage or slum; ancient blood and *noblesse oblige* give way to money and crime; the Sublime becomes sex, sensibility becomes sensationalism.

The chief reason for all this is the vastly different reader the Dreadfuls expected, and for whom the works were tailored. The typical reader of the Gothic novel seems to have been a young middle-class woman – or, rather, lady, as she herself would have insisted – of independent means, or dependent on a father or husband in a profession. (John Keats and Jane Austen, two avid fans of the genre, may not have been typical of the Gothic readership, but their class and circumstances are certainly right.) They could afford to buy a three-volume novel, or at least to subscribe to a circulating library; they had the leisure and the patience to read the long, long passages describing landscape; and they had the standard of literacy, the education, not only to cope with the language of the Gothic, but also to recognise the many literary references the authors offer the reader. Above all, perhaps, they had the background – through breeding or reading – that could understand and appreciate the *ethic* of the Gothic, the commerce of land and the feudal ties that either bind people together or tear them apart. They probably, also, knew what landscape looked like.

The Dreadful reader was very different indeed. Edward Lloyd's[22] manager had a simple system for deciding which new works to publish: he would take a sample downstairs and read it to the ten year old boy who worked in his steam-press room, and if he pronounced favourably, then 'we think it will do.' Lloyd was ahead of his time in market research; and fifty years before Northcliffe he

21 Louis James, *Fiction for the Working Man* (Harmondsworth: Penguin University Books, 1974) p. 71. See also Louis James, "The View from Brick Lane: Contrasting Perspectives in Working-Class and Middle-Class Fiction of the Early Victorian Period" in *The Yearbook of English Studies*, Vol. 11, Literature and Its Audience, II Special Number (1981), pp. 87-101.

22 Born Croydon, Surrey, 16 February 1815; died Westminster, 8 April 1890.

had correctly gauged the mental or reading age of his readers.[23] The demotic, therefore, serves as a more suitable standard for children than the High Style. Although *The String of Pearls* contains quotes from Shakespeare and Byron, the authors are not named: the child is not taxed to remember them, nor made to feel small for not doing so. And, as if to apologise for being clever, the authors are misquoted.

The readership of the Dreadful was urban, overwhelmingly so, and poor. Probably very few of them had ever seen a field, or a cow (unless in an abattoir), leave alone a mountain. It must have been extremely hard for them to imagine rural life, and more likely impossible.[24] Their standard of education may have been nil, and reading even four printed pages quite an arduous achievement. Many "readers" would have had to listen to other, older children, reading aloud to a hushed circle, which must have been great fun. Therefore the Penny Dreadfuls are set mainly in the world they know, the towns and slums of Industrial England,[25] and the stories are told in simple, repetitive language. Rather than long, leisurely accounts of landscape the Penny Dreadfuls offer incident upon incident, mounting in horror and excitement. A page without a visit to a charnel house is a wasted page. The heroes and heroines are more often children, or very young adults, with whom the reader can sympathise more directly.

Thus the Penny Dreadful might be defined simplistically as the Gothic, retold for semi-literate slum children; it removes all those things their readers cannot understand, and replaces them with things they know. Money as a motivation is one such thing, and one of the most important. But even if true, this definition is rather trite. For one thing very few Dreadfuls are mere "re-tellings for kids", and plenty of them remain close to the older style of Gothic novel – for example *Vileroy; or, The Horrors of Zindorf Castle* is set in a traditionally gloomy castle somewhere in Bohemia; it hardly mentions money at all in 166,000 words, and yet it was still a runaway success. If we want to see the root of money's importance in the Dreadful, we should look at how they were produced.

---

23 Thomas Frost, *Forty Years' Recollections: Literary and Political* (London: Sampson Low, 1880) p. 90. Lloyd's success as a publisher was partly due to a new process for making paper, which he made himself at his factory in Dartford. The new paper was made of esparto grass, and was so rough and porous that a blank had to be left on the other side of a picture, for fear of the ink seeping through.

24 At school in the 1950s, I knew children who had never seen a cow, and who would not believe that eggs came from chickens, as opposed to from the grocer's.

25 Even when they are set in the 17th century, the world is still recognisably that of the inner-city.

Production and Expansion of the Dreadful

Penny Dreadfuls were usually printed in weekly episodes, on both sides of a single large sheet of paper that was then folded and cut to form eight printed pages. Each issue commonly began with a wood-cut engraving (but rarely a mast-head) and was sold for one penny – hence "Penny Blood" or "Penny Dreadful", a coinage on "Penny Black". An issue was not necessarily an episode, much less a complete chapter, but just whatever could be fitted onto that week's allotment of paper. If it ran out in the middle of a sentence, so be it.

Edward Lloyd was the King of the Dreadfuls, and was both a publisher and his own printer, so his overheads were very low. He had a revolutionary system with newsagents: they would buy twelve copies from him for threepence, retailing each for a penny, thus making a very large profit on their outlay. Unsold copies were returned to Lloyd, and replaced without charge with the same number of copies of the next episode. Lloyd would store the returned copies, and if the story had been successful they would be bound together in single volumes and sold later, often for as little as a shilling each.

Unsuccessful stories were usually dropped, without bothering to finish them, so that some end in the middle of a word, with a terminal hyphen. Successful stories suffered a stranger fate. A money-earner could not be allowed simply to end where the author meant it to, or where the plot demanded, but must be kept going, at all costs to the story, for as long as people kept on buying it. The best example is *Varney the Vampyre*, and here we return to the point left unmade above.

It seems clear that the original author's intention had been to have Sir Frances Varney die there in the field where the Bannerworths left him, a just if brutal fate for a con-man and pretend vampire. But too many boys and girls were willing to spend their pennies on him for Lloyd to leave him in the mud: so, to the astonishment of all, himself not least, Varney turns out to be a real vampire after all, and goes on to new adventures. Apart from the Clara Croft episode, 600 pages in, the continuations are disappointing, episodic and often dull, and they show clear signs of being written by various different hands. The Bannerworths mostly fall out of view; Admiral Bell and Able Seaman Jack Pringle, who are set fair to be the most tedious characters in all literature,[26] now become the chief adversaries and pursuers of the Vampyre. Their tedious, tiresome, turgid, and above all unending nautical jargon is possibly, or probably, the work of Thomas Peckett Prest.[27] Each episode of the expanded *Varney* has roughly the same

26 Naturally I except Little Nell, whose tale is all shop and no curiosity.

27 Born Marylebone, London, 13 May 1810; died Islington, London, 5 June 1859.

structure. An ugly stranger (with a hissing voice) arrives in town; he attaches himself to a rich widow/ heiress; various women in the vicinity suffer strange and bloody attacks; the marriage is about to be celebrated when Bell and Pringle arrive (no, they never *arrive*, they *heave to*) and unmask the stranger as Varney. Varney flees, in the direction of the next heiress; Pringle and Bell weigh anchor, and set a course after him. In other words, Varney's motive in attacking people is not to obtain their blood – he does, but precious little – but *to marry into money*. For us the important point, and for Lloyd the only point, is that people bought it, in more senses than one. Lloyd's publishing philosophy was driven entirely by market forces, and so we get stories composed and re-composed on free-market principles – their plots revolve around the problems that arise when the market gets too free, and they are expanded or annulled as the market demands. Money becomes one of Lloyd's most valuable writers.

The Dreadful Writers

When we come to the *writing* of Penny Dreadfuls, these principles are even more clear. As we have seen, the writers of the High Gothic were often women of the professional middle-classes or above. They would put their books with a publisher who would bring them out in three or four volumes, and pay royalties on the profits. It was possible to earn a living from writing, if you wrote as prolifically as Parsons, but most did not need to, and indeed some, such as Lewis and Walpole, moved in circles where to discuss money would be "thought rather vulgar". Edward Lloyd liked money. He would buy completed stories outright, usually for 10 shillings, and he printed them in weekly parts, as stand-alone issues or in one of his many magazines. He paid no royalties, as far as we know, however much profit they made him, and he paid as little tax as he could. If he could avoid paying the author too, so much the better. His writers were hacks, mostly working also for other publishers at the same time. They would crowd into the ante-room of his offices in Salisbury Square, hoping either to sell a story to Lloyd or to borrow money from one of the other hopefuls. Anecdotes abound of these people, dirty, shabby, and frequently shaking for want of their next gin. If one of them was lucky enough to be working on a serial he would be paid at the rate of a penny for a double-column line. To ensure he didn't overpay them Lloyd provided the chosen hack with sheets of paper, ruled by Lloyd, that when filled with handwriting of ordinary size would fill the requisite eight pages of print. Very often the serial would originally have been the work of another, and the trick for the usurping penny-a-liner was to write as many lines as possible. This was achieved by a great deal of dialogue of the "Is he?" — "I believe so." —

"You surprise me." — "Indeed?" — "You do." — "Ah." variety, each utterance occupying a whole line, of course.

If Lloyd had something special, such as Varney or Todd, he would give it to one of his favoured hacks, Prest, or James Malcolm Rymer.[28] Prest was his chief plagiarist before the 1842 Copyright Act, re-working Dickens under the pen-name "Bos" and W. H. Ainsworth as "J.F. Hainsforth". Rymer arrived later, and worked on others' stories sold to Lloyd, as well as many original ones of his own. He trained as a civil engineer, went into publishing, and crashed rather badly with his *Queen's Magazine*. He met Lloyd, and agreed to follow Prest's example in "low" literature. The nautical sections of *Varney* are probably Prest's, as we saw, but the lengthy continuation of *The String of Pearls* was probably the work of Rymer.[29] Original authors disappear, their fame unsung, and the works are re-credited to Prest and Rymer. Ironically, a strong contender for the authorship of the original story of *String of Pearls* is Rymer's wife, Caroline (1821-1853).

Such a living is precarious, and it may be that the Dreadfuls' preoccupation with money and how to get it springs from this very closeness to the brink of poverty. It has usually been assumed, if tacitly, that the Dreadful writers were of middle class origin, or at least from "a comparatively affluent family". Thus their works are written *de haut en bas*, by educated, cultured men for semi-literate, uncouth children. Implicit in this belief is the view (again mostly tacit) that the working classes are necessarily uncultured, and if they have a literature at all it must be provided by their betters. It is the direct analogue of the unpleasant Victorian habit of assuming that poverty and crime go hand in hand, and equally spurious. Just as false, in fact, as the supposed middle-class origins of the writers.

Prest was a victim of the hack's life. Born in the slums of Marylebone on 13 May 1810, the son of a journeyman blacksmith, he spent most of his life in the crushing poverty of Shoreditch, in the East End of London. He was apprenticed to a printer, and was a journeyman type-setter by trade. He began as Lloyd's right-hand man, in the mid-1830s, and the discovery of a talented hack-writer who could set his own type must have been a God-send to Lloyd. But this same long association made him a poor companion in Lloyd's eyes. By the 1850s Lloyd had made enough money to go into serious (and legal) newspaper publishing, and he was eager to ditch the consumptive, working-class Prest. After 1850 Prest wrote very few titles for Lloyd, and after 1855 no more at all. He collected songs for

---

28 Born Holborn, London, 1 February 1814; died Shepherds Bush, Middlesex, 11 August 1884.

29 In 1850 Lloyd re-issued *the String of Pearls* in penny parts. It was so successful that it was expanded from 39 chapters to 179. It is as long as *Varney*, and as episodic, but not as dull.

song books, as he had before he met Lloyd, and probably also worked as a typesetter, but died of tuberculosis on 5 June 1859, in a lodging-house in Islington. A stranger reported his death to the Registrar. He was buried "on the rates" in a common grave, in the Saint Pancras and Islington Cemetery. It has no marker, just the number M3 2056. It wouldn't be surprising if such a man had worried about money, nor if that worry spilled out into his writing. He probably knew that his readers shared it with him. Perhaps the immense popularity of the Dreadful was due precisely to the coincidence of the writers' worries with those of their readers. He was, after all, very much one of them.

We must put away the idea, forever, that Penny Dreadfuls were written by louche, middle-class wastrels slumming-it among the working classes. Prest at least, and many others beside him, were of that class, and writing within their native culture.

The fate of the other men is chillingly different. James Rymer was born in St. Andrew's, Holborn, in 1814: it was the third most deprived parish in England. Although he always described his father as a "gentleman", he was probably a journeyman printer, like Prest. After Lloyd went respectable Rymer carried on writing for John Dicks,[30] a very different sort of publisher, with Socialist principles. Although he has family connections with Chartism, Rymer does not seem to have kept faith with his working-class roots. He rather despised his fate as a writer of Dreadfuls: he looked down on his production and he looked down on his readers. He published under the pseudonym Malcolm J. Errym, and disguised his identity so effectively that it was fifty years or more before his true name was known. In Street Directories he called himself a Civil Engineer. But he made enough from the children he sniffed at to buy a hotel in Worthing, Sussex. In 1882 he sold up and moved with his wife, Sarah Rebecca Rymer, to Lawn Cottage, 65 Shepherds Bush Green. He died on 11 August 1884, aged 70. He was buried in the family grave at Kensal Green Cemetery, London. Sarah Rymer lived on at Lawn Cottage for another twenty years or so, and died aged 85 in Brentford, Middlesex, in 1909. Her husband had made so much money from his writing that she never needed for it in 25 years.[31] She joined him in Kensal Green.

By the early 1860s George Reynolds had made so much from being the champion of the poor and oppressed that he could retire to 41 Woburn Square,

---

30 Born London 1818; died Menton, France 1881.

31 For fuller details see my article "The Pirates of Salisbury Square: Two Dreadful Writers and their Appalling Publisher" at Elizabeth Miller's Dracula Research Centre web-site at Memorial University, Newfoundland.

Bloomsbury, a very plush address indeed, where he lived until his death.[32] Towards the end of his life Reynolds became a Churchwarden of St. Andrew's, Wells Street. This decision by a committed atheist has puzzled and even annoyed commentators, but the post was political, not religious; and as the wealthy son of a Navy Flag Officer, Reynolds was exactly the sort of chap the Parish Council wanted to add to their number. The Churchwardens and Overseers of the Parish had been one of the favourite villains of the Penny Dreadfuls, including his own. He had come full circle.

Edward Lloyd went on to own a fine house in the fashionable suburb of Walthamstow, a huge paper-making plant in Kent, employing 250 men, as well as running several major newspapers. He died in 1890, in Westminster, surrounded by his children and live-in servants.[33] His chief money-spinner was the Liberal paper, *The Morning Chronicle*[34] and here perhaps we have our most significant clue to the link between the Penny Dreadful and money. For most of his early career Lloyd operated on the fringe of the law, his attempts at "newspapers" constantly being closed down by the Police for having no licence. He exploited his readers and his authors alike, amassing a vast fortune in the process. He seems to have had no interest in literature himself, but only in profit. In this, he is the very type of the mid-Victorian Liberal capitalist, and his publications show the nature of the breed, the Victorian feast naked at the end of our forks. He made a fortune sitting in his office, while ten-year-old children sweated at the boiler in his cellar. Yet, almost without noticing it, he produced the grand exposé of the system he so longed to join.

As cultural studies, the Penny Dreadfuls are invaluable. They tell us of the inner lives, the nightmares and even the aspirations of the London underclass, at the height of Victorian Glory. Their villains reduce the human being to an entry in a ledger, or the contents of a pie; but the writers, treated in the same harsh way,

---

32 Contrary to what we read he had, not three children, but ten: George Edward, Blanch, Edward, Frederick, Theresa, Joanna, Kossuth Mazzini, Louisa, Emily and Ledru. Unlike Edward Lloyd's (see note below) most of Reynolds' seem to have been legitimate. Reynolds was a great admirer of French culture, whence the Blanch; of the French radical, Alexandre Ledru-Rollin and of the Hungarian freedom fighter Lajos Kossuth; and of the Italian politician Giuseppe Mazzini, whence Kossuth Mazzini. I wonder if young Kossuth thanked him, when he went to school, for his name.

33 Lloyd fathered at least fifteen children, at least twelve of whom were illegitimate. Strangely, in the 1881 census three of his sons are put down as "farmer's sons".

34 Lloyd bought out the *Clerkenwell Chronicle* for £30,000 in 1876, re-named it the *Daily Chronicle*, then spent around £150,000 turning it into a national newspaper. It became the chief newspaper of the Liberal Party. It ran until well into the 20th century.

give out in their heroes' and heroines' voices the authentic cry of the Victorian poor. Reynolds does it directly through his polemic, the others more subtly through their sentiment and their horrors. The children who bought their weekly parts could never dream of green fields, but they could dream of growing rich: and since they were barred from wealth by all other means, they took as their heroes Jack Sheppard, Dick Turpin, Claude Duvall, Starlight Meg and all the other highwaymen and criminals that the Penny Dreadfuls told them of. It is no coincidence or mistake that Sweeney Todd is by far the wittiest, cleverest and strongest character in *The String of Pearls*. He, too, is the type of the Victorian businessman, the consumer of human life, the brutal user of child labour, as seen by the child. He embodies all the aspirations and admirations of the child, together with their loathing and their terrors.

As Marx almost put it, the Penny Dreadful is the cry of the soul in a soulless world. And all for a penny a week. The same as the human content of one of Mrs Lovett's pies.

Mary S. Pierse

George Moore, Sherlock Holmes and the Many Money Questions in Fin-de-Siècle English Fiction

In *Impressions and Opinions* (1891), George Moore remarked upon Honoré de Balzac's innovative literary acceptance of the importance of money, an element that Balzac had introduced into French novels much earlier in the century. Moore lauded Balzac's pioneering recognition "that money was as necessary to a young man in the nineteenth century as a coat of mail was in the fifteenth".[1] In terms of nineteenth-century English fiction, this development could be considered as one that was quite significant: money had not generally been acknowledged in this fashion in the romantic and adventure tales of the Victorian age. Where money did feature, its existence was often seen less as a usual or fundamental ingredient than as a matter that was more peripheral and of secondary importance to the progress, difficulties and success of a hero, the punishment of the villain, the safe containment of passion within marriage, or the adventures on voyages of discovery. This relative depreciation of the coin, fictionally, has been mirrored by a similar lack of critical attention; until recent years, treatment of money matters in Victorian fiction has not been prominent in critical focus either. However, in 1890s fiction by George Moore and by Arthur Conan Doyle, the treatment of money is obviously viewed as important by both authors although the nature of its appearances is surprising: its introduction is often subtle, it is frequently almost invisible, it surfaces in very diverse ways, and yet there is persistent engagement with several different money-related questions of the *fin de siècle*. This omnipresent money is, amongst other things, interconnected with patriarchy, so-called 'respectability', honesty, fair wages, investment scams, charity, gender, gambling, drinking and class. Shades of some of those issues and controversies arise in a Sherlock Holmes investigation into *The Man with the Twisted Lip*, a contemporary story by Arthur Conan Doyle, as well as in George Moore's novel *Esther Waters* and his story collection *Celibates*.[2] The literary approaches of the

---

1 George Moore, *Impressions and Opinions* (London: David Nutt, 1891), p. 4.

2 Arthur Conan Doyle, "The Man with the Twisted Lip", in *The Annotated Sherlock Holmes: The Four Novels and the Fifty-six Short Stories*, ed. William S. Baring-Gould (London: John Murray, 1968), pp. 368-387; George Moore, *Esther Waters* (London: Walter Scott, 1894); George Moore, *Celibates* (London: Walter Scott, 1895).

two authors to money questions may appear slightly camouflaged but they offer a fascinating picture of society in flux, and the methodology suggests that both men are determined to challenge late-Victorian opinions and to prompt debate on financial and social implications of having, getting and spending.

The three 1890s texts, all well-known in their time, provide illustration of variety in the complex approaches of Doyle and Moore: George Moore's book *Esther Waters* was a controversial novel, and a top seller in 1894; the story of *The Man with the Twisted Lip*, was in the first collection of Sherlock Holmes stories that was serialised in the *Strand* magazine between 1891 and 1892, was sold at railway station bookstalls and was exceptionally popular; Moore's 1895 volume *Celibates* contained three tales[3] and, being aimed at a higher end of the literary market, had a relatively small circulation. The apparent subject matter of each book and story was quite different: readers would have seen in *Esther Waters* the struggle for survival of a servant and her illegitimate son; in the Sherlock Holmes story, there are two missing husbands, and a display of detective skill is employed to find the husband who vanished from an opium den in the East End of London; in the stories of *Celibates*, the reader encounters the dissatisfaction of a young woman with her career options, a young girl's flight to a convent in order to prevent parental conflict, and the vacillation of an only son between the religious life and marriage, and the death of his fiancée before the latter course could be embarked upon. In no case would money be immediately identified as a matter of prime importance and yet each text is suffused with it.

Given Moore's praise for Balzac, it could be expected that money would loom large in Moore's 1890s fiction. However, throughout the story of *Esther Waters*, the references to actual sums of money are relatively few and seemingly incidental. Nonetheless, information is provided that a live-in scullery maid is not paid weekly or monthly but only every quarter[4] and that the wages might amount to between £14 and £16 per year, or approximately 6s.6d. per week.[5] While a butler would get £50 a year, a locomotive painter could earn £65-75 per year or 25 to 30 shillings per week, and the income of a stationer's clerk amounted to £78

---

3 *Mildred Lawson*, *John Norton* and *Agnes Lahens*.

4 Moore, *Esther Waters*, p. 3.

5 ibid. p. 153. This pre-decimalisation sterling currency was divided into pounds, shillings and pence, normally written as £.s.d., those letters being derived from the Latin, *Libri, solidi* and *denarii*. There were twelve pence in a shilling (1s. or 1/-), and twenty shillings in a pound (£1 or £1.0.0). A crown was the name given to a five-shilling piece and a half-crown was two shillings and six pence, usually written as either 2s.6d or 2/6. A penny was further divided into two half pence, variously called ha'pence or halfpennies, and into four farthings. Four pence would be written as 4d., one halfpenny as ½ d., and a farthing as ¼ d.

per year or 30s. per week.[6] These figures are somewhat buried in the story and receive no authorial comment but the poverty of a kitchen maid is unmistakable when it emerges that paying out five or six shillings per week for childcare could leave the mother with absolutely nothing to live on.[7] Only the very lucky ones might have up to £3 a year left, just over one shilling every week. If working as a servant does not allow a mother to bring in enough to support herself and her baby, as a wet-nurse she could earn between 15s. and £1, plus board, every week.[8] She would not be permitted to bring her own child with her to such a situation but would have to pay 6s. per week for its care, most probably by a possibly unscrupulous baby farmer who would be willing to ensure the baby's early demise for £5.[9] In this market, servants who are hired from the workhouse are obviously desperate to escape from it – and they are offered lesser wages.[10] Even small children work to supplement family income and are paid 3s.6d. for every gross (one hundred and forty four) of toy dogs they stuff; since they must buy some of the material themselves, the net income could be reduced by as much as twenty per cent.[11] A landlord who owns what is called a coffee shop but is obviously more of a slum doss house, pays his servant 7s. a week for round-the-clock slavery but he manages to rent rooms for 8s. a night, and beds in the cellar for 4d each per night.[12] The poor gamble desperately and illegally in public houses, with every one shilling bet accompanied by one shilling spent on drink.[13] At this time, newspapers cost just ½d., a glass of good whisky is priced at six pence, a short trip on a Thames pleasure boat is one penny, and a cheap novel – not the more usual expensive 3-decker – is sold at one shilling (1s. or 1/-).[14] The average cost of a cab journey in London is two shillings, and to escape from misery in London and England, an assisted passage to Australia is available at £2.[15] Although that list of actual sums of money might seem moderately substantial when put together, the allusions are relatively few in a novel of 377 pages and they are not at all conspicuous. The emphasis in the narrative does not

---

6 ibid., pp. 320, 23, 183.

7 ibid., p. 153.

8 ibid., p. 132.

9 ibid., pp. 134, 148.

10 ibid., p. 153. The rate was approximately £14 per year, instead of £16, a difference of £2 per year.

11 ibid., p. 96.

12 ibid., p. 361.

13 ibid., p. 325.

14 ibid., pp. 301, 241, 108, 116.

15 ibid., pp. 133, 113, 122.

seem to be on making income comparisons or pleas for fair wages but the cumulative evidence is ultimately persuasive of considerable injustices, and of the author's resolve to influence public opinion subtly in their regard.

The centrality of money matters is not, in this novel, confined to the lower classes. At the other end of the class spectrum, the former lady of the manor has what is called her "fortune" of £500 but the income generated by that capital (the actual amount coming to her is not stated) barely permits her to scrape by: she wears old clothes, her house is dilapidated, the knocker has gone from the door, lights are used sparingly, she no longer has a trap and engaging a man to cut down a tree is a major expense.. The family's fortune had been dissipated by gambling.[16] Another member of the more privileged classes is the judge whose one cameo appearance is perfect evidence of societal imbalance regarding money, and of an associated, cavalier hypocrisy: he could bet £300 on a horse – and lose – and, without a qualm, still hand down a jail sentence to an unemployed servant for a gambling debt of one tenth of that amount. He could also think of "the pint of excellent claret that lordship always drank with his lunch, and the thought enabled lordship to roll out some excellent invective against the evils of beer and spirits".[17] Those latter drinks were, of course, the tipples of the poorer classes. As befits an art critic – as George Moore was – the inclusion of such portraits is artistic, quite in the impressionistic mode rather than in photographic or realist style. The references are suggestive, they do not obtrude; rather they are infiltrated into the reader's consciousness. Thus, as illustration of gross disparities in income in contemporary society is gently furnished, a case for greater equity is never articulated in the didactic manner that had been customary in earlier Victorian times; yet, for a readership prone to pronounce on religious commandments, and schooled in biblical dicta and the concept of 'duty', the moral choices are utterly and uncomfortably clear.

The monies noted in *Esther Waters* provide some scale by which to assess the amounts found in the Sherlock Holmes adventure of *The Man with the Twisted Lip*. Although there are additional interesting connotations, 'Twisted Lip' in the title of this story refers ostensibly to the disguise that enables an erstwhile journalist to earn a lot of money by begging in the street. The totals are notable: Neville St. Clair had been a reporter on £2 per week but he could easily get as much in a day as a beggar. In fact, he could gather in more than £700 per year, about seven times a reporter's salary. St. Clair has a comfortable villa in the leafy suburbs, minimal debts and a credit balance of £220 in the bank.[18] On the crucial

---

16 ibid., pp. 205-206.

17 ibid., pp. 315-316.

18 Doyle, "The Man with the Twisted Lip", p. 373.

day in the tale, a load of coin is found in the pockets of his coat: 421 pennies (that is £1.15.1) and 270 halfpennies (11s.3d).[19] The full sum comes to £2.6.4. At that rate, it would take him just over a week to amass what a servant like Esther was paid in a full year. Arthur Conan Doyle does not provide costs for the various cab trips that Holmes and Watson take while they chase up and down on this case but it is evident that they do not baulk at the price, and although the source of income for Holmes is never clear, it is apparent from *Esther Waters* that a family doctor like Dr Watson might receive 5s. for a call. Holmes and Watson may not compete with the beggar on income but they are not impoverished. Whatever might be the messages Doyle wants to convey to his readers by detailing coin, salary and bank balance of Neville St. Clair – and some pertinent issues will be dealt with later – they do not concern the exploitative wages of domestic servants.

In *Celibates,* brief references to money deliver additional information on actual pounds sterling, as well as prompting thought on issues associated with them. In the story *Mildred Lawson*, accounting is at the level of hundreds and thousands of pounds. The affluence of the Lawsons permits Mildred to have hats, dressmakers, carriages, servants, art lessons and sojourns in Paris. Mildred's brother Harold (a distiller with business in the City) will not give consent to her marriage until Alfred, her current suitor can "settle five hundred a year" on Mildred.[20] Some years later, Alfred has increased his income from £300 to £500 per year. In the judgement of Harold, "that isn't much" but the progress "proves that he is a steady man".[21] When Mildred comes of age, rather than invest her £5000 capital in the 5% securities recommended by Harold, she entrusts her money to the Panama Canal scheme and to a French socialist newspaper where she fondly believes she might get a return of 20%.[22] Of course the money is lost. On Harold's death, Mildred succeeds to an income of £6000 per annum and Alfred, who had become a lukewarm acquaintance, is now very anxious not to lose Mildred and that money pot, and he indulges in subterfuge to achieve his ends. In this story twist, any trace of previous romantic Victorian fiction patterns is spurned by George Moore and, while the focus of the story appears to be primarily on Mildred's search for a meaning in life, money is discreetly, surely and inextricably linked to every move.

The allusion to the Panama Canal investment scandals is typical of an authorial literary strategy that might be described as aiming for maximum return from minimum investment. The word 'Panama' is briefly dropped into the text on

---

19 ibid., p. 377.

20 Moore, "Mildred Lawson", p. 5.

21 ibid., p. 275.

22 ibid., pp. 251-252, 267.

a few occasions and without further explanation, but its effect is carefully calculated and, for middle and upper class English readers, the echoes are multiple.[23] The associations and implications include blackmail, swindle, risks of foreign investment, duplicity of socialists, and the corrupt nature of French politicians, especially concerning sexual morality. It is possible that the mention of Panama contains an unspoken disapproval of ordinary workers buying shares, and that such investment should be the sole prerogative of the more privileged. While not explicitly provided in the story, a potential contrasting scenario that immediately suggests itself is the greater security that appears to obtain in Harold Lawson's conservative business world in the City of London, as opposed to risky Parisian ventures or socialist-linked ones. However, the constricting features of Harold's lifestyle and viewpoints are also intimated, and thus clarity of an attractive polar opposition is removed for the reader. This is particularly so for the female reader who, faced with the rigid patriarchal structures and cosy fraternity obtaining in financial and social affairs,[24] seems to be left with a restricted range of highly-policed investment options.

In *John Norton*, another of the stories in *Celibates*, comfortable financial circumstances obtain in the Norton household where John Norton's mother complains that John intends to spend £1500 on a window and an organ for a Jesuit church, and that he pays his solicitor £200 per year just to collect rents when he could do the job himself. While the coins given to the man with the twisted lip were mainly pence and halfpence, we find that John Norton throws a shilling to a beggar. The story seems to centre on John's gendering, on the allure of the clerical life and celibacy, on his attraction to Kitty and on her fate, but money matters are just beneath the surface. In John's absence, Mrs Norton's easy competence in managing the estate is evident and she ensures the maintenance of healthy returns from it. Her practicality contrasts with John's more fanciful notions, thus projecting the image of a woman in a position more usually occupied by a man. Those less-common, *de facto* circumstances are seen to undermine the assumptions behind the prevailing *de jure* and *de consuetudine* realities. The money concerns of Mrs Norton relate to the title of the property that

---

23 The Panama Canal investment scandal involved the loss of millions of francs by half a million investors, many of them peasants who placed their trust in the designers' reputations. Journalists and politicians (both deputies and ministers) were accused of taking bribes, both to encourage such investment and to cover up the overruns when they knew the position was hopeless. The company collapsed in 1889.

24 The family solicitors inform Harold Lawson of Mildred's withdrawal of money from her own funds, although they acknowledge that it is "a breach of professional etiquette". They repeat that misdemeanour, this time saying "we thought that we might venture on a confidential statement" (pp. 233-234).

generates their income. She is apprehensive lest John would assign it to the Jesuits and she fears that if John does not marry, the estate would pass to "to those terrible cousins of ours".[25] The fact that she and John would have shaken off the mortal coil at that point is irrelevant in her eyes. Money and what it buys are to be firmly clutched; they buttress the image, position and tradition the family has inherited and enjoyed, they are the shields and weapons by which they establish superiority.

The third family featured in *Celibates* is that of Agnes Lahens in the story bearing her name. Mrs Lahens (mother of Agnes) has money and a lover while Major Lahens, her husband, has been swindled out of his money and Mrs Lahens refers to him as "merely an expense".[26] In this Grosvenor Street household, he has been relegated to the attic room and reduced to buying the cast-off coat of the butler for ten shillings, a sum that he earned by typing. Mrs Lahens lends him an amount to buy a cheap suit and subsequently lends him £16 for the typewriter with which he attempts to earn a living. However, those monies must be repaid whereas Mrs Lahens actually bestows money on her titled, divorced lover and on a Mr Moulton. The latter is an idle young man who has a weekly allowance of 15s. from his uncle and who obviously finds that figure insufficient for his society needs. He does not seem to seek gainful employment and he would not be able to support a wife and household in the style that either would expect. His plight, and that of many young men of the time, might be summed up in the biblical phrase, "To dig I am not able, to beg I am ashamed".[27] Remaining unconcerned by her husband's status and options, Olive Lahens can voice understanding of Mr Moulton's predicament: "every day he finds himself face to face with the problem where he shall lunch, where he shall dine".[28] The contradictions inherent in her attitudes tend to steer the reader towards a distinct lack of sympathy for this man of "hollow cordiality".[29] The sum of £3 is mentioned as having been given to him by Mrs Lahens for an expensive pair of shoes.[30] In a short, whispered aside between Mrs Lahens and the suggestively-named Lilian Dare, it is conveyed that Lilian pays the princely sum of £30 every month to Lady Duckle who poses as her chaperone.[31] Once more, these monetary

---

25 Moore, "John Norton", pp. 322, 333.

26 Moore, "Agnes Lahens", p. 523.

27 Luke, 16.3.

28 Moore, "Agnes Lahens", p. 470.

29 ibid., p. 472.

30 ibid., p. 471.

31 ibid., p. 392. There is no further detail given concerning the profession, old or otherwise, of Miss Dare.

details are not prominent in the story but their implications are controversial for the period. In the Lahens home, it is the woman who has money and the associated power; she is clearly not an example of the 'Angel in the House' as wives were supposed to be. While Victorian society claimed that biological superiority fitted the man to be head of the house, here the lesson is that it is wealth that establishes supremacy and *that* notion could only be a very disturbing thought for patriarchal and aristocratic establishments. Without authority, position and money in the family and society, the moral rectitude and diligence of Major Lahens are made to seem pathetic. 19th-century society pays lip service to such values as laudable, essential and ever-present in idealised mothers but they go unappreciated in the male. More than that, their possession and exercise stigmatise a man as inadequate and insignificant.

Even in a relatively brief glance at three texts of the 1890s, it is apparent that money is shown to be critical for survival and for image. In *Esther Waters*, Moore injects a reality check into fiction with price and wage and legal inequalities, and he also touches on sensitive matters that are to the forefront in *The Man with the Twisted Lip*: the combination of respectability and wealth and charity. In that story, Neville St. Clair has the image of a successful man with business in 'the City', with wife (from a wealthy brewing family), children, and a large desirable suburban residence. The nature of his business in the city was not known to anyone, not even to his wife and it appears that she did not expect to know; he departed and returned regularly, just as did Harold in the story of *Mildred Lawson*. The misplaced aura of solid respectability that the financial centre of 'the City' bestows on the gentlemen who commute and work there is queried and undermined. The fact that St. Clair's comfortable income actually derives from disguising himself as a beggar is deemed to be shocking and unacceptable, both by Sherlock Holmes and by the police. They are in total agreement that such activity is to be instantly discontinued and that the police will "hush this thing up".[32] Neville St. Clair is to be removed from his lucrative begging career ("there must be no more of Hugh Boone") and restored to what is respectable. This is obviously of vital importance since it, rather than the source and security of any future income, is what merits mention. The beggar's obvious dramatic skills are not those deemed appropriate to his apparent domestic and social position, even if they are richly rewarded by those who continued to give him money. In the estimation of the time, donors would only have given their pence if they felt he was 'worthy' and the class element would have coloured their verdict on who could be labelled 'deserving'. In the case of St. Clair, it was thespian excellence that enhanced the beggar's image and enabled him to be

32 Doyle, "The Man with the Twisted Lip", p. 387.

perceived as falling into those categories. However, judgemental Victorian society placed a high premium on the rigidity of the existing class structure, and its boundaries were defensively policed. The joining of class and charity issues touched particularly sensitive nerves: with social standing often conveyed by dress and comportment, the safety of secure class identification was shattered if both could be altered so quickly and effectively by disguise. Arthur Conan Doyle's possible dissent from those views could be deduced from the use of disguise by Sherlock Holmes in the same story when he masquerades as a drug addict in an opium den.[33] Can there be clear distinctions drawn between Holmes' adoption of costume and make-up to solve a crime, and Neville St. Clair's impersonation of a beggar to earn a good living? The morality may be objectively equal but the social implications would have been perceived as disparate: Holmes was the superior policeman for the establishment; St. Clair was 'letting down the side' and disturbing the security of the villa owners. St. Clair was also well aware of how his actions would be judged ("a family blot" and "my miserable secret") and was most worried about the effect on his children: "I would not have them ashamed of their father".[34]

There are unspoken intimations in this text that readers should reflect on the arbitrary distinctions that are assumed between sources of income, whether the money be the meagre amount earned by the exploited employees of City industrialists, the revenues accruing to those same employers or to stockholders, the modest salary of the journalist, or the pence received in charitable donations that were freely given by the better-off to the seeming poor. In this particular Sherlock Holmes story, it is clear that the police are happy to countenance begging as long as the beggar pretends to be a poor match seller; it is the acceptance of pence by a middle-class man, rather than their donation by his unknowing peers, that is immediately worrying. For a contemporary readership, the matters of class confusion and class-appropriate behaviour are the more unsettling aspects of the tale and they are bound to be entangled with a questioning of the desirability of any charitable donations and the honesty of any beggar. Victorian attitudes to charity were openly challenged by Doyle in a book he published a couple of years later: "Why should people ever take credit for charity when they must know that they cannot gain as much pleasure out of their

33 The facility with which both Holmes and St.Clair disguised themselves also called into question the popular hypotheses of phrenology which allocated character traits according to physiognomy. As a medical doctor, Doyle would have been quite sceptical about some of Lombroso's theories.

34 Doyle, "The Man with the Twisted Lip", p. 377.

guineas in any other fashion?"[35] In George Moore's depiction of the lack of charity shown to Esther Waters by many pillars of society, whether hospital patrons, socialites, visiting ladies committees or Anglican clergy, the portrayals suggests a similar agenda of self-satisfaction and judgmental certainty on the part of several of the do-gooders.

Amongst the numerous money-linked aspects in each of these stories, several are closely connected to marriage and marriageability. The relationship between Neville St. Clair and his wife exhibits a separation of spheres that restricts communication to the pleasantly functional. Regenia Gagnier finds that the 1890s were a time of "economic, political, social, psychological"[36] crisis for males in England, and that intermingling of predicaments would seem to be the fate of Neville St.Clair, among others. Gagnier's diagnosis finds corroboration in the analyses of Joseph Kestner.[37] Catherine Belsey notes the recurrent presence of "shadowy, mysterious and often silent women" in the Sherlock Holmes tales.[38] Rosemary Jann's study of the Sherlock Holmes stories has suggested that, in them, only women with good social position and independent wealth can get married and that their money goes to preserve the economic and social power of men.[39]. Certainly, some fictional marriage prospects would seem to be in direct proportion to wealth, and the outlook is less good for those not so fortunately endowed. In *Mildred Lawson*, the opinion of Alfred, her suitor, is that Mildred poses a threat as a spouse; he sees "the danger of taking so flighty a minded person into the respectability of a British home";[40] she is not a compellingly desirable wife until her inheritance becomes irresistibly large. At that point, he is instantly willing and anxious to jettison the 'Angel in the House' criteria. An influence on Esther Waters in her choice of marriage partner is her urge to achieve greater security for her son, and her perception that William Latch (his

---

35 Arthur Conan Doyle, "Letter II", The Stark Munro Letters. Academic Search via Google. http://www.worldwideschool.org/library/books/lit/socialcommentary/TheStarkMunroLetters /chap2.html. The Stark Munro Letters was published in 1894.

36 Regenia A. Gagnier, *Idylls of the Marketplace: Oscar Wilde and the Victorian Public* (Stanford; Aldershot: Stanford University Press; Scolar Press, 1997), p. 98.

37 Joseph A. Kestner, *Sherlock's Men: Masculinity, Conan Doyle, and Cultural History* (Aldershot; Vermont: Ashgate, 1997).

38 Catherine Belsey, "Deconstructing the Text: Sherlock Holmes" in Arthur Conan Doyle, *Sherlock Holmes: The Major Stories with Contemporary Critical Essays*, ed. John A. Hodgson (Basingstoke: Macmillan, 1994), p. 384.

39 Rosemary Jann, *The Adventures of Sherlock Holmes: Detecting Social Order* (New York: Twayne, 1984), pp. 124-125.

40 Moore, "Mildred Lawson", p. 288.

natural father) might be able to provide more money for him than would Fred Parsons. One of the factors assisting her in reaching that conclusion is the attitude of Victorian society to children born out of wedlock.[41] In that same text, the relative contentment of the Parsons sisters in their single state might be read as resulting directly from their ability to survive economically without a marriage partner, while the obverse of the coin is apparent in the situations of Esther's mother, Sarah and others. Lord Chadwick, the lover of Mrs Lahens, is dependent upon her financially and is very aware of the chain of money-respectability-marriage linkages: "His name had been mixed up in questionable city transactions; his wife had divorced him, and he was over forty [...] Notwithstanding his title, he'd find it difficult to marry a girl with money; he couldn't marry one without".[42] There is no staple romantic fodder concerning love and marriage here. Despite the low-profile, and often tangential, nature of its mentions and inclusions, the crucial nature of money is admitted.

It might be suspected that George Moore's reason for introducing an example of the notorious half-crown entrapment ruse into Esther Waters was in order to draw more attention to his discreet inclusion of other money matters and to further underline the inseparability of money from morality. In this event, in which John, a "pasty-faced, despicable chap" leaves the coin on the floor of his room as a temptation to Esther; the intention is to induce her to steal it when she comes there to clean.[43] The motive in this instance is not to discover a dishonest servant, it is to create one. The snare is unsuccessful from John's point of view but by featuring the incident, Moore mirrored a contemporary practice and thoroughly discredited it. Moreover, he also manages to spread guilt by association to "Dissenters who exacted the uttermost farthing from their customers and their work-people" and to cast both doubt and aspersion on the sexual inclinations of John Bingley.[44] This technique of unvoiced suggestion with multiple implications is one that pervades many of the depictions glimpsed in Esther Waters: spending excessive amounts of money on drink and betting is variously and implicitly associated with lack of job security, self-indulgence,

---

41 Moore, *Esther Waters*, pp. 84, 100, 143.

42 Moore, "Agnes Lahens", pp. 465-466.

43 Moore, *Esther Waters*, pp. 155-156. The stratagem was often engaged in by the mistress of the house to test the honesty of servants. Cf. Frank E. Huggett, *Life Below Stairs* (London: John Murray, 1977), p. 111.

44 ibid., p. 153. In associating John with a custom usually enacted by females, further doubt is covertly directed at his sexuality. He is portrayed as something of a peeping Tom.

inability to confide in a partner, desperation to be married, belief in the 'happy ever after' scenarios of popular fiction, and clutching at the straws of omens and premonitions. Throughout the other texts, money-related topics are equally numerous and interconnected and they include the issues of power, gender, patriarchy, political corruption, property, class, image, investment and charity that have already been touched on. Those lists are lengthy but, such is the reverberation or ripple effect achieved by Moore and Doyle, they cannot be seen as comprehensive. Two further examples illustrate the multiple possibilities: the availability of inexpensively priced newspapers, fleetingly mentioned in Esther Waters, was at the heart of a debate over whether increased literacy facilitated reading the racing pages and thus encouraged gambling, or whether increased gambling opportunities increased literacy. The second example relates to the arguments that raged over sending the poor and the 'surplus' to the colonies, with or without the assisted passage rate of £2 mentioned in the same book. Particularly after the London riots of 1887 and the dock and gas strikes of 1889, and in the climate of the bombings in Paris in the early 1890s, it was believed that it was important for the security of England that the unemployed and young men from lower social classes should be encouraged to move to the colonies where they might earn more money and be less likely to destabilise the existing order at home.[45]

Given the presence of the many money questions in these examples of fin-de-siècle fiction, it would be reasonable to ask if there are answers. This study suggests that, rather than provide answers, the outcome of the authorial approaches results, in turn, in the generation of even more questions. Having departed from more traditional Victorian practice, Moore and Doyle may nudge and manipulate but they are not about to formulate explicit and easy prescriptions and resolutions for their readers. In every case, the money will be linked to social conditions and problems, and any answers will be reader-dependent ones. Thus, the responses will be individual and varied; they will only come later, and extra-textually. There is ample diversity in the authorial offerings: Balzac's focus on money might be called Marxism *avant la lettre*; Doyle's detective sniffs out problems with money and the capitalist image; Moore's variation on the Balzac example relentlessly but subtly queries societal structures, implicitly expanding

45 An example less directly connected to money, but still ultimately having financial implications, is the challenge posed to the theories of Darwin, and to the nature versus nurture argument, by the Whitney brothers in *The Man with the Twisted Lip*: one was principal of a theological college, the other was a drug addict. The import relates to the source of money for drugs, the income for the family, the disputes over degeneration and which class would decline and lose control over money and society.

the nineteenth-century necessity for money beyond the category of the "young man". A century later, when *libri*, *solidi* and *denarii* have vanished from common currency, the approaches and diagnoses from the Moore and Doyle stories must still be judged to be substantial and noteworthy. There is, perhaps, one question outstanding in the twenty first century: is there any change?

Hans-Walter Schmidt-Hannisa

Love for Sale. Men, Women and Money in Works by Arthur Schnitzler*

All you need is love.
John Lennon

Happiness? Pardon me, Fräulein, but there's no such thing. In general, it's precisely the things that are talked most about which don't exist... for example, love. That's another one.
Arthur Schnitzler[1]

Prelude at the bottom of the Rhine

In Germany, the 19th century saw two major and fundamental attempts to analyse the relationship between money and power and to criticise what has been called the capitalist system; one in the form of a philosophical theory of money and economy, the other as a myth in the form of an opera. Both were monumental critical manifestos: Karl Marx's *Das Kapital* and Richard Wagner's *Der Ring des Nibelungen* focus on the negative consequences brought about by the capitalist transformation of society.

Reflections upon the relationships between men and women are included in both Marx's and Wagner's works, and both authors consider what price 'capitalists' have to pay in order to acquire wealth. The accumulation of treasure is always based on sacrifice, renunciation and fetishism: gold is given fetish status and becomes something intrinsically valuable. It becomes a major object of

* This paper was originally given in German at Trinity College Dublin. I wish to thank Michael Shields who helped me so much to re-write this text in English, and Sheila Dickson for her valuable advice.

1 Arthur Schnitzler, *Round Dance*, in Arthur Schnitzler, *Round Dance and Other Plays*, trans. J.M.Q. Davies (Oxford, New York: Oxford University Press, 2004), p. 99. "Glück? Bitt Sie, Fräulein, Glück gibts nicht. Überhaupt gerade die Sachen, von denen am meisten g'redt wird, gibts nicht... zum Beispiel, die Liebe. Das ist auch so was." Arthur Schnitzler, *Reigen*, in Arthur Schnitzler, *Liebelei, Reigen* (Frankfurt a.M.: Fischer Taschenbuch, 1975), p. 141.

desire – *the* object of desire – and ultimately outstrips all other objects in this regard. Marx emphasises in particular the ascetic dimensions of amassing capital: "In order that gold may be held as money, and made to form a hoard, it must be prevented from circulating, or from transforming itself into a means of enjoyment. The hoarder, therefore, makes a sacrifice of the lusts of the flesh to his gold fetish. He acts in earnest up to the Gospel of abstention."[2] Whereas Marx's focus is on the pleasures of the flesh, Wagner's analytical opera is more subtle and reflects upon the interplay of gold, love and lust. The opening scene of *Rheingold*, the first opera of the *Ring* cycle, is particularly revealing. In it, Wagner's myth of the origins of the negative power of gold arises from a love-story. As a result, the relationship between love and lust is redefined, with far-reaching consequences.

The mythical point of departure is, as so often, a catastrophe, a fall from grace. Its scene is the riverbed of the Rhine. Here the Rhine gold still sparkles, safe in the bosom of Nature, under the admittedly careless guard of the Rhine maidens. These three mermaid-like females, with the attractively streamlined names Woglinde, Wellgunde und Floßhilde, are fully aware of the gold's significance. Whoever can forge a ring made of it will have "unlimited power" and "the world's wealth".[3] He has merely to fulfil one precondition, and that is renunciation. "Only he who forswears / love's power, / only he who forfeits / love's delight" will be able to manufacture the ring.[4] This is why the careless Rhine maidens fancy the gold is safe, since "everything that lives wants love: / no one will reject love."[5]

---

2 Karl Marx, *Capital. A Critical Analysis of Capitalist Production*. Trans. Samuel Moore and Edward Aveling, ed. Friederick Engels (London: Lawrence & Wishart, 1974), vol. 1, p. 133. – "Um das Gold als Geld festzuhalten und daher als Element der Schatzbildung, muß es verhindert werden zu zirkulieren oder als Kaufmittel sich in Genußmittel aufzulösen. Der Schatzbildner opfert daher dem Goldfetisch seine Fleischeslust. Er macht Ernst mit dem Evangelium der Entsagung." Karl Marx, *Das Kapital. Kritik der politischen Ökonomie* (vol. 1), in Karl Marx, Friedrich Engels, *Werke* (MEW), vol. 23 (Berlin/ GDR: Dietz, 1962), p. 147.

3 "Der Welt Erbe / gewänne zu eigen, / wer aus dem Rheingold schüfe den Ring, / der maßlose Macht ihm verlieh!" Richard Wagner, *Die Musikdramen* (München: Deutscher Taschenbuch Verlag, 1978), p. 533. All English translations of Wagner's libretto are from the online version, http://www.rwagner.net/libretti/rheingold/e-t-rhein.html.

4 "Nur wer der Minne / Macht versagt, / nur wer der Liebe / Lust verjagt", ibid.

5 "Wohl sicher sind wir / und sorgenfrei; / denn was nur lebt will lieben, meiden will keiner die Minne." Ibid.

However, the Nibelung Alberich is an unfortunate exception to this rule. Admittedly he too starts out in search of love and lust, setting his sights on the three Rhine maidens. But after encountering their mockery and realising his suit has no chance of success, he transfers his interest from their womanly charms to the gold. As the secret of the fascinating metal has already been betrayed to him by the Rhine maidens' careless talk, the Nibelung does something inconceivable. He curses love and steals the gold, thus initiating a chain of events that ends, as we know, in the *Götterdämmerung*, the *Twilight of the Gods*. Alberich's love-curse spreads to others and a loveless world ensues, in which money has become a universal fetish, the privileged object of all desires. In Alberich's words: "As I renounced love, / all living things / shall renounce it! / Allured by gold, / for gold alone shall you hunger."[6]

According to Wagner, the ring fashioned by Alberich from gold stolen from nature stands for a stockbroker's portfolio ("Börsenportefeuille") and is a symbol of the universal hegemony of money.[7] It transforms Alberich into an oppressor of human flesh, a capitalist beast of prey who uses his power to make others work and accumulate more and more wealth for him. This essay, however, will not focus on Alberich's capitalism but on his love life. Just before seizing the Rhine gold, Alberich addresses it and utters a very revealing remark: "The world's wealth / I could win for mine through you? / If I cannot extort love, / then by cunning can I attain pleasure?"[8]

In other words, even before Alberich has decided to renounce love he is thinking about ways of getting back what he has been forced to sacrifice. If the power of the ring symbolises the power of money, then it is clear that the only way of getting the sacrificed back, at least in part, is by buying it back. But what exactly is it that money can procure? Which things, of all the things possible between the sexes, can be bought? The dichotomous answer suggested by

---

6 "Wie ich der Liebe abgesagt, / Alles was lebt / soll ihr entsagen! / Mit Golde gekirrt, nach Gold nur sollt ihr noch gieren!" Ibid., p. 558.

7 Quoted in Dieter Borchmeyer, "Gold und Geld in Goethes *Faust* und Wagners *Ring des Nibelungen*", in Studium Generale der Ruprecht-Karls-Universität Heidelberg, *Geld* (Heidelberg: Universitätsverlag C. Winter, 2002), p. 56.

8 "Der Welt Erbe / gewänne ich zu eigen durch dich? / Erzwäng ich nicht Liebe, / doch listig erzwäng ich mir Lust?" Wagner, *Musikdramen*, p. 534. Alberich is even sure that he possesses the power to force the Gods' women to have sex with him, as he announces to Wotan: "For when once you men / serve my might / the dwarf will take his pleasure / with your pretty women / who scorn his wooing, / though love does not smile upon him." – "Denn dient ihr Männer / erst meiner Macht, / eure schmucken Frau'n, / die mein Frei'n verschmäht, / sie zwingt zur Lust sich der Zwerg, / lacht Liebe ihm nicht!" Wagner, *Musikdramen*, p. 558.

Alberich – love, no: lust, yes – is certainly over-simplistic. On the one hand, love is often regarded as *the* principle that eludes economic categorisations and subverts the laws of exchange, hence it is widely accepted that love is not something that can be bought. On the other hand, there is clearly much more for sale than the kind of pleasure that can be bought from a prostitute. What exactly can one get for money? And what are the limits on the purchasing power of money in encounters between the sexes? What is the person who is "for sale" selling, what can he or she offer as a commodity? What does 'selling oneself' entail, even if it 'only' involves putting one's body at the disposal of another person for libidinous purposes? What do such transactions signify for the (male) buyer/ (female) vendor? And how should we read the balance sheet of profit and loss when the transaction is complete?

Love for sale in works by Schnitzler

In order to provide answers to such general questions one would have to examine the anthropological dimensions of being available for purchase and establish, for example, what the gender-specific differences are. One would also have to take into account the different historical and cultural forms of sexual commodification. The aims of this study are far more modest. Using selected texts by Arthur Schnitzler, I will attempt to show how the concept of being for sale became a topic of major interest in a particular milieu, that of Vienna at the beginning of the 20th century. Why Schnitzler? In his analysis of the emerging crisis in (or rather: the collapse of) the ideal of monogamous love in *fin-de-siècle* Vienna, Schnitzler is more radical than most of his contemporaries. He has no particular interest in the romantic side of relations between the sexes beyond demonstrating that it does not exist and showing, again and again, that the notion of a romantic relationship is a farce.[9] His sustained criticism of the doctrine that men and

9 Cf. W. G. Sebald's apposite observation: "Schnitzler's literary work was written just as the bourgeois concept of love was beginning to enter a phase of dissolution. It derives its fascination from the fact that it describes – with regret, but without pathos – the calamities arising from an ideal of love that has become an *idée fixe*; but also from the fact that in so doing it renders the real social and mental state of his contemporaries more faithfully than the many contemporary works in which personification of love continues to be taken seriously." ("Das literarische Werk Schnitzlers entstand auf dem Punkt, an dem der bürgerliche Begriff von der Liebe ins Stadium der Dissolution einzutreten begann. Es hat seine nachhaltige Faszinationskraft daran, daß es mit Bedauern zwar, aber ohne Pathos die Kalamitäten beschreibt, die von einem zur fixen Idee gewordenen Ideal ausgelöst werden, und daß es solchermaßen den wirklichen

women should engage exclusively, within a single relationship, with one another in the four areas of love, lust, reproduction and everyday household living is still provocative to 21st-century readers. His great theme is double morality, the gaping void between pretence and reality, and nothing attracts his critical attention more than the institution of marriage. For Schnitzler, marriage is a concept that has become completely hollow in its romantic and moral senses. In his texts it is defined in economic terms, as are other relations between the sexes. After Eros, money is the most important basis on which men and women have relations with one another. And when money comes into it, there is always a variety of things on offer.

Doubtless Schnitzler is more inclined to side with Alberich's cynicism than with the Rhine maidens' naive faith in love. Prostitution, 'kept girls' (*süße Mädel*), and marriages of convenience are more frequently encountered in his works than happily united couples. Some of his texts can be read as a series of experiments – discrete sections of a project designed to probe the different ways and dimensions of being available for purchase and to analyse them – and Schnitzler's Vienna appears to be an ideal testing-ground for literary investigations of this kind.

A psychologically well-versed social diagnostician, Schnitzler cultivates a double perspective in his texts. They are sociological, economic and socio-psychological critiques of contemporary Viennese society, but, in addition, can almost be read as clinical case studies of individuals torn apart by the tensions and contradictions that existed between love, sex and commerce in Viennese society. I will outline this in greater detail, using three exemplary texts that describe characters who can be bought in three different forms, *Fräulein Else*, *Casanovas Heimfahrt* and *Spiel im Morgengrauen*.

These texts are not descriptions of prostitution in the classical sense, that is, of a transaction in which a woman offers sexual services through direct physical contact in return for payment. 'Classical' prostitution is, of course, the paradigm in these texts too, but it is interpreted anew in every text, with changed parameters that involve, for example, reversal of sexual roles, new definitions of the 'service' provided, or the portrayal of marriage for money as a form of prostitution – this last equation had already been made in Georg Simmel's *Philosophy of Money*.

---

gesellschaftlichen und seelischen Zuständen genauer Rechnung trägt als die weiterhin an der Hypostasierung der Liebe arbeitenden Werke vieler Zeitgenossen.") "Das Schrecknis der Liebe. Zu Schnitzlers Traumnovelle", in W. G. Sebald, *Die Beschreibung des Unglücks. Zur österreichischen Literatur von Stifter bis Handke* (Frankfurt a.M.: Fischer Taschenbuch, 1994), p. 39.

It is most clearly in the figure of the prostitute that the power of money becomes manifest. The prostitute makes possible an immediate transference between money and desire, money and lust. The lust that she puts up for sale is lust for a commodity. In this sense Walter Benjamin apotheosized the prostitute as an incarnation of Modernism with its subjugation to the power of money. She is characterised by a dual enslavement to the laws of a commodified world, because she is vendor and product at one and the same time.[10] Everything individual, personal or intimate about her withdraws, leaving an exchange object that can be put on the market. Her price, which can be expressed in abstract pecuniary terms, is the sign of her replaceability. While she is selling herself, the prostitute is forced actively to display her body in accordance with the principles of product aesthetics, for example by using make-up and clothes that emphasise her erotic features.

As in other cities, prostitution in Schnitzler's Vienna was a mass phenomenon. It would be impossible to write about the society of *fin de siècle* Vienna without mentioning how extraordinarily widespread, and how entrenched, this 'purchasable love' was. A statistic from the Morality Bureau (*Sittenamt*) of the Viennese Directorate of Police from 1920 may serve as an illustration. According to this, no less that 3,272 women were arrested for the "uncontrolled practice of prostitution" in that year. This total included 377 civil servants, 14 dental technicians and dentists' assistants, eight officers' wives, 571 members of the middle class, 255 qualified workers, and 446 housemaids. Among those arrested were also middle-class minors: the daughter of a dentist, an army doctor, a tax official (*Oberfinanzrat*) and a town councillor (*Stadtrat*) respectively.[11] It is clear from these statistics that prostitution was not the sole preserve of the working classes. According to a contemporary source from the turn of the century, 80 per cent of all men in Vienna had their first experience of sexual intercourse with a prostitute.[12]

A wide range of texts from the literature of the period deals with prostitution, documenting its importance as a social and cultural phenomenon.[13] In

---

10 See Walter Benjamin, *Das Passagenwerk*, in Walter Benjamin, *Gesammelte Schriften in sieben Bänden*, ed. Rolf Tiedemann and Hermann Schweppenhäuser (Frankfurt a.M.: Suhrkamp, 1992), vol. 5, p. 55

11 http://www.bmi.gv.at/oeffentlSicherheit/2000/11_12/artikel_12.asp.

12 See the chapters on prostitution in Wolfgang Maderthaner, Lutz Musner: *Die Anarchie der Vorstadt. Das andere Wien um 1900* (Frankfurt a.M., New York: Campus, 1999).

13 See Christiane Schönfeld, *Dialektik und Utopie. Die Prostituierte im deutschen Expressionismus* (Würzburg: Königshausen & Neumann, 1996); Dietmar Schmidt, *Geschlecht unter Kontrolle. Prostitution und moderne Literatur* (Freiburg i. Br.:

Schnitzler's texts, however, portrayals of prostitution, including prostitution in the classical sense, occupy a particularly prominent position.[14] Significantly, his most famous and most scandalous play, *Reigen*, which consists of a series of ten dialogues between couples from different social backgrounds, each culminating in sexual intercourse, opens with a dialogue between the prostitute and the soldier, and closes with a dialogue between the prostitute and the count. Despite their differences, both dialogues provide revealing examples of how the prostitute and her client deal with the economic nature of their relations. Each encounter is characterised by the protagonists' conscious and unconscious use of strategies to disguise the financial basis of the encounter. In the closing scene it is the count who is inclined to discount the fact that he has paid for the services the woman he has just spent the night with. Watching the prostitute, who is still in bed, he observes that one would not necessarily see that a woman can be bought by the look of her. "When all one can see is their little head like this... they all look innocent on waking up... God, one could imagine all sorts of things."[15]

This remark is the point of departure for subsequent 'romantic' gestures that belie the monetary nature of their relationship. He kisses her on the eyes and asks whether she is, after all, happy. But in order to be able to disengage himself from the encounter he has to remind himself that "it all comes down to money with such women".[16] There is no externally visible sign to indicate that a woman who has turned herself into a product is just that. In fact it is the social situation that brings about this transformation; it takes the market to turn a thing or person into a commodity. By contrast, in the opening dialogue it is the prostitute who tries to deny the financial nature of the relationship. Here her denial is a central part of her seduction strategy: "I don't want money", she reassures the soldier. "Civilians have to pay up. But a fellow like you can always come with me for nothing."[17]

Rombach, 1998); Isabelle Siemes, *Die Prostituierte in der literarischen Moderne, 1890-1933* (Düsseldorf: Hagemann, 2000). Most of these recent publications make reference to Schnitzler.

14 For a treatment of prostitution in Schnitzler's work see W. G. Sebald, "Die Mädchen aus der Feenwelt – Bemerkungen zu Liebe und Prostitution mit Bezügen zu Raimund, Schnitzler und Horvath", in *Neophilologus* 1/67 (1983), pp. 109-117.

15 Schnitzler, *Round Dance*, p. 104. "Wenn man nur das Kopferl sieht, wie jetzt ... beim Aufwachen sieht doch eine jede unschuldig aus ... meiner Seel, alles mögliche könnt man sich einbilden [...]." Schnitzler, *Reigen*, p. 150.

16 Schnitzler, *Round Dance*, p. 106. "Ich weiß doch, daß es solchen Frauenzimmern nur aufs Geld ankommt." Schnitzler, *Reigen*, p. 153.

17 Schnitzler, *Round Dance*, p. 51 "Ich brauch kein Geld. [...] Zahlen tun bei mir die Zivilisten. So einer wie du kanns immer umsonst bei mir haben." Schnitzler, *Reigen*, p. 72.

She raises expectations of a sexual encounter based on mutual desire, veiling the fact that her service is really a market product by giving the soldier the impression she is eager for his company because of her affinity to soldiers and not for the sake of his money. After completion of the sexual act, she does not ask him openly for payment but formulates her demand as a request: she has to give the concierge a tip.[18] This simple scene shows clearly that an act purchased for money is considered to be worth less than one in which money is not an intermediary. The devaluation of the act is a direct result of the fact that it has been assigned an exchange value, and that that value is money.

Fräulein Else

Reigen looks at a prostitute from the outside. She, like all the other characters in the play, represents a social role and acts out a series of socially 'typical' behaviours. *Fräulein Else* approaches the theme of being available for purchase from a very different angle. The novella depicts a young girl's struggle to assert herself in an extreme situation: those around her expect her to use her beautiful body to generate capital. Here the woman, mercilessly pursued and doomed to tragedy, is presented more clearly as a victim than in most of Schnitzler's works (except, perhaps, his novel *Therese*). The theme of selling oneself is positioned within a wider context, as the novella links the themes of prostitution and marrying for money. (Georg Simmel's *Philosophy of Money*, which appeared around the same time, operates along similar lines.) The plot of *Fräulein Else* can be briefly summarised as follows: Else, a nineteen year-old girl from a Vienna-based upper-class family is spending her holidays together with relatives in a luxurious hotel in the Italian Alps. There she receives a letter by express mail from her mother, urging her to ask an art dealer and friend of the family, Herrn von Dorsday, for a loan of 30,000 gulden. Her father, a lawyer and a notorious gambler, is in urgent need of the money, as he is about to be arrested for embezzlement. Motivated by loyalty to her family, Else overcomes her reluctance and speaks to Dorsday who, as it turns out, is prepared to put the money at their disposal. However, as might be expected, he proposes a deal: he stipulates that she let him see her naked for a quarter of an hour. Else cannot see any way of refusing this request and keeps her side of the bargain, though in an unexpected way. Instead of baring herself to Dorsday in private, she unveils her body in a public performance. In this way she satisfies the contract, but also violates it, since the sight of her naked body plummets in value as soon as it is freely

---

18 "Geh, ein Sechserl fürn Hausmeister gib mir wenigstens!" Ibid., p. 73.

available to all without payment. Apart from this, Else is able to use her public appearance to indulge her exhibitionist leanings. The price which Else pays for her transgression of bourgeois morality is high: the performance that she herself has organised ends in a hysterical breakdown and she commits suicide to avoid the ensuing scandal.

The letter from Else's mother brings her carefree life as an upper-class young lady abruptly to an end. Else realises that her parents regard her primarily as an exchange object that can be cashed in when needed. "They've brought me up only to sell myself one way or another".[19] As soon as Else accepts this role in principle, the question of her value acquires existential significance. During the hours after receiving the letter, Else's thoughts revolve around the possibility of an alternative form of self-definition. She searches for a means to escape from the necessity of recognising that her price in money is the key to her social identity. During her conversation with Dorsday, Else is negotiating not only the terms and conditions of Dorsday's loan, but also, more importantly, her own worth. Initially she tells Dorsday the loan is for a million gulden rather than 30,000 in order to gauge his reaction: it will tell her what her market value is.

It becomes clear how arbitrary such sums are when a telegram arrives containing the laconic disclosure that the required amount has risen from 30,000 to 50,000 gulden. Even before Else speaks to Dorsday she is searching for compromise solutions that will alleviate the disgrace of her 'sale', both socially and psychologically. She toys with the idea of offering herself to her cousin Paul, whom she finds attractive. Above all, it is the possibility of a marriage for money that she entertains as a socially acceptable means of "permanently prostituting oneself", as Simmel puts it.[20] After musing whether she would be prepared to sell

19 Arthur Schnitzler, Fräulein Else, trans. Robert A. Simon, in Arthur Schnitzler, *Viennese Novelettes* (New York: Simon and Schuster, 1931), p. 165. "[...] sie haben mich ja doch nur daraufhin erzogen, daß ich mich verkaufe, so oder so." Arthur Schnitzler, *Fräulein Else*, in Arthur Schnitzler, *Gesammelte Werke in Einzelausgaben. Das erzählerische Werk* (Frankfurt a.M.: Fischer Taschenbuch, 1978), vol. 5, p. 240.

20 Georg Simmel, *The Philosophy of Money*, ed. David Frisby, trans. Tom Bottomore and David Frisby (London, New York: Routledge, 1990), p. 381. German original: "chronische Prostituierung". Georg Simmel, *Philosophie des Geldes* [1900], Gesamtausgabe (Frankfurt a.M.: Suhrkamp, 1989), vol. 6, p. 522. On the other hand, Simmel points out that prostitution in principle can be as socially acceptable as marriage for money, if only the price charged by the prostitute is high enough: "With regard to prostitution we can observe that, once certain prices are exceeded, money loses its baseness and its incapacity to be worth the equivalent of particular values. The abhorrence in which the prostitute is held by modern 'better' society is more pronounced the more miserable and the poorer she is, and it becomes weaker as the price for her services increases [...]." Simmel, *Philosophy of Money*, p. 383

herself for a million, a palace or a pearl necklace, she decides: "If I marry some day I'll probably do it for less."[21]

Else is realistic enough to admit that she has no prospects of leading a financially independent life. Her preordained career path – that of a 'young woman of good family' destined to be married to a wealthy man – would guarantee a life without material worries, but would also mean a life of dependency. She laments: "O God, why haven't I any money? Why haven't I ever earned anything? Why didn't I ever study? Oh, I've learned something. [...] I play the piano; I can speak French, English and a little Italian; I've attended lectures on the history of art. – Haha!"[22]

Despite the practical limitations of her situation, Else's crisis has a catalytic effect: it prompts her to develop emancipatory thoughts and a desire for a life that is self-determined, at least sexually . She has repeated fantasies of having several lovers at once. Her idea that she can give rather than sell herself to the men suggests that sexual pleasure is not irreconcilable with personal dignity: "I'll be a wanton, not a prostitute."[23] Else's thinking is free, to an extraordinary degree, of the influence of bourgeois norms and conventions with their double standards.[24] As the time for her nude performance approaches, she repeatedly tries to view it as a fresh start, even as a rebirth. She feels as if she is about to "come into the

---

(translation modified). "Es macht sich übrigens für die Prostitution auch die Erscheinung geltend, dass das Geld über eine gewisse Quantität hinaus seine Würdelosigkeit und Unfähigkeit, individuelle Werte aufzuwiegen, verliert. Der Abscheu, den die moderne, 'gute' Gesellschaft vor der Prostituierten hegt, ist um so entschiedener, je elender und ärmlicher diese ist, und mindert sich mit der Höhe des Preises, um welchen sie sich verkauft." Simmel, *Philosophie des Geldes*, p. 524.

21 Schnitzler, *Fräulein Else*, p. 136. "Wenn ich einmal heirate, werde ich es wahrscheinlich billiger tun." Schnitzler, *Fräulein Else* (German original), p. 218.

22 Schnitzler, *Fräulein Else*, p. 135 (translation modified). "Ach Gott, warum habe ich kein Geld? Warum hab' ich mir noch nichts verdient? Warum habe ich nichts gelernt? O, ich habe was gelernt! [...] Ich spiele Klavier, ich kann französisch, englisch, auch ein bißl italienisch, habe kunstgeschichtliche Vorlesungen besucht – Haha!" Schnitzler, *Fräulein Else* (German original), p. 217.

23 Schnitzler, *Fräulein Else*, p. 158. "ein Luder will ich sein, aber nicht eine Dirne." Schnitzler, *Fräulein Else* (German original), p. 234.

24 "Down there they'll all think that I've gone mad. But I've never been so sensible before. For the first time in my life I'm really sensible." Schnitzler, *Fräulein Else*, p. 177. "Da unten werden sie meinen, ich bin verrückt geworden. Aber ich war noch nie so vernünftig. Zum erstenmal in meinem Leben bin ich wirklich vernünftig." Schnitzler, *Fräulein Else* (German original), p. 249.

world for a second time."[25] But in society the display of her naked body does not mean a return to innocence, to a state in which social compulsions have been shaken off like unwanted clothes, but rather Else's transformation into a commodity. And life has long since departed from the body, which has been turned into merchandise. "Yes, most certainly I'm dead", she senses; and again, before her encounter with Dorsday in the music room, she has to admit: "My heart is dead."[26] Else does succeed in turning her nude self-display into a kind of compromise by displaying herself to the entire company and not exclusively to her buyer. By this trick she sells herself and gives herself simultaneously; her actions are partly determined by others but also partly self-determined, since she is doing what she is told but not *as* she has been told by her 'business partner', and she is not acting in his interest. Still, what she reveals is not nakedness as the expression of her new, liberated life, but as the mark of her commodification; it is the nakedness of depersonalised flesh. As Else herself clearly states: "Herr von Dorsday has the right to see my body, my beautiful naked corpse."[27] Ultimately Else has no chance of escaping her own loss of self, and her only option is a retreat into hysteria and then into the last remaining arena where self-determination is possible: suicide.

Casanovas Heimfahrt

Whereas *Fräulein Else* is narrated from the woman's perspective and from the point of view of a victim who has been commodified, *Casanovas Heimfahrt* adopts the perspective of the male 'client'. *Fräulein Else* portrays contemporary characters; by contrast, in *Casanovas Heimfahrt* the reader is confronted with the portrayal of a quintessentially eighteenth-century man of the world. The choice of a historical setting and a character who has achieved mythic status makes it clear from the start that this story is not concerned with the everyday life of

---

25 Schnitzler, *Fräulein Else*, p. 179. "[...] bevor man zum zweitenmal auf die Welt kommt." Schnitzler, *Fräulein Else* (German original), p. 250.

26 Schnitzler, *Fräulein Else*, p. 179, 184. "Ja, ganz bestimmt bin ich tot", "Mein Herz ist tot", Schnitzler, *Fräulein Else* (German original), pp. 250, 254.

27 Schnitzler, *Fräulein Else*, p. 170. "Herr von Dorsday hat das Recht, meinen Leichnam zu sehen. Meinen schönen nackten Leichnam." Schnitzler, *Fräulein Else* (German original), p. 243. The transformation of the displayed body into a corpse is portrayed unambiguously in a dream Else has after her conversation with Dorsday: Else watches her own burial, at which she wears mourning but also feels she is being stared at by greedy eyes perceiving her as being naked. See Schnitzler, *Fräulein Else*, p. 163.

Schnitzler's contemporaries. This makes it possible for Schnitzler to treat the question of how someone can be bought as if it were a technical and organisational problem rather than a moral question. We shall see shortly that the plot is centred on a very special kind of transaction.

Schnitzler's Casanova is a miserable wretch. 53 years old, he is burnt out and disappointed, sapped of his energy and tired of his wandering life. Nothing is left of his wealth; his clothes are old and shabby. More than anything else it is the thought that he could return to his home city, Venice, and take up an official post that excites him – no matter how morally and politically dubious it may be. Casanova's most valuable asset is his name, which is known throughout Europe and is synonymous with erotic adventure, gallantry and freethinking. Casanova is the irresistible seducer and lover of the women he pleasures (erotically at least); he is not a careless cynic like his counterpart Don Juan.[28] At this stage in his career it is more the myth of Casanova's past seductions than his actual appearance that attracts women. Casanova is only a shadow of himself, a man who can no longer bear the sight of himself in a mirror.[29] He does however experience love and desire one more time, and the novella is centred on this encounter.

When the narration begins, Casanova is delayed on his homeward journey to Venice by a meeting with Olivo, whom Casanova had helped 16 years previously by, giving financial assistance that resulted in Olivo's marriage. Olivo is now a prosperous landowner, and invites Casanova to be his guest for a few days. Casanova agrees. It transpires that the family idyll of Olivo, who is the self-satisfied father of three daughters, is only a bourgeois façade. Casanova's donation of money before the marriage had not been an uninterested gift: on the evening before the wedding Amalia, the bride, had shown her "generous patron" ("edlen Gönner") gratitude, "in the manner prompted by her own heart"[30], and had been far from thinking that she was doing her future husband any wrong. For Casanova it makes little difference whether Olivo knows about this "consideration" offered by his wife or not; it seems equally possible to him that he knows nothing or that he knows everything and approves of it as something completely normal. When Casanova sees Amalia she spontaneously signals that

28 On the literary and cultural evolution of the figure of Casanova, see Hartmut Scheible (ed.), *Mythos Casanova. Texte von Heine bis Buñuel* (Leipzig: Reclam, 2003).

29 Arthur Schnitzler, *Casanova's Homecoming*, trans. Eden and Cedar Paul, revised by Caroline Wellbury, in Arthur Schnitzler, *Plays and Stories*, ed. Egon Schwarz (New York: Continuum, 2003), p. 198.

30 ibid., p. 161; "in einer Weise [...], die ihr das eigene Herz gebot" Arthur Schnitzler, *Casanovas Heimkehr*, in Arthur Schnitzler, *Gesammelte Werke in Einzelausgaben. Das erzählerische Werk* (Frankfurt a.M.: Fischer Taschenbuch, 1978), vol. 5, p. 38.

she would not be averse to a continuation of the liaison, after so many years. Obviously the household espouses loose morals that have little in common with the idealised codes of the bourgeois epoch. The fragility of the family idyll again becomes clear when Olivo's eldest daughter, the 13 year-old Teresina, is only too happy to let herself be seduced by Casanova. Although there is no need for him to do so, after they have had sex Casanova gives the girl a gold coin in the presence of her father. The following reason is provided to explain this gift: "In days gone by he had possessed the girl's mother and grandmother also, and he thought it a particularly good joke that he was paying the little wench for her favors under the very eyes of her father."[31] Clearly Casanova intends this as a lesson for the adolescent girl. Teresina is to learn that money and Eros go together like two sides of a coin; becoming a woman involves becoming a commodity. Quite independently of any desire or pleasure that one might feel, the granting of sexual favours creates a value that forms the basis for an economic claim. But Casanova also has a second lesson prepared for the "little wench":

> "You must not tell the abbot anything about this, Teresina, not even in confession. Some day, when you have a lover or a husband, there is no reason why he should know anything about it. You should in fact always lie [...] that it may be well with you on earth."[32]

This maxim extols hypocrisy and deception as the highest moral principles (articulated in a blasphemously biblical-sounding formulation). Casanova initiates the young girl into the disingenuous rites and processes that make it possible for a woman to satisfy the two main roles expected of her by men: to be a saint and a whore at one and the same time – and not, of course, in an exclusive relationship with one man alone, but within the promiscuous order of society; an order that we find depicted in exemplary fashion in Schnitzler's *Reigen*.

However, it is actually the encounter with another woman that causes Casanova's passions to rekindle. Olivo's beautiful and talented niece, Marcolina, has studied mathematics at the University of Bologna, and is staying with her uncle and aunt for a visit. In her Casanova finds a woman perfectly enlightened in

---

31 Arthur Schnitzler, *Casanova's Homecoming*. p. 214. "Es machte ihm einen ganz besonderen Spaß, das Dirnchen, deren Mutter und Großmutter ihm auch schön gehört hatten, im Angesicht ihres eigenen Vaters für ihre Gunst zu bezahlen." Schnitzler, *Casanovas Heimkehr*, p. 91.

32 Schnitzler, *Casanova's Homecoming*, p. 213. "Du mußt es dem Abbate nicht sagen, Teresina, auch in der Beichte nicht. Und wenn du später einen Liebhaber kriegst oder einen Bräutigam oder gar einen Mann, der braucht es auch nicht zu wissen. Du sollst überhaupt immer lügen, [...] auf daß es dir wohl ergehe auf Erden!" Schnitzler, *Casanovas Heimkehr*, p. 90f.

every respect, even though she is not yet 20. In the course of a philosophical discussion it transpires that she is far superior to him in intellectual acuity and rhetorical brilliance; she is moreover capable of using her reason so independently and freely that she remains unimpressed by the authority of state, church or academia. Possessed of a critical and independent mind, she is also unimpressed by Casanova's reputation. Contrary to first impressions, however, it turns out that she does live for more than just science and virtue. By chance Casanova observes a young man, lieutenant Lorenzi, climbing out of her window at dawn. He concludes that Marcolina, like all other women, is a hypocrite, a liar and a whore, but even so he is forced to admit to himself that he is in love with her.[33]

What can he do? Casanova can see clearly from the way she looks at him that his physical appearance repels Marcolina. As she is immune to his seductive arts, Casanova decides to use Amalia as a go-between. Amalia, who still loves and desires him, will take him to Marcolina, and will receive in return the favours she longs for. The plan fails, not because Amalia is shocked or angered, but because she is convinced Marcolina cannot be bought, declaring with conviction: "Had you a hundred thousand, you could not buy Marcolina."[34]

A second plan is more successful. Favourable conditions are created during an evening spent in exclusively male company. As so often in Schnitzler's works, it is gambling (in other words, culturally organised coincidence) that causes the tide to turn. Marcolina's lover Lorenzi starts to lose and borrows from a fellow-player, while Casanova wins again and again. Lorenzi's creditor insists upon being paid immediately, because Lorenzi's future is uncertain – his regiment will leave the following day. Lorenzi must find a way of saving his honour, and Casanova exploits his dilemma: Marcolina may not be bought, but her lover can be. When he offers Lorenzi the sum needed to pay off his debts and save his honour, the lieutenant is prepared to sell Marcolina's honour in return. What Casanova gets from Lorenzi for his money is the following: Lorenzi will prepare Marcolina for a farewell nocturnal visit, and will warn her that neither of them is to say a single word – both the pleasure of meeting and the pain of parting are to be shared in silence. Lorenzi is also to let Casanova have his coat so that Casanova, wrapped in it, can visit Marcolina in the guise of her lover. In this way Casanova hopes to circumvent the disadvantages of "normal" bought love. Paid women usually know that they are entering, as merchandise, into a relationship defined by economic parameters, and act accordingly by building up inner reservations that

33 Schnitzler, *Casanova's Homecoming*, pp. 196, 199.

34 ibid., p. 172. "Auch für hunderttausend bekämst du Marcolina nicht." Schnitzler, *Casanovas Heimkehr*, p. 50.

distinguish their "real" self from the commodity that is being sold. But during this nightly love encounter Marcolina will not know that her body has been transformed into traded goods; she will give herself to Casanova with the passion of a woman who fears that her lover will be killed on the battlefield. What Casanova hopes to acquire is authenticity: the authenticity of female passion and of a uniquely individual passion that cannot be expressed in terms of abstract economic value, and which consequently cannot be bought.

In principle Casanova achieves his aim of buying what cannot be bought, but at a high price. At the end of a night of ecstasy, in which bodies enjoy pure lust without language and without names or faces, a ray of half-light falls on Casanova's face, and he sees Marcolina's damning expression – one of nausea and horror. "Had it been within his power to annihilate himself by a spell, he would have done so".[35] In a moment of a sudden moral insight, the ladies' man Casanova realises that he has debased Marcolina twice in one night; once by turning her into a commodity, and a second time by persuading her lover to turn her into a commodity.

Ultimately, however, Marcolina's humiliation and the question of purchasable and authentic passion are of secondary interest in *Casanovas Heimfahrt*. The central focus is the tragedy of an old man who is forced to buy what he can no longer have by any other means. Whereas his legendary name has hitherto disguised his physical collapse, enabling him to seduce women by virtue of its reputation (as in the case of his landlady, of Amalia and of Teresina), now Marcolina's critical and enlightened gaze separates the name Casanova, his identification mark, from his naked, unencoded body, reducing the value of the latter to zero. His decrepit frame no longer has any exchange value on the love market, so that Casanova is forced to replace his most personal currency, that of his name, with the most general and abstract currency: money. The face value of his name can no longer be backed by that of his body.

Casanova tries in vain to hide from his partner the fact that he has become a buyer. That he has to depend on money as the defining medium of his sexual relationships, rather than on his name, marks the loss of his uniqueness. Subjection to the laws of the market de-individualises the male lover, who is reduced to the position of buyer, as well as the woman, who is transformed into a commodity. As a rule it is money and money alone, the sum that a man has at his disposal, that defines his status as a market player. However, since Marcolina is

---

35 Schnitzler, *Casanova's Homecoming*, p. 234. "Wäre es in diesem Augenblick in seiner Macht gestanden, sich selbst durch ein Zauberwort zu vernichten – er hätte es getan", Schnitzler, *Casanovas Heimkehr*, p. 111.

the commodity, not the vendor, her gaze is doubly humiliating for Casanova. It exposes his descent from seducer to customer, and it strips away his name and his reputation to reduce his individuality to a pitiful, naked old man's flesh and bones.

Spiel im Morgengrauen

Gambling is an essential component not only in *Casanovas Heimfahrt* but in many of Schnitzler's works. The last of the novellas to be discussed here, *Spiel im Morgengrauen,* contains an allusion to gambling in its title, and could be translated as *Gambling at Daybreak.* In both texts, gambling stands allegorically for fate and for the power of chance – a power that is invoked as soon as one stops believing in any kind of god. Gambling can be perceived as a summary of life's ups and downs: within the span of a few hours the gambler can be both winner and loser, experiencing the extremes of good and bad fortune. The hierarchies and power constellations of the gaming table, based solely on wealth, can be completely reversed in seconds. On the one hand the vicissitudes of a game represent the elevation of chance to a dominant principle; on the other, the players are playing for money, the most universal equivalent of all values; so what is at stake may decide about life and death. Gambling debts are debts of honour; so losing at gambling results in losses of honour, which, if they are great enough, involve sacrificing the reputation that is the basis for the bourgeois male's existence. We know from *Fräulein Else* and *Casanovas Heimfahrt* that honour can be more important than morality. On the other hand, he who wins gets the chance to enjoy everything money can buy. As in *Casanovas Heimfahrt*, winnings in *Spiel im Morgengrauen* are equated with power over women and with sexual conquests.[36] The corollary of this is that gambling losses correspond to loss of manhood. While the winner suddenly finds he can buy everything, what dawns upon the loser is that he can be bought. This inversion is a central theme of *Spiel im Morgengrauen*, as the male protagonist's gambling debts put him in a position where a former prostitute now pays him, her former client, for sex. However, *Spiel im Morgengrauen* is of interest not just because the text inverts the traditional gender role distributions within love for sale but also because it casts the female character in a dual role. This sexually and economically dominant figure appears both as an enterprising and successful spouse and as a *grande dame* who pays for her lover's services.

---

36 See Susann C. Anderson, "Shattered Illusions. Gambling in Arthur Schnitzler's Prose Works", in *Modern Austrian Literature* 25 (1992), pp. 241-256, here: p. 248f.

The plot of the novella can be summarised briefly as follows. The male protagonist, lieutenant Wilhelm Kasda, is jolted out of his modest and predictable existence by a visit from an acquaintance, an ex-officer who has been cashiered for embezzlement and who implores him to lend him 1,000 gulden. Kasda, he declares, or more precisely, his wealthy uncle Robert, is his last resort. This uncle has given Kasda financial support in the past, however, his behaviour has changed strangely in recent years; he no longer sends money and has broken off all contact with his nephew. Kasda promises to stake what money he has of his own (120 gulden) at cards on the Sunday afternoon, and does so with success. At this point, it must be emphasised that Kasda is far from being prone to excesses. He is well able to live within his means, doing without luxuries if necessary; even his encounters with women are subject to such economies.[37] As a gambler he is equally self-disciplined, and after he has won enough money to lend his friend 1,000 gulden he leaves the table. But a 'coincidence' drives him back, and the same thing happens on a second attempt; Kasda goes on winning, and by two in the morning has won 4,200 gulden. Then, in the next half hour, his luck changes. He loses steadily, but also loses control of the size of his wagers. By 2.30 a.m. he is 11,000 gulden in debt, the equivalent of three years' salary. His creditor, a shady consul, insists on being paid at noon on Tuesday, and this leaves Kasda with no option but to beg from his uncle, who is forced to explain that his circumstances have changed. He has married a prostitute a few years earlier, but is not living together with her. In their marriage, which is fundamentally a financial arrangement, he has transferred control of his fortune to her and is only entitled to a modest stipend for his day-to-day expenses. The infrequent meetings between the married couple are strictly defined by a marriage contract. Although the uncle assures his nephew he would like to help him, his financial dependency makes him incapable of doing so. The lieutenant, who realises from the uncle's narration that he has in fact slept with his new aunt in her previous life, decides to appeal to her directly for help. He discovers that the former prostitute, Leopoldine, is now a successful businesswoman and international financier. She promises to talk to her advisor, then she will inform Kasda what she can do for him. In the end she visits the lieutenant (her former client) in his flat and sleeps with him for a night, giving him 1,000 gulden on her departure – in payment for his love services, as she pointedly remarks. As she makes no reference to the

---

37 "[...] he had [...] determined that women, in the future, must not cost him anything." Arthur Schnitzler, *Daybreak*, trans. William A. Drake, in Schnitzler, *Viennese Novelettes*, p. 15. "[...] die Weiber durften einen überhaupt nichts mehr kosten." Arthur Schnitzler, *Spiel im Morgengrauen*, in Arthur Schnitzler, *Gesammelte Werke in Einzelausgaben. Das erzählerische Werk* (Frankfurt a.M.: Fischer Taschenbuch, 1978), vol. 6, p. 138.

11,000 gulden that Kasda had been hoping for, the novella ends with Kasda's suicide. The uncle, who arrives a few hours later with an envelope containing the required sum, finds his nephew already dead.

Here Schnitzler is clearly operating with two types of relationship involving a 'dominant' female partner, each of them conditional upon the man's economic dependency. At the start, the relationship between Leopoldine and the uncle is nothing more than a marriage of convenience, and Simmel's comment, that a prostitute who can sell herself dear enough can rid herself of social stigma, is most apt. Leopoldine has made the most of her husband's obvious enslavement to her ("I need her very badly, Willi; I can't exist without her!"[38]), and now she dictates the terms of their relationship. The marriage contract between the couple only concerns economic and sexual matters; it excludes romantic love completely. The uncle's acceptance of a comprehensive state of economic and sexual dependency appears as an emasculating transformation, a scandalous feminisation that violates the (apparently) sacrosanct norms of sex/gender roles in Viennese society. Since the uncle has entered into the contract as a free agent – "I did it really as much for my own sake as for hers"[39] – his story can be read as a case history; it is more an example of pathological dependency in the man than of tyrannical leanings in his wife.

If the uncle's story is an example of a free, if 'deviant' life choice, Kasda's experience of female dominance is an "unerhörte Begebenheit", an "unheard-of occurrence" of the kind that Goethe thought should form the centre-piece of the novella; the product of a combination of chance events, here within the context of gambling, which functions as a ritualistic tempting of fate. The reversal of sex roles that is forced upon Kasda results in the collapse of his system of values, causing a profound identity crisis. The idea that an Austrian royal and imperial officer *(k. und k. Offizier)* – by definition a man of honour – should receive financial remuneration for rendering love services goes beyond the limits of what was conceivable at the time. When Leopoldine lays the banker's note on the table in the morning, this is a humiliating act and an "unheard-of insult", an expression of "most insolent disdain"; Kasda reacts with "anger, aversion, and exasperation".[40] What makes the fact of payment seem particularly infamous is that it is an afterthought, and an economically unnecessary one at that:

---

38 Schnitzler, *Daybreak*, p. 81. "Ich brauch' sie nämlich, Willi, ich kann ohne sie nicht existieren." Schnitzler, *Spiel im Morgengrauen*, p. 180.

39 Schnitzler, *Daybreak*, p. 81. "Und ich habe es eigentlich mehr um meinetwillen getan als um ihretwillen." Schnitzler, *Spiel im Morgengrauen*, p. 180.

40 Schnitzler, *Daybreak*, p. 108. "unerhörten Schimpf", "frechsten Hohn"; "Abwehr, Zorn, Erbitterung", Schnitzler, *Spiel im Morgengrauen*, p. 89.

Leopoldine is not paying her former client an agreed fee that is now due; Kasda does not feel himself to be a seller of services or a commodity – on the contrary, during her nightly visit he tries again and again to adopt the masculine role of the seducer. Even though the matter of Kasda's gambling debts is present as an unspoken question, Kasda and Leopoldine are both at pains to give their encounter the appearance of an ordinary rendezvous, one in which both parties want pleasure, not money. When she pays him the following morning, Leopoldine provides the explanation for her behaviour. She reminds him of the night's love-making they had spent together years before. She had declared her love to him the next morning, but instead of answering, Kasda had paid ten gulden and left. Leopoldine's description demonstrates how violent and brutal the act of payment can be. Money used in this way is a rejection of the possibility of passion, a devaluation of it and of everything that bypasses the structured order of quantified values. The act of paying forces the female recipient to admit that as a prostitute she is a commodity; it is the sign that her presence is only required as merchandise that can be expressed in terms of its market value, not as a free agent in a relationship. Leopoldine pays Kasda back in the same currency for the hurt he had caused her long ago – though she uses a note of a considerably higher denomination. An interpretation of her behaviour as an act of revenge would, however, need to be revised in the light of the subsequent revelation that she does, after all, plan to save Kasda, and shortly after hands over the money he needs to his uncle. Either way, she teaches her former client a lesson, and the lieutenant grasps it in a moment of moral insight: he feels a "deep anguished shame, such as never in his life he had experienced".[41] This shame triggers a moral catharsis:

> But even as the foul word, which was due her, was finding its way to his lips; as he lifted his fist, […] the word failed him, his hand sank slowly to his side. For he suddenly became aware – perhaps he had suspected it all the while? – that he had been prepared to sell himself. And not only to her, to any other, to any one at all, who might have offered him the sum which could save him; and thus, in the cruel and treacherous wrong which had been added to his store of misery by an evil woman, he began to see,

---

41 Schnitzler, *Daybreak*, p. 106. "[...] überfiel ihn eine Scham, so tief, so peinigend, wie er sie niemals in seinem Leben verspürt hatte." Schnitzler, *Spiel im Morgengrauen*, p. 197. For a discussion of the significance of shame as the final resting point of male 'feminisation' in Schnitzler, see Elsbeth Dangel-Pelloquin, "Peinliche Gefühle: Figuren der Scham bei Arthur Schnitzler", in Konstanze Fliedl (ed.), *Arthur Schnitzler im 20. Jahrhundert* (Wien: Picus 2003), pp. 120-138. Dangel-Pelloquin also discusses the shame Casanova feels when his nude body is exposed to Marcolina's gaze on the morning after.

in the depth of his soul, despite himself, a hidden, inescapable justice, which had ensnarled him, not only in this sorry adventure, but in the very essence of his life.[42]

His insight into the injustice of traditional gender roles, which make it the exclusive right of the man to choose between romantic and bought love, culminates in an understanding of himself as a purchasable entity. Kasda's crisis reveals that it is not heroism and honour that form the core of his manly identity but a 'womanish' readiness to allow himself be transformed into merchandise. Schnitzler's text, however, leaves the exact reasons for Kasda's suicide open to interpretation: it might be that he simply despairs of ever repaying his debts and saving his honour, but it might also be that his suicide is an attempt to deny the truth of what he has learned about himself.

Conclusion

Arthur Schnitzler is the sceptic of romantic love. In many of his texts relations between men and women are determined essentially by money and sexuality, and often by a direct interplay between economic and erotic interests. Schnitzler is particularly interested in phenomena such as prostitution and marriages of (financial) convenience: paradigms for the triumph of purchasability over the ideal of selfless devotion. In the three texts examined here – two of which end in suicide – Schnitzler analyses different varieties of relationships involving the subjugation of characters, against their will, to commodification. In each case it is a coincidence that brings about the transformation of an individual into merchandise. What Schnitzler portrays are the resulting identity crises of individuals and their coping strategies; these fail in at least two cases, *Fräulein Else* and *Spiel im Morgengrauen*.

In *Fräulein Else* the protagonist tries in vain to avoid commodification by imagining herself as a 'wanton' who can preserve her independence by giving

42 Schnitzler, *Daybreak*, p. 108f.; "Doch während das Schmähwort, das ihr gebührte, den Weg auf seine Lippen suchte, während er die Faust erhob, [...] zerfloß das Wort ihm auf der Zunge, und seine Hand sank langsam wieder herab. Denn plötzlich wußte er – und hatte er es nicht früher schon geahnt? –, daß er auch bereit gewesen war, sich zu verkaufen. Und nicht ihr allein, auch irgendeiner andern, jeder, die ihm die Summe geboten, die ihn retten konnte; – und so – in all dem grausamen und tückischen Unrecht, das ein böses Weib ihm zugefügt –, auf dem Grunde seiner Seele, so sehr er sich dagegen wehrte, begann er eine verborgene und doch unentrinnbare Gerechtigkeit zu verspüren, die sich über das trübselige Abenteuer hinaus, in das er verstrickt war, an sein tiefstes Wesen wandte." Schnitzler, *Spiel im Morgengrauen*, p. 199f.

herself to men of her choice. In contrast, *Casanovas Heimfahrt* analyses what happens when a legendary seducer is forced to enter the market of love as a buyer, once his name and his ageing body have lost their erotic exchange value. Anyone who is forced, as he is, to buy his beloved with money – even if he manages to secure an arrangement that seems at first sight to conceal this fact from her – has lost his identity to money. Casanova's realisation that he cannot be Marcolina's lover as himself results unavoidably in the loss of his self-respect. Finally, *Spiel im Morgengrauen* highlights the extreme shock experienced by a man who is subjected to a reversal of the relations between buyer and vendor, and forced to understand his own status as commodity in matters of honour and love.

Brian Moloney

Exchange Rates in Italo Svevo's Later Narrative Fiction

In 1919, John Maynard Keynes, then head of the External Finance Department of the British Treasury, was sent to Paris as the Treasury's principal representative at the Peace Conference. An intelligent and far-sighted man, he soon found himself in fundamental disagreement with the terms in the peace treaty dealing with war reparations, which he saw as nothing less than a plot to destroy Germany as an economic power. He resigned and returned to England to write a book that soon became famous, *The Economic Consequences of the Peace*. He made it clear in his preface that the results of the policies pursued by the victors at Paris could have only disastrous consequences, describing what he had seen and heard in terms of tragedy:

> Paris was a nightmare, and everyone there was morbid. A sense of impending catastrophe overhung the frivolous scene; the futility and smallness of man before the great events confronting him; the mingled significance and unreality of the decisions; levity, blindness, insolence, confused cries from without, – all the elements of ancient tragedy were there.[1]

In the longer term, of course, Keynes was right: the harsh terms imposed on the vanquished helped to sow the seeds of World War Two. In the short term, however, Italo Svevo saw the possibilities of both tragedy and comedy. After all, Schopenhauer, his favourite philosopher, wrote that "Money is human happiness in *abstracto*; and so the man who is no longer capable of enjoying such happiness *in concreto*, sets his whole heart on money".[2]

Italo Svevo is the Italo-German pseudonym of the Italian novelist probably better known to his fellow-citizens at the time as the paint manufacturer Ettore Schmitz. Born in Trieste in 1861, Svevo was for most of his life an Austrian subject, becoming Italian only after the 1914-18 war. The shifting of the frontier, the change of nationality, fierce competition in industry and commerce and the

---

1 J.M. Keynes, *The Economic Consequences of the Peace* (Macmillan, London, 1920), p. 3-4. Subsequent references to this work will be given in brackets in the text.

2 Arthur Schopenhauer, *Parerga et Parolipomena. Short Philosophical essays*. 2 vol., trans. by E.F.J. Payne (Oxford: Clarendon Press, 1974), vol. 2, p. 590. See also vol. 1, p. 347.

wildly fluctuating currency market in the post-war period created problems for businessmen and industrialists, of whom Svevo was one.

Svevo began his working life as a modestly paid bank clerk, but in 1896 he married his second cousin Livia Veneziani. Her parents, Gioachino and Olga Veneziani, owned a company that manufactured a unique marine anti-fouling compound. Their customers included yacht-owners, shipping lines and the navies of the belligerents in the First – and later the Second – World Wars. They eventually became seriously rich, but in the 1890s the company was still in the early stages of its development.[3] In 1891, Trieste lost its privileged status as a free port, which had made it a great emporium for the whole of the Mediterranean and the Orient. To replace these sources of wealth, Triestines turned to new ventures, including financial services and insurance, as well as industry. The Veneziani company can be seen as part of this new expansion, which brought great wealth to the city but bound it even more closely to the Habsburg Empire just as it was about to disintegrate.[4]

In 1899, Svevo's parents-in-law took him into the family firm. In fact they recruited all their sons-in-law. The anti-fouling compound – the famous 'Moravia compound' – was manufactured according to a carefully guarded secret formula, entrusted only to senior members of the firm, which the Veneziani children, four daughters and one son, would inherit. Their sons-in-law thus had a double vested interest in ensuring that the secret and the attendant prosperity of the family were maintained. Svevo's financial, and perhaps also his linguistic skills may have been factors that made him particularly useful. Certainly he was very much involved in the financial side of planning the factory that opened in Charlton in 1903, and he travelled widely on behalf of the company, even as far as what was then Queenstown and is now Cobh, just down the road from Cork, where he supervised the painting of Lord Muskerry's yacht "Rita".[5]

---

3 On the Veneziani family and firm, see Fulvio Anzellotti, *Il segreto di Svevo* (Pordenone: Edizioni Studio Tesi, 1986).

4 The standard work on the history of Trieste is Elio Apih, *Trieste* (Rome: Laterza, 1988), but see also Anna Millo, *L'élite del potere a Trieste* (Milan: Franco Angeli, 1989).

5 Before going to Cobh, Svevo referred to it disparagingly as "that [...] hole in Ireland" (*'This England is so Different...' Italo Svevo's London Writings* edited, translated and introduced by John Gatt-Rutter and Brian Moloney [Market Harborough: Troubador, 2003], p. 23), but his wife, who joined him there, says that in the event the "wild beauty" of the Irish landscape "enchanted" him and that he was "delighted with all that beauty and peace" (Livia Veneziani Svevo, *Memoir of Italo Svevo* [London: Libris, 1989], p. 52).

For at least a decade after he joined the Veneziani firm, his mother-in-law, who was the effective driving force behind the firm, kept him on a very tight financial rein. Perhaps because he came from the less prosperous branch of the family anyway, and had earned only a modest salary at the bank, supplemented by teaching commercial correspondence at the Revoltella College of Commerce, Svevo was always acutely aware of the cost of everything. When his employer/mother-in-law gave permission for his wife – her favourite daughter – to join him in London in 1901, for example, his immediate reaction was not one of unmitigated joy: instead, he urged his wife to ensure, before she agreed to travel, that the expense allowances they would receive while in England together would be adequate before she agreed to travel.

As in life, so in literature: in all Svevo's works there are discreet but clear and important indications of his characters' social and financial status and of the part money plays in personal relationships. It is my contention that the theme of money and the use of money-related imagery occur more frequently in Svevo's post-war works and that this development is directly related to Svevo's perceptions of what Maynard Keynes called: "the economic consequences of the peace".

Since Svevo tended to cover his tracks, as it were, as far as his reading is concerned, I cannot demonstrate that he read Keynes: what I can say is that between 1920 and 1927 he spent a good deal of time each year in London, supervising the Charlton factory, as he had done between 1901 and 1914, when he became an 'enemy alien', and therefore unable to visit England. The crucial difference between his pre- and post-war visits was that after the war, the factory was much less busy than it had been before the war.[6] Before 1914, Svevo's working day had often stretched from 7 am to 7 pm, leaving him too exhausted to do anything more than have dinner and then collapse into bed to read a newspaper and smoke endless cigarettes until he went to sleep. After the war, he had a good deal of free time. He went sightseeing in the capital, he frequented the theatre and the new-fangled cinema, and he read a remarkable range of newspapers and books. Above all, he wrote. It is more than likely that a good deal of Svevo's later fiction was in fact written in Charlton, where he spent several months each year from 1920 to 1927.

It has now become almost conventional to distinguish between Italo Svevo the writer and Ettore Schmitz the industrialist. Svevo himself told the story of how, in

---

6 In a letter from London to his friend Giulio Cèsari, dated 28 January 1924, Svevo wrote: "I will be tied up here until mid-March if not beyond. Times aren't especially bad even if they aren't good." *'This England is so Different...'*, op. cit., p. 173, and I. Svevo, *Epistolario* (Milan: Dall'Oglio, 1966), p. 749.

the course of business negotiations, he was asked whether he was the author of a couple of novels. He claims to have denied it, saying that his brother was the author.[7] An almost identical story is told of Søren Kierkegaard, who also published his works under a pseudonym and denied having written anything himself. Following, for the moment at least, Svevo's distinction between his two identities, we can say that in the years following the First World War, Italo Svevo wrote *La coscienza di Zeno* and its unfinished continuations, as well as a number of short stories, some finished, some unfinished. Ettore Schmitz, on the other hand, wrote essays, reports and short items for the new Triestine newspaper *La Nazione*, which he had helped to found. The combined output of Svevo/Schmitz in the last years of their joint life is impressive in terms of both quantity and quality, especially if one bears in mind that Schmitz was by now a senior director of the Veneziani company, travelling to Austria, Italy, England, France and Germany, and had health problems. He signed his fictional works 'Italo Svevo', while items published in *La Nazione* were signed either with his initials, 'E. S.', or 'E. Sch'.

Schmitz wrote on a wide range of subjects, from Lloyd George's influenza attack to the Jack Dempsey-Georges Carpentier heavyweight boxing championship; from the surplus of shipping to falling wages; from British coal miners' strikes to Anglo-German trade competition; from trials of early forms of the helicopter to the world's first aircraft carrier; from war crimes trials in Leipzig to the effects of Bolshevik rule in Russia. His short reports have not yet been republished, but they will appear shortly.[8] The central economic themes running through his writings, however, mirror or parallel what Keynes saw as the economic consequences of the peace: the disastrous effects of the punitive reparations policy and the way in which that policy was distorting financial and commercial markets. Keynes focussed mainly on Germany: Schmitz was particularly but not exclusively concerned with Triestine-Austrian commercial relations in the post-war period.

In the introduction to his work, Keynes wrote: "Lenin is said to have declared that the best way to destroy the Capitalist System was to debauch the currency". Inflation was the way to achieve this aim. Keynes went on:

---

7 Svevo tells the story in the unfinished essay *Soggiorno londinese* ('My life in London') in '*This England is so Different*..., op. cit., p. 257, *Teatro e saggi*, edizione critica con apparato genetico e commento di Federico Bertoni (Milan: Mondadori, 2004), p. 904.

8 Brian Moloney and Fraser Hope, 'Italo Svevo giornalista triestino, con scritti sconosciuti', Quaderni Giuliani di Storia XXVII (2006), 2, pp. 7-62.

> By a continued process of inflation, governments can confiscate, secretly and unobserved, an important part of the wealth of their citizens. [...] and, while the process impoverishes many it actually enriches some. [...] Those to whom the system brings windfalls, beyond their deserts and even beyond their expectations or desires become "profiteers", who are the object of the hatred of the bourgeoisie, whom the inflationism has impoverished, not less of the proletariat. As the inflation proceeds and the real value of the currency fluctuates wildly from month to month, all permanent relations between debtors and creditors, which form the ultimate foundation of capitalism, become so utterly disordered as to be almost meaningless; and the process of wealth-making degenerates into a gamble and a lottery. (p. 220)

Later, describing the functions of the Reparations Commission set up by the Allies to administer their policy, he wrote:

> The Commission will liquidate the Austro-Hungarian Bank, and will supervise the withdrawal and replacement of the currency system of the Austro-Hungarian Empire. (p. 199)

Governments proved unable or unwilling to raise money through taxation and resorted instead to printing money. Keynes comments:

> In Russia and Austria-Hungary this process has reached a point, where for the purpose of foreign exchange the currency is practically valueless. The Polish mark can be bought for about 1½d. and the Austrian crown for less than 1d., but they cannot be sold at all. (p. 223)

This situation naturally attracted comment in Trieste, formerly Austrian and still with many commercial links with Vienna. From the Italian nationalists' point of view, indeed, it was cause for gloating. An (anonymous) article in *La Nazione* on 11 February 1920 crowed: "Finally, however much European currencies have been depressed in gold standard countries, the fact remains that with one of our modest little *lire* we can buy today 25 crowns!"[9]

The first two short pieces Schmitz contributed to *La Nazione* date from the beginning of the crown's free fall. On 6 October 1919, he sent two despatches from Vienna. In the first, he wrote that the Austrian government's likely solution to the excessive amounts of paper money circulating would be to withdraw existing notes from circulation, replacing them with notes reduced in value by 75%.[10] In his second despatch, he reported that British, American and French –

---

9 "E infine, per quanto sieno state deprezzate nei paesi dell'oro tutte le valute europee, resta pure il fatto che con una nostra modesta liretta si comprano oggi 25 corone!" 'Lira e corona', *La Nazione*, Trieste, 11 February 1920, p. 2, col. 2.

10 E.S., 'Per l'assestamento delle finanze austriache', *La Nazione*, Trieste, 8 October 1919, p. 1, col. 4.

even Italian – companies were able to buy up Austrian companies and properties very cheaply because of the exchange rates.[11] Later he wrote on the fall in the value of the *lira* as a result of strikes in Italy[12] and on attempts to set up a conference to stabilise exchange rates.[13]

Ettore Schmitz's perceptions of this topsy-turvy world provided grist to Italo Svevo's creative mill. What the journalist described in general terms, the novelist could relate to the individual lives and fortunes of his characters. This process began in *La coscienza di Zeno*, which was published in 1923. This novel takes the form of memoirs written for his psychoanalyst by a middle-aged neurotic who hopes to find in Freudianism a cure for his various ailments and problems. War interrupts his course of treatment. While his analyst takes refuge in neutral Switzerland, Zeno goes into business and proclaims that he has been 'cured' by commerce. The rest of the world is ill, not him. The credibility of Zeno's claim is undermined, however, by the fact that what he blandly describes as 'commerce' is in fact war profiteering.[14] His simple system is to buy almost anything, confident that in war-torn Trieste his unfortunate fellow-citizens will be forced to buy it in order to use it as a substitute for something that has become unattainable. There the novel ends, with the war still raging. But Zeno gets his come-uppance in the unfinished and perhaps unfinishable continuations written in the last couple of years of Svevo's life.

Immediately after the end of the war, Zeno continues to trade as before. He buys a trainload of cheap soap in Italy. The sheer stench of unwashed humanity on a crowded Triestine tram convinces him that he will find a ready market for it. But by the time the train reaches Trieste, peace has broken out and his market has disappeared. In any case, the soap does not satisfy Austrian regulations, still in force, governing its content. In the end, he sells it to an Austrian at a reduced price, with payment deferred, in Austrian crowns. By the time he receives the crowns, their value has fallen catastrophically and he makes a loss that wipes out his ill-gained wartime profits. He has been neatly hoisted with his own petard.

---

11 E.S., 'L'Austria tedesca e il capitale internazionale', *La Nazione*, Trieste, 8 October 1919, p. 1, col, 5.

12 'Le conseguenze degli scioperi in Italia'. *La Nazione*, Trieste, 9 June 1921, p. 1, col. 3.

13 'Per i cambi'. *La Nazione*, Trieste, 12 October 1921, p. 1, col. 4.

14 On the theme of war in *La coscienza di Zeno*, see B. Moloney, 'La coscienza di Zeno come romanzo di guerra', in *Italo Svevo narratore: lezioni triestine* (Libreria editrice goriziana,: Gorizia, 1998), pp. 95-113.

There are two versions of this episode, one in the chapter known as "Un contratto", the other in "Le confessioni del vegliardo". Details of the episode differ in the two versions, but exchange rates are used in the same way in both.[15]

The dramatic way in which exchange rates collapsed in the post-war period is exploited more fully in a delightful story entitled *Una burla riuscita*, recently translated by J.G. Nicols as *A Perfect Hoax*.[16] Svevo published it in the Florentine review *Solaria* in early 1928, when he was finally enjoying international fame. No doubt it is this circumstance that enables the story's narrator to accompany his account of events with a sustained series of wry reflections on the unpredictable quality of celebrity.

The story's central character is Mario Samigli, a bachelor who lives in genteel poverty with his invalid brother Giulio. Mario, who is now almost sixty, had in his youth published a novel entitled *Una giovinezza*, which was a complete flop. Since Svevo had at one stage used the pseudonym E. Samigli and had published a novel entitled *Una vita*, the self-irony is obvious. Mario, like his creator, writes fables – in his case about the sparrows he feeds in the courtyard overlooked by his apartment. But unlike his creator, Mario has a very modest job as a clerk and is resigned to his failure, although still proud to be an author. His apparent self-satisfaction provokes Enrico Gaia, a commercial traveller addicted to practical jokes, to decide to hoax Mario. Almost at the end of the war, on 3 November 1918, the very day when the first Italian troops land in Trieste and when there is naturally considerable confusion and turmoil in the city, Gaia tells Mario that he has by coincidence met the local representative of the Viennese publisher Westermann, who wants to buy the translation rights to his novel. He even persuades a colleague to pose as Westermann's agent and give Mario a false contract and cheque for his fee. Gaia's idea is that Mario will boast of his unexpected success, only for Gaia to reveal the hoax and humiliate him. But Mario is both more naïve and more ambitious than Gaia realises: he decides to keep quiet about his impending fame until the translation appears, because that will create more of a stir in local literary circles. Meanwhile, he gives the cheque for safe keeping to his office supervisor, Brauer, who is also a good friend.

News of the hoax reaches Mario before Gaia had intended. The angry Mario confronts him on what was then the footbridge over the Canal Grande and engages in an unseemly bout of fisticuffs in which Gaia is humiliated. There is a delightful account of Gaia's hat blowing off his head into the water and later

---

15 For the two episodes, see Italo Svevo, *Romanzi e Continuazioni* edizione critica con apparato genetico e commento di Nunzia Palmieri e Fabio Vittorini (Milan: Mondadori, 2004), pp. 1090-91 and pp. 1118-20.

16 London: Hesperus, 2003.

being seen by Mario propelled out towards the sea by Trieste's notorious *bora,* a fierce wind that blows through the mountains from north-north-east. As Clotilde Bertoni points out, this is a marvellous Triestine variation on an episode from *The Pickwick Papers,* one of Svevo's favourite comic masterpieces.[17]

Mario's humiliation, of course, should be greater than Gaia's, since he is the victim of the hoax. But Brauer had taken the fake Westermann cheque for 200,000 crowns to the bank, where he had received an advance of 75 *centesimi* per crown, that is, 150,000 *lire,* subject to the cheque being honoured. In the end, the cheque is not honoured, of course, and Mario has to repurchase his 200,000 crowns, but at the new, lower exchange rate, with the result that he is left with a net profit on the transaction of 70,000 *lire.* The crown has lost just over half its value in a few days and Mario is left with just under half of what he would have received had the fake cheque been honoured by the real Westermann. News of the hoax has not leaked out more widely and Mario is not only spared public embarrassment but is able to convince himself that literature is profitable. First Mario and then the narrator wryly reflect:

> When he collected that large sum, Mario was full of wonder. How strange and mysterious man's life was: the bargain Mario had almost unconsciously made was the beginning of the post-war surprises. Prices shifted unpredictably, and many other innocents, like Mario, received the reward of the their innocence or, on account of their very innocence were destroyed. Things like that had always happened, but they seemed strange because they were happening so frequently as to appear life's norm.[18]

In the third example I wish to look at, exchange rates are not in fact mentioned. *La novella del buon vecchio* is the story of a wealthy elderly widower's affair, in wartime Trieste, with a young working class girl. It is not simply the story of wealth corrupting poverty, however: all the indications in the text suggest that the girl enters very willingly into the affair, that the old man is not her only client, and that her mother initially promotes her 'career'. The old man dies, the victim of a heart attack, leaving his whole estate to the girl. Some time later the old man's doctor sends her a bill for services to his late patient. She

---

17 I. Svevo, *Racconti e scritti autobiografici*, edizione critica con apparato genetico e commento di Clotilde Bertoni (Milan: Mondadori, 2004), pp. 259-60, 993.

18 "Incassato il grosso importo, anche Mario fu pieno d'ammirazione. Strana vita quella dell'uomo, e misteriosa: con l'affare fatto da Mario quasi inconsapevolmente, s'iniziavano le sorprese del periodo postbellico. Il valori si spostavano senza norma, e tanti altri innocenti come Mario ebbero il premio della loro innocenza, o, per tanta innocenza, furono distrutti; cose che s'erano viste sempre, ma parevano nuove perché si avveravano in tali proporzioni da apparire quasi la regola della vita." I. Svevo, *Racconti e scritti autobiografici*, op. cit., p. 263.

asks him to visit her and tearfully asks his advice. On her mother's advice, she has kept all her money in cash and has a chest full of Austrian crown notes. She also explains that her fiancé has borrowed money from her, but now will neither repay it nor marry her. It is too late to take the money to the bank that day, and the doctor consoles the girl in the only way he can think of, by putting an arm round her and caressing her.[19] At that point the story breaks off. What continuation and conclusion could Svevo have had in mind?

One has the impression that another cycle in a Triestine Schnitzler-like *ronde* is about to begin, with the doctor taking the place of his patient, while the narrator's insistence that the girl's money was in Austrian crowns and that it was too difficult to take all that paper money to the bank that day certainly leaves open the possibility that the crown is about to fall in value, significantly reducing the girl's wartime profits, although perhaps not reducing her to her previous poverty. But that is pure hypothesis.

In the three cases I have discussed, the vagaries of the exchange rate are not, as it were, tacked on to the story: on the contrary, they represent a twist whose introduction has been carefully prepared by the consistent use throughout the tales of the language and imagery of money and financial relations. The most frequently recurring images in Svevo's narrative works are those of struggle and conflict, of victory and defeat, since his art has its intellectual roots in philosophies of conflict: Schopenhauer and Nietzsche, Darwin and Spencer, Marx and Freud. But his working life was spent in the world of finance, industry and commerce, and he would have noticed with wry amusement that Schopenhauer turns to commercial imagery on occasion. Making the point that the Will-to-life's constant blind struggle merely produces humans destined to die after a brief existence, Schopenhauer comments: "[...] a seeing will would have made the calculation that the business does not cover the costs."[20] Svevo, too, turns to the imagery of finance and commerce – even to express tender gratitude to his wife, as when he expresses gratitude that his old affection for her has yielded interest year after year, or that he returns her kisses at a usurious rate of interest.[21]

In *La coscienza di Zeno,* Zeno Cosini is frustrated by his father's decision not to allow him to manage the family firm. He enters into partnership with his rival in love, Guido Speier, in whose business he is supposed to act as accountant, and then becomes a successful war profiteer. In the unfinished fourth novel, he not only looses his wartime profits, he is forced to negotiate a new contract with his

---

19 I. Svevo, *Racconti e scritti autobiografici*, op. cit., pp. 497-98.

20 A. Schopenhauer, *The World as Will and Representation.* Trans. by E.F.J. Payne (New York, Dover, 1966), vol. 2, p. 579.

21 *'This England is so Different...'*, op. cit., p. 49, *Epistolario,* pp. 300, 192.

manager, young Olivi, who receives a basic salary and a substantial share of the company's profits. In *Una burla riuscita*, the narrator not only illustrates the straitened circumstances in which the two brothers live, he also reflects continuously on literature as a commodity in a market whose mechanisms are unpredictable.[22] *La novella del buon vecchio e della bella fanciulla* is one of Svevo's bleakest tales, a quality it achieves by the constant use of financial imagery to describe the relationship between the lovers. The girl complains that her wages as a tram-driver are inadequate and asks the old man to help her find a better paid job: he in turn reflects that he will have her, if she is for sale. Money and luxury food are the basis of their relationship. When he has his first angina attack, he sends her every week 'a certain sum', which she finds inadequate, so that she asks for an increase in her wage. She clearly regards herself as being contractually bound to supply certain services, in return for which he is bound to pay her adequately. The introduction of the exchange rate mechanism – or in the case of *La novella*, its hypothetical introduction – serves to give the plot an unexpected but perfectly convincing twist while maintaining the language and imagery of the story. Italo Svevo's later narrative works are the ironic expression of one aspect of the chaotic economic consequences of the peace, which Ettore Schmitz faithfully reported to the Triestine public in the pages of *La Nazione*.

In Svevo's narrative fiction, exchange rates become a striking metaphor for the unpredictable and the surprising. Guido Speier, in philosophising and self-pitying vein, tells Zeno that life is "unjust and hard", to which Zeno replies that it is neither beautiful nor ugly, but "original", by which he seems to mean that it is full of surprises. He is so impressed by the originality of this rather banal thought that he adds: "Very original!" Guido merely laughs and asks him: "Life is original! […] Where did you read that?"[23] Zeno, in his memoirs, denies having read it anywhere, obviously thinking it a profound conclusion that he had reached without assistance: Svevo would, of course, have read it in one of his favourite philosophical texts, namely Schopenhauer's *The World as Will and Representation*. There he would have read that surprise is indeed a very philosophical emotion, but that it is merely the beginning and never the conclusion of philosophical enquiry.[24] Precisely because they are philosophically naïve, unlike their creator, Svevo's characters are constantly surprised by the unpredictable turn events take. Post-war exchange rates are a perfect metaphor for life's unpredictability.

---

22 E.g., I. Svevo, *Racconti e scritti autobiografici*, op. cit., pp. 225-26, 228.

23 I. Svevo, *Romanzi e Continuazioni*, op. cit., pp. 972-73.

24 A. Schopenhauer, *The World as Will and Representation*, op. cit., vol. 2, pp. 70-71 and 160-61.

Guy Snaith

All Because of Money: Money and Culture in Gabrielle Roy's *Bonheur d'occasion*

Gabrielle Roy's first novel, *Bonheur d'occasion*, was published in Montreal in 1945, and was immediately hailed as a major literary event not just in Quebec but in Canada as a whole. It was published in Paris in 1947, when it was also translated into English under the title *The Tin Flute* and published simultaneously in Toronto and New York. By then it was being hailed as 'the great Canadian novel' and Roy was thanked for showing the world that Canadian literature could have universal resonances.[1] Honours and awards rained down upon her to the point that she remained haunted by the success of this first novel for the rest of her life,[2] at one point even wishing that it would be forgotten.[3]

And yet from our standpoint, when bestsellers tend to be of the sex-and-shopping or international conspiracy variety, it is a curious novel to have reached international bestseller status, dealing as it does with problems of unemployment and poverty amongst the urban proletariat of Montreal during the early days of the Second World War. *Bonheur d'occasion* depicts a Canadian francophone family which has fallen on hard times because of the Great Depression. The consequences of the Wall Street Crash of 1929 were, of course, felt as keenly in Canada as everywhere else. The father, Azarius, loses job after job. The family moves from poor to poorer accommodation, and, like good francophone families, continues to produce children. By 1940, when the novel begins, Rose-Anna has had 11 children, three of whom have died (another dies and another is born during the course of the novel). At 19, the eldest daughter, Florentine, who works in the diner of a 5 and 10 cent store, is, for the most part, the only breadwinner. In the course of the novel she becomes pregnant and marries someone she does not love for the sake of respectability. In the background men are enlisting to serve in the Canadian forces fighting in World War II.

From 1939 Roy had been working in Montreal as a jobbing journalist. In her spare time, she would take long solitary walks, during one of which she found herself in the down-at-heels neighbourhood of Saint-Henri. She has since said

---

1 François Ricard, *Gabrielle Roy: une vie* (Montreal: Boréal, 1996), p. 285.

2 ibid., p. 268.

3 David Cobb, "'I have, I think, a grateful heart'", *The Gazette*, sec. The Canadian, May 1, 1976, p. 12.

that indignation was what pushed her to write her novel: indignation at the poverty she saw in Saint-Henri, indignation at the human cost of unemployment, and indignation that war should be welcomed with open arms as the only solution to the crises of the 1930s.[4] Indignation, too, at the effects of urbanisation and industrialisation; indignation that the booms and busts of the capitalist system mean that recessions and depressions do occur, bringing with them redundancies and layoffs, so that in urban industrial societies social, political, and economic forces all contrive to deprive human beings of their dignity. And ultimately, indignation that the only thing capable of restoring dignity to Azarius and the other unemployed men is war.

Bonheur d'occasion was seen as "the expression of the tragic, almost revolutionary, realisation of the misery and the social conflicts gnawing away at a French-Canadian community lost in a city that was too big and with which it was not in tune".[5] Looking at Roy's journalism from 1939, one can see the novel as the culmination of the social preoccupations she had as a journalist. There, in piece after piece, she passionately denounced an industrial system that exploited its workforce, that created social inequalities, and that perpetuated injustice. In contrast to the individualism of the capitalist system, she came to admire "the dignity of collective man"[6] which she saw through the work of unions and co-operatives across Canada. As Novella Novelli writes:

> By following the march of industrial progress through the different provinces of Canada, the reporter came to realise that modernity, instead of having created a society founded on participation and equality, had produced inequality and division. Henceforth, this assessment was joined by Gabrielle Roy challenging the system and calling society to account, as she would do in *Bonheur d'occasion* where she exposed a similar situation.[7]

---

4 Réjean Robidoux and André Renaud, *Le Roman canadien-français du vingtième siècle* (Ottawa: Editions de l'université d'Ottawa, 1966), pp. 76-77.

5 André Brochu, "Thèmes et structures de *Bonheur d'occasion*", *Ecrits du Canada français* 22 (1966), p. 165. "L'expression d'une prise de conscience tragique, presque révolutionnaire, de la misère et des conflits sociaux qui rongeaient un quartier canadien-français perdu dans une ville trop grande, à laquelle il n'était pas accordé."

6 Novella Novelli, *Gabrielle Roy: De l'engagement au désengagement* (Rome: Bulzoni, 1989), p. 56: "cette dignité de l'homme collectif".

7 Novelli, ibid., pp. 60-61: "En suivant la marche du progrès industriel dans les différentes provinces, le reporter se rend compte que le modernisme, au lieu de créer une société fondée sur la participation et l'égalité, produit l'inégalité et la division. Dès lors, ce constat s'accompagne chez Gabrielle Roy de la remise en question du système. Elle met en cause la société, ainsi qu'elle le fera dans *Bonheur d'occasion* où elle expose une situation similaire."

Gabrielle Roy is a realist, and, as she takes her society to task, *Bonheur d'occasion* would seem to have all the credentials that a good card-carrying social realist novel should have. One might even ask whether it had a Marxist agenda. Certainly Ben-Zion Shek has shown that Roy was sensitive to socialist thought and moved in circles and wrote for publications which were left-leaning, calling the novel "a skillfully aestheticised charge against the capitalist system",[8] and Gilles Marcotte has discussed it in the light of Lukács's theories of realism, exploring Jean and Florentine as Lukácsian types.[9] It could even be said to fit that prescription of Russian "revolutionary democratic" critics that "art reflects social reality, and must portray its typical features".[10] *Bonheur d'occasion* is certainly socially reflective. In Lukácsian terms, Roy takes "burning problems of the community" as her starting point, her pathos as a writer "stimulated by those sufferings of the people which are the most acute at the time".[11] In chronicling how it feels to find oneself in certain situations at a specific time, she "penetrates through the accidental phenomena of social life to disclose the essences or essentials of a condition"[12]: the struggle of men and women to survive in a twentieth-century urban environment. In doing so, she offers insights into the realities of human experience at one point in the twentieth century. Writing in the early 1940s, at a time when history is manifestly being made, Roy engages with the significant forces, movements and dynamics of Canadian society at that time. By so doing, she allows us to see the nature of the ideology at work in that society. Roy does not need to betray any overt political commitment; it is sufficient that her representative characters act out the conflicts and struggles of the time. She imposes no solution. Indeed, for solutions one has to look to her journalism rather than to the novel where any partisanship is inherent in the realities depicted. As Novelli writes: "the description itself amounts to a denunciation".[13]

---

8 Ben-Zion Shek, "De quelques influences possibles sur la vision du monde de Gabrielle Roy: George Wilkinson et Henri Girard", *Voix et images* 42 (1989), p. 437: "une charge habilement esthétisée contre le système capitaliste".

9 Gilles Marcotte, "*Bonheur d'occasion* et le 'grand réalisme'", *Voix et images* 42 (1989), pp. 408-13.

10 Terry Eagleton, *Marxism and Literary Criticism* (London and New York, Routledge, 2002), p. 41.

11 Georg Lukács, *Studies in European Realism*, trans. Edith Bone (London: Hillway Publishing Company, 1950), p. 12.

12 Eagleton, *Marxism and Literary Criticism*, p. 27.

13 Novelli, *Gabrielle Roy*, p. 70: "sa description équivaut à une dénonciation".

As capitalism is the ideology of the society depicted, Roy takes it to task and, as monetary profit is the aim of capitalism, so much of what happens in *Bonheur d'occasion* is all because of money. There has not been any money for ten years. Of the Lacasse family, the father Azarius has been out of work for that length of time, the brother Eugène is also out of work, and the only member earning a regular pay packet is the eldest child, Florentine. In the cramped quarters of the dingy flats of the Lacasse family, the children sleep on couches, campbeds or makeshift beds of two chairs put together. They have no change of clothes, so that they cannot go to school if their clothes are not dry after washing. Florentine is thin, drawn, carrying about with her an air of poverty. Her mother Rose-Anna scrimps and saves, constantly calculating the household money, knowing that she cannot count on her husband. The realisation that the family's welfare is up to her has taken its toll. Rose-Anna is weary, careworn, without hope, "suffering and courage inscribed on her features" (p. 115).[14]

Roy's sympathies are with the downtrodden. Just behind the drama being played out by the central characters is a whole backdrop of secondary characters through whom Roy gives a voice to the marginalized and disenfranchised, to a whole generation of young men who had every right to expect a bright future for themselves but who have been doomed to vegetate because, during the Thirties, the capitalist system seemed unable to right itself. The novel's periphery thus underscores the themes of the main narrative. Roy presents us with a representative sample of such a lost generation in Alphonse, Pitou and Boisvert, who haunt a bar in Saint-Henri, each with a similar past but with different futures. Having left school at 13 or 14, they have been looking unsuccessfully for jobs for the last five years. For Emmanuel, "they had seemed to him to be the true expression of his generation – confused, wise-cracking, indolent" (p. 51),[15] "their faces marked by disappointment and hardship" (p. 302).[16]

For over ten years there has been no work, fifty men have battled to get one job. Never having worked, Pitou would sit in the bar asking: "Is there one job in this town? One lousy job?" (p. 318)[17] When Azarius puts his head in his hands

---

14 The English translation used is *The Tin Flute*, translated by Alan Brown (Toronto: McClelland & Stewart, 1989); the French edition is *Bonheur d'occasion* (Montreal: Boréal, 1993); "la souffrance, le courage écrits sur ce visage" (p. 121). All references will be to these editions.

15 "Chez eux, il avait trouvé la véritable expression, tourmentée, blagueuse, indolente, de sa génération" (p. 53).

16 "Toute une série de visages marqués par la déception, marqués par la rudesse de la vie" (p. 317).

17 "Y en a-t-y une job dans la ville, une seule job dans la ville? Y en reste-t-y une job dans la ville?" (p. 335)

and asks: "What on earth had happened to him?" (p. 156),[18] one hears the voice of the damaged and the disempowered, of the ordinary working man not understanding the great socioeconomic forces which have brought him to this and which he is uncomprehendingly unable to harness. Rose-Anna knows the difference that having a job makes to a man and, at one point when Azarius briefly has a job, she imagines him after a day's work: "he's coming home, he's done his day's work, he's got his self-respect back and a line of sweat on his face..." (p. 164).[19] But this job is soon lost. The eldest son of the family, Eugène, explains his reasons for joining the army to his mother:

> Listen, Ma, a guy gets fed up, you know, bumming ten cents here and a quarter there. You get fed up always hanging around looking for work. The army's the right place for a guy like me. No trade, not much school, it's the best place. (p. 71)[20]

When he reassures her that she will receive $20 a month, Rose-Anna bursts into tears:

> She was holding back a sob, tugging at her apron. Suddenly all her resentment about money, her misery for lack of it, her fright, and her great need for money poured out in a pitiful protest.
> "Twenty beautiful dollars a month!" she was murmuring through her sobs. (p. 72)[21]

Later that night as she attempts to pray, uncontrollable visions of dollar bills crowd out the image of the statuette of a *mater dolorosa*: "she saw paper money, rolls of bills peeling off one after the other, flying, twisting, disappearing in the night, carried away by the wind" (p. 73).[22] This is Rose-Anna at her lowest ebb, and Roy's indignation over what poverty has reduced a well-meaning, caring person to is obvious.

---

18 "Que lui était-il donc arrivé? [...] Oui, que lui était-il arrivé?" (p. 164)

19 "Il va rentrer, son labeur de la journée accompli, avec sa dignité retrouvée, la trace de la sueur sur son visage..." (p. 173).

20 "Mais écoute, donc, sa mère. Un gars vient qu'il en a assez, tu sais, de quêter un dix cennes pis un vingt-cinq cennes. Écoute, sa mère: un gars se tanne de rôder d'un côté pis de l'autre pour se trouver de l'ouvrage. Écoute, sa mère: l'armée c'est la vraie place pour un gars comme moi. Pas de métier, pas gros d'instruction; c'est encore là que je suis le mieux" (p. 74).

21 "Un sanglot lui vint aux lèvres. Elle tira sur son tablier. Et, soudain, toute sa rancune de l'argent, sa misère à cause de l'argent, son effroi et sa grande nécessité de l'argent tout à la fois s'exprimèrent dans une protestation pitoyable. --- Vingt belles piasses par mois! se reprit-elle à murmurer à travers ses hoquets" (p. 75).

22 "Tout un rouleau de billets qui se détachaient les uns des autres, s'envolaient, roulaient, tombaient dans la nuit, le vent soufflant très fort sur eux. Les billets. Le vent dans la nuit..." (p. 76).

For all the despair that a lack of money causes, money itself is magical in *Bonheur d'occasion*: when Eugène tells his mother about his $20 a month pay packet, for the first time in the novel he is filled with "a sort of innocent, proud, astonished joy" (p. 72);[23] money has the power to transform, to make people feel better, to give them confidence. The coda to this episode happens late in the novel when Eugène, having given his mother $20 to help with the household expenses, now returns, when Rose-Anna only has $10 of the money left, and asks if she cannot lend him some of the money back. Rose-Anna has no smaller notes and so has to give Eugène the $10 bill. From being hangdog, ashamed, down in the dumps without money, with the bill in his pocket, he is transformed. He becomes cocky, he offers to buy all sorts of things for his mother, he throws coins up in the air for his younger siblings to catch or chase. The atmosphere in the house is magically changed to one of high spirits and excitement, and Eugène leaves, whistling. For someone like his mother, such ostentation, such frivolousness, such waste is actually physically hurtful.

Money may have transformative powers but it does not necessarily make for better people: Eugène becomes vain, self-important, uncaring, even sadistic, all because he has $10 in his pocket, a $10 bill that he cracks at the bar in front of men still unemployed just as he used to be. And as he casually picks up his change, his eyes are described as sparkling with vanity. One of the ironies about money is that indifference to it is a sign of having it. Florentine likewise admires the way that Jean Lévesque casually leaves his tip on the lunch counter, again apparently indifferent to how much he is leaving. At such times of economic hardship, superfluity inspires awe.

One of the first things mentioned about Jean is what he is wearing: a well-fitting suit of English cloth, a wristwatch which catches the light with every movement of his hand, a rich silk scarf and fine leather gloves, all of which he must have bought on fashionable St Catherine Street in downtown Montreal. Part of his attraction for Florentine is therefore that his clothes set him apart from the usual men she encounters in Saint-Henri. The sign-exchange value of such clothes is that they guarantee respect and prestige and hold out the promise of future success.

Money's magic does not just lie in its physical self, but in the promise the coins and bills hold of what you can do with them. Jean obviously spends what he earns. For other characters as well, once they have a little money, they buy things and feel better for it. Having joined up, Eugène produces an engraved cigarette case which he admires and looks on as a marvellous acquisition.[24] Consumption

---

23 "Une sorte de joie naïve, orgueilleuse, émerveillée" (p. 74).

24 "Ses yeux tombaient sur cette merveilleuse acquisition" (p. 245).

boosts self-esteem and increases feelings of self-worth. Florentine too is caught up in the politics of consumption and materialism, believing that happiness and popularity can be ensured by having the latest and the newest. Searching for reasons for Jean's disappearance, she later feels that she would not have lost him if she had been better dressed. As she tries to seek him out where he used to live, she worries that she is wearing last season's styles. Consumerism thrives on obsolescence. Once married and with more money than she has ever had, she is elated that everything she is wearing is new: a new coat, a new hat: "Everything's new [...] I bought all new things this spring..."[25] Not only new, but expensive: she has moved from the leatherette handbag she carried at the beginning of the novel to a new one in suede. As she slips on a new pair of gloves, she "gazed at them on her hands, her eyes shining with satisfaction" (p. 332).[26] Florentine spends hours trying on all her new clothes. But "for consumerism there is no such thing as enough",[27] and so Florentine, "in her grasping way" (p. 382)[28] wants more and more: "consumerism consumes".[29] And at the end of the novel, as she sees Jean at the station, she craves a kind of sartorial revenge on him. Their reciprocal success can be measured by the clothes they are wearing: his "well-cut new suit [...] his tie, the same colour as his summer shoes, and his soft felt hat pushed carelessly back"; her "pretty silk print dress and the dainty shoes Emmanuel had bought her before he left. And the beautiful suede purse" (p. 380).[30] It would be a battle of commodities, of sign-exchange values, but Florentine opts to walk away unseen.

Roy takes an anti-consumerist stance. Early in the novel there is a setpiece on consumerism delivered by one of the unemployed, Alphonse. He describes how, if you walk down St Catherine Street, all of the shop windows are designed to tempt you with consumer goods. And the commodities he describes are not the necessities of life either, but are luxury goods geared to fun and enjoyment and the good life: fast cars, evening dresses, sporting goods. But as an unemployed

---

25 "Tout est neuf, [...]. J'ai acheté tout du neuf ce printemps..." (p. 350).

26 "Elle les regardait à ses mains, avec une sorte de contentement qui faisait briller ses yeux" (p. 349).

27 Jay Griffiths, "Consumerism Consumes", in *Resurgence*, p. 185. http://www.resurgence.org/resurgence/articles/griffiths.htm.

28 "Apre au gain" (p. 404).

29 Griffiths, op. cit.

30 "Il portait un complet neuf de bonne coupe [...], sa cravate qui était de même teinte que les souliers d'été, et le chapeau de feutre souple mollement rejeté en arrière."; "Et aussi pour qu'il la vît bien dans la jolie robe de soie imprimée que lui avait achetée Emmanuel, et les fins souliers qu'il lui avait apportés la veille de son départ. Et le ravissant sac de suède encore!" (p. 401f.).

person, "all the fun we get is looking" (p. 57)[31]. As he says, society tempts us: "They put all that under our noses, all the very best. [...] They tell us to buy, as well. You'd think they're afraid we won't be tempted enough. [...] Yeah, temptations, that's what they've given us [...] Nothing else but" (pp. 57-8).[32] Society even ostensibly tries to help us become consumers by offering us loans. Advertising keeps reassuring us that no-one should be without anything, that everyone should be having fun. As a consumer, society welcomes you with open arms, but exclusion awaits those with nothing to spend.

As Novelli writes: "The protagonists as well as those in the background struggle to become integral members of the consumer society which wants nothing to do with them".[33] The character of Boisvert is one who succeeds. Unemployed and railing against society at the beginning of the novel: "But what about us, what did we get from society? Look at me, look at Alphonse. What did it ever do for us? Nothing." (p. 55),[34] Boisvert has, by the end, found a job and a fiancée, new clothes, a downpayment on a house, and is acquiring consumer durables via hire/purchase. Now a consumer, he is welcomed into the fold as a fully-fledged member of society. Alphonse, on the other hand, unable to find work in a factory and rejected by the army because of his physical state, remains excluded because of his inability to consume. Ironically, he ends up frequenting the rubbish tip, the dump at Pointe-Saint-Charles, himself part of the detritus of the consumer society.

Victims of economic forces beyond their control, for the most part the characters of *Bonheur d'occasion* are buffeted by such forces, unable to harness them, or turn them to their advantage. The one character who does succeed is Jean Lévesque, the man Florentine falls for, and who she hopes will be her ticket out of Saint-Henri, but who leaves before she realises that she is pregnant. He studies at night, with the aim of bettering himself. Saint-Henri is just a rung on the ladder of success he is climbing. He aspires to Westmount, the English bastion of wealth which shimmers up on the mountain above Saint-Henri. He reappears at the end, glimpsed at the station as the boys go off to war. He has got

---

31 "Le seul fun qu'on a, c'est de les regarder" (p. 59).

32 "La société nous met toute sous les yeux; tout ce qu'y a de beau sous les yeux. [...] A nous conseille d'acheter aussi. On dirait qu'a peur qu'on soye pas assez tentés. [...] Oui, des tentations, c'est ce que la société nous a donné, [...]. Des tentations d'un boutte à l'autre." (p. 59).

33 Novelli, *Gabrielle Roy*, p. 75: "Les protagonistes ainsi que ceux qui servent d'arrière plan, luttent pour s'intégrer à la société de consommation qui n'a que faire d'eux".

34 "Mais nous autres, qu'est-ce que'on a eu de la société? Regarde-moi, regarde Alphonse. Qu'est-ce qu'a nous a donné à nous autres, la société? Rien" (p. 57).

on, but the implication that he has done so through profiteering directs us to disapprove of Jean's achievement.

Those that get on in *Bonheur d'occasion* are not sympathetically portrayed. Jean may be hard-working and driven to self-improvement but he has become hard in doing so, sacrificing friends, going it alone, contemptuous of the normal run of mankind. Marcotte declares him to be the purest exemplar of urban industrial civilisation.[35] It is not difficult for Emmanuel to imagine Jean's future: "When you're not hampered by scruples, you succeed" (p. 302).[36] In the critique of capitalism in *Bonheur d'occasion,* the depiction of the self-made man is at its core. Nor is Jean the only character in the novel whose personal values have been the price one pays for getting on in a capitalist society. Boisvert, who suddenly has a job thanks to the war, is on the point of getting married, the implication being that, no longer single, he will not be called up. Always selfish, his philosophy summed up by Alphonse as: "What's yours is mine and what's mine's my own" (p. 304),[37] he could serve as a lesson in how to get on. Alphonse bitterly comments: "He shoulda been a capitalist. [...] If you want a three-lesson course in how to succeed in life [...] go see Boisvert. [...] A small-time Rockefeller with three dimes to his name" (p. 304f.).[38] Those who do get on in *Bonheur d'occasion*, therefore, are those who are willing to sacrifice decent human qualities. An extreme example of a successful businessman is Lachance who during the Thirties hired men on relief so that he could pay them next to nothing and, if they left him, he then denounced them to the authorities so that they would lose their relief. For the above men, people are commodities. Jean abandons Florentine because she is not going to be of benefit to him in his advancement up the ladder of success; she has no sign-exchange value. Éveline Rochon has exchange value for Boisvert because, as his wife, she guarantees immunity from conscription. The unemployed men that Lachance can pay rock bottom wages to have exchange value in providing work for very little outlay on the boss's part. Roy's critique of capitalism thus resolves itself into a critique of a selfish ideology that promotes the survival of the fittest, requiring the commodification of people, and demanding the exploitation of the weakest.

Roy's most admirable characters are those untouched by acquisitiveness: Rose-Anna who would rather have her husband by her side than his pay packet, if

---

35 Marcotte, "*Bonheur d'occasion* et le 'grand réalisme'", p. 411.

36 "Quand on ne s'encombre pas de scrupules, on réussit" (p. 318).

37 "Ce qui vous appartient m'appartient et ce qui est à moué est rien qu'à moué" (p. 321).

38 "Un petit trustard manqué. [...] Si tu veux recevoir un cours en trois leçons pour savoir comment réussir dans la vie, [...] va trouver Boisvert. [...] Un petit Rockefeller de trente bidous." (p. 321)

it means him going off to war; Emmanuel, the idealist who hopes for a different kind of society after the war. They are also the characters who think beyond themselves, who are moved by the plight of others: Rose-Anna by the fate of Norwegian women when she hears of the fall of Norway, Azarius, going all sentimental over the fall of France, Emmanuel touched by universal humanity. Given what de Grazia calls "the antinomies of private and public and of market and state",[39] it is Florentine, Jean, or Boisvert who are focused on acts of private well-being, "of individual purchasing and consuming", who are "unfamiliar with co-operation, civic participation, [or] sacrifice for the common good".[40] Jean believes in profit rather than patriotism, Boisvert manages to marry so he will not have to enlist, Florentine is preoccupied with resolving her immediate situation. Roy favours the poor and the powerless and the object-less, the Alphonses and Azariuses and Rose-Annas and Emmanuels of this world over the object-laden Jeans and Florentines and Eugènes and Boisverts. By the mid twentieth century, as de Grazia states, the dominant model was that of the United States, a model that "established the predominance of individual acquisitiveness over collective entitlement and defined the measure of the good society as private well-being achieved through consumer spending".[41] Roy raises a critical voice against this model.

And yet is *Bonheur d'occasion* not ideologically conflicted? Because money *is* sexy in *Bonheur d'occasion*. Jean is far more handsome than the noble Emmanuel: broad-shouldered, slim-waisted, powerful, potent and indeed procreative: he is, after all, the father of Florentine's baby. And the place he aspires to is the luxurious English enclave of Westmount, perched up on the side of Montreal's Mount Royal and continually contrasted with the rundown neighbourhood of Saint-Henri at the foot of the mountain: "Millionaires up on the hill and guys out of work down below, fighting with each other" (p. 60).[42] We catch our first view of Westmount as Jean suddenly glimpses it through a gap in the buildings of Saint-Henri:

> But beyond [St. Henri station], in a large notch in the suburb, the town of Westmount climbs in tiers toward the mountain's ridge in its stiff English luxury [...] an invitation

39 *The Sex of Things: Gender and Consumption in Historical Perspective*, ed. by Victoria de Grazia and Ellen Furlough (Berkeley, University of California Press, 1996), p. 8.

40 Philip Cushman, "The Politics of Consumption", in *Seattle Times* (19 October 2004) via http://www.commondreams.org/views04/1019-28.htm.

41 De Grazia and Furlough, *The Sex of Things*, p. 5.

42 "Les millionaires sur la côte et les chômeux en bas à s'engueuler" (p. 61).

> to the infinite travels of the mind. Here poverty and superfluity will stare tirelessly at each other, as long as Westmount lasts, as long as St. Henri lies at its feet. (p. 34)[43]

For someone like Jean, Westmount is an aspirational place, a neighbourhood where those who have succeeded live. In the lushness of the image: "an invitation to the infinite travels of the [soul]", Roy attributes a kind of magic to this wealthy world. Above the smoke and soot and grime of Saint-Henri, the air is fresh, the lawns are manicured, the gravel of the drives is untrodden, the stars shine more brightly. Indeed, at night, looking up from Saint-Henri, the lights of Westmount can even get confused with the stars. So attractively is Westmount described during the novel that it seems a testimonial to the power of commodity and a vindication of the success one can attain within the capitalist system. Emmanuel, the character most given to empathy with the downtrodden, and the spokesman of humane values in the novel, has never borne any resentment against the rich, neither envying them nor hating them. The fact that there are rich people is accepted simply as the way things are in capitalist societies. Nevertheless, as he wanders about Westmount's quiet streets on his last visit before going off to war, Emmanuel is moved to damning thoughts about wealth and poverty: "Wealth, accepting the offering of the poor, was unable to see their tormented face",[44] and he questions whether the wealthy are really giving as much to the war effort as the poor are: "Are these people giving all they have to give?" (p. 320)[45] The very materials out of which Westmount is built seem to scoff at Emmanuel and his humanistic values, whispering to him: "Stone and steel and iron, gold and silver –

---

43 "Mais au-delà, dans une large échancrure du faubourg, apparaît la ville de Westmount échelonnée jusqu'au faîte de la montagne dans son rigide confort anglais. Il se trouve ainsi que c'est aux voyages infinis de l'âme qu'elle invite. Ici, le luxe et la pauvreté se regardent inlassablement, depuis qu'il y a Westmount, depuis qu'en bas, à ses pieds, il y a Saint-Henri" (p. 36). In his translation Alan Brown considers the antecedent of the pronoun *elle* in the second sentence to be the station, 'la petite gare', mentioned at the beginning of the paragraph in the original; in his seminal study "Thèmes et structures de *Bonheur d'occasion*", André Brochu thinks similarly (op. cit., p. 187). Grammatically, however, the pronominal antecedent must be the last feminine noun, "la ville de Westmount". It is thus the sight of the city of Westmount which inspires aspirational thoughts rather than the humdrum, workaday, red brick railway station of Saint-Henri. Brown also chooses to translate *âme* as *mind* rather than *soul*.

44 "La richesse, acceptant l'offrande du pauvre, ne pouvait voir sa face tourmentée" (p. 337); my translation; the English version omits the last three sentences of this paragraph.

45 "Eux autres, est-ce qu'ils donnent tout ce qu'ils ont à donner?" (p. 337)

we're the things that last, and cost the most!" (p. 320).[46] In contrast to the fragility of human beings, such vocabulary, aligning Westmount with the hardness of capitalist values, could be seen to condemn the ruthlessness of the ideology itself. Willing to pay the price, Jean may well aspire to Westmount.

The fact that Westmount is an English enclave bears witness to the fact that class relations have traditionally been ethnically based in Quebec. The English words in the text relate, for the most part, to work: *job, truck, factory, trade, business, overtime*. Indeed, the firm which Jean works for is called "Montreal Metal Works". It is thus easy to see where the money lies in this second-largest French-speaking city in the world. The vocabulary of war is predominantly English as well. Not only are the barracks situated in Westmount, but when Emmanuel by chance comes upon Pitou doing guard duty there, the latter's speech is suddenly peppered with chirpy phrases like "thumb's up" and "you bet" (p. 316). And at the station as the men depart, it is to the sound of jingoistic phrases like "We'll fight to the last man for the British Empire" and "There'll always be an England" (p. 377). Clark criticises Roy for not revealing that the roots of the poverty seen in the novel lie "in our political and economic subservience to U.S. imperialism and Anglo-Canadian colonialism".[47] He comments that "the ethos of Jean Lévesque is that of the comprador bourgeois class",[48] and, of course, he could add mimicry to his criticism of Jean in his having chosen English cloth for his suit and his slipping in to English whenever he refers to getting on. In *Bonheur d'occasion* one never sees "the coloniser": there is never anyone in Westmount; at the Montreal Metal Works it is just the francophone foreman one meets. The absence of any physical English presence seems indicative of relations between workers and bosses in the city. The English have 'othered' the French, who can do all the mundane work and go to war for them. So secure are they in their superiority that they can afford to be a non-presence in the novel, the consequences of their enormous economic power tangible in the use of their language and the names of their firms, and the magnificence of their houses, set, close to the stars, above the scene of the production of their wealth.

On 8 September 2002 the London *Sunday Times* had the headline on the front page of its 'MONEY' section: "War on Iraq 'will boost stock market'". The article began: "Investors are being urged to prepare for a stock-market rally if

46 "Nous autres, la pierre, le fer, l'acier, l'or, l'argent, nous sommes ce qui se paye cher et ce qui dure." (p. 337)

47 J. Wilson Clark, "Pro-Imperialist Ideas in Gabrielle Roy's *Tin Flute*", *Literature and Ideology*, 13 (1972), p. 33.

48 Ibid., p. 33.

America and Britain decide to launch a full-scale war against Iraq. American share prices have soared by an average of 36% in four recent wars".[49] Roy would be saddened to think that in sixty years nothing has changed. On 10 September 1939, a week after Britain's declaration, Canada declared war on Germany and suddenly business picked up. For Jean, at the Forge, there is overtime and more men are being taken on. Rose-Anna predicts that Azarius will soon be working again because war will boost the construction industry, and it is envisaged that another son, Philippe, could get a job in the munitions industry. And if you cannot find a job, you can always join up. So, for all the years of the Depression, there has been no work, there has been no money, governments have seemed incapable of helping their people. As the barkeeper Sam Latour thunders:

> Money [...]. There was none for the old folks or for schools or orphans. And none to give people work. But just take a look right now, there's money for the war. It's there now, all right. (p. 148)[50]

Even Emmanuel says: "A guy never had a better chance than nowadays" (p. 305).[51]

As the novel begins, Canada has only been at war for six months and Florentine rushes to see a parade of recruits. What she sees is a ragged bunch of men looking like tramps, men who, like her father, have spent years on relief, and "she had the vague intuition of a wretched poverty which looked upon [the war] as a last resort" (p. 19).[52] At the end of Alphonse's castigation of the consumerist society, he mentions how an acquaintance of his has joined the army just to get a winter coat (p. 58). For those who have enlisted, Alphonse later comments, it is as if they have discovered a goldmine, another Klondike (p. 310). Once in the army, the physical transformation of the new recruits is plain to see: they are all so well dressed, so well fed. When Eugène returns on leave he is scarcely recognizable. His complexion now ruddy, he carries himself better, and, no longer indecisive, he has been mentally transformed as well: "He felt that he was master of his life and floating sky-high" (p. 244).[53] When Emmanuel comes across Pitou on guard duty, he finds him smiling and excited: "His grin almost

---

49 *The Sunday Times*, London, sec. 6, "MONEY", September 8, 2002.

50 "Y en avait pas pour les vieux, ni pour les écoles, ni pour les orphelins, ni pour donner de l'ouvrage au monde. Mais à c'te heure marque ben qu'il y en a pour la guerre. A se trouve à c'te heure, l'argent" (p. 157).

51 "Jamais un garçon a eu autant de chance que de nos jours" (p. 321).

52 "Elle eut la très vague intuition d'une horrible misère qui reconnaissait là sa suprême ressource" (p. 21).

53 "Il se sentit soudain maître de sa vie et porté sur des nuages" (p. 254).

burst open his round cheeks, shining like polished apples" (p. 316),[54] all because he is happy. But the irony of the situation is not lost on Emmanuel: in being handed a rifle, Pitou "was handling his first working tool" (p. 318).[55] And when Azarius enlists, he is rejuvenated; Rose-Anna, having just given birth to her eleventh child, looks at her husband and is astonished to see how young he looks. Indeed the narrator slips into the most fundamental Christian imagery to describe the transformation: "He had a sensation of accomplishment and resurrection" (p. 372).[56]

As the men leave for war in the last chapter, Emmanuel cannot get over the laughter, the singing, the look of joy on so many faces. Azarius, now strong, vigorous, authoritative, is beaming with enthusiasm; Pitou's face is glowing. And Emmanuel can scarcely believe his eyes:

> Emmanuel thought he must be dreaming. Were these yesterday's unemployed? Were these the men he had seen so lifeless, miserably submissive, discouraged to the marrow? [...] Salvation through war! (p. 375)[57]

And yet as Emmanuel surveys the crowd getting on to trains and making their farewells, "through that breath of liberation rising from the crowd", he hears "the chink of money" (p. 376). It is the sound of blood money. "They've been bought, he thought. They've been bought too. They, above all, he thought" (p. 376).[58] Earlier, Jean had pronounced that they were all profiteers, even those who were joining up or getting jobs in munitions factories, all having their own best interests at heart. At the end, Emmanuel realizes that Jean was right, that they are indeed all profiteers now: by providing jobs, by putting money in men's pockets, the war is serving everyone's purpose, but Emmanuel makes the distinction between the ordinary footsoldier as "the least of the profiteers" as opposed to the Léon Boisverts and Jean Lévesques "who'll owe their personal advancement and

---

54 "Le sourire faisait presque éclater les joues rondes, lisses et brillantes sous les yeux, comme des pommes longtemps frottées" (p. 333).

55 "Pitou avait entre les mains son premier instrument de travail." (p. 335)

56 "Mais il avait sur ses lèvres une sensation d'accomplissement, de résurrection" (p. 393).

57 "Emmanuel croyait rêver. Étaient-ce là les chômeurs d'hier? Étaient-ce là les petits gars qu'il avait vus sans ressort, misérablement soumis, et découragés jusqu'à la moelle de leurs corps? [...] Le salut par la guerre!" (p. 397)

58 "Il lui sembla entendre, loin, dans le grand souffle de libération qui montait de la foule, comme le son de l'argent qui tinte. 'Eux aussi, pensa-t-il. Eux aussi ont été achetés.' 'Eux surtout!' se dit-il" (p. 398).

maybe their fortunes to the war, without running any risks" (p. 376).[59] And for Emmanuel this is "the supreme bankruptcy of humanity. Wealth had spoken the truth [...] on the mountain":[60] the capitalist system has won out again: men, when desperate enough, can be bought; self-interest or sheer survival does motivate; immediate relief blinds people to the consequences. Only the one left behind, Alphonse, is thinking of the number of men who will not return, whose lives will be forfeited just so that they can have a few coins in their pocket or a winter coat. Emmanuel is indignant, and this was the source of Roy's indignation: that life should have sunk to such a desperate level that for thousands of men war should be seen as a salvation.

Roy does not preach revolution. *Bonheur d'occasion* has never prompted anyone to man the barricades in Westmount. One of her more left-wing critics can even write that "Miss Roy's interest in poverty stems from her pro-imperialist comprador outlook".[61] Roy's sensibilities are compassionate, humanist, conceptually sympathetic to socialism. And one cannot deny that the novel displays explicit criticism of the crudeness of capitalism shown by its boom-or-bust mentality, its woeful inability to deal with a crisis like that of the 1930s, its sheer lack of imagination resulting in the waste of the potential of a whole generation of young people, and the fact that only something as equally crude as war is able to resolve the situation by giving a kick-start to economies dormant for a decade.

At the station, Florentine feels inside her handbag and experiences an intense satisfaction on touching her cheque book and feeling a roll of dollar bills. But, "where would they all have been without the war" (p. 383),[62] she asks on the last page of the novel. She cannot understand her mother still being inconsolable about Azarius going off to war because "Pappa did the right thing, he did well to join up. It's the most beautiful thing he ever did in his life. [...] Funny how hard she takes it! She never had so much money in her life!" (p. 382)[63] And money allows Florentine to think about the future: she's beginning a new life, another life...

---

59 "Ceux qui partent, ce sont les moindres profiteurs. Il y a une infinité de Léon Boisvert, de Jean Lévesque qui devront leur avancement personnel et peut-être leur fortune à la guerre, et qui courront aucun de ses risques" (p. 398).

60 "Et il lui apparut qu'il constatait de ses yeux la suprême faillite de l'humanité. La richesse avait dit vrai sur la montagne" (p. 398).

61 J. Wilson Clark, "Pro-Imperialist Ideas in Gabrielle Roy's *Tin Flute*", p. 33.

62 "Sans la guerre où seraient-ils tous?" (p. 404)

63 "C'est la plus belle chose qu'il a faite dans sa vie. [...] C'est drôle quand meme qu'elle prenne ça si mal... Pourtant jamais elle a eu tant d'argent!" (p. 404)

Throughout the novel Emmanuel has been thinking about the future too. He has hoped that the war will destroy the power of money. He says to Pitou in what Marcotte has called "a truly socialist speech" wherein Emmanuel pours forth "the pure doctrine of the exploitation of the masses":[64]

> You know, Pitou, what keeps us all in the circus behind bars, it's money. The guys who have the money decide if you're going to work or not, depending how it suits them. But the war, this war, it's going to destroy that damned power of money. […] Money invested in destruction destroys itself. Great! That's just fine! 'Cause money isn't wealth. Wealth is our arms and our brains, the masses. And that's the wealth that'll last after the war. That's what's going to feed the world, and all men, in justice. (p. 60)[65]

Although he may be disappointed at the end of the novel that all of these young men are just commodities for the same "guys who have the money" who rule their working lives, Emmanuel nevertheless hopes for an end to such a system after the war and for a bright new world of humane values, peace, and the equitable distribution of wealth. But as the title of the novel indicates, no happiness therein is totally unalloyed, no joy unadulterated, no hope totally fulfilled.[66] Indeed, one could hardly call the last line of the novel inspirational: "Low in the sky, dark clouds heralded the storm."[67]

---

64 Marcotte, "*Bonheur d'occasion* et le 'grand réalisme'": "un discours proprement socialiste […] la pure doctrine de l'exploitation des masses". Between the first and second editions, Roy excised much of the more radical social criticism, but Shek considers that even before the deletions Roy "stops short of explicitly proposing a socialist solution" (ibid., p. 83).

65 "C'est l'argent qui nous tient tous au cirque derrière les barreaux. Les gars qui ont de l'argent, c'est eux autres qui décident si vous allez travailler, vous autres, oui ou non, selon que ça fait leur affaire ou bien qu'ils s'en fichent. Mais la guerre, c'telle-ci, va te le détruire le maudit pouvoir de l'argent. […] L'argent s'en va pour la destruction pis se détruit elle-même. Eh ben! tant mieux ! Parce que l'argent, c'est pas la richesse. La richesse, c'est le travail, c'est nos bras, c'est nos têtes à nous autres, la grande masse. Et c'est c'te richesse-là qui va faire vivre le monde, tous les hommes dans la justice" (p. 62).

66 The French title is difficult to translate; *Broken Dreams* and *Borrowed Bliss* were thought of as possibilities. Of course, the term *d'occasion* meaning *second-hand* is one with links to buying and selling. *The Tin Flute*, which was finally settled on, refers to an episode which is symbolic of hopes and dreams in the novel: as Daniel, the youngest son, is dying of leukaemia, he finally gets the tin flute he has long wanted, but once he has it, he finds that possessing it is not as wonderful as he imagined it would be.

67 "Très bas dans le ciel, des nuées sombres annonçaient l'orage" (p. 405).

In June 1945 when *Bonheur d'occasion* is published, the war has been over for a month. The novel thus perches on the cusp of the post-war world, looking backwards and forwards, and Emmanuel's questions hang in the air: is society going to be reconstituted after the war or are we just going to revert to ideologies that have proved wanting? In 1947, in her acceptance speech for her admission to the Royal Society of Canada, Roy paid an imaginary visit to Saint-Henri and saw the whole sorry cycle beginning again. The Jean Lévesques of this world are still selfish, are still avoiding social responsibilities, are still intent on profit. And yet Roy could not bring herself to have Emmanuel return from the war: "He was the spirit of intransigent youth who wants nothing less than perfect justice, and he was thus marked out for sacrifice".[68] Rose-Anna and Emmanuel are still held up as the ideal, as people who live for others, or offer themselves to a higher purpose, and as such we should not be totally devoid of hope of a better society and a better humanity. The speech was welcomed by socialists, trade-unionists, everyone on the left; communists even printed it in their weekly paper *Combat*. But it was to be the last word that the author had to say on social issues. For Ricard, it is a kind of testament to the social ideas and ideals which Roy had had from her days as a journalist and which had culminated in her novel, but it was thus "a farewell, if not to the ideas themselves, at least to their public expression".[69] Henceforth Gabrielle Roy would stay clear of obvious commitment.

And yet the novel has been credited with a potency that Roy could not have imagined in 1947. As Eagleton writes of Lukác's critical concepts: "All great art is socially progressive in the sense that, whatever the author's conscious political allegiance [...], it realizes the vital 'world-historical' forces of an epoch which make for change and growth, revealing their unfolding potential in its fullest complexity".[70] Having appraised Florentine according to Lukácsian theories, Marcotte asks the meaning "for a literature, for a culture, of placing on the shoulders of a young woman showing all the signs of fragility, the weight of its historic transition towards modern life, towards the city".[71] In an article the title

68 "Il était l'esprit de l'intransigeante jeunesse qui ne veut rien de moins que la justice parfaite, et ainsi il était marqué pour le sacrifice": "Retour à Saint-Henri: Discours de réception à la Société royale du Canada" in *Fragiles Lumières de la terre, écrits divers 1942-1970* (Montreal: Quinze, 1978), p. 174.

69 Ricard, *Gabrielle Roy: une vie*, p. 304: "un adieu, sinon à ces idées elles-mêmes, du moins à leur expression publique".

70 Eagleton, *Marxism and Literary Criticism*, p. 27.

71 Marcotte, "*Bonheur d'occasion* et le 'grand réalisme'", p. 413: "...que signifie pour une littérature, pour une culture, le fait de confier à une jeune fille portant toutes les

of which translates as "Thresholds of Modernity", Brigitte Faivre-Duboz sees the modernity of *Bonheur d'occasion* and Ringuet's novel *Trente Arpents* as lying in "the depiction they give us of a turning point in the history of Quebec, a moment when a new reality appears, a reality characterised by instability, movement, a diversity of points of reference and within which move people whose ways of interacting with the world spring from a more traditional way of life".[72] And in 1975, thirty years after the publication of the novel, an hour-long radio homage was paid to the novelist on St Jean Baptiste Day, Quebec's annual holiday, and during which the commentator suggested that "all Quebec emancipation sprang from *The Tin Flute*". Roy commented: "It was a profoundly emotional hour for me. It stilled a lot of pain in my heart".[73]

Any text is both a social and an economic production, authors working up their chosen materials into a product to be sold. As her material, Roy took the ordinary ideological experience of the people of Saint-Henri, as she witnessed it during the early 1940s, transforming it by giving it shape and structure. As Eagleton sums up Macherey: "It is by giving ideology a determinate form, fixing it within certain fictional limits, that art is able to distance itself from it, thus revealing to us the limits of that ideology. In doing this, Macherey claims, art contributes to our deliverance from the ideological illusion."[74] As a work of art, *Bonheur d'occasion* contributes to our deliverance from any ideological illusions we may have about capitalism. And yet art is a commodity in a capitalist society. No matter the content, the finished work is an object, a piece of property to be bid for, bartered for, bought, printed, packaged, advertised, promoted, all with the aim of shifting it off the shelves and on to someone's coffee table. Book sales, bestseller lists, film rights, awards are all generated by the work. Ricard describes the implications of *Bonheur d'occasion* being chosen for the American 'Book of the Month Club' for May 1947 in terms which could well have found themselves into the novel itself: "her book in the hands of millions of readers, and money,

---

marques de la fragilité, le poids de sa transition historique vers la vie moderne, la ville?"

72 Brigitte Faivre-Duboz, "Seuils de la modernité: *Trente Arpents* et *Bonheur d'occasion*", *Quebec Studies* 32 (2001-2002), p. 81: "... la représentation qu'ils nous livrent d'un moment charnière dans l'histoire du Québec, celui où apparaît une réalité nouvelle caractérisée par l'instabilité, la mouvance, la diversité des repères qu'elle produit et au sein de laquelle se meuvent des personnages ayant une façon d'entrer en rapport avec le monde qui relève du mode traditionnel."

73 Cobb, "'I have, I think, a grateful heart'", p. 14.

74 Eagleton, *Marxism and Literary Criticism*, p. 17.

money such as she could never have imagined, even in her wildest dreams".[75] This deal guaranteed an initial print run of 750,000 and provided leverage with Parisian publishers for the French rights. At about the same time the film rights were sold to Universal Pictures for $75,000, and, although the film was never made, Roy still made $67,000 on the deal.[76] The irony of *Bonheur d'occasion* is that a novel about such dire poverty became a worldwide bestseller and, for Roy, a money-spinner. No, Roy is not anti-capitalist. However, as Lukács writes: "from the point of view of history and posterity, what matters is the picture conveyed by the work".[77] The picture conveyed by *Bonheur d'occasion* of ordinary people struggling to make ends meet during desperate times still has truths to reveal about how we live, how we confront the realities of our existence and how we survive.

---

[75] Ricard, *Gabrielle Roy: une vie*, p. 283: "son livre entre les mains de millions de lecteurs, et de l'argent, de l'argent comme jamais elle n'a imaginé en avoir, même dans ses rêves les plus fous".

[76] Ricard, *Gabrielle Roy: une vie*, p. 287.

[77] Lukács, *Studies in European Realism*, p. 10.

Ekkehard Knörer

Counterfeit: Of Signs and Money in Robert Bresson's Film *L'argent*

Prologue – Genesis

L'Argent (1983) is the last film Robert Bresson made, at the age of 82 and after a lifetime of only thirteen feature films, but it is not the last one he intended to make. The one he had planned for quite some time to realise and still hoped to make after *L'Argent*, the one that got into pre-production but never beyond, was to be a film version of the Biblical *Genesis*. Robert Bresson intended to film paradise and, according to some reports, he even wanted to leave Adam and Eve out of the story and focus on animals, or even, according to a report by Serge Daney, on traces of animals alone; traces of the real presence they leave in the ground. This, of course, might not have been as absurd as it sounds, as there already is one film in Bresson's oeuvre with an animal protagonist, *Au Hazard Balthasar*, featuring a donkey and his suffering at the hands of humans.

It seems, however, not quite imaginable how a *Genesis* could have fitted into a work that seemed to get darker with every film, ending with a serial killer protagonist in *L'Argent*. How could Bresson have found a back door to paradise, following up his presentations of a world dominated by *Le Diable probablement* (the film he made before *L'Argent* in 1977) with a vision of a world not yet fallen. Bresson was a director who always had a lot of trouble finding the money to get his films financed, but in the case of *Genesis*, there might be another factor contributing to its failure. The one thing you can say about the world in the Jansenist Catholic Bresson's films is that it is never not fallen. His protagonists sin, they suffer, they are trapped or literally imprisoned (*Un Condamné à mort s'est échappé ou Le Vent souffle où il veut*, 1956), they commit suicide (*Mouchette*, 1967), they are burnt at the stake (*Procès de Jeanne d'Arc*, 1962) and sometimes they are redeemed by acts of grace, which are as inexplicable as you would expect them to be within the predestinarian frame of Jansenist Catholicism. There is, however, more than this level of subjects and plots in Bresson's art; there is, as I will try to show, another kind of redemption going on – a redemption that lies precisely in the art itself, and more specifically in the kind of images and signs Bresson painstakingly and with theoretical aforethought produces – an aesthetic of redemption that follows a very precise semiotic logic of transubstantiation. This logic, I want to argue, finds its precedent in the Jansenist *Port Royal Logic*.

Money

In the post-adamic beginning of *L'Argent* there is money. In the end there is a bloody axe. *L'Argent* tells the allegorical story of the transformation of the one into the other. Let me sum up the plot, which Bresson derived from Leo Tolstoy's story *The Forged Coupon*. It is interesting to see, however, how Bresson not only transposed it into the present but also simplified its meandering plot and especially left out Tolstoy's rather explicit comments on the religious implications of what is going on. This is Bresson's version: Norbert, a young man from a rich family, needs more money than his father is willing to give to him. A friend has money, a note of 500 francs, but it is counterfeit. This counterfeit money is passed on. After a series of transmissions it gets into the hands of Yvon who is completely innocent but becomes a criminal when he is falsely accused of forgery and then dismissed by his employer. After a botched bank robbery Yvon is imprisoned and in one of the letters he receives from his girlfriend, she tells him that their daughter died and that she will never see him again. When released Yvon finds accommodation in a cheap hotel. He kills the operators and steals the money from the cash desk. Later on he observes an old lady withdrawing money from a cash machine and follows her home. She gives him shelter in her house and says that if she were God she would forgive everybody. A few days later he kills her and members of her family living in her house with an axe. The question "Where is the money?" remains unanswered. The last image shows Yvon in a restaurant when the police enter the room.

This is the abbreviated version of the film's plot. What should not go unnoticed is Bresson's change of title from Tolstoy's *The Forged Coupon*: that the fact of the forgery is no longer announced may seem slight but it is, I would argue, of great importance, as it really signals a fundamental indifference in Bresson's film. *L'Argent* is not about counterfeit money and it is not titled "The Forged Coupon" or "Counterfeit Money" because money as such is fundamentally counterfeit in Bresson's vision of a fallen world. Money, paper money, almost obsessively framed again and again in shots throughout the film, is for him a "contrefait", a false simulation of the truth. The innocent man becomes a sinner – which, as a human being, we must add, he is from birth. There is nothing like true innocence in the Jansenists' view to which Bresson explicitly subscribes. So, we could say, Yvon does become what he is from birth, in much the same way as money turns out to be what it essentially is: counterfeit. The hand that was introduced filling gas into a tank becomes the hand that holds the money and the hand that holds the money becomes the hand that holds the devastating letters announcing Yvon's daughter's death and his girlfriend's goodbye. And in the end this hand becomes the hand that holds the axe and kills exactly the person ready to forgive every sin. Before that, however, this hand in a rather scandalous turn of religious imagery becomes the hand of Jesus Christ in the last supper, offering not bread and wine but – in a gesture *reminiscent of* the Eucharist's "hoc" – a hazelnut flower to the woman Yvon will soon kill with the bloody axe in his hands.

Jochen Hörisch once wrote that "money is the medium of the remarkably successful attempt of simulating the world as a whole".[1] He added that, for this reason, negating money was an exercise as futile as negating the world. It is an exercise, one could further add, as futile as negating language in its representative functions or negating signs as that which connects words/images and things. What lies at the core of *L'Argent* as well as Bresson's oeuvre as a whole is exactly this most fundamental negation of representation, of signs and therefore also of money. Money, for him, in the last film he made, is more than just an example. It is the prime example of a counterfeit sign, of a sinfully false simulation of a world in need of redemption from exactly these simulations. This redemption, however, is thinkable only as a miracle, a miracle done by an always inscrutable god – or by a (not) altogether different instrument: the art Bresson insistently calls cinematography.

Hoc

This miracle of cinematography is a miracle of transubstantiation. To prepare this argument, I will make a short detour to the 17th century, which leads straight to the heart of Robert Bresson's Catholic aesthetics. There is a famous passage in Antoine Arnauld's and Pierre Nicole's Jansenist *The Art of Thinking*, better known as *The Port Royal Logic*. What they develop in this book is a subtle semiotic theory – and in a key passage they apply it to an analysis of the words spoken in the Eucharist, the words effecting transubstantiation: "hoc est corpus meum", "this is my body". Their interpretation is explicitly directed against a Calvinist reading of this sentence that understands it as merely symbolical. Arnauld and Nicole, on the contrary, insist on the logical possibility of a religious necessity: the real presence of Jesus Christ's blood and body in the Eucharist. The

1 Jochen Hörisch, *Kopf oder Zahl* (Frankfurt a.M: Suhrkamp, 1987), p. 179.

whole argument hinges on the semiotic logic of the *hoc* in the words Christ speaks at the Last Supper. I quote from *Logic or the Art of Thinking*:

> [The Calvinists] claim is that in Jesus Christ's assertion, "This is my body," the word "this" signifies the bread. Now the bread, they say, cannot really be the body of Christ, and therefore Christ's assertion does not mean "This is really my body". [...] It remains only to be said, following the principle we have established, that the word "bread", indicating a distinct idea, does not correspond exactly to the term *hoc* which indicates only the confused idea of a present thing. Rather it is clear that when Christ uttered this word, and at the same time drew the Apostles' attention to the bread he held in his hands, they probably added to the confused idea of a present thing signified by the term *hoc*, the distinct idea of bread which was only prompted and not precisely signified by this term.[2]

So, according to their reading, the *hoc* did, at the moment of utterance, prompt the distinct idea of "bread", but it did at this moment not distinctly *signify* the "bread". This is because the *hoc* does not signify any *distinct* idea at all, but only the indistinct or confused idea of a "present thing". The "present thing" of the *hoc* is neither the bread nor the body, but only the presentation of something, of some thing still and always open to a distinct signification: i.e. it can without difficulty refer first to the bread and then to the body, remaining semiotically open to the miracle of trans-substantion. In other words the *hoc* cannot saturate the presence of the thing with a distinct meaning. It is therefore at the same time empty and most present; it takes the place of a presence that is open to different significations. Christ (or the priest) can *not* possibly say, to put this more bluntly, "the bread is my body" – because with these words he would utter a semio-logical contradiction. It is only the *hoc*'s emptiness that neither distinctly refers to nor represents something absent (or present) that opens up the possibility of a trans-substantiative logic of real presence. Only in this *hoc* can the bread become the body, which happens in the exact moment the transubstantiating word "body" is spoken, thereby replacing the idea of "bread" by the idea of "body". Only in the sheer presence of the word that refuses to signify distinctly can Jesus Christ's real presence find its way into the scene and the host of the Eucharist.

Bresson's Jansenist cinematographic aesthetics, I will now venture to say, are an aesthetics that at every moment aims at the *hoc* of the Eucharist, at the emptiness of a real thing present but not *distinctly* signified, an aesthetics that at every turn avoids the lapse to the distinctiveness of representation – in order to remain open for a miraculous redemption. Such an aesthetics, however, might seem completely impossible for one very simple reason: the iconicity of the

---

2 Pierre Nicole, Antoine Arnauld, *Logic or the Art of Thinking* (Cambridge: Cambridge University Press, 1996), p. 71.

image. In our Western tradition deriving from concepts of iconicity and the *vera icon* we have a tendency to take the image as a symbol that makes us see what it refers to. Within the broad context of cinema as a basically realist art this tendency certainly is even more enduring than in the arts in general. The one question Bresson's aesthetics which aim at something fundamentally different to realism, have to answer then becomes: "How can the cinematographic image that always seems to refer very distinctly to a thing it resembles – to the point at which it seems to be the thing it shows – be turned into a sheer *hoc*-ness, into the presentation of a thing that is most present and remains semiotically absent at the same time?" "How can the "iconic" cinematographic image ever not signify in the sense of a representation?", "how can it, in the parlance of Arnauld and Nicole, attain the status of the *hoc,* a signifier of confused ideas, open to the bread at one moment and Jesus Christ's body the next?"

Bresson's aesthetics: Hands

I will begin my preliminary attempts to find an answer to this question with the significant observation that Bresson is interested in hands rather than faces. You can see it, to take a striking example, in his *Procès de Jeanne d'Arc*, which seems to be, among other things, a cinematic counter-proposal to Carl Theodor Dreyer's more famous version of the historic events. Where Dreyer composes his film from a series of highly expressive close-ups of Maria Falconetti's face, Bresson does not give us a single one. There are, indeed, close-ups – as there always are in Bresson – but they are of Jeanne's feet, shackled to a stone and on her way to the fire, and of her shackled hands, or her hands holding a makeshift cross. Consider also the more famous case of *Pickpocket* (1959) in which the hero by profession, if not conviction, is a master of theft with his moving, taking and feigning hands. Once, in a series of fast cuts we see these hands at work, picking purses, catching purses, and handing them on to the accomplice's hand (see image 2). And in *L'Argent* the first time we see Yvon, its protagonist, is when we see his hands in a close up, filling a tank with petrol, a service which is part of his job. Bresson shows hands at work, without a face, a context, or any kind of background. To get to the core of Bresson's aesthetics, I would argue that this way of introduction by showing only the hand and not the person is not intended as either metaphor or metonymy. In terms of rhetoric, it can, of course, not be anything else, but in a way all of Bresson's *oeuvre* runs counter to the idea of rhetoric in its most basic sense and therefore to the ways in which, rhetorically speaking, meaning can be made. In an interview the director refers to Montaigne, saying: "Montaigne has a marvelous chapter on hands in which he says that hands go where their owner does not send them."[3]

The focus on hands (or feet) in movement and at work, then, in Bresson's aesthetics is what allows him to show human beings not as beings of intellect and will primarily, to show their actions as things that are not explicable by mere psychological insight and to show bodies not as a whole, but as things at the mercy of powers they cannot control, or rather, as things that work mechanically, controlled not by a will but by a body. It is the body that is trained in *Pickpocket*, with the hands learning by repetition and exercise to make their own ways in the ways of the world, to move with and against other bodies. Bodies in the world, observed by a camera, do not move in accordance with any language of signification – the actions of hands do not form a language, properly speaking. They have to be taken as they are. Hands, in close-ups, bring bodies in contact with the world; they are the means of very concrete transactions. Images of hands, in Bresson's view, escape rhetoric and representation (and therefore the merely symbolic) in much the same way that the Eucharist's *hoc* escapes being bound to the realm of merely symbolical representation.

I will soon come to another important point: Bresson's work with his actors. Let me, however, just mention that you can find other means of avoiding symbolical signification in his films. The general emphasis on sounds is another very important part of his aesthetics, which would certainly deserve further elaboration. In *L'Argent* it is mostly the sound of steps, a sound that, like the movement of hands, tends to emphasize transition rather than duration, offers a rhythm of being there and being gone, of never being at the same place in consecutive moments of time. Another striking feature of *L'Argent* is the importance of doors, which function not as metaphors of transition, but rather as events and instances of the threshold-like character of signification in Bresson's film.

Representation

Bresson negates money by supposing that it is counterfeit from the beginning. Money is the signifier that does not signify in the way of the *hoc*, open to distinct ideas and therefore open to the miracle of transubstantiation. As the signifier that can signify all or nothing, it actually seems very close to this openness, but it is exactly this proximity that makes it so thoroughly and irredeemably counterfeit.

---

3 Bresson in an interview, quoted in: http://www.mastersofcinema.org/bresson/Words/CTSamuels.html.

Money is, you could say, the exemplary signifier of language, basically empty in a way that is strictly opposite to the openness of the *hoc*. The *hoc* would completely lose its sense and use when disconnected from the body it ends referring to, i.e. from its inherently deictic moment. In its deixis the *hoc* can refer to the bread and the body, but only in connection with the priest's "I" (or "my" as in "my body") that speaks of itself in the manner of the *hoc*. The priest's "I" becomes the "I" of Jesus Christ and only by the performative power of this "I" performs the transubstantiation.

Money then, in Bresson's Jansenist reading, is the *hoc* that has disconnected its association with *any body*. It is counterfeit because it is open to any kind of signification, of completely arbitrarily representing one thing at one moment, and another the next. Money therefore has to be negated, just as the sign has to be negated insofar as it functions as representation. The sinful image is the image as rhetorical representation, representation being the production of a persuasion that what is represented is real, but not real in the sense of a real presence. And the manifestation of a real presence is exactly what Bresson – rather perversely – aims at. From early on in his career he refused to work with professional actors, abhorring the calculated delivery of words, as well as bodies and gestures, that comes with the training. Actors in his opinion are virtuosos of using their own bodies and words as tools and instruments of signification; they know how to do and represent things with gestures and words. He, however, wants to catch his "models" (that is the word he uses instead of actors) unawares – but he is no Pygmalion in disguise, because he does not want them to follow his intentions, but wants to be caught by the lack of awareness that only the camera brings to the fore. So indeed he does model – or rather prepare – his actresses and actors, but not by giving them psychological instructions. His instructions are, on the contrary, of a very material banality: Bresson very meticulously dictates gazes, gestures, movements, flat line delivery, and by sheer repetition of takes (twenty takes for one single shot were common) pushes the models into a state of automatic "acting". That there is a deliberate logic behind this becomes obvious when you read the aphorisms Bresson collected under the title *Notes on the Cinematographer*. The following is just one typical example:

> Models who have become automatic (everything weighed, measured, timed, repeated ten, twenty times) and are then dropped in the medium of the events of your film – their relations with the objects and persons around them will be *right*, because they will not be *thought*.[4]

4 Robert Bresson, *Notes on the Cinematographer*. Trans. by Jonathan Griffin (Copenhagen: Green Integer, 1997), p. 32.

And, in the same gist:

> To your models: "Don't think what you're saying, don't think what you're doing." And also: "Don't think *about* what you say, don't think *about* what you do".[5]

Only by fitting the models and their actions, words, gestures, gazes, and movements into a background of images and sounds that is supposed to be on the same "semiotic" level as the gestures of acting is the apparition of a real presence made possible, a real presence, more precisely, that is something like the re-emergence of a real nature. Behind this idea – which Bresson followed with unprecedented strictness –, there is, no doubt, a paradox to be found, which the director himself articulated like this: "Nature: what the dramatic art suppresses in favour of a naturalness that is learned and maintained by exercise."[6] Or: "Nine-tenths of our movements obey habit and automatism. It is anti-nature to subordinate them to will and to thought."[7]

The movement Bresson imagines here (and in his films) is a movement that goes back to nature (or, rather, a paradise of real presences) by going beyond the artificial naturalness that enters the world by words and actions that are thought and not merely done. This state of redemption from naturalness, however, can be made visible, according to Robert Bresson, only by the cinematographer's work. This suggests that in questions of vision the human eye and its preconceived perceptions can never be trusted. According to Bresson, our natural ways of seeing are always already too close to the intellect as a faculty of abstraction. He believes that it is the mechanical and therefore neutral camera that becomes the medium of truth and revelation. It reveals that which cannot be seen by the unaided human eye, it reveals that which can be perceived only in the proper vision made possible by the camera image:

> There are so many things our eyes don't see. But the camera sees everything. We are too clever, and our cleverness plays us false. We should trust mainly our feelings and those senses that never lie to us. Our intelligence disturbs our proper vision of things.[8]

Bresson's editing and his narration aim at a complicity with the camera, not with the intellect. The cinematographer can never know what will become visible in his film; he has to wait, in other words, for a miracle to happen. This miracle,

---

5 ibid., p. 25.

6 ibid., p. 18.

7 ibid., p. 32.

8 Interview, op. cit. And, even more explicitly: "What no human eye is capable of catching, no pencil, brush, pen of pinning down, your camera catches without knowing what it is, and pins it down with a machine's scrupulous indifference." Bresson, *Notes on the Cinematographer*, p. 36.

however, takes place without flourishes, but possesses a certain Jansenist matter-of-factness, which is not a matter-of-factness in the sense of the matter and fact of materialism, though. Bresson is not at all interested in the material world, or only insofar as what is at stake in his aesthetics is the overcoming and redemption of this material world. Bresson's aesthetics are all about this possibility of redemption.

Aesthetics of Transubstantiation

All the fundamental decisions of Bresson's aesthetics, his attempts to counter the counterfeit rhetorical and representational signs of language and of money, his determination to elicit gestures instead of expressions from his actor-models: all this works towards an aesthetics of transubstantiation that hinges on the non-arbitrary emptiness of *hoc*-like images that do not distinctly refer to or represent anything. Bresson himself wrote about the status of the image in his films:

> If an image, looked at by itself, expresses something sharply, if it involves an interpretation, it will not be transformed on contact with other images. The other images will have no power over it, and it will have no power over the other images. Neither action, nor reaction. It is definitive and unusable in the cinematographer's system.[9]

This theory and practice of the image's serial transformation and lack of definition lies at the core of its possible transubstantiation. The *hoc* of every image can be transformed by its progress towards an ever-open horizon of possible interpretations or readings. This openness, however, is by no means what we have learned to regard as a 'postmodern' openness that sees the sign as something that evades distinctness for the sake of a never ending play of meanings. The semiotics of the *hoc* does not presuppose a rift between the signifier and the signified that can never be overcome. The openness of the *hoc,* the openness of Bresson's images and transformations, is an openness to only one thing: the miracle. It would be a hubris from which Bresson refrains ever to say that the transubstantiation truly takes places in his films – as, of course, he would have to assume Jesus Christ's place to posit with any certainty that the miracle took place. The transubstantiation, however, will never be acted out by a Eucharist that – as in the Calvinist version – has to be taken merely metaphorically. Metaphor is never enough, signs are never enough, rhetoric is never enough for Bresson. They always are as counterfeit as money – because they make meaning in merely human ways. Money, you could say, is the most

---

9 ibid., p. 21.

extreme form of metaphor (and the sign), as it connects what has no true connection; it is a virtuoso of equivalence that posits value, but has value only as long as you believe in it. What makes it counterfeit, is the necessity of belief. Belief, however, is never enough for the Jansenist Bresson. There is, in this world, no guarantee that the miracle will happen. However, as long as we believe in monetary and metaphorical semiotics, Bresson says, we are not even open to the miracle that is never guaranteed, but always possible. If we believe in the workings of money and metaphor we believe too easily and too soon.

The aesthetics of Bresson, and of *L'Argent*, then, are an aesthetics that remain open to the miracle of transubstantiation by insisting on the non-metaphorical and non-distinct *hoc*-ness of its cinematography – cinematography for Bresson being much more than merely a production of images. Bresson searches for images and gestures and words that, like the *hoc* of the Eucharist, are not representative or expressive, neither metaphor nor metonymy. He shows hands that present – just as the deictic word *hoc* presents –, but do not represent, hands that hand on meaning from one sense of the *hoc* to the other, hands that go where their owner does not send them. Only when the hands and the models and their gestures come together in cinematography might an aesthetic redemption possibly have taken place:

> If, on the screen, the mechanism disappears and the phrases you have made them say, the gestures you have made them make, have become one with your models, with your film, with you – then a miracle.[10]

Coda: Allegory of Transubstantiation, Paradise

I admit that I have hardly mentioned the story told by *L'Argent*, the story of an innocent man turned into a serial killer by the machinations of money. It is a complex, even baffling, story that has been read as a complete darkening of Bresson's views, which had never been assumed to be very bright ones, anyway. I think, however, that this interpretation might be completely wrong, in a sense. There is no doubt that the world Bresson depicts is always a fallen world, waiting for and in dire need of redemption. The more miserable our lives, the more necessary this redemption. I have tried to describe his aesthetics as, in their own way, extremely optimistic: redemption is possible in the transubstantiating miracle of the Eucharist. Only an aesthetics that aims to repeat the Eucharist by artistic means can itself remain open to redemption. (There is no denying that

---

10 ibid., p. 43.

Bresson puts his cinematography in a singular place; the rest of movie history in his explicitly stated opinion just confirms the fallenness of a fallen world.)

What is most baffling about *L'Argent,* however, is the heretic daring, with which it not only aims at a trans-substantiative aesthetics but also tells an allegorical story of a material transubstantiation. The *hoc* and the hands work as shifters in a transformative series that in its own very serious way retells, in a skewed, even perverted version, the story of Jesus Christ. The money that starts it all, counterfeit from the beginning, the money in Yvon's innocent hands, is first replaced by the hazelnut flower he offers to the innocent woman with a presenting gesture, the nut lying in his open hand, which can be read as the equivalent of the *hoc*. This hazelnut flower, Yvon seems to say, is my body. And this hazelnut flower that replaced the money is in the end replaced by the bloody axe, with which Yvon killed the woman and her family, as if to say: this is my blood. So *L'Argent* retells the gospel in replacing the saviour by a serial killer. Bresson surely does not mock his own beliefs here. What he rather wants to make thinkable is the scandalous idea that redemption can be effected by the hands even of this serial killer. And the serial killer is by no means a metaphor, he has to be taken as crassly literally as the transubstantiation, which itself, taken literally, by dint precisely of its character as a miracle, is an act of cannibalism. Bresson demonstrates nothing less than the possibility that in the *hoc* of Yvon's, an innocent killer's hands, the transubstantiation of money into blood can take place in front of our very eyes.

So, to come back to the beginning, where does all this leave us with regard to Robert Bresson's project of retelling the story of *Genesis*? There is, I would still argue, no way he could have done it – at least not without completely reinventing his cinematography. His aesthetics are always already post-adamic and fit only a world in urgent need of redemption, in need of the transubstantiating sacrifice taking place in the bloody deed of the Eucharist. According to Bresson, we live in the world of the counterfeit that is a world of money and false signification. You can believe in redemption and Bresson figured out ways of presenting things in their *hoc*-ness in the most austere and sinister ways imaginable. The paradise before the fall, however, would have to be beyond presentation, it would be the sheer presence of things, not the real presence of Christ in the bread and the blood. There is no image to show that. There is no back door to paradise for Bresson's cinematography.

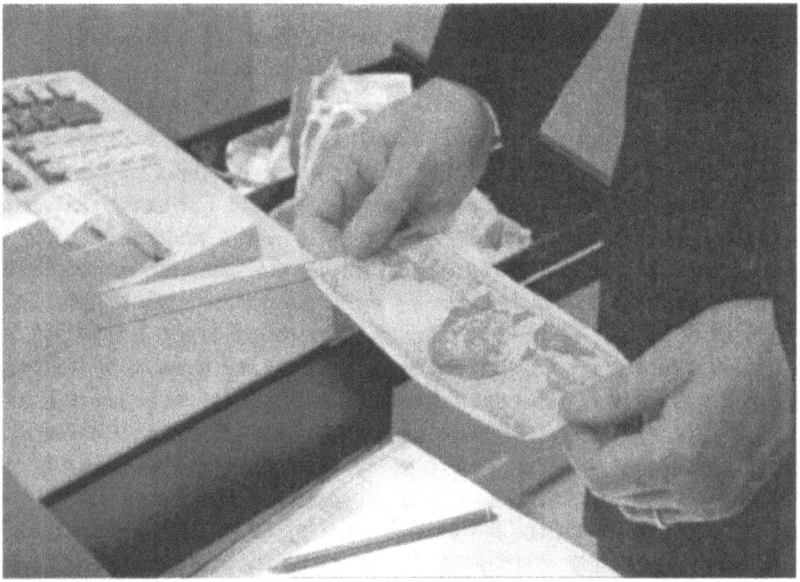

Image 1

Image 2

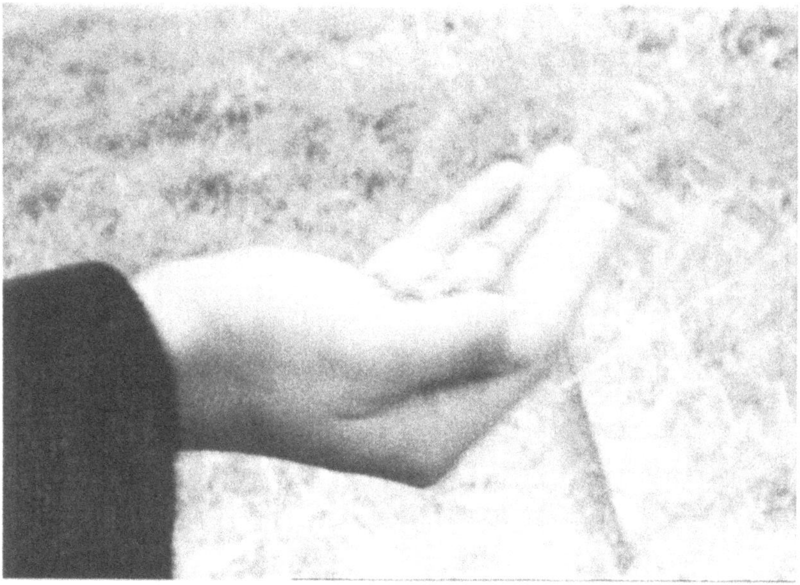

Figure 3

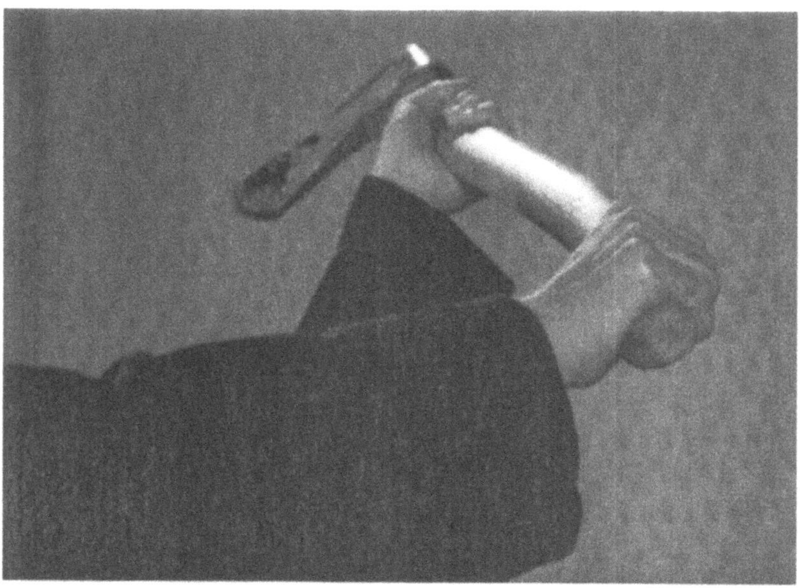

Figure 4

Ailbhe Thunder

Honour in the Dollar? Filming the Virtual Economy from *Wall Street* to *Boiler Room*

Money has always involved signification and thus is homologous with other representational forms, as seen in the work of Marc Shell or Jean-Joseph Goux. While gold money appears to embody the value it claims to represent, the development of paper money underlined the role of credit in what was an inherently unstable signifying structure, a development apparently mirrored in the instabilities of modernism. Virtual or electronic money marks a further shift, thus the uncertainty generated by the endlessly deferred cybercapital of the virtual economy seems to mirror the crisis of representation prevalent in postmodern literary theory. Despite such apparent parallels, fictional representations of stock market speculation typically rely on conventional narrative structures in order to contain the crises of speculation engendered by the virtual economy. The bull markets in the American stock market of the mid 80s and late 90s provide two such moments of crisis, and are represented in two remarkably similar film narratives: Oliver Stone's *Wall Street* (1987) and Ben Younger's *Boiler Room* (2000). In either case the conventional narrative structure is used to convey a cautionary tale about the temptations of illicit market behaviour. However, treated together, the similarity between these tales exposes their conventionality. Through both its explicit and unacknowledged references to Wall Street, along with other financial fictions, *Boiler Room* poses as a counterfeit – a tale which troubles the real/fictional distinction upon which both plots depend. In so doing, it also investigates the relationship between financial selling and storytelling and inadvertently questions the credibility of all narrative, economic or otherwise.

Financial trading, the arcane world of stocks, securities, indexes and derivatives, poses a particular challenge for the fictional representation of economic institutions. The obscure language of trading often seems too impenetrable to be grasped by the reader unversed in such texts. In the fiction of market culture attention is often paid, therefore, to the culture of consumption which attends the character who finds success in this obscure world, avoiding the challenge of narrating market transactions themselves. In Oliver Stone's *Wall Street*, however, a serious effort is made to represent the world of stock market speculation in the cut-throat 1980s.[1] Thus, the action of the film is concentrated

---

1 *Wall Street*, dir. Oliver Stone, Twentieth Century Fox, 1987.

within the corporate offices of investment bankers, lawyers and risk arbitrageurs, cutting from trading rooms selling stock to public investors to the trading floors of the New York Stock Exchange itself. On at least two occasions protracted sequences narrate the history of a single equity's journey through the market, capturing in cinematic form the kind of information typically represented by a single undulating line on a financial chart. To this end, Stone constructed elaborate facsimile sets of bank trading rooms, and employed numerous technical advisers including investment banker Kenneth Lipper, with whose help he gained access to the New York Stock Exchange and was permitted to film scripted scenes using real brokers "during trading hours"[2].

This effort to attain verisimilitude on the part of the film's makers inevitably risks alienating the viewer. Writing on the critical reception of *Wall Street* Martin Fridson notes that some reviewers complained that the "meticulous fidelity to details of securities industry practices and language" made it "inaccessible to a lay audience".[3] In order to illuminate the obscurities of market speculation, then, *Wall Street* relies on the conventions of classic realist narrative. The plot is constructed around a dominant central character with whom the viewer can identify and who acts as a tour guide through the unfamiliar world which the film portrays. Our guide is Bud Fox, whose oxymoronic name manages to suggest both naivety and guile, a combination essential for his role as market neophyte. From the opening sequence, we trail Bud on his lengthy commute to Wall Street, his transport changes and the escalating crowds increasing the sense in which he takes the viewer deep into the heart of things, the centre of the financial world. Our identification with Bud is emphasised as the sequence culminates in a long tracking shot where we follow him into the confusing environment of his office at investment bank Jackson Steinem, where he works as an account executive selling stock to public investors on the phone.

The earnest verisimilitude of the film is carefully managed so as not to risk alienating the viewer entirely. Bud's day at the office thus unfolds with a lengthy sequence which alternately depicts the world of financial trading and inducts the viewer into that world. As the market opens the camera tracks away from Bud and enters into the frenzy of Jackson Steinem's salesroom, the rising babble of unexplained terminology and flashing LED screens apparently offering the

---

2 Stone's quest for accuracy is described in detail in Martin S. Fridson, "Wall Street", in Robert Brent Toplin (ed.), *Oliver Stone's USA: Film, History and Controversy* (Lawrence: University of Kansas Press, 2000), pp. 120-134; and in Oliver Stone "On Seven Films", in Toplin (ed.), op. cit., pp. 219-248, in which Stone recalls that "The scripted scene from the movie was played by real brokers on the floor *during trading hours*." (p. 235)

3 Fridson, "Wall Street", op. cit., p. 120.

unmediated access of reportage. The documentary effect is extended as the film cuts between Jackson Steinem and the trading floor at the New York Stock Exchange. However, the establishing crane shot gives the viewer a point of view above the pandemonium of the frenzied action. For the plot to unfold the viewer must be made familiar with some of the tools of market analysis; thus, we return to Bud, and watch him check on the price of a stock for a client. He does this by typing the three letter 'ticker' by which any stock is identified into his computer keyboard and the camera zooms in to note this, then cuts to the scrolling LED screen on which tickers and prices are displayed, so that the viewer can make the connection between the stock named by the client and the market convention of abbreviation. This point is reinforced throughout the film as the camera cuts continually back to the scrolling LED as each of the plot's main trades are played out. The visual narrative is thus carefully constructed both to expose the viewer to the confusion of this unfamiliar world, and to manage that confusion through the intervention of traditional cinematic techniques.

Employing conventional cinematic techniques, then, the narrative of *Wall Street* is also traditionally constructed in order to engage the interest of its viewers. *Wall Street* is a morality tale where forces of good and evil do battle for the soul of Everyman; as such its generic antecedents stretch back to classical and religious mythology. Further, a series of binary oppositions structure the narrative and operate in parallel to the good/evil dichotomy informing the film's moral code. The most obvious of these is the distinction between rich and poor as the plot is also one of reversed fortunes. Our Everyman, Bud Fox, is not part of the Wall Street elite but is the son of an airline maintenance worker, who grew up in Queens and won a scholarship to NYU. Despite the 'account executive' title, he is, as his father says, "a salesman" who spends his day cold-calling customers in order to sell them stock. This is entry-level stock-broking, despite Bud's ambitions to be a major "player" in the financial world – like Gordon Gekko, the billionaire financial mastermind whom Bud admires. Gekko is an aggressive and, we soon learn, corrupt market investor: a corporate raider, of the kind who were both vilified and praised in the 1980s for embodying the spirit of neoliberal free-market economic philosophy. The character of Gekko is at least partly modelled on Ivan Boesky, an infamous corporate raider who was convicted for dealing in insider information in 1986 and served a term in prison.[4] The crime of insider dealing, into which Gekko eventually inducts Bud, was prosecuted with increasing severity in the 1980s and is depicted in the film as an evil distortion of normal market practice.

4 Commentators note that Gekko is most likely a composite of Boesky and other infamous characters from the 1980s such as Michael Milken and Carl Ikahn.

On an obvious level, then, Bud's paternalistic role models – his actual father and his idol, Gekko – embody the dichotomies of poor/rich, honest/dishonest upon which the film is structured. A lifelong union representative, Bud's father also represents the voice of labour as opposed to that of capital, represented by Gekko. This, more interesting, dichotomy can further be read as an opposition between what can be referred to as the real (or old) economy of production and the virtual (or new) economy characterised by the inflated financial sector. Main Street versus Wall Street. The real/virtual binary is signalled in *Wall Street* through the character of Lou Mannheim, a gentlemanly older broker who exhorts the younger traders not to forget the "fundamentals" of financial trading: "The money you make for people creates science and research jobs. Don't sell that out."

Mannheim's approach appears as quaint as he does, however, and is evidently out of step with market conditions based on, as he complains, "too much cheap money sloshing around the world." He blames this on the abandonment, by Nixon, of the gold-standard, which had fixed the price of dollars in relation to gold, and thus in relation to all international currencies, since the end of the Second World War. The removal of the dollar from the gold-standard in 1971 led to a devaluation of the dollar in world markets intended to re-balance an international goods market which had no longer been operating in America's favour. A system of fixed values, anchored by the convertibility to gold was thus replaced by one of fluctuating values, and the deregulated financial sector was equipped to capitalise on such fluctuations. The comprehensive restructuring of the US Economy in the period following the devaluation gave rise to the mergers and acquisitions mania which proved so profitable for corporate raiders like Ivan Boesky. This seemed to accelerate the perception, so dominant in the film, of a virtual economy which is increasingly divorced from the real world of production. As one historian of the US Economy, Tom Kemp, puts it, increased market activity occurred alongside de-industrialization so that high interest rates designed to attract overseas investors to the American financial markets had the effect of "pushing up paper gains and favouring a proliferation of financial transactions which had little or no relationship to production."[5]

In fact, then, Lou Mannheim misrepresents the relationship between the financial sector and industry. While the trading of stocks was originally intended to guarantee a flow of funds from business to industry, the original *raison d'être* of the financial sector has long been superseded by its ability to manufacture money independently of the worth of the goods initially traded. It is in this sense

---

5 Tom Kemp, *The Climax of Capitalism: The U.S. Economy in the Twentieth Century* (London: Longman, 1990), p. 87.

that I refer to the financial sector as the virtual economy – as a discursive locale which claims a relationship to the real but continually threatens to supersede it. Writing on the fictionality of financial trading Sandra Sherman notes that "credit entails narrative". She continues:

> Within a regime of credit, where reality-in-time is configured by imagination, reality is recessive, a speculation on what might be. It "exists" as a representation. [...] [C]redit is always a potential cipher, a fiction with nothing behind it. Credit narratives, homologous with literary counterparts, appeal to imagination for consent to their truth claims.[6]

While I wish to argue for the narrative basis of stock market values which Sherman outlines, I would like to point out that I disagree with her characterisation of credit, here, as a "fiction" with nothing behind it. The virtual economy is not simply fictional, in the superficial sense she describes – rather it generates fictions which have real effects, and these fictions are stable only as long as they acquire credit by passing themselves off as real. *Wall Street* and *Boiler Room* are both texts concerned with this tension between the fictional and the real which lies at the heart of the uncertainties of financial speculation. It is their differing responses to this tension which I discuss further here.

The homological relationship described by Sandra Sherman exists, she argues, between the paper credit instruments of the early eighteenth century and the newly developing novel form – particularly the work of Defoe.[7] The apparent parallel which she uncovers between financial selling and literary tale-telling is reminiscent, however, of the work of French theorist Jean-Joseph Goux who claims to ascertain homologies between the money form and other signifying forms of any particular historical period.[8] Goux finds, for example, that modernist experimentation with the rules of realism in art and literature in the early years of the twentieth century has its corollary in the concurrent shift to a paper currency no longer grounded in the real or intrinsic value previously represented by metal money-forms[9]. Like Sherman, Goux does not claim that this homology is straightforwardly causal, with one field simply determining the other in a Marxian base-superstructure model. Thus, by placing emphasis on both art

---

6 Sandra Sherman, *Finance and Fictionality in the Early Eighteenth Century: Accounting for Defoe* (Cambridge: Cambridge UP, 1996), p. 28.

7 Cf. op. cit.

8 Jean-Joseph Goux, *Symbolic Economies: After Marx and Freud*, trans. Jennifer Curtiss Gage (New York: Cornell UP, 1990).

9 Jean-Joseph Goux, "Ideality, Symbolicity and Reality in Postmodern Capitalism", in Stephen Cullenberg, Jack Amariglio, David F. Ruccio (eds.), *Postmodernism, economics and knowledge* (London, New York: Routledge, 2001), pp. 166-81.

and money as modes of signification which may (or may not) display similar tendencies within any particular "sociosymbolic moment",[10] Goux's work offers one method for exploring the apparent disciplinary borderlines which we are concerned with here. My question, then, is what form might this homological relationship between art and money take in current (or relatively recent) cultural texts. What effect, for example, does the further abstraction of electronic money have upon Goux's model? Gesturing towards the contemporary domination of share capital – of the virtual economy over the 'real' economy – Goux asserts that a further shift has now taken place, whereby "money is no more than a mere trace in the indefinite circulation of debt", ushering economy into a "deconstructive regime of the sign, of value, of the real and time – and maybe, in the long term, the deconstruction of economy itself".[11] Thus Goux finds a historical homological encounter between the virtual economy and the poststructuralist philosophy of Jacques Derrida, whose account of the deferral of meaning in language Goux draws upon as expressive of the "sociosymbolic moment" of postmodern capitalism.[12]

What remains to be seen then, is whether this apparent historical conjunction is accompanied by similar shifts in the field of cultural representation. With its steadfastly binary structure and classical realist narrative, *Wall Street* seems to belie Goux's expectations. In fact, the representational strategy of Wall Street does engage with the uncertainties of market speculation in the virtual economy, but contains them through the imposition of the conventional structure. Thus Bud's narrative trajectory, and success in the financial sector, is only finally achieved when he illegally passes Gekko confidential information on the airline for which his father works, an action which results in his recruitment by Gekko for the crime of insider dealing. The episode illustrates the rigidity of the film's moral code. In order to fully transfer to the rich/capitalist/virtual economy side of the film's binary structure, Bud *must* also cross the honest/dishonest line, becoming an accomplice of the evil Gordon Gekko. Neither hard work nor education can guarantee him success, and he must betray his own real economy roots in the process. Bud's eventual downfall, brought about by his misplaced efforts to get Gekko to invest in the airline, rather than simply liquidating it, emphasise the film's artificial separation of the virtual from the real. The narrative resolution of *Wall Street* seeks then, to reaffirm the values of the real economy which had been under threat from an avaricious and speculative financial sector. In the closing moments of *Wall Street*, as Bud walks up the steps

10 ibid, p. 180.

11 ibid., p. 179f.

12 ibid., p. 180.

of the New York City Courthouse, preparing to face charges for his crimes, an extravagant crane shot pulls out to a position high above him emphasising the imposing edifice of the neoclassical justice building. The majesty of this shot, which then pans across the city to gaze at the towers of Wall Street, attempts to underline the centrality of the justice system in the proper working of the financial sector. While *Wall Street* may trouble the binaries slightly, they are ultimately re-imposed. The fact of their imposition is in itself troubling, however, and suppresses an underlying uncertainty regarding market speculation which gained new ground in the decade following the film's production. This uncertainty returns in *Boiler Room*.

Seth Davis, the rookie stock-seller and narrator of Ben Younger's 1999 film *Boiler Room*,[13] lives in a world saturated with economic narratives about shortcuts to financial success. His voiceover, as the film opens, emphasizes the ersatz quality of these get-rich-quick tales, drawn from popular culture and urban myth:

> I read this article a while back that said that Microsoft employs more millionaire secretaries than any other company in the world. They took stock options over Christmas bonuses. It was a good move…
>
> …..and then you turn on the TV and there's just more of it. The eighty-seven-million-dollar lottery winner, that kid actor that just made twenty million on his last movie, that internet stock that shot through the roof – you could have made millions on it if you just got in early.

In each of these stories financial success is largely a matter of good timing in a world where millions appear as if by magic, multiplying themselves in the hands of these lucky individuals as they go about the business of their everyday lives. For Seth, the effect of these endlessly repeated fictions is that they reinforce each other, insisting upon their own realisation: "I remember there was this photograph of one of the [Microsoft] groundskeepers next to his Ferrari – blew my mind. You see shit like that and it just plants seeds, makes you think it's possible, even easy." By mutual reinforcement the stories accumulate credit and enter the bounds of possibility – the fictional becoming real.

The period to the end of the 1990s, during which *Boiler Room* is set, was that of the longest bull market in American economic history. Despite the high-profile criminal cases of the mid-eighties and the 1987 'Black Monday' crash, both of which generated market mistrust, the bull market of the 1990s saw a return to economic investment conditions based on mergers, flotations of new internet based companies, and reinstated public optimism in the ability of markets to

---

13 *Boiler Room*, dir. Ben Younger, New Line Cinema, 2000.

generate easy money. This boom in market speculation, partly derived from the new possibilities of internet trading, saw an unprecedented rise in the number of individual Americans investing in stock,[14] and created a culture of credibility in financial storytelling such as Seth describes in the opening voiceover. The discursive field of *Boiler Room* is thus similar to *Wall Street*, as in both cases the rising market encourages a proliferation of economic storytelling which exacerbates the tension between the fictional and the real at the heart of the virtual economy. The similarities between the two films are marked by more than their economic backgrounds, however, as *Boiler Room* depends upon the same narrative conventions as *Wall Street*, orienting the viewer though the use of a central character, Seth, who is inducted into the gendered world of financial selling, where he is tempted to engage in illegal activity in return for untold wealth. With similarities extending, for example, to the subplot concerning Seth's relationship with his father, and even the use of stock characters, specific shots, and framing devices, it is possible to argue that *Boiler Room* amounts to a remake of *Wall Street*.

Writing on the Hollywood remake industry, Lucy Mazdon notes that remakes are often critically dismissed as evidence of the triumph of commercialism over creativity. This response, she argues, fails to engage with the pertinent issue of why certain kinds of stories get remade, nor does it pay attention to the significant issues raised by remakes concerning the relationship between an "original" and its "copy".[15] Moreover, bearing in mind David Wills' broad definition of the remake as "the possibility that exists for a film to be repeated in a different form,"[16] *Boiler Room's* repetition can thus be accounted for in the decisive differences between the texts as much as in their similarities.

The most obvious difference between the two films is the change in location. Just as the opening sequence in *Wall Street* emphasises Bud's journey into the

---

14 "An unprecedented boom in the stock market, combined with the ease of investing in stocks, led to a sharp increase in public participation in securities markets during the 1990s. The annual trading volume on the New York Stock Exchange, or 'Big Board', soared from 11,400 million shares in 1980 to 169,000 million shares in 1998. Between 1989 and 1995, the portion of all U.S. households owning stocks, directly or through intermediaries like pension funds, rose from 31 percent to 41 percent." – "How the U.S. Economy Works", http://usinfo.state.gov/products/pubs/oecon/chap5.htm.

15 Lucy Mazdon, "Introduction", in *Film remakes*, spec. issue of *Journal of Romance Studies* 4, no. 1 (2004), pp. 1-11.

16 David Wills, "The French Remark: Breathless and Cinematic Citationality", in Andrew Horton, Stuart Y. McDougal (eds.), *Play It Again, Sam: Retakes on Remakes* (Berkeley: UCP, 1998), p. 148.

centre of the financial universe, an early sequence in Boiler Room depicts Seth's opposing drive outwards – to a call centre located "off exit 53 of the Long Island Expressway, a good hour away from Wall Street" an opposition highlighted, as Seth repeatedly notes, by the diminishing skyline of Manhattan in his rear-view mirror. The opposition is further emphasised by the brokers with whom Seth works: coarse, grasping Wall Street hopefuls who lack the education and social skills which Bud Fox has acquired and who, despite their apparent wealth, are still riven by the racial insecurities which do not hamper their WASP counterparts. Completing the outward and downward dispersal of the social structure which comprises *Wall Street*, Seth's firm, J.T. Marlin – a financial scamming "boiler room" which employs high-pressure cold calling to sell unappealing stocks – draws its clients from the flood of new individual investors who were attracted to the market as it reached its peak at the end of the 1990s.

This extension of *Wall Street* is marked in *Boiler Room* by a further reversal which complicates the relationship between the two texts. Whereas, in Stone's film, the real economy of production seemed to provide a viable alternative to the speculative working of the financial sector, such an alternative is no longer possible in *Boiler Room*. Further, the moral economy of Wall Street is reversed – whereas Fox and Gekko are depicted as transgressive criminals, exploiting the rules of an imperfect but ostensibly honest marketplace, in *Boiler Room* all rules are in abeyance as the entire firm is engaged in a financial fraud about which only Seth seems to be even curious. The con, Seth eventually discovers, consists in their selling stock for companies which do not exist. The boiler room operates as a closed unit, issuing the shares in the name of a small group of individuals, who are all associates of J.T Marlin's creator Michael Brandtley, and then promoting them to its unlucky customers. In the discursive field of *Boiler Room* fake stocks are traded like Sherman's early credit instruments of the eighteenth century, perpetually deferring the question of their authenticity in order to remain in circulation. The fraud depends upon a structure of repetition which allows the stocks to pass as real – thus the fictional firm's name J.T Marlin plays upon its similarity to the real and celebrated financial house of J.P. Morgan in order to gain credibility when cold-calling clients. Equally, when Seth questions the legality of his trainer's instruction that he can lie about his market experience in order to "be whoever [he] want[s] to be" on the phone, he is assured that everyone does it, even on Wall Street. The effect is to emphasise the role of narrative at the heart of the financial transaction – as Seth hones his script, so his success increases. Such apparent ascendancy of the fictional over the real is further emphasised by the film's dependence on intertextual references to other financial fictions, such as David Mamet's *Glengarry Glen Ross* and, most notably, Stone's *Wall Street*. The explicit and unacknowledged presence of these fictions in *Boiler Room* emphasises the discursive field in which they all reside. Thus the conventionality of *Wall Street*, I wish to argue, once re-iterated in *Boiler Room*, becomes relativised, so that the real-fictional oppositions upon which its moral narrative depends become no longer tenable.

According to the editors of *Play it Again Sam: Retakes on Remakes*, texts which in some way announce to us that they are borrowing from other texts, call the relationship between original and copy into question with a particular intensity.[17] *Boiler Room's* remake of *Wall Street* exists at this level also, in an arresting sequence which I would now like to examine. As Seth becomes more committed to his new job at the boiler room, several sequences depict his integration with his new colleagues. On the first such occasion Seth arrives at a colleague's house where a number of J.T. Marlin's employees are already gathered, watching a movie and eating pizza. The soundscape of the sequence is complicated as Seth's voiceover is first overlaid with the intermittent strains of hip-hop which make up much of *Boiler Room's* soundtrack. As Seth enters the house, the voiceover ends, while the soundtrack continues to play against the new sound of film dialogue emanating from a television within the house. The camera pans through empty rooms to represent Seth's point of view as he searches for the source of the off-screen TV noise. The source, it turns out, is Oliver Stone's *Wall Street*, which is playing on the widescreen television around which Seth eventually finds his colleagues seated. The roving camera is finally arrested, as Seth pauses to take in the reverential audience, who are all viewed from behind and slightly above Seth, giving the impression of a congregation absorbed in the object of their gaze. At this moment, as the hip-hop theme fades away, a crescendo from *Wall Street* swells, so that the soundtrack of the earlier film is borrowed for the later one.

This merging of the two soundtracks foreshadows the action to follow, in which Seth's senior colleagues, for whom the viewing of *Wall Street* is evidently a ritual, begin to recite Gordon Gekko's dialogue in turn, reproducing not just the script but also the delivery, tone of voice and character of Gekko. As the momentum builds, Chris Varick, soon to be Seth's mentor, rises and crosses the floor to stand next to the television, taking up the position of gazed object and addressing the younger traders (seated on the floor) as though they were Bud Fox, to whom Gekko is speaking. The move may simply serve to emphasise the extent to which the young men have internalised Gekko's character; Chris, smoking a cigarette in the exact manner of Gekko, is able to mimic Michael Douglas without missing a beat, even though he is not looking at the screen. However, like the merging of the soundtracks, Chris' move also denotes a potential transgression, or

---

[17] Horton/McDougal (eds.), *Play It Again, Sam*, op. cit, p. 3.

invasion, from one film to the other, as Chris figuratively crosses the fourth wall and enters the filmic reality of *Wall Street*, embodying the character of Gekko, and becoming the object of his audience's attention. In so doing, he also takes up the subject-position offered to him by the world of the boiler room in its representation of the realm of finance, that of a broker by repetition, who maintains his position in the market by ritualistically embodying the traits which the 'real' broker Gekko represents. This subject-position is consequently offered to the younger brokers to whom he speaks, just as Gordon Gekko does to Bud Fox. Their collective response: "How do you do, Mr. Gekko, Bud Fox," is delivered in a chorus which evokes both twentieth century rap and classical Greek drama, indicating their shared adoption of the role offered.

On one level the younger traders' faithful repetition of Gekko's persona demonstrates the extent to which *Wall Street's* morality tale aspirations have backfired. Despite his portrayal as the devilish embodiment of market corruption, Gekko is resurrected here as a hero for the following generation of aspiring stockbrokers. The extent to which this has indeed occurred can be measured in the fact that Gekko's mantras such as "Lunch is for wimps" or "Greed is good" became slogans for the whole decade. However the excessive quotation of Gekko also emphasises the artificiality of the character, his status as a type which can be endlessly repeated. This alternative reading of the sequence draws upon the work of Jacques Derrida who, in his seminal essay "Signature Event Context", argues that citation can be a radical, subversive force. This subversion derives from the iterability of the signifying mark which enables it to be repeated in the absence of its original referent. Such iterability both constitutes the mark as a unified entity and inevitably subverts that unity through the fact that it can be repeated differently from itself.[18]

Through their careful re-enactment of Gekko's character, then, Chris and the others exemplify Derrida's initial assertion that "a certain self-identity" is recognizable within any signifying form, consisting, in the case of spoken language for example, of "empirical variations of tone, voice, etc., possibly of a certain accent" which "permit its recognition and repetition".[19] As they compete with each other to capture more accurately Michael Douglas' tone and speech pattern, Seth's colleagues conversely illustrate Derrida's subsequent assertion that the self-identity of the mark is also "paradoxically the division or dissociation of itself."[20] In his response to John Searle's critique of "Signature Event Context",

---

18 Jacques Derrida, "Signature Event Context", in *Limited Inc*, trans. Samuel Weber (Evanston, Illinois: Northwestern University Press, 1988), pp. 1-21.

19 ibid., p. 10.

20 ibid.

"Limited Inc a b c ...", Derrida re-clarifies the paradox which the condition of iterability imposes on all texts:

> For the structure of iteration [...] implies *both* identity *and* difference. Iteration [...] contains *in itself* the discrepancy of a difference that constitutes it as iteration.[21]

The self-identity of any mark or text is, Derrida tells us, merely an illusion. In order to be communicable, hence repeatable, it must draw upon conventional structures which make possible its re-iteration in a different context. As Chris mimics Gekko he communicates to himself and others not only that they can all, to some extent, be Gekko, but also that Gekko can never uniquely be himself. This effect is achieved, not because they succeed in their efforts to embody Gekko's character but because they embody his character differently from what Stone or Douglas apparently intended. This "discrepancy of a difference" is, Derrida tells us, constituted in the primary text itself, or, the possibility for a mark to be reiterated in a manner which preserves its identity while activating its difference "constitutes it as iteration."

As with Gekko, so with Stone's *Wall Street. Boiler Room's* excessive dependence on the earlier film exposes not simply the extent to which the characters in *Boiler Room* are inauthentic copies, but also the iterability of *Wall Street* itself – its ability to be repeated, hence its own dependence on conventional types such as the evil Gordon Gekko. This iterability is, Derrida suggests, a condition of all narrative, although, as a classic realist text, *Wall Street* avoids drawing attention to this, concentrating on chastising the fictionality of deviant market behaviour, but ignoring the fictionality at the heart of its own construction. In his later work *Given Time 1: Counterfeit Money,* Derrida reworks the trope of iterability more specifically in relation to the monetary form. He draws attention here, to the way in which counterfeit money – an almost perfect copy of an apparent original – is only able to circulate as money by not drawing attention to its status as a copy.[22] Like the circulation of fake stocks in *Boiler Room*, the circulation of counterfeit money exposes, Derrida says, the conventionality of a system which can only consist in passing itself off as real. In emphasising and exploiting the dependence of financial selling on narrative exchange, *Boiler Room* destabilises the apparent opposition between the fictional and the real, hence demonstrating the wider uncertainties at work in the financial

---

21 Derrida, "Limited Inc a b c ...", in *Limited Inc*, op.cit., p. 53.

22 Jacques Derrida, *Given Time: 1. Counterfeit Money*, trans. Peggy Kamuf (Chicago, London: University of Chicago Press, 1992).

economy. In the process, it undermines not just *Wall Street's* efforts at realism but also the truth claims of all narrative – fictional or financial.

Wall Street depends, then, on the opposition between the real and the fictional, in order to make a moral point about market corruption. But, since narrative exchanges are the condition of possibility of all markets, the opposition between reality and fiction, or honest and dishonest, is not as clear-cut as the film implies. In *Boiler Room*, the strict opposition between reality and fiction is removed, and everyone is caught up in the potentially illegal credit fraud – by the end of the film even Seth's father, a judge, has become partially involved. Despite the eventual intervention of the FBI, and a narrative resolution similar to, though lacking the power of *Wall Street's*, it is clear that the fraud works not because the boiler room operates outside the law, but because it operates within the discursive field of the financial economy, its fictions reinforced by everyday stories of financial success. While Seth may ultimately discover that the stocks he is selling are indeed fake, significantly he is reluctant to act upon the knowledge – asking his girlfriend whether in fact it makes any difference. Her response: "You tell me, Seth – you tell me" only defers resolution further into narrative, and prompts the continuous re-telling in which Seth's first-person voiceover is engaged. His credibility as the narrator of his own story is ultimately problematised by the narrative which he relates – a tale about his success as a teller of tall tales. The final resolution of *Wall Street* is thus less tenable once repeated in *Boiler Room*, a text which, in turn, destabilises the artificial opposition between the fictional and the real upon which *Wall Street* relies. In highlighting the extent to which all market systems depend on the production and circulation of narrative, *Boiler Room's* critique proves more troubling than *Wall Street's* unconvincing morality tale.

Joyce Goggin

Casinos and Sure Bets: *Ocean's Eleven* and Cinematic Money

The 2001 remake of *Ocean's Eleven*[1] opens as Danny Ocean, played by George Clooney, is released from prison after a three-year sentence. Ocean, whose ambition seemingly knows no bounds, immediately sets to work recruiting eleven highly specialised criminals with whom he executes the heist to end all heists in Las Vegas. Banking on the skills of his team, Ocean concocts a strategy to break into a vault beneath the three thousand block of Las Vegas Boulevard where cash holdings for The Bellagio, The Mirage and The MGM Grand are deposited. Naturally, the job is virtually impossible to pull off because, as Ocean explains to his team of con artists and pyrotechnical experts, the Bellagio's vault is located 200 feet below ground making it the "least accessible ever built". What is more, the vault boasts a "security system that rivals a nuclear weapons silo"; is approachable only by an elevator equipped with voice, finger print and motion detectors; and, once they've managed to reach it, the thieves will have to deal with the "most elaborate vault door ever constructed".

But the "good news" is the size of the haul and the assurance that the money will be in the vault once they crack it. According to Ocean, on weekdays the vault contains 60-70 million, on weekends this figure climbs to 80-90 million and on fight nights – like the night of the cinematic caper in question – casinos are required to hold 150 million or more in anticipation of extra traffic. The money will be there, Ocean explains, because "the Nevada Gaming Commission stipulates that a casino must hold in reserve enough cash to cover every chip played on the floor" at any given time.[2]

---

1 *Ocean's Eleven* directed by Steven Soderbergh (Warner Bros. 2001) is a remake of the film with the identical title, directed by Lewis Milestone (Warner Bros. 1960).

2 The movie version of the law is not entirely accurate since the bankroll requirement is not based on outstanding chips but rather on total games and gaming devices and potential jackpot exposure:
"**6.150 Minimum bankroll requirements.** Each nonrestricted licensee and each person licensed as an operator of an inter-casino linked system shall maintain, in such manner as the chairman may approve or require, cash or cash equivalents in an amount sufficient to reasonably protect the licensee's or operator's patrons against defaults in gaming debts owed by the licensee or operator [...]. Failure to maintain the minimum bankroll required by this section, or a higher bankroll as required by the chairman

In what follows I will argue that Ocean's reference to the Gaming Commission's stipulation that casinos cover every chip in play bears a wealth of information concerning contemporary constructions of money. For instance, what the gaming commission's regulation means is that *unlike* banks, casinos must be able to cover all the financial markers it issues at any given time. In the world of post-modern finance presented in the film, Ocean's 'good news' amounts to a proclamation that Vegas casinos are a safer bet than banks. In this article I will also have occasion to discuss how casino space since the original *Ocean's Eleven* (1960) is portrayed as being somehow analogous to bank space, replete with signifiers of high culture such as priceless works of art. The purpose of my argument is ultimately to show how the representation of casino space and policy in relation to that of banks in the film, conveys a number of remarkable notions about money and how it is secured, how it circulates and what it signifies.

Banks and Casinos

My first observation is directly related to Ocean's 'good news' about casino holdings on fight nights and how the presence of sufficient holdings is required by law under the Nevada Gaming Commission. The thinking behind this stipulation, however conscious or unconscious, is a reaction to past disasters in the history of banking that accompanied the advent of paper money. Most western European Banks began to circulate paper money late in the 17th century as a convenience because paper has the singular advantage of being more portable than coins and quantities of precious metals.[3] The function of early paper money was to stand in for coin and specie as a written assurance that the holder would be able to collect its value in hard currency. In its initial phases then, paper money was a sort of I.O.U., which might subsequently be signed over to second and third parties in exchange for goods or services.

---

pursuant to this section, or failure to notify the board of any deficiencies, is an unsuitable method of operation (Adopted: 10/87. Effective: 1/88. Amended: 11/90; 5/00)."

3 Earlier examples occurred in Italy in the 14th century and other incidental cases have also been cited. I refer to the late 17th century as a significant moment because it was then that paper money became an increasingly common mode of exchange whereas earlier it was still an exceptional practice. On bills of exchange and early paper money in 14th-century Italy see Jack Weatherford, *The History of Money* (New York: Three Rivers Press, 1997), pp. 72-79.

The Amsterdam bank, established in 1609, was among the first European banks to experiment with the expanded circulation of paper notes of credit. These notes were issued as a receipt to an original depositor who entrusted the bank with his hard currency. This sedentary deposit could then be loaned out in the form of another bank note, which in principle could also be redeemed for hard currency. If all went well, the hard currency remained in the bank as a sedentary deposit, while credit notes were drawn up for the depositor and subsequent borrowers who paid interest on these loans. The borrower might then purchase goods with the loan note as opposed to redeeming it for hard currency, which in turn the recipient might choose to use in payment of goods. "Meanwhile back at the bank", wrote Galbraith, "interest was being received on the original loan" and therefore, new money was being miraculously generated.[4] In this way, notes written on loans were able to circulate more or less uneventfully provided no one, or at least few investors in the chain, wished to redeem their notes for real specie at the bank of issue.

Problems did arise however with this system later in the 17th century, because the owners of the Bank of Amsterdam also happened to be the directors of the Dutch East India Company. In their role as colonial traders, the directors of the East India trading company were frequently in need of money to outfit their merchant fleet or to cover their costs until ships returned from ports of call with saleable goods. This contingency forced bank owners to draw directly on the deposits with which they had been entrusted, or to circulate more paper money than specie contained in the bank's vaults. Although enormously appealingly, the practice of simply printing a little more paper money as a strategy for raising funds had the unfortunate consequence of making depositors nervous. And when a group of suspicious investors arrived at the Bank of Amsterdam in 1672 demanding hard currency for deposit notes in excess of what the bank actually held, disaster was narrowly averted by allowing the irate mobs to inspect the bank's vaults in small, staggered groups.

Less than a century later in France, a similarly delicate financial structure was instituted by John Law who founded the Banque Générale de la France in 1716. Law's system was based on a plan for refinancing the royal debt through a system of credit founded on paper money or *billets d'État*. At the same time he developed the *Compagnie d'Occident* – also known as the Mississippi Company, which was financed through the sale of shares paid in the new paper money. Like the founders of the Bank of Amsterdam, Law printed paper money in excess of hard currency available to back it, giving rise to the well-founded fear that he had

4 See John Kenneth Galbraith, *Money: Whence it Came, Where it Went* (New York: Houghton Mifflin, 1975), p. 19.

gambled with investors' trust.[5] In order to rally investor trust, Law assembled more than 6000 impressed men, equipped with pikes and shovels, who were to be sent off to mine gold in New Orleans. The men quickly "[d]ispersed themselves over the country, sold their tools [...] and returned to their old course of life".[6] Law's system finally collapsed in December of 1720 as hundreds were trampled to death while attempting to redeem their inflated paper money for specie at the Banque Générale.

Some two hundred years later in 1933, however, the United States made the bold move to sever paper money from the gold standard for domestic trade and by 1971 Richard Nixon had done the same for all international trade within the United States. At this point, paper money began to circulate definitively and on its own without the indexical safety net of specie to back it.[7] Hence today, as Brian Rotman has pointed out, paper money no longer makes any pretence of being redeemable for the amount of precious metal that it would formerly have guaranteed, so that "a dollar bill presented to the U.S. Treasury entitles the holder [only] to an identical replacement of itself" (89).[8] In a similar vein, Jean Baudrillard read New York's former Twin Towers as the perfect icon of the American economy, because the towers reflected this new concept of paper money by referring to nothing save their own identical twin.[9] "The most interesting thing about them" he has since written, "was that there were two of them, and the way they were positioned, not exactly next to each other, but north

---

5 See Charles Mackay, *Extraordinary Popular Delusions and the Madness of Crowds* [1841] (New York: Barnes & Noble, 1993), p. 31f. On John Law's System see Thomas Kavanagh, *Enlightenment and the Shadows of Chance: The Novel and the Culture of Gambling in Eighteenth-Century France* (Baltimore and London: John Hopkins U.P., 1993), pp. 67-104. See also Mackay, op. cit., pp. 1-46.

6 Mackay, *Extraordinary Popular Delusions and the Madness of Crowds*, p. 32.

7 See Marc Shell, *Art & Money* (Chicago: The University of Chicago Press, 1995), p. 108, John Kenneth Galbraith, *Money: Whence it Came, Where it Went*, p. 48, and Brian Rotman, *Signifying Nothing: The Semiotics of Zero* (Stanford: Stanford U.P., 1987), p. 88f.

8 Brian Rotman, *Signifying Nothing: The Semiotics of Zero* (Stanford: Stanford U.P, 1987), p. 89.

9 Jean Baudrillard, *Simulacra and Simulation*. Trans. Sheila Faria Glaser (Ann Arbor: The University of Michigan Press, 1981), pp. 75-79. Note as well that the Tower One of the Twin Trade Towers was built in 1972 while Tower Two was built in 1973. In other words, their construction coincides with the economic developments to which I refer above.

and south [each] at the perfect angle in relation to the other [...] they seemed to echo one another other, an exercise in architectural repetition".[10]

In *Ocean's Eleven* 2001 the effects of what Baudrillard would call duplication without representation are amplified. Yet at the same time the film seems to call nostalgically for some kind of standard or representational baseline. For while in the 'real world' in which *Ocean's Eleven* was produced, money has been severed from its original signified, namely the gold standard, for some time and has become a gliding signifier whose value is contextually determined, Ocean and his friends expect that paper money itself will now act as the standard for chips in circulation on the casino floor. In other words, in the world of postmodern finance presented in the film where the notion of value has become abstract in the extreme, paper money has taken on a sort of false indexicality as an ersatz gold standard, guaranteeing payment for casino money. More strikingly still, the concept of Ocean's heist rests on the notion that casinos may be counted upon to follow the law to the letter, ultimately making them a better and more secure bet than a bank.

In the cinematic context of *Ocean's Eleven* therefore, the notion that casinos might be more secure than banks begins to make sense. This may be read as the logical extension of the current synergy between gambling and public finance, which has taken hold in most countries in the western world. What I am referring to is the growing trend to generate funds for old age pensions, medical insurance and public education through lotteries and casinos, as well as the practice of paying off pensions in volatile stocks as a means of transferring risk to the recipient.[11] On a grander scale, the generation of funds through currency markets, futures trading and hedging all seem to have more in common with gambling than with their somewhat tamer cousin, speculation.

Likewise, investment has also undergone significant change since paper money has been severed from its gold referent, particularly with respect to the notion of what constitutes an investment. As economist Jim Davis has explained, where once tangible assets such as real estate, equipment and inventories

---

10 See the Mississippi Review: http://www.mississippireview.com/2004/Vol10No1-Jan04/1001-0104-00-percesepe-intro.html

11 On the transfer of risk to the individual see Ulrich Beck, *Risk Society: Towards a New Modernity* (London: SAGE Publications, 1992), in particular chapter "On the Logic of Wealth Distribution and Risk Distribution", pp. 19-51.

represented 78 per cent of the assets of US non-financial corporations, 70 percent of trade is now based on intangible commodities such as intellectual property and goodwill.[12]

Gambling, Vegas and Art

Ocean's Eleven has further deep ties to the arguments I have been making about money that might be somewhat more obscure and in need of explanation.

Steve Wynn, Las Vegas entrepreneur and art collector, opened his private collection of art masterpieces to the public in the Wynn Vegas Resort, a casino Wynn built as an homage to himself. His collection of impressionist and post-impressionist works includes a Van Gogh a Picasso, a Renoir, a Manet, a Monet, Matisses and a Cézanne, but not Cézanne's famous red *Card Players*, a painting of gamblers that appears behind Julia Roberts throughout a scene in a casino art gallery. In her role as Tess Ocean, Roberts curates and buys paintings for a collection much like the one housed in Wynn's Bellagio gallery. That the set designers for the movie chose this particular painting of all the paintings that Wynn *does not* own is significant.

Cézanne painted the two gamblers that appear behind Julia Roberts in the gallery scene to which I am referring three times, and the paintings have had a long and interesting history, including a stint as the anti-counterfeiting device on the last French 100 franc bill to circulate before the Euro. Moreover, Cézanne's *Card Players* along with other paintings of gamblers appeared not only on the French franc but also in countless advertisements, as well as on novelty items, T-shirts and telephone cards throughout the 90s. Given this, it is probably safe to say that the makers of *Ocean's Eleven* chose the painting to signify high culture and lots of money because it depicts gamblers. and they knew that audiences would recognise the painting and have certain associations with it. At the same time, I would like to read the cinematic use of the Cézanne as a pun on art as the perfect commodity, which comes to be worth enormous amounts of money based on vague notions such as artistic value. Because the price of artistic commodities

---

12 "Fifty years ago, tangible assets such as real estate, equipment and inventories represented 78 per cent of the assets of US non-financial corporations. Today, the proportion is 53 per cent, according to Federal Reserve data. Much of the shift is due to growth in intangible assets such as patents, copyrights and goodwill [...]". From *The Wall Street Journal* (4 November 2002). Cited in Jim Davis, "Speculative capital in the global age", in *Race & Class*, Vol. 44 (3), (2003), pp. 1-22, here: p. 20.

is so very arbitrary it can be inflated at will, hence art's tremendous popularity as a preferred investment with bankers and entrepreneurs like Steve Wynn.[13]

Such notions concerning money and representation may also be extended to *Ocean's Eleven* and its lack of an indexical referent outside of itself, as well as to the film's place in the history of canonical Hollywood films. After the early discovery that film could serve more fanciful and lucrative purposes than simply documenting events, Hollywood began staging adaptations of well-know novels whose familiarity and popularity were to act as the guarantors of a film's success.[14] As George Bluestone pointed out in *Novels into Film*, "about one-third of full-length" feature films from 1935-1945 were "derived from established novels", but this figure has continued to decline ever since.[15] In fact, by the time the 2001 version of *Ocean's Eleven* was made, the decline in the number of films based on pre-existing novels or stories may have been at an all-time low, with many popular movies being made from screen plays such as *Adaptation*, which itself was a self-conscious movie about adapting novels for the screen. In other words, in earlier decades of Hollywood production, movies were connected to literary antecedents in much the same way that paper money was once tied to the gold standard. A film's literary antecedent provided a base or originary index of value, serving as the standard of a film's quality, entertainment value and most importantly, its potential to make money.[16]

Likewise, more and more of the movies currently produced are based neither on a work of literature nor on a screen play, but rather on what might be seen as a somewhat less authoritative antecedent, namely old T.V. sitcoms, detective shows, videogames and of course, old movies like the 1960 version of *Ocean's Eleven*. In this last case it is important to keep in mind just what kind of cultural capital served as the 'original' for the 2001 remake. The first *Ocean's Eleven* was produced to showcase the rat pack and provided an excuse to film Frank Sinatra, Dean Martin, Sammy Davis Jr. and Peter Lawford joking around and generally charming the public as they talked-the-talk.

---

13 For more on the relationship of banking to art, collecting and the market see Bzdak's contribution to this volume.

14 On this point see David A. Cook, *A History of Narrative Film*, (4th ed., New York and London Norton, 2005), pp. 1-27 ("Origins").

15 George Bluestone, *Novels into Film* (Baltimore and London: John Hopkins U.P. 1959), p. 3.

16 In the same section Bluestone also points out that adaptations from novels such as *Gone with the Wind* ranked among Hollywood's "all time money makers" when he wrote the book in 1959; see ibid., p. 4.

Based on the same logic, advertisers predicted that the 2001 version would be a huge box-office hit, which is, needless to say, the Hollywood euphemism for 'to make a lot of money'. What the producers had banked on was the same strategy that made the 60s version a hit despite mediocre acting and a plot that went quite literally nowhere; they banked on viewers' enjoyment of watching their favourite stars having fun and not their desire to see a great work of literature brought to the screen. And in fact, crowds did rush to the theatres to see George Clooney flirt with Julia Roberts, while Brad Pitt and Matt Damon developed site-gages involving food. In other words, the *Ocean* movies, including the recently released *Ocean's Twelve* featuring many of the 'original' cast members, thematise money while thematising and mirroring themselves – potentially to infinity.[17] The *Ocean* films do this moreover, while performing the central activity they portray, namely, obtaining large sums of money by taking a risk on what audiences want to see.

Hollywood and Vegas

In this section I will focus briefly on the history of Las Vegas and its obvious relationship to money, gambling and Hollywood, in light of what I have been arguing thus far. Las Vegas was originally founded by the Mormons in the 1850s as a watering post for travelers from Los Angeles to Salt Lake City through the desert.[18] The Paiutes natives drove the Mormons out in 1858 and reclaimed their land, with the result that the town of Las Vegas remained an obscure outpost for the next 70 years. In 1928 however, plans were approved for the construction of the Hoover Dam just 30 miles from Vegas, at which time entrepreneurs began to look at the town as a playground for construction workers with surplus cash who might enjoy a little legalised gambling and a little less legal prostitution.

---

17 It is interesting to note that Liese Spenser in her review of *Ocean's Twelve* (Dir. Steven Soderbergh. Warner Bros. 2004) suggests that the trouble with the last film in the series is that it is a "knowing sequel to [a] remake"; Liese Spencer, "Ocean's Twelve". *Sight and Sound*, 15,2 (February 2005), pp. 62-64, here: p. 64. By this I take her to mean that *Ocean's Twelve* is somehow one step too far removed and that thus, the notion of an original, much like collective memory of the gold standard, still persists in popular culture.

18 On early Las Vegas see Alan Hess, "Cowboys 'n' Cadillacs: 1855-1940", *Viva Las Vegas: After-Hours Architecture* (San Francisco: Chronicle Books, 1993), pp. 14-25; and Robert D. McCracken, "Early Exploration", *Las Vegas: The Great American Playground*. (Nevada: University of Nevada Press, 1997), pp. 7-13.

It was not, however, until Bugsy Siegel, entrepreneur and mafia wise-guy, brought air conditioning to the Las Vegas desert that the town became a lucrative resort and get-away spot for Hollywood stars as well as for the general public. Siegel's popularity with the stars in the 1940s launched the beginning of a long, profitable and mutually sustaining synergy between Hollywood and Las Vegas. Taking advantage of the town's propinquity to Los Angeles and the lure of cash, casino owners began booking the endless list of stars who have performed there, from Ronald Reagan to Debbie Reynolds and David Cassidy.

Just as Bugsy Siegel left his mark on the 1940s and 50s, Vegas of the 60s was stamped by the style of Howard Hughes who owned landmark casinos like the Silver Slipper, the Desert Inn and the Frontier. It was also in the 60s that the Sands, owned by Howard Hughes, became the favourite haunt of the rat pack, and the setting for *Ocean's Eleven* 1960, which was created to show-case their talents.

But nothing lasts forever, especially in Vegas, one of the only places in the world that makes money by blowing things up. In fact, just ten years before the filming of the first *Ocean's* picture, the US government commenced above-ground atomic testing in the desert immediately outside the gambling centre. Casino owners, who were initially worried that the blasts might detract visitors from the city's charms as a recreational centre, came up with a way to turn a profit on the blasts. Not easily stymied, Vegas developers capitalised on the explosions by opening the Stardust Casino-Hotel featuring an atomic age sign, which has since become the symbol of the city.[19] So by 1958, the year in which a record 77 above-ground tests were made just ten miles outside of Las Vegas in the Mojave desert, most in-town casinos were serving atomic cocktails and offering really explosive deals.[20]

While Howard Hughes owned Vegas in the 60s and 70s, the era was followed by a particularly drab, faceless corporate 80s in which the town was known almost exclusively as the world centre for bad taste. At about this time Steve Wynn, then a young slot machine and keno manager showed up determined to give Vegas a facelift by developing casino-hotels in themed family parks such as Treasure Island and The Excalibur. Wynn was also determined to give the place a little class, which he did by upgrading casinos as simulacra of culture capitals such as Paris, New York, Venice and Bellagio.[21] In order to make space for his

---

19 Note that the Stardust was imploded March 13, 2007.

20 See McCracken, op. cit., p. 48f, and Hess, op.cit., pp. 66-71.

21 Interestingly enough, George Clooney has invested an undisclosed amount for a new 'high-class' casino which has the working name of Las Ramblas. According to the *Ocean's Eleven* star, the casino will have a dress code, will not cater to children and

dreams, Wynn devised a plan to clear the path for progress and make money at the same time. Wynn's strategy for accomplishing both is what reporter Jeff Simpson has called "one of Las Vegas' most impressive spectacles – [the] hotel implosion".[22] Since Wynn's entrepreneurial arrival, an impressive list of casinos have been imploded and captured on videos sold everywhere in Vegas.[23] Wynn's greatest hits list includes The Dunes (1993), The Hacienda (1996) The Old Aladdin (1998), El Rancho (October 2000) and most importantly the forty-four year old Sands, opened in 1952 and the home to Frankie, Dean and Sammy.[24]

The brunt of all the criminal antics in *Ocean's Eleven* 2001 is a character named Terry Benedict played by Andy Garcia, based on Steve Wynn. Like Steve Wynn, Terry Benedict comes from humble beginnings, collects art, is obsessed with security and surveillance and, most importantly, he implodes casinos and makes events of the implosions.[25] In the film this takes the form of a dramatisation of the moment that Steve Wynn pushed a detonator at Treasure Island that set off fire works and made it look like he had bombed the Desert Inn casino hotel, causing it to implode.

Hence, like the segment in *Ocean's* 2001 that contains embedded narratives of attempted heists in Vegas in the 50s, the 60s and the 80s, (the mafia years, the Hughes era, the corporate strip) this is Hollywood taking yet another sidelong self-conscious glance at the historical and economic high points of a city to which it has meant so very much. And because Steve Wynn was the man responsible for

---

will evoke Vegas' glamour years. See the actor's site at http://www.lasramblasvegas.com/news/clooney-building-in-las-vegas.html.

22 See "Next DI implosion planned. Tower to come down by Halloween; Wynn Las Vegas expansion on tap", in the *Las Vegas Sun*, April 27, 2004. http://www.lasvegassun.com/sunbin/stories/business/2004/apr/27/516758770.html.

23 One such video is titled *Blasted in Las Vegas* and features "Dunes Pyrotechnics", "Sands Breathtaking", and "Hacienda Earth Shaking".

24 As a sentimental gesture, Warner Brothers now include documentary information and footage of the Sand's implosion with the DVD as a tribute to the old casino that served as the location of *Ocean's Eleven* 1960.

25 The fictional vault in the film also hints at Wynn's own obsession with heightening security measures. In his latest hotel-casino, Wynn Las Vegas, players will be issued radio frequency identity (RFDI) chips, which make it easier to "identify counterfeit chips, keep track of markers, rate players for comps, and deter casino cheats". http://honeymoons.about.com/od/lasvegashotels/a/Wynn_Las_Vegas.htm.

imploding the Sands, a move not popular with Hollywood performers, aficionados and Vegas residents who are "concerned about how disposable [their] history is", the movie in which the Steve Wynn character gets stung is something of a good natured, self-conscious poke in the ribs.[26]

Conclusions

What I have tried to show here is how money is represented in both versions of *Ocean's Eleven* as an indication of how it circulates in tandem with changing notions of value, speculation, security and risk in the 'real' world. Over-arching all of these considerations is how the *Ocean* films work together as a self-conscious subgenre and I have tried to trace the process of semiosis that drives them. As I see it, these films form a knot of auto-parodic intertextuality, referring always only to themselves, while mobilising Vegas and casino culture as the perfect metaphor of this brand of selfconsciousness. As Clooney explains in *Ocean's* 2001, "casinos are built like labyrinths to keep people in". So if the catch phrase for the first *Ocean's Eleven* was "In any other town they'd be the bad guys", it might now be revised as "in any other town they'd just be movie stars and casino owners", a line which adequately expresses the claustrophobic nature of these films and indeed of the sister cities, Vegas and Hollywood.

But most importantly, while the *Ocean* films generate all of this, they reside resolutely in the present moment which I take to be no coincidence. As Georg Simmel explained almost a century ago, gamblers' time is about "unconditional presentness, the quickening of the process of life to a point that possesses neither past nor future".[27] Similarly Gerda Reith has written that gambling is always about "the time of the eternal present", the moment at which when the dice land, one's fate is revealed and past and future collide in the present moment.[28] And this is precisely what Sammy Davis tells the viewer when he sings directly into the camera at the close of *Ocean's* 1960 in front of a marquee that self-consciously announces that he's currently playing the Sands with Frankey, Dean, Peter and Joey.

---

26 See Simpson http://www.lasvegassun.com/sunbin/stories/business/2004/apr/27/516758770.html.

27 Georg Simmel, *Essays on Sociology, Philosophy and Aesthetics*. Ed. K.H. Wolff (New York: Harper and Row, 1965), p. 254.

28 Gerda Reith, *The Age of Chance: Gambling and Western Culture* (London and New York: Routledge, 1999), p.140.

In this last take, Davis explains that E.O. Eleven is just a state of mind when you're waiting to find out if you get "four score years or go to heaven". This is to say that the *Ocean* films are devoted to the gambler's decisive present moment, to gambling time, to trembling on the brink of decision, and this is indeed a timely notion in the current age of casino economics.

Christina Oldman

Financial identities in the American tycoon autobiographies by Andrew Carnegie and John D. Rockefeller. Credit negotiations as creator of masculinity

The business autobiographies by Andrew Carnegie (1920) and John D. Rockefeller (1909)[1] tell stories of male self-actualization and success illustrated by the acquisition of money and management of monetary flows. 'Financial identities' is the term I have chosen to demonstrate how Carnegie's and Rockefeller's senses of self are ultimately defined by money. Private investors, banks and other financial institutions provide the means for these men to run their businesses. In their narratives, money moves in and out of the corporation through loans, investments and expenses, which means that money is in a constant state of flux. Identities based on money are therefore consequently relational, as money moves in never-ending flows between a great number of individuals. These autobiographies show constant social negotiations between people and moneyed identities in a structure based on the opposition of static and fixed, and unstable and fleeting. These are primarily shown in situations of credit negotiations.

Money is characterized by its volatile nature. Yet there have continually been attempts in Western societies to "fix" the value of money. The introduction of money to create a common denominator producing a shared understanding of value is but one example of people's attempts to ascribe a fixed value to a transient entity, even though in modern societies a fixed value will only last for milliseconds. Both tycoons are conscious of the fact that they live in a society where fluctuation in values are perpetual and refer to, for example, panic striking the financial world. It is essential for them to monitor these changes and create as secure a foundation for business finances as possible. Carnegie stresses that secure finances are achievable only by investments in one's own corporation instead of diverting one's attention to outside speculation: "Most business men

---

1 Andrew Carnegie, *Autobiography of Andrew Carnegie* (Boston: Houghton Mifflin Co, 1920) and John D. Rockefeller, *Random Reminiscences of Men and Events* (London: Doubleday, 1909). Subsequent references to these books will be given in brackets in the text, with the abbreviations "Autobiography" and Random".

whom I have known invest in bank shares and far away enterprises, while the true gold mine lies right in their own factories." (*Autobiography*, p. 177). The image of the gold mine represents a form of stability in a world where the value of money fluctuates.

Discussing money as a foundation for identities, as I do, indicates that identities built on such a shaky and unstable base as money constitutes, must, as a consequence, share money's qualities of incertitude and non-finality. In the tension between the static and unstable, Carnegie's and Rockefeller's money-based identities seem, in many respects, to be constructed in order to privilege static and controllable versions of the self.

The paradox of financial lives is, however, that wealth cannot be treated as a fixed state. Carnegie and Rockefeller may have written their autobiographies as white, bourgeois billionaires, but that position was made permanent only when retiring from an active business life. In their autobiographies, they describe a process of moving from poverty to affluence and that process describes numerous transient identities in between these polar positions. They portray how they started as workers, went from small-business partners to large corporate magnates, and ended up in their final role as philanthropists. Both autobiographies illustrate a process of negotiation between multiple and shifting identities, despite their introductory statements that they will provide a uniform and linear portrait of themselves.

In a culture destabilized by money, both businessmen respond by attempts to stabilize the constructions of their identity. Investments in infrastructure and natural resources which are interpreted as long-term investments are examples of how both businessmen try to manifest themselves as stable actors. These tycoons describe businessmen, and thus themselves, as constructors and builders who transform landscapes, build cities in the vicinity of oil fields, and connect cities through the construction of railroads. Thus, individually instigated projects are described more in terms of projects for communal or national benefit than projects undertaken to make a profit. Carnegie depicts the commitment of businessmen to national projects as infinite and stresses the durability and permanence of the bridges his company constructs: "We never built and we never will build a cheap bridge. Ours don't fall" (*Autobiography*, p. 116). By this, Carnegie promises that he is equally solid. Both men call themselves "industrialists" which are solid, in comparison to "speculators" who are transitory. Carnegie, for example, defines speculation as "a parasite feeding upon values creating none." (*Autobiography*, p. 54). Rockefeller goes so far as to call money from speculation a curse: "Money which comes to him without effort on his part is seldom a benefit and often a curse." (*Random*, p. 152)

Stability, consistency and predictability is the prescribed path of money-making in these tycoon autobiographies. While acknowledging that fluctuations are prevalent in society, both authors paradoxically find those who make profits of fluctuations to be morally reprehensible, individualistic, and lazy, as the generated profits are not shown to provide employment opportunities for other people. In both accounts the "manly" businessman is described as an industrialist who manages large sums of money for the benefit of the nation. After depicting this ideal of the moneyed man, they set about to describe how they themselves conform to their established ideal.

Despite resenting speculation in paper credit, Carnegie sometimes relied on bonds to secure credit, for example, when building the Keystone Bridge. Paper credit points to the fictionality of finance as stocks and bonds have values which are only verifiable in the future when they are sold. Contrary to land and real estate, paper credit reinforces the impression that value changed from a steady variable into to a mobile one, as Catherine Ingrassia states: "Paper credit and the mechanisms of speculative investment shifted the nature of property from material, immovable and stable forms such as land to fluid, immaterial and multiple ones." Ingrassia concludes, "property became increasingly unreal."[2]

Credit transactions illustrate how immaterial value had become in that it no longer could be easily measured and assessed, so instead, the debtor becomes the one to represent a fixed value. Credit originally meant "belief, "trust" and "reputation", significations which reinforce the impression that credit is regarded as means entrusted to those who present themselves as believable and trustworthy. Credit is generally negotiated through personal encounters between creditors and debtors who try to estimate their opponent's strengths and weaknesses on a more personal level beside estimations of actual financial means. Craig Muldrew describes how in early modern England "the majority of transactions were transacted on credit which was also largely oral and informal, with only a token amount of cash used to set a seal on the bargain."[3] Both tycoons give detailed accounts of credit negotiations where the personal contacts replace the notion of anonymity and alienation so frequent in discussions on money.

In situations of credit negotiations each side is thus involved in a process of marketing their own credibility. It becomes a matter of negotiating one's identity whilst deducting what the other party ranks as the highest qualities which would

---

2 Catherine Ingrassia, *Authorship, Commerce, and Gender in Early Eighteenth Century England: A culture of paper credit* (Cambridge: Cambridge U P, 1998), p. 5.

3 Craig Muldrew, "Hard food for Midas': cash and its social value in Early Modern England", *Past & Present*, Issue 170 (February 2001), p. 83.

merit the loan. Loan negotiations are relational in that the debtor adapts to the expectations of the creditor. Presentation is essential. Carnegie refers to an interview where he depicts his skills in the "American" language as a sign that he is reliable and presentable: "But in speech and in address the broad Scotch had been worn off to a slight extent and I imagined that I could make a smarter showing if alone with Mr Brooks than if my good old Scotch father was present, perhaps to smile at my airs" (*Autobiography*, p. 37f) To market one's credibility means to project an image of permanence and predictability.

Margot C. Finn illustrates that "character" is a term which appropriately illustrates the trust and personal attributes involved in the negotiation of credit. In her book on consumer credit in Victorian England, Finn demonstrates that credit negotiations were socially negotiated where the creditor estimated the creditworthiness of the debtor through a range of personal attributes:

> Determinations of individual creditworthiness [...] only rarely reflected precise knowledge of individual wealth: personal credit was a fluctuating identity concocted by a shifting range of interested parties from a fluid series of representations of the self. Creditors sought constantly and unsuccessfully to read a debtor's personal worth and character from their clothing, their marital status, their spending patterns and their perceived social status, attempting to assign stable cash values to consumers in markets continuously buffeted by the vagaries of credit.[4]

The "stable" forms Finn mentions correspond well to my claim that moneyed identities aim to represent a fictional stability in an environment characterized by fluidity. For Carnegie, this meant, performing like a "manly man" through a change of clothes: "Up to this time I had been, perhaps, careless in dress and rather affected by it. Great heavy boots, loose collar, and a general roughness of attire were then peculiar to the West and in our circle considered manly" (*Autobiography,* p. 97f). Both tycoons express a constant need to borrow money and situations of loan negotiations are so frequent, that Rockefeller sees the need to explain: "I was a great borrower in my early days; the business was active and growing fast, and the banks seemed very willing to loan me the money" (*Random,* p. 19). It is clear that Carnegie and Rockefeller interpret acquired loans as a validation of their stable worth.

In early 18th-century Britain credit had feminine connotations and was associated with desire, passion, disobedience and speculative self-interest. Male creditors were considered to be unvirtuous, and even effeminate. Credit threatened to undermine both mens' personal autonomy and their very

---

4 Margot C. Finn, *The Character of Credit: Personal Debt in English Culture, 1740-1914* (Cambridge, Cambridge UP, 2003), p. 21.

masculinity. Later in the century, Susan Kingsley Kent demonstrates how politicians rendered

> a commercial system based on credit virtuous on the one hand, and they had to subject the unruly, and potentially effeminizing, passions and appetites of commercial capitalism to masculine discipline and management on the other. The first necessitated the removal of the feminine [...] from the public arena; the second required transforming passions into interests.[5]

Men were then encouraged to prove their masculinity in the commercial world, where credit became synonymous with a sense of enhanced masculinity.

It is apparent that Rockefeller does not view credit as feminized. The fact that he emphasizes the bank's willingness to loan him the money illustrates how Rockefeller describes himself as the debtor, without any reference to the company on whose behalf he negotiated, and whose reputation might have had an equally important share in the acquisition of the loan. He claims that he was anxious to "establish myself favourably with the banker" (*Random*, p. 42) which suggests that loan negotiations were situations where moneyed masculinities were performed and enhanced. Moneyed men were required to pronounce and "sell" their own significance. For both men, each acquisition of a loan, consequently translates them into businessmen. Rockefeller expresses that immediately after he acquired a loan his male status changed: "As I left the bank my elation can hardly be imagined. I held up my head – think of it, a bank had trusted me for $ 2,000! I felt that I was now a man of importance in the community." (*Random*, p. 42) Hence, in these narratives credit negotiations are masculine rites of passage into the business community.

The acquisition of credit was consequently interpreted in terms of a male achievement rather than an acknowledgement that Rockefeller's demands for funding were greater than he could provide for himself. "Trust" is a word commonly used by these businessmen to describe credit negotiations. Trust is interpreted as an assurance of a predictable monetary performance in the future where the acquisition of loans to both men are moments of self-realization and increased male worth.

Credit negotiations in both autobiographies illustrate that credit reflected their notion of self more definitively than actual money does. Credit is paradoxically described as a matter which can be controlled, taken charge of, and acquired more easily than profits from sales. The market of industrial enterprise is depicted as more volatile, as competitors and customers are described as more unpredictable

---

5 Susan Kingsley Kent, *Gender and Power in Britain, 1640-1990* (London: Routledge, 1999), p. 61.

counterparts than bankers. Credit negotiations are described as situations providing both men with a sense of stability, and affairs where they are personally responsible for success, and thus, personally entrusted with loans. Carnegie illustrates this as he quotes Banker Thompson saying: "Remember Andy, I look to you in this matter. It is you I trust, and I depend on your holding all the securities you obtain and seeing that the Pennsylvania Railroad is never in a position where it can lose a dollar" (*Autobiography*, p. 163f).

In the end, financial identities in these tycoon autobiographies are construed masculinities aimed at securing a stable construction in sharp contrast to a financial environment characterized by fluidity. Credit negotiations feature as one of the more striking examples where Carnegie and Rockefeller attribute their personal status, although fictitious, to the successful acquisition of loans. Equally, they have presented the credit market as a male club imbued with male socialization in their narratives.[6] Credit is given by men to men, and Rockefeller stresses that male friendships ought to be based on business in order to survive: "It was a friendship founded on business, which Mr. Flagler used to say was a good deal better than a business founded on friendship, and my experience leads me to agree with him" (*Random*, p. 12). The way that credit holds a prominent position in both narratives is also reflected in how Carnegie treats his means, namely that debt, and not revenue, should be prioritized: "A man's means are a trust to be sacredly held for his own creditors as long as he has debts and obligations" (*Autobiography,* p. 174f.). Ultimately, Rockefeller who began by describing credit as something "mysterious" (*Random,* p. 69) in a later argument stresses that the cultivation of moneyed identities, and its "permanent success" is not at all mysterious, in that "the confidence in the man himself [...] is the real capital we all prize and work for" (*Random*, p. 133).

6 In the same context, I would also like to emphasize that credit transactions for household economies have largely been conducted by women in Western societies, to an equal extent as men have dominated the business credit markets.

Matthias Weiss

The Trading Floor in the Display Case: Stock-Exchange Capitalism as expressed through the Medium of the Museum Exhibition

> Some suspicious persons maintain that the stock exchange was invented by Lucifer in order to trick speculators with the promise that they, like God, could create something out of nothing.
>
> Jose de La Vega[1]

Introduction

For as long as the stock exchange has existed, opinions have been divided as to whether it is a good or a bad thing. Nonetheless, given the fascination exerted by the promise of being able to create "something out of nothing", it comes as little surprise that faith in this institution is clearly far more widespread than doubt: plenty of people still speculate, and keep on speculating, on the stock exchange.

Equally, the trading floor becomes a stage – one on which rituals and symbols are transformed into an enactment of the lives of the protagonists. Their success is measured by the wealth they accumulate, and shown by their possession of status symbols.[2]

However, there are places where the representation of the values of stock exchange capitalism is not restricted to this arena. Should the budget of a trading centre stretch that far, the venue will often include an exhibition taking the stock exchange as its central theme. There is no more effective medium for communicating feelings and information than an exhibition – a world that can readily be accessed and entered. These are places where capitalism puts itself on

---

1 Joseph de La Vega, *Confusión de confusiones: diálogos curiosos entre un philosopho agudo, un mercader discreto, y un accionista erudito, descriviendo el negocio de las acciones, su origen, su ethimologia, su realidad, su juego, y su enredo* (Amsterdam, 1688).

2 Heiner Goldinger, *Rituale und Symbole der Börse: Eine Ethnographie* (Münster: Lit, 2001).

display, presenting itself to the public in a manner that is surprising, given the degree of rationality called for in economic activity: companies and prominent figures in business become icons, speculators become missionaries and the act of financial investment becomes something very much like a holy pilgrimage. The stock exchange and stock exchange capitalism belong to the cultural inventory of our society, and as such they influence our lives, not solely on a monetary but also on a metaphysical level – a level akin to that of a religious faith. On closer examination, we can discern in these presentations a form of covenant: the promise of affluence. It therefore comes as no surprise that the museum-style exhibitions presented below support the notion of capitalism as religion.[3]

In the first section of this article, the most up-to-date research on the topic of "Capitalism as Religion" is examined in greater detail and summarised. The second section is given over to the museum and/or exhibition as a medium, and to their particular features as a forum for learning. The third section contains a consideration of three exhibitions taking the stock exchange as their theme, together with the results of a qualitative analysis carried out by the author. This entails an examination of the contents, messages and intentions of exhibitions mounted by the *New York Stock Exchange*, the *NASDAQ* Stock Market and the *Museum of American Financial History* (Smithsonian).

1. Capitalism as Religion

It was Max Weber who developed the thesis that it had not been possible for capitalism to develop as an economic system until after the Reformation had brought about the creation of Protestantism in Europe. Essentially, Weber represents the viewpoint that profit-based trading was rendered possible and indeed promoted by Protestantism's belief in a form of salvation attainable in this world. There is no doubt that religion and capitalism were seen as co-existent yet separate, falling into two discrete categories: the sacred and the secular.[4]

This approach was further developed by Walter Benjamin in a text fragment entitled *Capitalism as Religion*. Like Weber, Benjamin proceeds from the assumption that capitalism did not emerge until after the appearance of Protestantism. In making this assertion, Benjamin discovers capitalism to be a

---

3 Cf. Dirk Baecker (ed.), *Kapitalismus als Religion* (Berlin: Kulturverlag Kadmos, 2003).

4 Cf. Constans Seyfarth and Walter M. Sprondel (eds.), *Seminar: Religion und gesellschaftliche Entwicklung. Studien zur Protestantismus-Kapitalismus-These Max Webers* (Frankfurt a.M.: Suhrkamp, 1973).

religion in itself; however, in contrast to Weber, he comes to the conclusion that Protestantism did more than simply promote capitalism – it actually transformed itself into capitalism.[5]

This is the point where the current discourse gets underway, further developing Benjamin's ideas. Deutschmann gets right to the heart of the definition of capitalism as religion when he identifies the "self-exploiting value as a procedure-related unit of money" as being "the religion of modern society". The culmination of this belief in capitalism is neo-liberalism, with its doctrine that "financial success [...is...] the direct measure of all dealing."[6]

This discourse cannot be overlooked when conducting a qualitative analysis of exhibitions taking the stock exchange or stock exchange capitalism as their theme. Deutschmann goes on to say:

> Just as – with the exception of a handful of masterly mystics – the man or woman of faith believes that he or she would be incapable of enduring the direct presence of God and therefore requires the mediation of prophets, priests, holy scriptures and rituals, so too protagonists in the economic arena are unable to endure direct confrontation with the infinite nature of the possibilities of money.
> They cannot find the correct path without the help of scientists, inventors, experts, consultants and management gurus, and of the constructions and symbolic interpretations created by these parties.[7]

And it is in precisely this light that the three exhibitions under consideration here should be viewed. These New York exhibitions serve as a medium for the creation of these very "constructions" and "symbolic interpretations". Here, stock exchange capitalism is depicted as a source of redemption, and the onlooker is exhorted to have faith in speculative investment.

2. The Exhibition as a Medium

It is sometimes claimed that nowadays the meaning of the term "museum" has become entirely negative – that it is associated with adjectives like "immobile, static, boring, unimaginative, dull, dry, indistinct and impersonal, unfathomable,

---

5 Walter Benjamin, "Kapitalismus als Religion", in Walter Benjamin, *Gesammelte Schriften*, ed. Rolf Tiedemann and Hermann Schweppenhäuser (Frankfurt a.M.: Suhrkamp, 1985), vol. VI, p. 100.

6 Christoph Deutschmann, "Die Verheissung des absoluten Reichtums", in *Kapitalismus als Religion*, op. cit., p. 145.

7 ibid., p. 163.

dead, lifeless, devoid of sentience".[8] This baseless prejudice has caused some experts to impute to museums a low value.

The fact that this notion is highly presumptuous and untenable is demonstrated by attendance figures at museums – among other things. A survey commissioned by the American Association of Museums (AAM) in the United States showed that more trust is placed in museums than in any other medium. 87% of the US citizens taking part thought museums were a trustworthy medium, as opposed to the 61% who trusted books. Television, meanwhile, is mistrusted by 50% of Americans, newspapers by 65% and magazines by 76%.[9]

Among communications media, therefore, museums are considered authoritative.[10] That means that messages disseminated through museum exhibitions are taken seriously and considered credible. A museum or an exhibition acquires this air of authority if it can consistently generate and maintain the public's perception of it as authentic. Equally, the public will readily express its confidence in this medium: often, a work of art by a well-known master, an artefact or a building associated with a historical event, or an interactive animation in a technology centre, will be sufficient to engender this impression.[11]

The fact that a company may take responsibility for the conception and creation of a museum presentation need not prevent an exhibition from being perceived by its visitors as being every bit as authentic and credible as one mounted by an independent museum, even if the intentions of the said exhibition are quite clearly commercial. By adopting a presentational style that properly reflects the seriousness of a state-run museum, a commercial exhibition will be able to engender this confidence in its visitors. The precondition for this is an appropriate presentational manner – this may, for example, be achieved through the integration of original objects. A further means of achieving this is the use of the same types of displays and presentation methods as those found in "museum-style" presentations. Likewise, such elements as the style in which the accompanying publications are presented or, indeed, maintaining one's own personnel to guide and inform single visitors and groups before, during and after

---

8 Friedrich Waidacher, *Handbuch der Allgemeinen Museologie* (3rd ed. Vienna: Boehlau, 1999), p. 25.

9 American Association of Museums, press release (May 5, 2001). http://www.aam-us.org/pressreleases.cfm?mode=list&id=21.

10 Anja Dauschek and Gail Dexter Lord, "Museen – Portale zur Welt?" in *Museumskunde* no. 2 (2001), p. 62.

11 Barry Lord and Gail Dexter Lord (ed.), *Manual of Museum Exhibitions* (Walnut Creek: Altamira, 2002), p. 16.

their visit, can also help to create this appearance.[12] In such cases, the presentations can only be differentiated from regular exhibitions by close scrutiny of the contents. The deceptive similarity in form between commercial exhibitions on the one hand and scholarly presentations on the other may be among the reasons why various associations of museums are now instituting codes of ethics for museums and insisting on adherence to these, over and above the standards already associated with museums.[13]

The key difference between independent museums and commercial exhibitions lies in their aims. The first of these interpret a theme with the intention of educating, while the second present objects with the intention of stimulating sales.[14] As early as 1959, Lang was able to see that exhibitions of this kind had an intriguing objective:

> Exhibiting starts to pay off when the product and corporate name become not only identical but firmly connected with warm, pleasing corporate identity as expressed by the exhibit and its staff. This result is one which is difficult if not impossible to achieve in other media, [...].[15]

The world of commerce makes deliberate use of exhibitions as one medium within its corporate communications mix – and because of the specific manner in which exhibitions convey information, they have come to occupy a place of special significance among such media as books, newspapers, radio or television.

3. What makes exhibitions so effective as a medium?

Dauschek characterises exhibitions as follows:

> This form of presentation does not just interpret its [...] subject matter by means of objects – it also *forms a statement* within the space itself by means of the setting given to objects, text, graphic design, photographs and other visual materials.[16]

---

12 George E. Hein, *Learning in the Museum* (New York: Routledge, 1998), p. 157; Barry Lord and Gail Dexter Lord, *Manual of Museum Exhibitions*, op. cit., p. 15.

13 American Association of Museums, *Code of Ethics for Museums* (2000). http://www.aam-us.org/aamcoe.cfm

14 Barry Lord and Gail Dexter Lord, *Manual of Museum Exhibitions*, op. cit., p. 15.

15 Rudolph Lang, *Win Place and Show – Effective Business Exhibiting* (New York: 1959), p. 17.

16 Anja Dauschek, *Die Entstehung des historischen Museums in den USA. Museumsgeschichte und Material Culture Studies als Ansätze zur Bewertung historischer Ausstellungen* (unpublished M.A. thesis, Munich: 1992), p. 2

Information conveyed by a space-shaping medium of this kind has a lasting impact, the value of which cannot possibly be overestimated. The viewers immerse themselves in the interpretations, with all their senses engaged. Whether the contents actually get through to the visitor – and if so, to what extent – will depend primarily on his or her perceptions of the exhibition. Occurrences that evoke strong feelings in us leave behind a greater imprint in our memory than those that leave us emotionally unmoved.[17]

The primary criterion by which a museum's scholars judge the success of an exhibition is whether it generates enthusiasm for the subject matter and can motivate visitors to find out more about it.[18]

Even if some museologists continue to adhere to Waidacher's belief that museum visitors behave like Pavlov's dog (according to Waidacher, learning is a "targeted alteration of attitudes by means of conditioning"[19]), the study of museums has, thankfully, used the century that has elapsed since Ivan Pavlov's experiments to apply other educational theories to the museum environment.

The educational scientists Falk and Dierking, who specialise in the field of museums, are one good example of this. They adopt a constructivist viewpoint, considering learning to be a dialogue between the individual and his environment, or an environmentally-conditioned search for meaning intended to ensure one's own survival and the development of one's personality.[20]

Here, learning is seen not as conditioning, or as the simple accumulation of knowledge, but rather as a sustained, cumulative process, the objective being interpretation ("making meaning") and the recognition of interrelations. The information required for this may be derived from school, newspaper and magazines, books, conversations with friends and family, television programmes, observations of the world and, last but not least, from visits to museums.[21]

Working on the basis of this insight, Falk and Dierking have developed a theory of learning in museums. They proceed from the assumption that such learning always takes place within three contexts and over a period of time. In

---

17 Barry Lord and Gail Dexter Lord, *Manualof Museum Exhibitions*, op. cit., p. 17: "[...] transformative experiences [...] can occur only if the museum visitors are truly enjoying themselves."

18 David Dean, *Museum Exhibition* (London: 1994), p. 7; Barry Lord and Gail Dexter Lord, *Manual of Museum Exhibitions*, op. cit., p. 18.

19 Friedrich Waidacher, *Handbuch der Allgemeinen Museologie*, op. cit.

20 John Falk and Lynn D. Dierking, *Learning from Museums. Visitor Experiences and the Making of Meaning* (Walnut Creek: Altamira, 2000), p. 136.

21 ibid., p. 12.

what they call their "Contextual Model of Learning", the following names are given to these contexts:

Personal Context
Sociocultural Context
Physical Context

The *Personal Context* is made up of the motivation and expectations that precede the learning process and the museum visit. This includes knowledge already acquired by the visitor and his or her interests and existing perceptions of the subject matter, together with the way the visitor selects and thus controls the information he or she absorbs.

The term *Sociocultural Context* refers to the way the visitor's social environment evaluates and communicates the subject matter.

By *Physical Context*, Falk and Dierking mean the place where the museum is located, and within the museum, the systems by which the visitor is guided around and the design of the exhibition itself.

And the learning process is far from over when the visitor leaves the exhibition. It also incorporates any incidents and experiences related to the subject matter that may occur following the exhibition visit:

> [...] consider learning as being constructed over time as the individual moves through his sociocultural and physical world; over time, meaning is built up, layer upon layer.[22]

Therefore the decisive elements for the use of museums or exhibitions for communicating information and ensuring that it has a sustainable impact are as follows:

1. Learning, as a process of interpretation, is not a process restricted to specific events. Learning and interpretation take place over a long period of time – indeed, a period covering one's entire lifetime. It is an interaction of knowledge that we have acquired and continue to acquire by means of a) sensory perception, b) personal experience, and c) our sociocultural environment. In this context, the term interaction means that new information is continually being evaluated in comparison with that stored in our memories.
2. The transfer of information from our environment to us, and the storage of such perceptions, may be made easier by the fulfilment of certain preconditions. For this to occur, points of connection for our system of perceptions and concepts must be supplied. Light, temperature, colours, sounds, odours, the selection and arrangement of objects and the formulation and composition of text all exert a

---

22 John Falk and Lynn D. Dierking, *Learning from Museums*, op. cit., p. 11.

direct influence over our readiness to engage with the interpretations presented.[23] If our emotions are stirred by a museum exhibition's themes, or indeed just by certain parts of it, they leave behind a greater imprint in our memory than those that address us little or not at all on an emotional level.
3. Exhibitions are media that present us with the opportunity to experience selected elements from our environment and from its history. By means of the way the contents are processed and prepared, they provide the visitor with points of connection and opportunities for identification. They impress through their apparent authenticity and shape the visitor's memories by means of lasting impressions.

4. Representations of money and the stock exchange in exhibitions and in museums – three examples from New York

It is not absolutely essential for museums to have an independent, non-commercial background in order to convey messages successfully. The manner in which this medium operates has for a long time now been used for other purposes too. The interpretation and exhibition of objects and symbols is part of a long tradition. Since time immemorial, objects of special significance within the religions of their respective cultures have been preserved in sacred locations, and later in temples, and presented to the people on special days. And for just as long, the medium of the exhibition has served as a location for "making meaning" and for the elucidation of power structures. The purpose of displaying the objects was (1) to make an impression on the visitor, (2) to provide him or her with opportunities for identification, in order (3) to win him or her over to the exhibitor's cause.

The continuity of this form of communication can be seen in such examples as the relic collections of the secular feudal lords of the Holy Roman Empire (who claimed to rule by divine right), or the museums maintained by modern states containing works of art plundered by colonial powers, as well as the exhibitions of capitalism under consideration here. These demonstrate particularly clearly what interpretations and perspectives relating to money and the stock exchange, and/or to capitalism itself, the organisers wish to impress upon their visitors.

---

23 David Dean, *Museum Exhibition* (London: 1994).

5. The messages and intentions of the exhibitions under examination

Until the year 2001, *NYSE*, *NASDAQ* and the *Museum of American Financial History* maintained presentations explaining the topic of the stock exchange to visitors. *NYSE* and *NASDAQ* are institutions whose livelihood is bound up in the trading of securities. Being a participant in the *Smithsonian Affiliate Program*, the *Museum of American Financial History* has committed itself as an institution to the education of society. All three exhibitions were closed in the wake of the September 11 bombings, and only the *MoAFH* exhibition has since reopened.

NYSE and its Interactive Education Center

On April 14, 1939,[24] the *New York Stock Exchange* (*NYSE*) opened an exhibition aimed at explaining stock exchange dealings to visitors in greater depth than a mere glimpse of the trading floor from the gallery could provide. Nothing now remains of this first exhibition (1939), which was regularly subject to revision over the years. This happened during the 1950s, 1970s and 1990s. In each case, the old exhibition was removed in its entirety and a new one put in its place. The presentation under discussion here was opened in 1996 and closed in 2001. It was not called an *exhibition* or a *museum*, nor was it called a *presentation*. Its official name was the *Interactive Education Center* (*IEC*). The mandate of the *IEC* is "*to inform and educate the general public*".[25] The *IEC* belonged to the Department of Education, a branch of the Communications Department, whose annual budget amounts to around 40 million US$. In addition to maintaining the *IEC*, the Department of Education has supplied schools, groups of visitors and investors around the world with informational material and publications from its own publishing concern.

Visitors to the 1996 exhibition were greeted with the words:

> *NYSE* – The world puts its stock in us.[26]

A display showed this sentence spanning the globe. There was a play here on the various meanings of the word "stock". We know that in addition to a share, it can also mean an inventory, a lineage, an origin and a derivation. But in addition to its semantic meaning, this statement also conveyed information about its

24 Private archives of the author: New York Stock Exchange, *Chronology* (unpublished historical key data for the exhibition: 2001).

25 Private archives of the author: New York Stock Exchange ed., *IEC at a Glance* (New York: 2000).

26 Private archives of the author: transcript of the text of the display panels at the *Interactive Education Center* (New York: 26 Juni 2001), p. 1.

originators: the institution here depicted was one that credited itself with a crucial role – if not, indeed, the crucial role – in the process of civilisation.

It would therefore seem only logical that this institution, and those institutions that attain power and riches through it, be accorded due homage. What was once represented by the relics – that is, the proximity of their owners to God and thus to power and authority – was here replaced by the contextual juxtaposition of the stock exchange with the icons of capitalism.[27] The religious character of this presentation becomes even clearer when we consider the framing context in which it took place. As with the majority of stock exchange buildings dating from the 19th or early 20th century, the façade of the New York Stock Exchange resembles that of a temple from antiquity. And just as temples and churches were once the dwelling-places of gods, and repositories for relics, this temple is "Home to the World's *Best Companies*". [28]

In addition to the façade, the messages conveyed in this exhibition were also the equivalent of religious themes. The promises that were made here had a quality that recalled the kind of promises we find in the Bible: both are linked to conditions. For example: "If a man love me, he will keep my words: and my Father will love him, and we will come unto him, and make our abode with him." (John 14:23), "I am the way, the truth, and the life: no man cometh unto the Father, but by me." (John 14:6). The counterparts to these in the exhibition carried such legends as: "Investors come First", or "for the ultimate benefit of all who participate." [29]

To the ears of those without property, who were unable to participate in stock exchange dealings for economic reasons, or on the other hand to those who remained sceptical and opposed to such dealings, these declarations must have sounded like a threat.

During the Middle Ages, the faithful were given an understanding of the stories in the Bible by means of scenes acted out in front of churches. The central message to visitors to the *Interactive Education Center* was conveyed in a video shown at short intervals in the so-called *NYSE Theater*. This short film carried the fitting title: "It all starts here."[30]

---

27 Cf. Anton Legner, *Reliquien in Kunst und Kult zwischen Antike und Aufklärung* (Darmstadt: Wissenschaftliche Buchgesellschaft, 1995).

28 Private archives of the author: transcript of the text of the display panels at the *Interactive Education Center* (New York: 26 Juni 2001), p. 1.

29 ibid., p. 2.

30 Private archives of the author: New York Stock Exchange (ed.), *It All Starts Here.* Video/self-presentation.

In this video Richard Grasso, former president of the NYSE, plunged directly into an explanation of the evolutionary principle of the stock exchange: someone has an idea, meets investors, the idea is realised and becomes part of the common cultural stock. That was his explanation of the provenance and generation of the world in which we live.

But the visitors had not yet reached the destination to which they all aspired – namely, the visitor's gallery of the NYSE. They were separated from this balcony by a guarded door, and only after much ostentatious surveillance of the door, and enquiries and confirmations via walkie-talkie, were the waiting visitors granted access. They were then permitted to view, from the gallery and through a bullet-proof glass screen, the holiest of holies of stock-exchange capitalism: the trading floor of the NYSE.

In short: at the *Interactive Education Center*, stock-exchange capitalism was presented in a manner similar to the ritualised ceremonies of many religions.

NASDAQ and the Market Site Experience

NASDAQ has a problem: unlike the NYSE, it has neither a world-famous building nor a world-famous trading floor.

The NASDAQ Tower in Times Square "[...] is strictly a public relations facility".[31] In a populist manner, NASDAQ is reaching out to people in probably the most famous square in New York. There is no trading of securities in this building. All securities trading is conducted via two large computers outside New York. The tower in Times Square houses a media centre for market reporting and, until 2001, a visitor centre containing an exhibition. The NASDAQ exhibition was called the *MarketSite Experience*. The exhibition's creators took virtual trading as their subject matter, endeavouring to make the invisible visible. The visitor was meant to immerse themselves in the virtual world of NASDAQ. The creators summarised their task as follows: "NASDAQ wanted to create a theatrical environment that lets visitors feel as if they where inside the network."[32]

Immersion in the virtual securities market takes place when visitors pass through a tunnel, called the *Information Screen Tunnel*. It is impossible for visitors to enter the exhibition without passing through this walk-in tunnel, which is illuminated with glass fibre-optic cables – cables of the very same type as those

---

31 Private archives of the author: notes taken during a guided public tour of the *MarketSite Experience* (New York: July 18, 2001).

32 David Barbour and French Liz, "NASDAQ MarketSite". *Entertainment Design* no. 7 (2000), p. 32.

used for data transfer. The tour guide ushers us inside with the words, "On the other side – in the *Global Connection* – we will meet again".

On the other side – the *Global Connection* – we are greeted by a film about the "Vision of the Global Networking of Financial Markets in Pursuance of Worldwide Trading". The message is one of a progressive world without need, in which all human beings have equal access to the capital market, wherever they may be and 24 hours a day.

The *tunnel motif* is familiar to us from reports of near-death experiences. During such dream experiences or visions, persons struggling against impending death have passed through a tunnel – or have felt themselves pulled through one. The enactment of this theme in the *MarketSite Experience* links the stock market to connotations of the "inevitable", and the act of trading on the stock exchange is imbued with a significance that renders it, for the investor, an obligatory station along the path to salvation. At the same time, the investor is given a promise: that NASDAQ is the one "enabling individuals to achieve their long-term investment goals".[33]

The inventions that are then presented, such as Bluetooth, etc – inventions that have become widespread thanks to capitalisations on NASDAQ – demonstrate the positive power that the stock exchange has over our everyday lives. The view of the trading floor – as presented at the NYSE – is here replaced by a view of the media centre, the so-called "Fishbowl". The name is said to have arisen from the impression created by the glass offices of the stock exchange reporters who, like goldfish in glass bowls, send out their NASDAQ reports to all four corners of the world.

Finally, a station is reached housing conventional computer terminals with Internet access.

These last three stations tie in directly with the visitor's own experiences. Bluetooth, the media and the Internet already have their connotations and these are here expanded within the context of NASDAQ. Thus we learn that NASDAQ is already a part of our lives, and that we too belong to the "[...] truly global community of investors".

---

33 Raymond Moody, *Leben nach dem Tod* (Hamburg: Rowohlt, 2001), pp. 46-49; (Original: Life After Death: Investigation of Phenomenon – Survival of Bodily Death (Covington, GA: Mockingbird Books, 1975); Bernard Jacoby, *Auch du lebst ewig* (Hamburg: Rowohlt, 2000), pp. 35, 39, 41; Hubert Knoblauch, *Berichte aus dem Jenseits: Mythos und Realität der Nahtod-Erfahrung* (Freiburg: Herder, 1999), pp. 61, 194, 198.

Museum of American Financial History – MoAFH [34]

Like other institutions bearing the title "museum", the MoAFH has a "mission statement", a collection and a permanent exhibition; it puts on temporary exhibitions, employs a curator and so forth. But in terms of content, the MoAFH does not live up to the notion that it houses academics carrying out research into the world of the rich.

> THE MUSEUM OF AMERICAN FINANCIAL HISTORY is committed to teaching the power of a democratic free market economy to better the financial lives of individuals, companies, and nations.[35]

This is not the mission statement of an *independent* museum – rather, we are dealing here with a statement of a political position. In his introductory note to the MoAFH – which, incidentally, is situated in the basement of the Standard Oil Building, the former power centre of John D. Rockefeller's business empire – Bill Clinton wrote this: "In teaching a new generation of Americans vital lessons about finance, you are helping to lay the foundation for our country's economic success." And the advertising leaflet states that "the Museum of American Financial History is the nation's only independent public museum dedicated to celebrating the capital markets."[36]

In keeping with these statements, and within a setting whose appearance is borrowed from that of a private library (shelves with a mahogany veneer, red plush carpet), the visitor learns about (1) the functioning of stock market dealing, (2) the importance of capitalism to the American Dream, and (3) some exemplary practitioners of the rules of capitalism.

All the above categories are dealt with in a manner consistent with this "dedication to celebrating the capital markets". Not only are the giants in the history of capitalism duly chronicled (General Electric, AT&T and many more), but other symbols of wealth are displayed too:

A plate from J.P. Morgan's yacht, a bottle of wine from Morgan's wine cellar, one of Morgan's cigars, Morgan's lighter and a bust of Morgan's secretary –

---

[34] Please note: this article deals with the MoAFH and its premises as experienced by the author in the year 2001. In fact, in November 28, 2005 the MoAFH changed its name to the "Museum of American Finanace", and at the same time issued a press release announcing its planned move from the Standard Oil Building at 26 Broadway to new premises, the former headquarters of the Bank of New York at 48 Wall Street. The new premises are expected to open by the end of 2006.

[35] Private archives of the author: Museum of American Financial History (ed.), *Mission Statement*.

[36] Private archives of the author: Museum of American Financial History (ed.), *Museum of American Financial History* (brochure).

these are objects from the life of a man who was, in the capitalist sense, successful. Here, they are raised to the status of relics, symbolising wealth and status.

The MoAFH makes no effort to conceal the nature of the picture of reality being painted here and the manner in which this story is being told. The advertising leaflet already cited makes it plain:

> It's the story of the American dream.[37]

And that is precisely the message of the MoAFH: the *American Dream* – if not necessarily the *American Reality* – is within the visitor's grasp.

Closing remarks

Exhibitions are media in which information may be imparted in a way that creates a sustained impact. There is no more engaging and intensive medium than that of a world that can be accessed and entered.

In the case of the exhibitions cited here, their creators, be they stock exchanges or museums, have used this medium in order to communicate their interpretations of stock-market capitalism. In the process, all three spheres of Falk and Dierking's model of "Contextual Learning" are touched on. Thus, for example, (1) the *Personal Context* sphere includes connections established with desires tied to financial circumstances, such as provision for old age or the education of one's children; well-known stories about personalities; and also the acceptance of status symbols (cigar, wine, yacht). (2) the *Sociocultural Context* category is represented by familiar media such as the Internet or by special news media and so forth. In terms of the (3) *Physical Context*, the location and its design are crucial. Wall Street, the view of the trading floor, the interior of the NASDAQ-Towers and the basement of John D. Rockefeller are locations charged with emotion, which radiate authenticity and remain securely fixed in the visitor's memory.

These New York exhibitions depict for us a reality in which the creative, supporting and fulfilling element is stock-exchange capitalism: the covenant of affluence becomes a reality for all who believe in it and participate in stock market capitalism.

The religious character here attributed to stock-exchange capitalism is clear to see, as is the manner in which these exhibitions elevate it to a doctrine of

---

37 ibid.

salvation, while at the same time raising to iconic status listed companies and successful speculators, these latter frequently being designated as *gurus*.

The New York exhibitions are descended from the tradition of the exhibition as a location for "making meaning". Firstly, they impress the visitor with their authenticity; secondly, they provide the visitor the chance to identify with the process of speculation by establishing connections with his or her needs for prosperity, success and social recognition. And thirdly, these exhibitions most certainly do win people over to their cause – that is, the belief that it is possible to realise one's objectives in life through speculation, or perhaps, like God, to "create something out of nothing".

Michael Bzdak

Money in the Bank? Corporate Support of the Arts in Twentieth-Century American Art

Over the past seventy-five years, Americans have become accustomed to seeing "corporation" and "the arts" in the same sentence. In reality, these two elements of American culture are antithetical and should create more discomfort than they do. In simple terms, business and the arts are not very compatible. The primary goal of the corporation is to create wealth for its shareholders while the typical arts non-profit exists to provide a cultural benefit to society. The fact that the corporation and the arts occur together regularly in our culture is perplexing and worthy of greater scrutiny. In fact, the history of twentieth-century American art is incomplete without a better understanding of the business influence on the art world.

Corporate, or private sector, involvement in all facets of our lives has raised the suspicions of many cultural observers. Most recently, Joel Bakan in his 2004 book, *The Corporation: The Pathological Pursuit of Profit and Power* has provided some rather dramatic examples of corporate power, greed and influence.[1] Bakan offers many reasons for the public to be much more critical and wary of the corporation's role in public life. Most important, he questions the practice of corporate philanthropy. However, very few writers have ventured specifically into the world of corporate art collecting and corporate philanthropic support of the arts. Chin-tao Wu casts recent corporate support of art in a critical and negative light in her 2002 book chronicling the privatization of culture since the 1980s in the US and Great Britain.[2]

The idea of business people influencing the production of art might be considered old news since the Medici family, as business leaders, embraced the arts many centuries ago.[3] In fact they, along with other prominent businesspeople, helped to make possible some of the great works of Renaissance

---

1 Joel Bakan, *The Corporation: The Pathological Pursuit of Profit and Power* (New York: Free Press, 2004); see also Clive Crook, "The Good Company", *The Economist*, January 22, 2005, pp. 11-19. The filmmaker Michael Moore has also taken criticism of big business to a new level and medium.

2 Chin-tao Wu, *Privatising Culture: Corporate Art Intervention since the 1980s* (London: Verso, 2002).

3 Tim Parks, *Medici Money: Banking, Metaphysics, and Art in Fifteenth-Century Florence* (New York: W. W. Norton & Company, 2005).

art and literature. Although this is true, the Medici were not organized according to the same rules and regulations that govern the modern corporation; most notably, they did not answer to many shareholders. However, the Medici, as bankers, are a particularly cogent example since they were bankers who were deeply involved in the culture of Italy and, through business relationships, the cultures of other countries.

Of all of the business sectors with critical relationships with the arts, banks provide us with the greatest number of noteworthy and recent case studies.[4] Financial institutions have been the dominant players ever since formal American corporate art collecting began in the 1960s. Given that, in many ways, art is like money, it is only natural that banks and bankers would have an interest in the arts. These interests, demonstrated over the past century, are multi-dimensional. The following essay examines the banking industry's relationship to the art world. The first section provides an introductory history of corporate art collecting in the United States with a focus primarily on three banks: 1) Chase Manhattan Bank; 2) Citibank; 3) FirstBank. The motivations for these banks to become arts patrons will also be addressed. Finally, corporate patronage and its effect on the worlds of art and/or business will be discussed. Chase Manhattan Bank, Citibank and FirstBank provide the opportunity to discuss three ways in which corporations have acquired art and supported the arts to influence various constituencies. These different constituencies include customers, employees, communities and stockholders.

The formal history of American twentieth-century arts and business collaborations begins in the 1930s. Three significant events occurred that have affected and shaped the relationship of art to business. First, early in the 1930s, the Rockefeller Center real estate development group, under the leadership of the Rockefeller family, made the decision to integrate art into their architectural complex.[5] Most notably, Diego Rivera was commissioned to paint a mural for one of the prominent public spaces. Not only was this a grand public statement by the private sector, it also emphasized the power and status of the Rockefeller family. Although the commission was not executed as planned, it has provided us with an important lesson on the limits of free expression when the expression is funded by corporate money; Rivera's expression was censored.

The second event, occurring in 1935, was the passing of a federal law that allowed corporations to deduct up to 5% of net income for charitable

4 Banks also provide models on how companies with affiliates, or branches, engage in community responsibility on a local as well as global level.

5 Ron Chernow, *Titan: The Life of John D. Rockefeller* (New York, Random House, 1998), pp. 669-670.

contributions.[6] This prompted increased business support of the non-profit sector in general. The third event was the formation of the IBM collection in 1937. The collection was started when the company purchased the work of artists from the 79 countries where they did business as well as acquiring two works from each of the United States.[7] Until this time, businesses had supported the arts mainly through commissioning art through advertising agencies.[8]

The banking industry entered the art world in a sustained and formal manner under the leadership of David Rockefeller. David Rockefeller deserves much of the credit for single-handedly forging a path where corporations could feel secure in publicly aligning themselves with the arts. His family's affiliation with the Museum of Modern Art and his leadership position at Chase Manhattan Bank in 1959 gave him the corporate and commercial clout to create one of the first American corporate art collections that actually rivalled public museum holdings.

Chase's collection evolved from the personal patronage of David Rockefeller, a style of patronage common among wealthy American families in the early twentieth century. Under his leadership, Chase began their formal collection in an era when public faith in the business world was very low.[9] It was in 1959 that the bank made the decision to organize an art acquisition committee to work in tandem with architects from Skidmore, Owings & Merrill to commission and buy art for a new headquarters in lower Manhattan that would include provisions for public art and a museum-quality art collection.[10]

Commissioning a large building in Lower Manhattan made a bold statement, while placing art inside and outside the building was even bolder with at least one half million dollars spent on public art alone. Few people realize, however, that Chase occupied only the lower half of the building leasing the upper half, except for the top floor, to tenants willing to pay high prices.[11] Chase's venture was not

---

6 Gideon Chagy, *The New Patrons of the Arts* (New York: Harry N. Abrams, 1972), p. 43.

7 Marjory Jacobsen, *Art for Work: The New Renaissance in Corporate Collecting* (London, Thames and Hudson, 1993), pp. 12-13.

8 Michele H. Bogart, *Artists, Advertising, and the Borders of Art* (Chicago: University of Chicago Press, 1995). Bogart provides a revealing and detailed history of advertising and art. In fact, many prominent visual artists began their careers in a commercial art studio. Andy Warhol is the most obvious example but many artists preceded him in this world of art and commerce.

9 See also Leonard Sloane, "Collecting at the Chase: Fine Art Stands for Good Business", *ARTnews*, Vol. 76, no. 4 (May, 1979), pp. 47-51.

10 *Art at Work: The Chase Manhattan Collection* (New York: E.P. Dutton, 1984).

11 Carol Willis, *Form Follows Finance: Skyscrapers and Skylines in New York and Chicago* (New York: Princeton Architectural Press, 1995), p. 151.

only a progressive step for bank architecture but more so for corporate art collecting. Hiring progressive architects to design bank buildings was not a new phenomenon, but buying major works of art was a relatively new idea.[12]

Chase management sought to assemble a museum-quality collection for its new building. Although the collection was meant to be of high quality, Chase never intended to compete with museums and always planned to maintain the art for the enjoyment of those in the building. Today, the J.P. Morgan Chase Collection includes more than 20,000 objects housed in over 350 locations worldwide. The Bank recently celebrated their 40th anniversary of acquiring art by publishing an elegant book.[13] Interestingly, while the Bank's original intent was to keep the works in the building, numerous travelling exhibitions have been organized over the past few years to take the Chase cultural message to many parts of the world. According to a company spokesperson, "The adventurous impulse that sparked the first acquisitions continues. The J.P. Morgan Chase collection mirrors the firm's values and its innovative approach to doing business."[14]

Chase deserves credit for sustaining their collection as well as their visible philanthropy to, and involvement in, the arts community. In a sense, Chase has helped to blur the distinction between the roles of community arts organizations and businesses.[15] Museums and banks play a major role in our lives and our

---

12 For a discussion of lower Manhattan architecture and bank architecture in particular, see Daniel W. Abramson, *Skyscraper Rivals: The AIG Building and the Architecture of Wall Street* (New York: Princeton Architectural Press, 2001); Lower Manhattan is home to experimental bank architecture from previous generations. For example, Voorhees, Walker and Gmelin's Irving Trust Building from the early 1930s was quite progressive for its time. The Irving Trust's stepped monumentality made a new statement in the vocabulary of modern skyscrapers and stood in obvious contrast to the neighbouring Bankers Trust Building and Bank of Manhattan Company building. Most important, the public space interiors were treated with lavish materials including a ceiling mural in the elevator lobby and an expressively abstract mosaic in the banking hall. This attention to interior detail enhanced the environment for employees and customers and increased the value of the real estate.

13 William B. Harrison, Jr., *Art at Work: Forty Years of the J. P. Morgan Chase Collection* (New York: J. P. Morgan Chase & Co., 1999); the book contains many photographs and very little explanatory text.

14 Harrison, *Art at Work*, p. 7. It is safe to say that David Rockefeller's family heritage gave him the cultural and social capital to lead Chase Manhattan in this new direction. The efforts were closely anchored in the legitimacy of cultural institutions such as the Museum of Modern Art and the Guggenheim Museum.

15 Chase actually used one of their SoHo branches as an art gallery in the 1980s; see Wu, *Privatising Culture*, p. 207f..

economy and have a ubiquitous presence in virtually all of our communities; they are visible symbols of responsibility and security. To complicate matters, most banks, including Chase, offer investment advice to wealthy art collectors. Since art has become something of a commodity, the return on art investments has evolved to a point where there are analysts who value art in the same way as they look at bond and stock market performance.

Since art is like money, it is not surprising that scholars and economists have attempted to tie the investment value of art to the stock market. Two professors from NYU have developed an index going back to 1960 that compares the performance of art sold at auction to the Standard and Poors 500.[16] According to their index, an investment of art, over the past 40 years, has yielded a slightly higher rate of return. Similarly, William Goettesmann from Yale has published extensively on the value of art as a commodity. Another economist has developed an investment tool that has proven that works by artists with Yale degrees fare much better in the art market. A further affirmation that art is indeed a commodity was announced in July 2004 when Fernwood Art Investments L.L.C. was founded as "the first independent firm to develop a comprehensive suite of art-focused investment, research and financial products...."[17] The fund will actually buy art but the client will not take the art home. Not surprisingly, the founder of the Citibank Art Advisory is one of the experts hired by the fund.

How can buying corporate art or supporting arts organizations with corporate dollars harmonize with a corporation's mission to maximize returns for its investors? Many argue that supporting the arts through collecting and corporate philanthropy is part of a company's social responsibility to their communities. Not so, according to Milton Friedman, the Nobel Prize winning economist, and many others who claim that a corporation's only true responsibility is to the stockholders.[18]

The growth of Corporate Social Responsibility (CSR) in the last 10 years has been dramatic. Business schools have created curricula around it, corporations publish CSR reports, and the Wall Street Journal and Business Week use the term freely and publish stories regularly on the topic.[19] One scholar has suggested that

---

16 Tim Gray, "When Beauty and Value Are in the Beholder's Eyes", Business Section, p. 8, *The New York Times*, August 29, 2004. Michael Moses and Jianping Mei have created an index of works dating back to 1875 including 13,000 transactions.

17 Carol Vogel, "Stocks, Bonds And Now Art", Weekend Arts Section, *The New York Times*, July 23, 2004, p. 2.

18 Friedman cited in Bakan, p. 34.

19 For example, Jessi Hemple and Lauren Gard, "The Corporate Givers", *BusinessWeek*, November 29, 2004, pp. 100-103.

we have entered a new economic phase that he calls "capitalism with a conscience."[20] This is a new twist on the theme of enlightened self-interest, a term used in earlier decades to justify and describe corporate philanthropy.

It can be argued that collecting art and philanthropically supporting arts organizations, when done correctly, actually return benefit to the stockholders and stakeholders of large corporations as well as the community. The most obvious and possibly the most complex return comes in the form of enhanced corporate reputation. As consumers, we make daily choices at the cash register and our decisions represent profit and loss for the makers of the products that we consume. Research has shown that consumers are willing to spend more for a product that they perceive to be made by a company with a conscience.[21] On a grander scale, a corporation seeking to do business in a new part of the world may find that they are unwelcome based on their reputation as an uncaring corporate citizen.

Few critics or arts writers ever consider the effect that a corporate collection has on employees. By commissioning good architecture and design and maintaining art within a facility, corporations make very explicit statements to employees, potential employees, the public and to stakeholders. Many job seekers are increasingly looking for employers who stand for something beyond the bottom line while in many cases, certain industry groups are engaged in a competitive search for talent in trying to hire the best new recruits.

More recently, another human resources issue that has become critical to all corporations is diversity. Corporate art, in some cases, has been called in as an ally as corporations are eager to show how they are diverse and engage in cultural awareness. In a 1999 Chase Manhattan publication on the company's art collection, William Harrison, Chairman and CEO writes: "Assimilating 'difficult' art into our daily lives is a potentially instructive and rewarding process. Face to face with our differences, we're given the opportunity to affirm the uniqueness of individual voices while discovering what unifies the diversity of backgrounds that makes up our institution."[22]

---

20 Ira Jackson cited in Bakan, *The Corporation,* p. 31f. The design and content of Chase's 2003 Community Partnership publication creates the impression that Chase is less like a large corporation and more like a small community-based non-profit organization; See *Impact: 2003 Community Partnership Report* (New York: J.P. Morgan Chase & Co., 2004).

21 See *The 2004 Cone Corporate Citizenship Study*, http://www.coneinc.com/Pages/pr_30.html.

22 Harrison, *Art at Work*, p. 7.

As previously mentioned, the history of American art includes some fascinating examples of artists who helped to create advertising for American companies. Not surprisingly, the companies that hired artists were primarily makers of consumer brands.[23] Citibank, now Citigroup, known for its arts patronage and art collection throughout the twentieth century, also engaged artists in helping to define its commercial mission. Although not as well known to the art public as Chase, Citibank's efforts, in some ways, preceded Chase's very visible entry into the art world.

A little-known Citibank advertising project, initiated in 1945 and continuing through 1958, engaged 20 artists and illustrators in the creation of more than 130 works of art.[24] Prominent American artists such as Thomas Hart Benton and Charles Sheeler took part in this visual campaign to promote Citibank's growing global presence as a financial services leader. Reproductions of the original works appeared in *Fortune*, *Time*, *Newsweek* and *BusinessWeek*. In addition, the images were accompanied by texts that spoke to the economics of the paintings' subjects. Many of these paintings continue to hang on the walls of Citibank, while few people are aware of the paintings and very little is known today about the advertising campaign. Not only did this remarkable group of paintings represent a wide variety of commercial activities, the art also represented the global reach of this bank. As a growing multinational company, Citibank executives engaged artists to help communicate the diversity of their business and cultural interests.

Today, the Citigroup collection includes more than 15,000 works from around the world. Citibank built a high profile skyscraper in the late 1970s but unlike Chase, decided to build in mid-town. Designed by Hugh Stebbins, the monumental Citicorp Center, with its triangular profile, has become an iconic element of the New York skyline. In 1979, Citibank created a unique new addition to their financial advising capacity by establishing its Art Advisory Service. According to their website, the specialists within the Art Advisory Service could provide the following services to their clients: "Create personalized strategies to build or disperse collections; identify acquisition opportunities around the globe; research attribution, condition, quality and value; and represent clients in transactions. [...] Evaluate and manage preservation and maintenance of art collections, including: insurance, conservation and framing, research,

---

23 Examples include Pepsi Cola, Dole pineapple juice and various automobiles and auto accessories.

24 CitiGroup curator Suzanne Lemakis graciously shared archival information on this campaign. Also, research was conducted by Rutgers University graduate student Betsy Parkyn in 2002. Citibank also published an internal article, "Citibank's Art Collection: Worldwide Search locates Missing Pieces", *Citibank World*, Vol. 1, No. 6, December 1992.

cataloguing, providing loans to exhibitions, shipping and security. […] Art Finance. Pioneered by Citibank to enable collectors to leverage their art collections. In most cases, the art remains in a client's home or office."[25]

This interesting marriage of art and culture provides wealthy art collectors with one-stop shopping for all facets of their art interests from collecting to advice on how to maximize tax advantage upon death. It would be fascinating to determine how customers of this service were drawn to the bank for their ability to deal with art as an asset. Is it possible that Citibank's reputation as a corporation that supported the arts both philanthropically and by collecting had any effect on clients and potential clients?

Most major banks today follow Rockefeller's model and are philanthropic leaders in supporting arts organizations. Certainly supporting the arts (especially grass roots arts non-profits) is seen as a sincere form of caring for the community. The philanthropists also have the potential to gain something from the relationship. Traditionally, business executives use non-profits as training grounds for their high potential employees. By serving on non-profit boards, future mangers are given real world experience in a context outside the walls of the corporation. At the extreme, CEOs and upper management often serve in leadership positions on the boards of major cultural organizations.

In most cases, the non-profit benefits not only by the generosity of the individual and his or her company but also by the influence the executive brings to the organization. This practice has come under criticism due to accusation that the executive and his or her company receive a benefit also. Chin-tao Wu sees corporations using cultural capital to influence, and ultimately, to convert this social influence into economic influence.[26]

It is often difficult to separate the style of an individual CEO and that of the corporation. One example is former Citigroup CEO Sandy Weil. During his tenure as CEO, Weil was extremely visible at high-profile exhibition receptions, ballet premieres and arts events of all types.[27] Many of his, and likely the bank's, favourite charities were dance companies and museums. Did the positive press attention accrue to Mr. Weil or to the bank? While impossible to quantify the benefits of cultural visibility, Mr. Weil's appearances in the press so often evoke

---

25 See Wealth Advisory section on the Citigroup web site, http://www.citibank.com/privatebank/wealth_life.htm.

26 Wu, *Privatising Culture*, pp. 6-9; the author, citing Paul DiMaggio's work, is particularly wary of this aspect of corporate power and influence.

27 A review of the *New York Times Sunday Style Section* from 1990-2000 would confirm and document Weil's almost weekly presence among the New York cultural elite.

David Rockefeller's monolithic presence as Chase Manhattan Bank's emissary in the 1960s and 1970s.

In more self-serving terms it is in the corporation's best interest to strengthen the communities in which it does business. Schools, hospitals, theatres and museums are all key elements of healthy urban communities. It is easy for corporations to justify civic philanthropy on this basis alone. It is this self-interest combined with very visible acts of generosity that define corporate philanthropy in this century. Likewise, by making the art hanging on the walls of corporations more publicly accessible, businesses can demystify and humanize the corporation. Certainly by buying the works of living artists, corporations can demonstrate their community responsibility in a very visible way.

A third American "bank as arts patron" example comes from outside of New York City. First Bank System was headquartered in Minneapolis, Minnesota and served customers in the upper mid-west and northwest. Their art collecting began in 1981 and was self-consciously designed to symbolize change- one change at hand was the deregulation of the banking industry- since deregulation was underway in the early 1980s. The collection was spearheaded by the bank president for whom the art collection became a personal project.

The bank's collecting strategy created controversy but company literature explained that the art was simply a reflection of its time and was purchased to provide "stimulus to thought."[28] From existing literature, it is clear that FirstBank Art Program leaders viewed the art program as a tool for change. They also formally solicited employee feedback through surveys and seminars. In their own words, the art program sought to "create a model structure in which the art [in this case] could act as a catalyst for dissent, discussion and encouragement of alternative operational styles which are vital to the health of the organization."[29]

In 1987, the collection comprised 3000 pieces. However, in 1988, the bank's profits began to decline and this decline marked the beginning of the end for this experiment in corporate art collecting. They acquired many of the most notable artists of the1980s art market. The works were often controversial in content and style. Coming to work and encountering aggressive, large-scale art became a jarring experience for employees and visitors. The managers of the Art Program designed many responses to the employee feedback on the art collection. In one case, reacting to worker dissatisfaction, employees were artificially empowered to banish works to what was called Controversy Corridor. According to their

---

28 Jacobson, *Art for Work*, p. 18.

29 ibid., p. 11.

published brochure, "The rules are simple: six people can 'banish' a work of art to Controversy Corridor; six people can retrieve it."[30]

This exercise, as at least one critic has pointed out, was blatantly artificial since the employees had no voice in the initial selection of art.[31] As part of their efforts to make the art more palatable to the employees, the FirstBank staff created feedback surveys. In one case, out of 10,000 employees (30% responded), 69% disliked the art, 25% liked it and 22% said that they thought it improved the workplace. Seventy percent said they stopped to read the didactic wall labels.[32] Some of the most controversial pieces were Andres Serrano's *Bloodstream, Milk Cross* and *Piss Elegance*; the collection also included Andy Warhol's *Mao* print portfolio.

Not surprisingly, the company faced increasing pressure after losing $300 million in the bond market in1988. During 1988 and 1989, the Art Program was sustained by selling works from the collection. The collection's demise can be attributed to five factors: 1) the program and collecting practices were not linked to the employees and the local community in meaningful ways; 2) there was a perception that the Art Program was a folly of the CEO; 3) the collection demonstrated that art culture and corporate culture are not compatible; 4) the bank was losing money; 5) people do not like to be the subjects of experiments, especially in the workplace. Their investment in art, however, did pay some dividends: works purchased over 10 years for $5 million were worth $10 million in 1990.[33] First Bank's unusual decade-long experiment also perfectly exemplifies the frenzied art world of the 1980s. Artists gained rapid and monumental notoriety and acquired rock-star like personae. The new wealth derived from the stock market was in many cases converted into the acquisition of art. In 1986, more than 800 corporations collected art and many hired art historians and museum professionals to manage them.

In conclusion, it can be argued that some good has come from corporate America's cultural interventions, ranging from sponsorships to commissions and acquisitions in the twentieth century. In the area of philanthropy, corporate support has allowed many non-profit cultural organizations and / or artists to

---

30 Lynne Sowder, *The Second Year: Controversy Corridor* (Minneapolis: First Bank Systems, 1989), p. 1.

31 Richard Bolton, "The Contradictions of Corporate Culture: Creative Collecting Proves Risky Business", *New Art Examiner*, April, 1990, pp. 18-21.

32 ibid.; also, John Herzfeld, "Take this Art and...", *ARTnews*, Vol. 86, no. 4 (April, 1987), pp. 12-13.

33 Walter Robinson, "Minnesota Bank Loses Interest in Provocative Art", *Art in America*, Vol. 78 (March, 1990), pp. 35-37, 239.

flourish. For example, Liz Claiborne hired prominent artists to participate in a social issues/ cause-related marketing campaign in 1991-92 – ranging from literacy in Chicago to domestic violence in San Francisco and to land reclamation in Atlanta – using contemporary art to expose social issues in their major retail markets.[34] In other cases, many museums have relied on corporate support to organize and/or host major exhibitions. Corporate support, both financial and in-kind, has helped organizations to develop sustainable practices, actually applying basic business practices to their operations. A small number of organizations have gone so far as to develop business-inspired, for-profit satellites that fuel their core cultural mission.

Another outcome of the growth of corporate art collecting in the 1980s was the development of new markets for specific types of art. Printmaking and photography enjoyed increased attention from buyers. Prints and photographs proved to be accessible on at least two levels to collectors. Primarily, the cost of prints by known artists was affordable compared to painting and sculpture. Secondly, the subject matter of prints of photographs was, in most cases, considered safe for corporate consumption.[35] There is also evidence that the corporate art boom in the 1980s enabled many women artists to have their works purchased by corporations. It is also safe to say that employees of the more enlightened companies have actually become better art consumers and art supporters as a result of their exposure to art in the workplace.

A survey was conducted in 2003 by the Business Committee for the Arts and the International Association for Professional Art Advisors to determine the value of art in the workplace from the employee perspective. Some of the findings include: a large majority of employees believed that art served to reduce stress; it increased creativity and enhanced morale; and it encouraged diversity. Not surprisingly, the survey also showed that employees believed that the art enhanced the work environment and also helped to further the business through

---

34 Margery Jacobson provides a good summary of these interventions; see note 7 above.

35 On the downside, one of the negative outcomes of the growth of corporate art collecting was the proliferation of a new class of decorative art that was created to fill the miles of walls in new corporate buildings. Mostly abstract and primarily geometric, this art has become a category of decorative art now known pejoratively as corporate art. For a discussion of some of the issues associated with the boom in corporate collecting see Rosanne Martorella, *Corporate Art* (New Brunswick: Rutgers University Press, 1990); on the positive side, the prevalence of corporate collecting may have helped to open up sales of art for women artists; see Randy Rosen, *Making Their Mark: Women Artists Move into the Mainstream, 1970-85* (New York: Abbeville Press, 1989), p. 220.

customer and community relations.[36] Unlike the very public corporate sponsorships of the 1980s, banks today tend to focus their cultural presence on projects and institutions in their key communities and increasingly focus on international markets. Chase, unlike many others, also has the power of its art collection to demonstrate the company's commitment to the arts

Philanthropy also serves to help banks continue to position themselves within the world of culture. Today, J.P. Morgan Chase and Citibank are among the nation's most generous corporations as well as two of the largest supporters of art and culture. In a 2003 survey of cash giving conducted by BusinessWeek, three of the top 10 givers were banks.[37] The 6th most generous corporation was J.P. Morgan Chase at $86 million while Bank of America weighed in at the number 7 spot at $85.4 million and Citigroup was number 10 at $81.4 million. While these numbers seem dramatic, the money donated still only represents less than 1% of pre-tax net income for each company.

Corporate philanthropy is only now receiving the scrutiny it deserves. As shareholders voice concerns about the amount of money a company may give, consumers in general have expressed an increasing interest in what a company stands for. How much a company gives is one simple measure of a company's social responsibility. How much they talk about it is an entirely different story. This increased scrutiny comes from customers, employees, community members and stockholders.[38]

To understand better what consumers actually think about companies, Harris Interactive and the Reputation Institute embarked on a fascinating research project in 1999.[39] Their method was to ask a large sample of random consumers a number of specific questions about their perceptions of about 60 companies. Their goal was to develop a Reputation Quotient for each of these companies. Consumers rated companies on 20 attributes in 6 categories. These categories are Emotional Appeal, Financial Performance, Products and Services, Social

---

36 The survey results can be found at the IAPAA's web site: www.iapaa.org/news.

37 Hemple, "The Corporate Givers", p. 102.

38 For a discussion of the various surveys and measures of corporate social activity, see Christy Eidson and Melissa Master, "Top Ten... Most Admired... Most Respected", *Across the Board*, Vol. XXXVII, No. 3, March, 2000, pp. 16-22.

39 In an attempt to quantify corporate reputation, Harris Interactive, in collaboration with Charles Fombrun and Cees von Riel, have developed an assessment tool that looks at six elements of a corporation's public face ranging from Emotional Appeal to Vision and Leadership. Complete information can be found on the Harris Interactive web site: www.harrisinteractive.com.

Responsibility, Vision and Leadership and, finally, Workplace Environment.[40] Findings indicate that consumers are interested in how corporations embrace social issues. These enlightened consumers are not afraid to vote with their wallets. According to one survey, 86% of consumers claim that they would switch brands to another associated with a social cause.[41]

There are many examples of how art and commerce have collided in the past fifty years with the banking industry leading the way. As perennial symbols of wealth and power, banks have always been prominent fixtures in the civic life of American cities. As they have become more global, banks have strategically used their affiliation with culture to demonstrate their social responsibility.[42] This essay has examined three different approaches to marrying art and culture taken by the private sector and more specifically by American-based banks. These examples represent an aspect of American culture that has not been studied in depth. Given the limited access to the company's collections and to their archives, scholarship on art and commerce is challenging. However, in an age of increasing calls for transparency and corporate social responsibility, more scholarship on this important chapter in the history of art will be forthcoming.

We have entered an era where the most enlightened corporations are strategic philanthropists. It is not enough to collect art or support arts organizations. It has become a question of what you do with your art collection and how your arts giving makes an impact on a community. The practice of social responsibility has taken on a new level of importance as stakeholders and the general public demand more transparency from corporations. New models of social responsibility whereby corporations can acquire art and help an organization at the same time are beginning to surface. In some cases, corporations have donated their collections to public institutions.

The reason that Chase and Citibank have managed to thrive as corporate cultural leaders is due to their success at integrating their art collections and support of the arts into their corporate cultures. FirstBank failed miserably since their approach underscored the differences between the world of art and the world of commerce as well as the danger of not engaging stakeholders. As the study of

---

40 In 2001, of the 60 companies, only 2 were banks. This is not surprising given that consumers are much more cognizant of companies that make things like Microsoft, Coca Cola and Unilever.

41 Summary of communication company Cone's research can be found at http://www.coneinc.com/Pages/pr_30.html

42 More recently, Deutsche Bank has also stepped up its collecting and social responsibility efforts. They published this elegant coffee table book in the year 2000. Alistair Hicks, *Art Works: British and German Contemporary Art 1960-2000* (London: Merrell Publishers Limited, 2000).

art and commerce in the United States is still in its infancy, it is important to study the lessons that our major banks have provided. Their bold experiments in bridging two seemingly antithetical worlds can serve as lessons for both the corporate world and the art world as they seek to co-exist and benefit from one another.

Mary O'Neill

Art and Money: Experience Destruction Exposure

The relationship between art and money is, at times, a tale of domination and censorship so subtle that even those producing the art works and the audience are frequently unaware that they are being influenced. I do not wish to suggest that commerce automatically corrupts the world of art or that all art should address this issue. Nor do I wish to suggest that this tangled relationship is a recent phenomenon.[1] I would suggest, however, that as users, producers, and commentators we should be aware of the system in which we operate. Pierre Bourdieu, in his conversation with the German artist, Hans Haacke discusses patronage and describes the hidden nature of the relationship, he states:

> Patronage is a subtle form of domination that acts thanks to the fact that it is not perceived as such. All forms of symbolic domination operate on the basis of misrecognition, that is, with the complicity of those who are subjected to them."[2]

He also refers to a lack of awareness and remarks how so few artists and writers are sensitive to the forms of domination that are exerted on the art world. There are many reasons for this insensitivity and I would suggest that it is a combination of pragmatism, helplessness, and lack of interest – however that is a concern for another paper. What I wish to focus on are those artists who were and are sensitive to the relationship between art and money and the risk to the independence of art posed by the hidden nature of this relationship. I have chosen to look at works by three artists, Lygia Clark, Hans Haacke, and Gustav Metzger, who have addressed this relationship very directly, but in very different ways.

---

1 There are numerous historical examples of attempts to address this relationship e.g. Roger Fry's article "Art and Commerce" (*Journal of Cultural Economics* 22, 1998, pp. 49-59, first published in 1926); Robert Hughes, "On Art and Money" *The New York Review of Books* 31, No. 19 (1984). In his review, "Co-opting the arts" (*Art in America*, October 2002), Robert Atkins discusses two recent books that address this issue; he states "we are long overdue for a new 'institutional critique' of the intertwined relationship of art, money and power".

2 Pierre Bourdieu and Hans Haacke, *Free exchange* (Cambridge: Polity Press in association with Blackwell, 1995), p. 54.

Ian Burns, co-founder of the Society for Theoretical Art and Analyses,[3] in his essay *The Art Market: Affluence and Degradation* discusses the influence of economics on art production:

> While it may once have seemed an exaggeration of economic determinism to regard works of art as 'merely' commodities in an economic exchange, it is now pretty plain that our entire lives have become so extensively constituted in these terms that we cannot any longer pretend otherwise. Not only do works of art end up as commodities, but there is also an overwhelming sense in which works of art *start off* as commodities.[4]

Burns is echoing Adorno's remarks in his essay *Culture Industry Reconsidered* when he states: "Culture entities typical of the culture industry are no longer *also* commodities, they are commodities through and through."[5]

The Brazilian artist Lygia Clark (1920-1988) addressed the notion of art as commodity. Her work examined the various roles within the art world – the artist, the mediating object, and the spectator – and relationships between these. Her works were largely un-saleable and could often be recreated using cheap, easily available materials. The American artist Daniel Buren argues that: "If the artist has anything against the art system, he should start by rebelling against himself as an artist, i.e. against his own product as a culture-gadget."[6] Clark attempted to transform the role of artist and spectators and to create an in-between state of joint participation in which both were responsible for the creation of the work.[7] Clark offered what she termed 'propositions' rather than complete artworks, which the participant could complete. The presence of the participants' body was essential and the work only existed in the moment of participation. The critic and writer Guy Brett, one of Clarks' fiercest advocates, says of her work: "The object made no sense without the living body, the present act, and therefore to alienate it as a commodity, to preserve it as an art work, was meaningless."[8]

---

3 Founded in New York in 1969.

4 Ian Burns, "The Art Market: Affluence and Degradation" *Artforum* (April 1975), pp. 34-37, here: p. 34.

5 Theodor W. Adorno, *The Culture Industry: Selected Essays on mass culture* (London: Routledge, 1991), p. 100.

6 Daniel Buren is quoted in Barbara Reise (ed.), "Gurgles around the Guggenheim" *Studio International*, no. 181 (June 1971), pp. 246-250. Buren's work had been removed from the Guggenheim International 1971.

7 She was critical of the idea of the artist as a demiurge and criticised those artists who fostered a shaman-like image, for example her contemporary, Joseph Beuys.

8 Guy Brett, "Six Cells", in *Lygia Clark. Exhibition Catalogue* (Barcelona: Fundacio Antoni Tapies, 1997), pp. 17- 35, here: p. 19.

Clark's work de-emphasised the visual and, in some cases, went as far as obscuring the sense of vision altogether. This forced the participant to experience the work through other senses, again rendering the notion of a passive 'viewer' obsolete. These works were not meant to be viewed but to be experienced. Brett writing in the *Third Text* describes Clark's *Air & Stone* as being simultaneously one of Clark's simplest and most complex works.[9]

> What is the sensation of first inflating it and putting it between one's hands? Its utterly simple communication of emptiness and fullness, of weight and lightness? Its open sensuality which seems to merge the attributes of male and female? An experience of the tenderness of one's own hands, or handling? It is all these things at once. At the same time, you realize it could just as easily be dismissed as 'nothing'. It has the Zen-like quality of a paradoxical initiation in 'life'.[10]

Clark, always concerned with the use value of her work, eventually stopped making work for a gallery setting and began making objects that were used in therapy session for her 'clients'.

Clark's works also raises the issue of the fate of these works when acquired by galleries or when documented, and the documentation itself becomes a commodity, highlighting the difficulty of avoiding the market and the art world's ability to commodify everything.[11] This issue is also significant in relation to the work of Gustav Metzger.

Gustav Metzger's career has been one of resistance, to the commodification of his work, to the pressure to make permanent art which the market exerts on artists, and to commercial art venues. And yet his output demonstrates not distaste for the art world but a love for the world of art and a desire to protect and repair it. Metzger had good reason to be concerned about art, for he had seen for himself how art could be used as a powerful political weapon. Metzger was born in Nuremberg in 1926 into an Orthodox Jewish family. Metzger was aware, for example, how the Nazi uniforms became more stylish year by year, creating and reinforcing an impression of an increase in power and influence. The infamous Party rallies which took place in Nuremberg made a big impression on the young Metzger. From these, he learnt about the power of art, the way that events can be orchestrated to achieve a desired effect. The Nazis manipulated these events in

---

9 To make *Air & Stone* inflate a small clear polythene bag and tie it with an elastic band. Place a smooth stone in a depression made in one corner. Gently press the sides of the bag so that the stone rises and falls in the depression.

10 Guy Brett, "Lydia Clark: The Borderline between art [and] life", in *The Third Text*, (Autumn 1987), pp. 65-94, here: p. 84.

11 There is of course the economy of which I am a part that includes catalogues, photographs, reproduction rights, conferences and research focusing on their work.

part to impress their followers but, like all military parades, they were also designed to instil fear in their enemies. Metzger and one of his brothers Mendel escaped to Great Britain on a "Kindertransport" in 1939 when he was twelve years old. His parents, grandparents, and older brother perished in a concentration camp. These traumatic early experiences coupled with his experience of political activism through his successful North End Protest and his involvement with the Committee of 100, a militant splinter group of CND, had a significant effect on the shaping of Metzger's worldview and his art.[12]

If Gustav Metzger is known at all, it is for his Auto Destructive Art Manifestos and demonstrations. "Auto Destructive Art is art which contains within itself an agent which automatically leads to its destruction within a period of time."[13] In the third of his manifestos, he links destruction to creativity. This use of destruction for what he saw as beneficial ends is clearly illustrated in Metzger's call for 'Years Without Art'. In 1974 Metzger was invited to participate in a group show at the ICA in London: *Art into society/Society into Art: Seven German Artists.*[14] Metzger decided not to include a piece in the show and instead he demonstrated his disillusionment with the art world by his catalogue inclusion – *Years without Art, 1977-1980.* This piece is indicative of Metzger's work of the period in that it is what is absent that is significant. His work could be seen as performing two related functions – to use art as an agent of social change and as a way of reforming the artworld itself. However he was aware of the acute difficulty of making political work when the artworld is so closely bound to the possessors of power, and in his call to down tools he describes the predicament facing artists. In Metzger's view:

> The use of art for social change is bedevilled by the close integration of art and society. The state supports art, it needs art as a cosmetic cloak to its horrifying reality, and uses art to confuse, divert and entertain large numbers of people. Even when deployed against the interests of the state, art cannot cut loose the umbilical cord of the state.[15]

Given his belief in the benefit of destruction as a route to change – destruction for improvement, it is not surprising that he should eventually call for an outright Art

---

12 Biographical details are taken from Clive Philpott's chronology in Gustav Metzger et al., '*damaged nature, auto destructive art*' (London: Coracle, 1996) and comments in Ken McMullen's documentary film *Pioneers in Art and Science: Metzger* (London: Arts Council, 2004).

13 From Gustav Metzger's *Manifesto Auto-Destructive Art*, first issued on 10th March 1960 and reprinted in Metzger et al., '*damaged nature, auto destructive art*', op. cit.

14 Hans Haacke was one of the artists included in this show.

15 Gustav Metzger, *Art into Society/ Society into Art.* ICA. Exhibition Catalogue, 1974.

Strike – the cessation of all art activity for three years. Like a chronically ill patient whose heart is stopped momentarily in the hope that once restarted it will have a sustainable rhythm, Metzger's Strike was a desperate measure in an attempt to save the art world, what Metzger described as 'deep surgery', a germination or fallow period. This act then was to be a sacrifice; it might not have seemed productive at the time, but was in fact something given up for a greater long-term gain. Metzger highlights the benevolence of this action when he describes this as a 'reformist' rather than a 'revolutionary' action.

Metzger gave three-year advance notice of the proposed strike. He first issued his call in 1974, proposing that the strike be held between 1977-1980, thus giving adequate time for artists to find other ways of making a living. Metzger did point out that most artists were not in fact supported by their work, but produced it at a loss and would thereby save money as a result of the strike. There was provision within the scheme for artists who were overwhelmed with the need to be creative – "These artists will be invited to enter camps, where the making of art works is forbidden, and where any work produced is destroyed at regular intervals."[16] Metzger was criticised for this suggestion as it appeared to represent an authoritarian attitude that was in contradiction with Metzger's philosophy. He has since remarked that this section of the call was meant to be a joke.[17] He suggested alternative outlets for the artist's energies in the consideration of the artworld and the construction of a new and more equitable system that could be put in place at the end of the period. Metzger himself observed the three year abstinence; however, his call was not met with enthusiasm. In fact, when asked how other artists responded to his call, Metzger replied "nobody took the slightest notice" and concluded that "artists were 'disgusting bastards'". Inspired by what he viewed as Freud's greatest success – that he forced the world to face up to the challenge of self-examination, Metzger shares that desire. "I need to take up that function of saying to myself and others ... face up to what is instead of denying ... [and ask] What is the source of you being an artist, where does the money come from? What are the implications of accepting that money, that patronage?"[18]

Another German-born artist, Hans Haacke, also takes up these questions. Haacke was born in Cologne in 1936. As with Metzger, a pivotal piece by Hans Haacke was a work that didn't happen. This was Haacke's 1971 exhibition highlighting the hidden relationship between the art world and commerce, which was cancelled by the Guggenheim for fear of offending the museum's patrons.

---

16 ibid.

17 McMullen, *Pioneers in Art and Science: Metzger*, op. cit.

18 ibid.

One of the themes which runs through Haacke's work is an attempt to expose the invisible manipulation of public opinion exercised by multinational corporations by their use of patronage of art to create an image of humane and enlightened cultural values, often masking suspect political affiliations or unethical business practices.

The specific contemporary danger to the independence of art is identified by Ian Burns in a 1975 *Artforum* article:

> What we have seen more recently is the power of market values to distort all other values, so even the concept of what is and is not acceptable as 'work' is defined first and fundamentally by market and only secondly by 'creative urge' (etc.).[19]

This issue is highlighted by two encounters between Haacke and the superstructure of art in the 20th century, The Guggenheim and the Museum of Modern art in New York.

In MOMA-Poll 1970, 'installation for audience participation' in the Museum of Modern Art's *Information* exhibition, visitors to the exhibition were faced with a question: "Would the fact that Governor Rockefeller has not denounced President Nixon's Indochina policy be a reason for you not to vote for him in November?" They were given ballot papers and asked to cast the vote into one of two boxes each of which was fitted with a counting device. This piece highlighted the relationship between the Rockefeller family, who had helped found and financially support the Museum of Modern Art and Richard Nixon. Nelson Rockefeller was the then Republican Governor of New York and had been on MoMa board of trustees since 1932. This led to a correspondence between the director of the museum David Hightower and David Rockefeller who was also a museum trustee.[20] David Rockefeller agreed that Haacke's work should not be removed or changed, because this would interfere with the artist's freedom of expression; however, what he did question was whether in fact this work could be called art at all. This objection is the very nub of that subtle influence of patronage, the risk to art as described by Bourdieu, the power to determine what is and is not art.

Given the controversy surrounding the MOMA poll it seems surprising that the Guggenheim were unprepared for the territory they were getting into by agreeing to exhibit a work by Haacke in 1971. Haacke's proposed exhibition consisted of three systems – social, political, and biological. It was the social system, *Shapolsky et al. Manhattan Real Estate Holdings, A Real Time Social*

19 Ian Burns, "The Art Market: Affluence and Degradation", in *Artforum* (April 1975), pp. 34-37, here: p. 34

20 Reise (ed.), *Gurgles at the Guggenheim*, op. cit.

System, May I 1971, which proved problematic for the Guggenheim. This section consisted of photographs of the façade of Manhattan real estate holdings, which were accompanied by business information relating to these properties. All the information had been collected from the public record office of the County Clerk and was therefore freely available. Thomas Messer, director of the Guggenheim Museum, again raised the question of what is a suitable and appropriate subject for art:

> I would say that at the point at which the intention and the result of a work is no longer general, summary, metaphoric and symbolic, by the point it addresses itself to a known specific topical situation, its status as a work of art – or at least its immunity as a work of art – is in question.[21]

In his correspondence with Haacke, Messer states:

> [...] under our Charter we are pursuing [a]esthetic and educational objectives that are self-sufficient and without ulterior motive. On those grounds, the trustees have established policies that exclude active engagement toward social and political ends.[22]

Taken to its logical conclusion this argument would prevent the Guggenheim from exhibiting works by Picasso, Goya, and all religious art.

Haacke entered into correspondence with Messer in the hope of arriving at an acceptable compromise. Messer replied to changes suggested by Haacke: "the implied changes that you propose to inject would render the same displays inappropriate for presentation in this museum though not necessarily elsewhere since it would hopelessly confuse assumptions under which we now function."[23] Interestingly, this suggests that the work itself is of a museum standard and therefore confirms its status as art, but it is the context that is at issue. This then created a completely new category of art – art that is offensive in the context of the Guggenheim. This is perhaps not very surprising, given the subsequent history of the Guggenheim as a global art brand, with branches in Bilbao, Berlin, Venice, and Las Vegas as well as two branches in New York. This has led some critics to refer to these galleries as part of the 'McGuggenheim' franchise.

Donald Kuspit in his article *Regressive Reproduction and Throwaway Conscience* is a harsh critic of what he terms "confrontational representation". He discusses the work of Jenny Holzer, Barbara Kruger, and Hans Haacke; and refers to their indebtedness to reproductive technology, which he sees as inconsistent with their aims. He states:

---

21 Benjamin Buchloh, "Hans Haacke: Memory and Instrumental Reason", in *Art in America*, vol. 76 (1988), pp. 97-159, here: p. 99.

22 Reise (ed.), *Gurgles at the Guggenheim*, op. cit., here p. 249.

23 ibid., p. 250.

> Neo-moralist art falls short of its goal without knowing it, because of its distrust of the humanism of imagination – its preference for the illusions of reproductive representation.[24]

He describes them as being no different from any other "creative novelty" in the social machine. This criticism however does not take account of the imagination of the viewer, who can distinguish between the dehumanising global media and when those media are used to highlight the issue. Bourdieu suggests that artists have an ability to manipulate the media in a way that political movements do not, and that this gives the artist a particular power. He argues as follows:

> This is where the specific competence of the artist is so important, because a person cannot just suddenly become a creator of surprise and disconcertion. The artist is the one who is capable of making a sensation, which does not mean being sensational, like television acrobats, but rather, in the strong sense of the term, putting across on the level of sensation – that is – touching the sensibility, moving people – analyses which would leave the reader or spectator indifferent if expressed in the cold rigor of concept and demonstration.[25]

Not only does Kuspit criticise these artists for their means of production but also he does so on grounds that must strike fear in the heart of anyone who objects – the fear of being co-opted, of being used as a pawn by the very system to which one is objecting, so that one comes to represent that bit of acceptable self-criticism that shows just how broadminded and open a particular society or institution is.

> The social moralist artists become more manipulated than manipulative: they are used "creatively" by the social machine. They become a tic within the social machine, a minor malfunctioning, easily corrected yet allowed to exist at the whim of the powers that be. It uses them to show the full extent of its powers.[26]

Kuspit is echoing a wider argument that the avant-garde is always assimilated and co-opted to support the status quo, that, in fact, the avant-garde is the new establishment. However, I would suggest an alternative way of looking at this assimilation, which would also apply to artists making political work. Within any group of artists there will be those who will be less committed to autonomy than others, there will be those who can more easily reconcile their art to the market, and those who succumb to the charms of canonisation. Among those who achieve some sort of success and reputation but retain their political commitment there

---

24 Donald Kuspit, "Regressive Reproduction and Throwaway Conscience", in *Art Scribe International* (Jan/Feb 1987), pp. 26-31, here: p. 31.

25 Bourdieu and Haacke, *Free exchange*, p. 28.

26 Kuspit, "Regressive Reproduction and Throwaway Conscience", p. 30.

may well be those artists whose message is understood and has an impact in a positive sense of adding to and improving rather than begin engulfed by the institution they address. An example of this would be work that addressed the political situation in South Africa prior to the end of Apartheid.

To say that artists such as Clark, Haacke and Metzger would inevitably be used to reinforce the *status quo* suggests that they are/were working naively and uncomprehendingly within a system. On the contrary, all were well acquainted through personal experience with the symbolic power of art and how it could be used both for good or ill with repercussions far beyond the world of art. Although working in different countries and at different times, they have an underlying belief in art and the ability of art to be a vehicle for social and personal change. They were/are also aware of the risks of art being used for propaganda and each strove to make their public aware of this. Interestingly, to achieve a degree of independence, all three found sources of income other than directly from their work, which freed them to some extent from the constraints imposed by the art market.[27]

If one looks at Haacke's career there is a sense in which he is the acceptable revolutionary within the art world. He is an insider, having exhibited in Documenta and participated in the Venice Biennale – these are not the career moves of an artist who has alienated those with power within the system. However, after the Guggenheim cancellation of his show he was not invited to show in an American public gallery for fifteen years.[28] Like Clark and Metzger, his work was more successful in Europe.[29] If he is the acceptable face of art's self-examination, he has proved to be a force to be reckoned with and only institutions confident enough to endure a high level of self-examination and exposure can risk an encounter with him.

Metzger says himself that his work was largely ignored and critics Guy Brett and Yve-Alain Bois state that Clark did not in her lifetime receive the recognition she deserved. This however, may have its advantages. Patricia Bickers, referring to Lucy Lippard's[30] comments in *The Dematerialization of Art*, states "it would seem that Conceptual Art's best hope of avoiding commodification lay in the likelihood of it, and its agenda, effectively being ignored."[31]

---

27 Haacke taught at Cooper Union. Lygia Clark taught at the Sorbonne 1968-1976.

28 From an interview with Ilana Stanger of TheArtBiz.com, found on www.nyfa.org.

29 Possibly reflecting the difference between American and European art funding.

30 Lucy Lippard was a co-founder of The Art Workers Coalition along with Hans Haacke in 1969.

31 Patricia Bickers, "'Oh Politics Schmolitics!' Art in the Postmodern Age", in *Third Text*, vol. 16, Issue 4 (2002), p. 337.

Metzger is enjoying a resurgence of interest in his work. For example, the call for *Years Without Art* was taken up by other artists some years later – Stewart Home organised an 'Art Strike' between 1990 and 1993[32] and Gavin Wade curated the exhibition *'Strike'* in 2002, both of which referred to Metzger's *Years Without Art.*[33] Increasingly, exhibitions that reflect on the legacy of the art of the 60's now include Lygia Clark.[34] This does not necessarily mean that they have been co-opted but rather that their messages are even more pertinent now that we have lived through two decades of the legacy of Reagan and Thatcher when the art world surrendered to market forces.[35] It suggests a looking back to the sixties as a golden age of engagement when art had a social and political value and was seen as part of society, not merely a commodity or part of a celebrity culture but a field of intellectual inquiry.

These artists highlighted questions of value within the art world; a world that prioritizes exchange value over use or experiential value, where big business (one thinks of Saatchi and Saatchi) can subtly influence the type of art that is appropriate to represent our age, the type of work that will be purchased by institutions and will form the 20th and 21st century sections of the museums of the future. They produced work that is performative, in much the same way that Eve Kosofsky Sedgwick describes knowledge as performative i.e. "knowledge does rather than simply is".[36] Haacke, Metzger and Clark are concerned with knowledge and power in their works, which 'do' rather than 'are'. We are not being asked to simply look, but to think, to feel, and to act. They ask us to take art seriously, to appreciate that it has a value beyond its role as a marketable commodity, to be bought, sold, and kept safe for investment purposes. This is not autonomous art but art that has a value for our culture. They offer an opportunity, as Metzger says, to face up to things, to see and question those things which we take as given. These works encourage, lead, and stimulate the viewer/reader/participant into an interactive participatory mode of perception and collaboration.

---

32 Stewart Home The Art Strike papers are available at http://www.stewarthomesociety.org/artstrik.htm. *About the Art Strike* can be accessed at http://www.thing.de/projekte/7:9%23/y_About_the_Art_Strike.html.

33 Wade asked artists to submit text in response to two questions: "How does/could/would the withdrawal of art affect the world? And, does the answer to the question reveal ways that art can affect the world or strike a blow on the structures of the world?"

34 A forthcoming symposium at Tate Modern will include a discussion of Clark's work.

35 Discussed by Patricia Bickers in 'Oh Politics Schmolitics!", op.cit.

36 Eve Kosofsky Sedgwick, *Touching feeling: affect, pedagogy, performativity* (Durham, N.C.; London: Duke University Press, 2003), p. 124.

Sina Vatanpour

Money, Language and Identity in Paul Auster's *City of Glass* and *Ghosts*

On a first reading of *City of Glass* and *Ghosts*, money – which appears as cash, check or money order – seems to be a mere formality, something that has to be mentioned rather than a structural component of the story. The payment by the client and its acceptance by the detective seal the contract between the two parties; their engagements mark the start of the story and set the elements in motion.

In *City of Glass*, the protagonist Daniel Quinn, ex-poet and now writer of detective stories is woken up in the middle of the night by phone calls that ask to speak with a detective named Paul Auster. The following night, Quinn decides to play the role of Paul Auster, the detective, for motives that are not clearly explained. He meets Peter and Virginia Stillman, who commission him to protect them against Peter's father who will be released from prison the next day. As Quinn explains, he does not do "any of this for money" (p. 37)[1], yet in order to put himself in the clear and make things look real he fixes a price for his work.

> My fee is one hundred dollars a day plus expenses, if you could give me something in advance, it would be proof that I am working for you – which would ensure us a privileged investigator-client relationship. (p. 36)

Mrs Stillman makes out a check for five hundred dollars to Paul Auster, then as in a traditional detective novel, she throws her arms around him and kisses him passionately. The kiss and the check are both promises to pay, neither of which will materialise. Quinn, who is not Paul Auster, cannot cash the check and he does not meet Virginia Stillman again.

Such a contract has several obvious and immediate effects. Firstly, it provides the characters with economic existence; it brings them to life, makes the story and the characters credible.[2] Secondly, the act of paying is a means of acquisition of

---

1 All quotations in the text are from Paul Auster, *The New York Trilogy: City of Glass, Ghosts, The Locked Room* (New York: Penguin, 1990).

2 As Christian Arnsperger remarks, division of work and circulation of merchandise has structured our lives so profoundly that today no human existence is possible without economic existence. Christian Arnsperger, "L'inestimable valeur de l'Autre: argent, altérité et socialite", in *L'Argent, croyance, mesure, spéculation,* ed. Marcel Drach, *Recherches* (Paris: La Découverte, 2004), p. 42.

power; it becomes the instrument through which the 'employer' exercises his will on the employee. He buys the other's time and work and making money becomes the motivation that justifies the detective's actions that consequently unfold the plot. Thirdly, being paid or paying mark the characters as separate and independent identities. This last point, despite its triviality, is of crucial importance in the novel. As we shall observe, in *The New York Trilogy*, the characters and their identities overlap in such a way that in the end they seem to be fragments of an entity. One flagrant example is the name Peter Stillman that simultaneously refers to the father and the son, the man who hires Daniel Quinn and the person he is supposed to investigate. As we shall observe, Paul Auster puts in place a mechanism that has the objective of cancelling the differences between the characters in favour of a non-specific totality, a consciousness which like that of the writer encompasses all of the characters.

Moreover, the author purposefully blurs the boundaries of fiction and reality through the interplay between the author, the real Paul Auster, and the fictional Paul Auster in the novel. The question of identity, who is writing, what is an author and why he writes, become central in the novel. Such an approach recalls Michel Foucault's work entitled "What Is an Author?" in *Language, Counter-memory, Practice*, which describes the function of the author and the position that he occupies within a discourse. Several scholars such as Dennis Barone, Denis Mellier, Madeleine Sorapure and others have already remarked that Foucault's different texts were possible sources of inspiration to Auster.[3] *The New York Trilogy*, as we know, borrows the structure and appearance of a detective novel; however, the mystery is not who committed the crime, but who is who in the novel.

In *Ghosts*, the second story in *The New York Trilogy*, Paul Auster names his characters by colours, which in the reader's imagination become simultaneously associated with the identity and appearance of the characters. A man called White hires a detective named Blue to spy on Black for reasons that he does not determine. Blue writes weekly reports and mails them to White who sends him postal money orders. After some time, Blue "finds it a little perplexing, however, that the methods of payment should be anonymous. Why not a personal check

---

3 See Dennis Barone, "Paul Auster and the Postmodern American Novel", in Dennis Barone (ed.), *Beyond the Red Notebook* (Philadelphia: University of Pennsylvania Press, 1995); Madeleine Sorapure, "Detective and the Author: *City of Glass*", in Barone (ed.), *Beyond the Red Notebook*; Denis Mellier, "Tuyauteries et theories à la noix: métafiction et signification dans *Cité de Verre*", in Annick Duperray (ed.), *L'oeuvre de Paul Auster* (Paris: Actes Sud, 1995); Bertrand Gervais, "Au pays des tout derniers mots: une *Cité de verre* aux limites du langage", in Duperray (ed.), *L'oeuvre de Paul Auster*.

from White?" (p. 157) he wonders. The anonymous money order dissimulates White's identity just like the make up and the disguise that he wears when he first meets Blue. In order to discover White's identity Blue goes to the post office where he mails his reports, but when White appears Blue cannot see his face because he is wearing a Halloween-like mask.

Little by little, Blue identifies with Black and in the end he understands that Black is in fact a part of himself. Moreover, he discovers that Black and White are one and the same person. The revelation of identities leads to a complex, even an impossible, situation where Blue, Black and White become fragments of a totality. Two important questions emerge in this context, the first concerns the definition of this total identity that seals the fragments, the second concerns the significance of the payment and the money that circulates between the different parts of the same entity.

One is tempted to say that the entity cannot but be a narrator with a split personality, or one whose consciousness encompasses that of all other characters. The money that circulates among the different parts of the entity seems to serve several purposes. First, it creates the illusion of separate and independent characters, one pays, the other is paid. Secondly, in a reverse movement, the anonymous payments dissimulate and question the identities of the payer and the payee. In this scheme the reader, like a detective, follows the author's clues and signs in order to find out who is who. In this sense, money seems to be the substance that ignites and feeds the mechanism that leads to the discovery of the global identity that includes the different parts. White, who pays to find out, activates the process, Blue, who is paid, acts to discover and put the information together, and Black, who is being observed, is in possession of the knowledge that the fragments constitute one entity.

Money and language seem to be the currencies that make the transfer of knowledge between the different parts of the entity possible. The money order brings Blue to question himself about White's identity, and the weekly report leads him to the post office where he sees White wearing a mask.[4] When Blue omits reporting the incident at the post office, White sends him a note with the money order asking him why he lied. Consequently, Blue begins to have serious doubts about White's true identity since his job is to report on Black and not White.

Let's consider another scene. In order to observe Black more freely, Blue disguises himself as Jimmy Rose, an old tramp with white hair and white beard, and asks Black for some change. Black gives him a coin. The next day Black

4 The number of White's mail box is 1001, which clearly conveys a mirror image that sets one against one.

gives him another coin without being accosted and asks Blue whether anyone has ever told him that he "look(s) just like Walt Whitman" (p. 205). White's observation puts forward the subject of identity and disguise and places it in a historical and cultural American context. The commerce that follows between them centres on American writers and personalities such as Whitman, Thoreau, Henry Ward Beecher and Hawthorne. The names and references are significant in the context and seem to establish an alternative coded language in which names function as semiotic boxes.

The allusion to Whitman operates on two different registers simultaneously. From a historical point of view, it recalls *Leaves of Grass*, which incorporates two parts, I Sing the Body Electric and Songs of Myself, and thus puts forward the idea of the self as the centre of the world. At a literary level, Whitman's name becomes a pun on the word 'whit', meaning a very small part of something, which suggests fragmentation of a shattered identity. Furthermore, Whitman's name suggests white-man. Such a reading of the name becomes particularly meaningful in relation to another American historical character listed in the same paragraph, Henry Ward Beecher. The interconnection between Whitman and Beecher is clearly confirmed through the description of the street where the rented hide out is situated.

> Walt Whitman handset the first edition of *Leaves of Grass* on this street in 1855, and it was here that Henry Ward Beecher railed against slavery from the pulpit of his red-brick church. So much for the local colour. (p. 163)

The reference to Beecher and his radical character once again emphasises the importance of personal identity and the self. Furthermore it clearly alludes to slavery which sets white against black and thus picks up on the colour pattern and representations of the characters in *Ghosts*. The humorous remark, "so much for the local colour", confirms such supposition. Furthermore, Hawthorne's name refers to the shrub with white or pink flowers with dark fruit and thus picks up on the novel's colour pattern.[5]

Mireille Hardy has shown the importance of the colour white in *City of Glass*, its growing presence and its association with the snow that covers New York at

---

5 Hawthorne on account of the multiple and various references ranks high on the scale of Auster's hermetic language. In the third book in *The New York Trilogy*, Auster uses the name Fanshawe which brings to mind Hawthorne's first novel *The Blithedal Romance and Fanshawe*. William Marling has discussed the problem of the father's absence and the similitude between *The Locked Room* and Hawthorne's *The Blithedal Romance and Fanshawe,* in "Le Fanshawe d'Hawthorne: La filiation avouée d'Auster", in Duperray (ed.), *L'oeuvre de Paul Auster*, pp. 128-139.

the end of the novel.[6] A similar pattern occurs in *Ghosts*, in the sense that the colour white, like snow, conceals things from the eye and functions like darkness. Moreover, in a later scene Blue impersonates a character named Snow with white hair and a white beard. In a similar spirit, Auster uses Hawthorne's name not only to refer to the writer, but also the colours that his name evoke. In American slang 'snowing someone' connotes dissimulating the truth or deceiving. On this reading the protagonist and the reader who act as detectives try to discover signs and read meanings into them. In *Ghosts* Blue discovers the truth when he finds out that Black is White in disguise.

The transfer of money from Black to Blue, both fragments of the same entity, becomes analogous to language and a transfer of meaning and consciousness. Money – a sign that stands for value – like words, circulates in a close circuit among the different parts of the entity to bring them to a stage where unity or dissolution becomes possible. Once this process has been completed, Blue kills Black, and consequently White, who is Black in disguise, disappears. One may wonder whether from a clinical point of view Blue becomes a saner person.[7]

In *City of Glass*, a similar interaction occurs between black and white, darkness and light. When Quinn meets Peter Stillman junior, Peter is wearing a white shirt, white pants with white socks and shoes. (p. 17) He has white blond hair, milky blue eyes, and his skin is transparent. He sits in a red velvet armchair and when his eyes meet Quinn's, he becomes "invisible" to Quinn. He and his wife simply disappear when Stillman senior commits suicide and Quinn's mission as detective Auster ends.

As we near the end of the novel, the two contrasting colours black and white dominate. When Quinn and the Stillmans disappear, the whole city is covered by snow. As the protagonist Daniel Quinn gradually loses consciousness and physically vanishes in the end, darkness grows until in the end there are just a few minutes of day light during which Quinn can write.

Stillman's whiteness is in complete contrast with Virginia Stillman who was his speech therapist before becoming his wife. She has dark hair, dark eyes and wears a black dress and a very red lipstick. The description of Peter and Virginia

---

6 "Le blanchiment des repères dans la Trilogy New Yorkaise", in Duperray (ed.), *L'œuvre de Paul Auster*, pp. 114-127.

7 Roy C. Caldwell writes that "La destinée de Quinn, comme celle de Fanshawe, suit la trajectoire du saint. Pour fortifier l'âme, pour arriver au centre de soi, il faut nier le monde matériel, il faut châtier la chair. Il faut arriver au vanishing point: point de fuite d'identité. C'est un projet qui correspond à la vision puritaine fondatrice du pays, l'obsession des origines, caractéristique, selon Baudrillard, de la culture américaine." "*New York Trilogy*: Réflexions postmodernes", in Duperray (ed.), *L'oeuvre de Paul Auster*, p. 81.

Stillman's physical appearance and clothes is restricted to colour, which points to the essence of their character in the novel and their literary *raison d'être*. Here the colour pattern, the combination of white and black with the red armchair in which the Stillmans sit, in turn evokes Quinn's red notebook and his writing about the characters. From this standpoint the entire existence of the Stillmans seems to be the consequence of Quinn's fantastic literary imagination; and, simultaneously, they mirror Quinn's own fictional existence. They are words – characters – in black and white written in a red notebook.

Paul Auster seems to place the characters on the same register as signs. Like words empty of their meanings, money without real value or the check with no backing, names are hollow and meaningless. The characters cancel out their identities as soon as this has been established. Peter Stillman says: "I am Peter Stillman. That is not my real name. Thank you very much." (p. 26) Similarly, after the meeting with Peter Stillman, Daniel Quinn says: "All I can say is this: listen to me. My name is Paul Auster. That is not my real name." (p. 49).

The theme of the fall of language as a result of the original sin and paradise lost is central to the very construction of *City of Glass*. Quinn discovers that Peter Stillman senior wrote a thesis entitled *The Garden and the Tower: Early Visions of the New World*. The work is divided into two equal parts "The Myth of Paradise" and "The Myth of Babel". According to Stillman, the Tower of Babel episode is just a "recapitulation of what happened in the Garden", and "The story of the Garden, therefore, records not only the fall of man, but the fall of language" (p. 52) as one and the same thing as the fall of man. With the fall of man and language, it becomes impossible to discover the true meaning of things; all signs – language, colours, and names – are questionable and open to interpretation.

The search for God's heavenly language and the truth of things becomes a major theme in the novel. Stillman believes that language is false, "it hides the thing that it is supposed to reveal (p. 78) His major occupation is to rename things and invent a new language. Peter Stillman locked up his son at the age of two and a half in a dark room with no windows for nine years in the hope of discovering man's language before the fall. The result was a total failure and when the police discovered Peter, he had to receive speech therapy in order to speak.

Language is emphatically linked with money and personal identity through the check that Virginia Stillman makes out to the name of Paul Auster. Quinn, we know, cannot cash the check since it is not made out to his real name. Later, Quinn meets the 'real' Paul Auster, who is not a detective at all but a writer. Quinn shows Paul Auster Mrs. Stillman's check as the proof that makes his story about the Stillman's credible and asks Auster to cash the check for him. The check is, however, no good and bounces when Auster deposits it in the bank.

The meeting that takes place between Daniel Quinn and Paul Auster is the turning point in the novel which marks Quinn's descent and dissolution. He withdraws 300 dollars out of a total of 349 dollars that he possesses in his bank account and camps in the street opposite Stillman's hotel to be able to observe him permanently. From this moment on, the remaining money in Quinn's pocket acts as a countdown to the dissolution of his identity. As Quinn spends his last dollars his metamorphosis into a tramp is fully established and when he moves into Peter Stillman's apartment he is gradually transformed into a different person with no name and no consciousness.[8] As Roy C. Caldwell has remarked, the destiny of Quinn is similar to that of a saint, who in order to purify the soul must give up the material world and reach the centre of his self, which is the vanishing point when all identity is dissolved.[9]

In the Auster/Quinn equation, the question of identity in relation to money emerges with great simplicity at first, ironically as transparent as a city of glass. The bouncing check establishes a parallel between false identity and a check with no funds behind it. However, the art of Paul Auster lies precisely in blurring the transparent structure by multiplying it infinitely. The complexity emerges through overlapping identities and characters that mirror one another. The Paul Auster in the novel is not the real Paul Auster, but then he is, if we consider things in the light of Lejeune's analysis of autobiographies.[10] Yet the novel, despite the autobiographical dimension, is not an autobiography but a reflection of the real life Paul Auster's consciousness as a writer. Quinn, on the other hand, quintessential as his name indicates, also incarnates certain aspects of Paul Auster's life. Daniel Quinn, although a poet, writes detective stories under the pseudonym of William Wilson[11] in order to make a living, like the real Paul Auster who wrote detective novels under the pseudonym of Paul Benjamin before

8 Quinn's disappearance corresponds to the appearance of the narrator in the last few pages of the novel, who takes possession of the red notebook in which Quinn recorded his detective work.

9 See Roy C. Caldwell, "*New York Trilogy* : Réflexions Postmodernes", op. cit. p. 81.

10 Philippe Lejeune, *Le pacte autobiographique* (Paris: Seuil, 1975).

11 Madeleine Sorapure comments that "in Quinn's description of the 'triad of selves' through which he writes detective stories, we see his desire to assume different identities and thus 'lose' himself [...]. She comments that "Poe's *William Willson* highlights the doubled, divided status of the artist, the paradox of creativity in which 'creation implies destruction, ultimately destruction of the artist himself'. By 'becoming' William Wilson, itself a fractured persona, Quinn creates his detective hero, Max Work." – "The Detective and the Author: *City of Glass*", in Dennis Barone (ed.), *Beyond the Red Notebook*, op. cit. p. 77.

becoming a celebrity. Money and identity seems to become fully significant at the conjunction between detective work and writing.

Daniel Quinn draws a parallel between the act of writing and the work of a detective. He places the 'I' with its double meaning – as the self and as the organ that sees – at the heart of this equation.

> Private eye. The term held a triple meaning for Quinn. Not only was it the letter "i," standing for "investigator," it was "I" in the upper case, the tiny life-bud buried in the body of the breathing self. At the same time it was also the physical eye of the writer, the eye of the man who looks out from himself into the world and demands that the world reveal itself to him. For five years now, Quinn had been living in the grip of this pun. (p. 9f)

The work of the writer becomes one with detection, looking into the world and into himself, trying to understand who he is and to define his identity in relation to the world around him. On this reading the narrator and the characters in the novel become reflections of the writer's self, fluctuating and overlapping into one another. Money in this conjunction finds its full significance, firstly as payment for writing, secondly as a sign which has to be interpreted and investigated in the text, and leads the reader to discover the writer's intentions and consciousness.[12] In this sense Quinn's pun on I/eye recalls Emerson's idea of the "inward eye" or "transparent eye-ball". In this inward quest for identity, money as sign and symbol and as the general equivalent of all values becomes significant.[13]

The check is script that represents value, like words that disclose meanings, like the book itself that by unfolding the plot is to provide the key to the riddles in the reader's mind and consequently earn money for the writer. However, both money and language prove to be deceptive and void of significance. When the check made out to the name of Paul Auster bounces, all promise of making sense

---

12 Quinn's first name, Daniel, once again evokes the problem of writing and interpretation. In the *Old Testament*, the first part of *The Book of Daniel*, contains stories in the third person about the experiences of Daniel and his friends; the second half, written mostly in the first person, contains reports of Daniel's three visions and one dream.

13 Viola Sachs has advanced that "in the United States, absence of money and absence of identity go together." – "Money and the Covenant: the Destruction of the American Dream", in *Letterature D'America*, Bulzoni Editore, Anno XIII, n. 50 (1993), pp. 5-17, here: p. 5.

or discovery evaporates.[14] To use Melville's words in *Moby-Dick; or, the Whale*, both language and money prove to be "nothing but empty ciphers".[15]

The recurrent references to American writers and their texts in Auster's work seem to situate his work in a historical continuity of a literary tradition. It strives to establish an American cultural identity through the permanent intertextual dialogues, which in the end proves to be illusory. However, the American national and cultural identity seems to be just as multiple and misleading as the identities of Auster's characters in the *New York Trilogy*. It is a shattered identity with many particles that negate and cancel out one another. Like Melville's Bartleby and his much quoted sentence "I'd rather not", Auster's characters negate their identities and say that they are not who they say they are. In the end, the American national identity, if any at all, seems to be anchored in its very absence and the possible existence of a multitude of identities.

14 The check with no backing may be compared to the advent of paper money and the analogies it evoked. Emerson for example wrote that, "a man's power to connect his thought with its proper symbol, and so to utter it" is corrupted when "new imagery ceases to be created, and old words are perverted to stand for things which are not; a paper currency is employed, when there is no bullion in the vaults." Ralph Waldo Emerson, "Nature", quoted by Marc Shell, *Money, Language and Thought*, (Berkeley: University of California Press, 1982), p. 19.

15 Marc Shell comments on the expression used by Melville in *Money, Language and Thought*, "The fear that all literature was, like money, in this sense a merely passable 'naught' – a mere cipher – troubled Melville, an expert on confidence, for whom the tropic centre of symbolization is an 'algebraic x' threatening language and money with devaluation and annihilation". Shell, *Money, Languageand Thought*, p. 7.

Joachim Schwend

"Pecunia non olet" – Money and Consumer Cultures

Money has no smell, but how about us? Do we smell, in a metaphorical sense, differently according to whether we have money or not? Thorstein Veblen argues in his study on the leisure class that the motive at the root of ownership is emulation.[1] Ownership confers social prestige and thus it is after all "pecuniary strength"[2] that determines our standing in society or, to put it differently, whether we smell of poverty or of wealth. According to the *Collins English Dictionary* you can be "stinking rich" but not 'stinking poor'.

Poverty should be conceptualised not only in terms of money and wealth – "economic poverty"[3] –, but also in terms of deprivation and, above all, in social exclusion. The question remains of whether we can afford to belong to the peer group we would like to belong to. Social deprivation can take different shapes and forms. There is the impossibility of constructing the kind of identity which we would like to have and which would thus enable us to join the desired peer group. Matthew Hilton asks the following questions: "Are we more conscious of money as a financial return on our labour, or as the goods into which it can be converted? Are we wage-conscious or price-conscious? Do we produce to earn, or earn to spend? Are our identities structured around production or consumption?" And he gives the answer: "The answer must surely be that production and consumption are entirely intertwined in our economic lives, if not our social, political and cultural lives as well."[4] Consumerism contributes to the construction of flexible identities fit for unstable worlds. The notion of 'lifestyle' implies that we can construct a particular identity and change this lifestyle and by doing so also our identity if we want to. This means clearly that it is more important how we spend our money than how we earn it. Money and the consumer goods and activities money can buy are part of our identification

---

1 Cf. Thorstein Veblen, *The Theory of the Leisure Class* (New York: Dover Publications, 1994), p. 234.

2 ibid., p. 236.

3 Hilary Tovey and Perry Share, *A Sociology of Ireland* (Dublin: Gill & Macmillan, 2000), p. 129.

4 Matthew Hilton, *Consumerism in 20th-Century Britain. The Search for a Historical Movement* (Cambridge: Cambridge University Press, 2003), p. 27.

processes. We live in a time of "postmodern consumer subjectivities"[5] and we construct our identity by means of the goods we buy and the activities we choose to undertake. These activities may include the refusal to buy certain goods or undertake certain activities. We do not simply buy goods, as Naomi Klein argues, but lifestyles, or to put it differently, we buy "patterns of association that we call lifestyles".[6] When you buy a BMW you do not simply buy a car to take you from A to B but you buy a status symbol which carries the desired associations. It is a question of the brand or the superbrand, as Hugh Oram argues:

> Quantitatively, the premium paid [for a superbrand] is the difference between the price a consumer will pay for a Superbrand versus a lesser brand or commodity with similar values. That premium is often as high as 30%. Superbrands may also account for over 50% of their company's total value and have often valued their owner's companies at twenty to thirty times their book value.[7]

A so-called Superbrand offers the consumer significant emotional and/or physical advantages over its competitors and consumers are prepared to pay an extra sum of money for this advantage. Emotional satisfaction is a central argument in the purchase of a brand.

In Leipzig you could also argue from a patriotic or regionally conscious perspective that you buy a mark three BMW because it is manufactured in Leipzig and you want to support the local industry and safeguard jobs in the region. BMW as a superbrand stands for a lifestyle and you construct your identity around this car and the peer group of those who drive the same make and model. Chaney argues: "the increasing significance of lifestyles derives from a re-evaluation of material culture, away from the immediate monetary value of objects and towards their social or cultural value".[8] The sign-value is relevant, the use-value takes second rank.[9] In the case of expensive consumer goods such as a car the monetary value is of course relevant as well. In consumer society status is opposed to class as an indicator of social difference. Differences stem rather from using than from producing goods. Identity construction works either by imitation or differentiation and the consumer can decide either to imitate the others or to differentiate himself/herself from the others. You differentiate yourself by the

---

5 ibid., p. 27.

6 David Chaney, *Lifestyles* (London: Routledge, 1996), p. 152.

7 Hugh Oram, ed., *Ireland's Superbrands. An Insight into Ireland's Strongest Brands* (London: Superbrands Ltd., 2000), p. 7.

8 Chaney, *Lifestyles*, p. 43.

9 Cf. Jean Baudrillard, *The Consumer Society. Myths and Structures*, trans. Chris Turner, (London: Sage Publications, 1995), p. 21.

manner of consuming and the lifestyle you can buy with your money. It is a question of "moving from quantitative ostentation to distinction, from money to culture".[10] Consumption is not only the consuming of goods, it is extended to "all life's activities" which gain a certain "symbolically malleable" [11] social value and imply a pattern of associations which are defined by the social and cultural code of the society we live in and by the time frame in which it is enshrined. The consumer must have the proper social knowledge to use both the product and the activity in the right way or to read them in their social context. The goods and activities of our consumer culture must be considered as "hermeneutic texts embedded in larger, although frequently incoherent, narratives".[12] It is a dialogic process of decoding and encoding in which the meaning is created in the discourse. Meaning is not fixed once and for ever; it is changed all the time; it is part of hegemonic power politics and thus part of a social competition which relies on the sign-value of goods in relation to other goods. Money transforms objects from their intrinsic use-value to having an exchange-value in a "new, cultural discourse that is independent of functions and individual tastes".[13] The code for this value-system is determined by the cultural code of our consumer society. In order to have a certain lifestyle you need the necessary resources and a willingness to use your resources, in other words to apply your "disposable income"[14] in the way necessary for the lifestyle you long for. This means that social groups with lower incomes will feel excluded from pursuing certain lifestyle fashions. Lifestyles thus gain both an aesthetic and a hierarchical significance in social structures. The ephemeral character of such value-systems and thus also of the identification processes is self-evident when we look for instance at the world of fashion. The value-system depends on the changing structures of society and its cultural codes. Consumption is, however, not only a matter of resources and disposable income, but also a matter of taste and thus of what is called cultural capital, that is: "the existence of dominant and socially legitimated ideas about what is culturally valued and desirable in our society".[15] Very often the decisions about what is valued and desirable are made by the dominant groups in society which might come from different backgrounds but are often linked to financial and economic power.

10 ibid., p. 55.

11 Chaney, *Lifestyles*, pp. 34, 45.

12 ibid., p. 139.

13 ibid., p. 49.

14 ibid., p. 97.

15 Tovey/Share, *A Sociology of Ireland*, p. 138.

Peter Corrigan places the beginning of consumer society in the Elizabethan age when the Queen made aristocrats come to London to her court where they had to compete with London society and differentiate themselves from others. They began to spend money on clothes and other consumer goods: "a consumer boom in Elizabethan England, and an eighteenth-century explosion in the fashionable use of consumer objects such as pottery (Josiah Wedgwood is an important figure here)".[16] Both the aristocrats as well as the middle classes – among the rest of the well-off sections of society, the loaded and the landed classes[17] – tried hard to emulate their betters and to show off their aestheticism and their status in society. The absentee landlord in Ireland or Scotland is an example of the consuming spirit as are the expensive attractions of London, which reflect also the conflict between the core and the periphery, especially the core in its function of lifestyle creator. The 18th century is usually considered to be the age when consumer society really began, when mass production was introduced into British society and when the service nexus was finally replaced by the cash nexus. People had more money and more opportunities to spend their cash. Daniel Defoe writes in *A Plan of English Commerce*: "Father gets the Food [...] Mother gets them Clothes."[18] This is the time of entrepreneurs who made a lot of money and created empires of commerce. The protestant work ethic helped capitalism to rise; everything and everybody had a price. It is said about Beethoven, that he hurled away a novel by Sir Walter Scott with the cry: "Why, the fellow writes for money".[19]

In our postmodern times with a more flexible value system the pursuit of a lifestyle is not an "irrational exploitation but an existential search for distinction in a deeply secular culture".[20] Alissa Quart argues in a similar way in her study *Branded*: "Affluenza invaded the realm of all traditional religions".[21] Loyalty to a brand satisfies the desire for security and stability because brands stand for values and offer the consumer a given certainty in a world otherwise lacking stable

---

16 Peter Corrigan, *The Sociology of Consumption. An Introduction* (London: Sage Publications, 1998), p. 2.

17 Roy Porter, *English Society in the Eighteenth Century. The Pelican Social History of Britain* (Harmondsworth: Penguin, 1986), p. 67.

18 Cf. Margrit Schulte-Beerbühl, "Die Konsummöglichkeiten und Konsumbedürfnisse der englischen Unterschichten im 18. Jahrhundert", in *Vierteljahresschrift für Sozial- und Wirtschaftsgeschichte* 82 (1995), vol. 1, pp. 1-28, here p. 16.

19 Cf. Paul Du Gay, ed., *Production of Culture/Cultures of Production* (London: Sage Publications, 1997), p. 110.

20 Chaney, *Lifestyles*, p. 17.

21 Alissa Quart, *Branded. The Buying and Selling of Teenagers* (London: Arrow, 2003), p. 90.

values. Brands continue to represent a solid base especially in view of the flood of advertisements which confront us, the invasion of the public space by products and their adverts. Brands tell stories, they are narratives, about themselves but also about us, the consumers who buy and use them. Coca Cola used to be the "American dream in a bottle"[22] and Baileys was marketed with its Irishness, evoking connotations of everything that is considered typically Irish. Or: "I have a Mercedes, therefore I am."[23] The brand is a sort of emotional coat which clothes us, protects us and constructs our identity. Brands and the lifestyles they represent are patterns for the specific behaviour of peer groups. The tribal myths of old are being reorganized to "identify and explain wider complexes of identity and affiliation"[24]. The lifestyle in consumer culture has the additional advantage that it can be changed at a whim. Spending money is part of being alive and of finding one's place in a postmodern society with all its insecurities. The traditional religions and the so-called Victorian values of austerity and thrift have lost most of their attractions and people are willing to invest money in the pursuit of enjoyment and style. Consumer society replaced established class distinctions and shrank social differences based on class structures. We have to look for new alternatives to differentiate ourselves from the others, or to integrate ourselves into the peer group we would like to belong to in the course of the above-mentioned imitation process. Up to a certain degree, and this is where money in the shape of the disposable income comes into it, it is up to the individual to choose a peer group and the tribe of consumers he or she would like to follow. We have a choice between peer groups, but have we all the same range of choices? Certainly not. Zygmunt Bauman argues:

> All commodities have a price-tag attached to them. These tags select the pool of potential customers. [...] But they draw the boundary between the realistic and the feasible, the boundary which a given consumer cannot overstep. Behind the ostensible equality of chances the market promotes and advertises [...] the practical inequality of consumers – that is the sharply differentiated degrees of practical freedom of choice.[25]

It is certainly too simple to reduce the possibility for choice on money, but money does play a role in our choices. Conrad Lodziak expresses a comparable point of view but goes a bit too far in his study *The Myth of Consumerism* when he writes: "money has become the main currency of freedom."[26] One cannot, however,

---

22 Oram, ed., *Ireland's Superbrands*, p. 15.

23 ibid., p. 8.

24 Chaney, *Lifestyles*, p. 12.

25 Quoted in Celia Lury, *Consumer Culture* (Cambridge: Polity Press, 1997), p. 5.

26 Conrad Lodziak, *The Myth of Consumerism* (London: Pluto Press, 2002), p. 76.

ignore the fact that consumption and thus our identification process is after all also dependent on income levels.

The far-reaching removal of traditional class barriers and the relative homogenisation of life in our society at the level of essential goods, so-called necessities, is opposed by the subtle differentiation in lifestyles which are expressed in prestigious logos or in the absence of logos, as Naomi Klein makes it clear in her study *No logo*. The differentiation process is transferred away from the work sphere and from everyday consumer objects satisfying our bare necessities, because they "are becoming less and less expressive of social rank. And incomes themselves, in so far as the great disparities are being reduced, are losing their value as a distinctive criterion".[27] Relevant is no longer the quantity but the quality of goods and their inherent sign structures of a specific lifestyle. The best example for this trickle-down process which transforms former luxury items into everyday products are probably so-called colonial goods such as coffee, tea and sugar or gadgets such as washing machines or even refrigerators. Consumption is a process of signification and communication which is based on a cultural code generated in society and ordered as status symbols in a social hierarchy. This also includes questions of health because a healthy lifestyle has gained a new relevance. "Health today is not so much a biological imperative linked to survival as a social imperative linked to status".[28] Keeping fit and healthy has become a matter of social concern. The discussion about obesity and binge-drinking shows how much it is considered a problem in our society. In the 18th century the potbelly was considered a sign of social distinction, the hard-drinking so-called "three-bottle man"[29] was perfectly acceptable. Buying and eating health food is more expensive than mass produced foodstuffs. The so-called muesli belt is comparable to the Volvo belt in big cities; both products represent lifestyles and it is not the cheapest form of survival having a bowl of organic muesli for breakfast and travelling in a Volvo.

Healthy food is also linked with regional food and thus carries the ecological advantage of shorter transport. The Irish brand "Donegal Catch" with the trawler as the immediately recognisable trademark uses the Celtic Tiger image in connection with its quality frozen foods. Inherent in the advertising campaign is the implication that the contemporary Irish consumer wants quality and is prepared to spend more money on it. The consumer is time-conscious which

---

27 Baudrillard, *The Consumer Society*, p. 57.

28 ibid., p. 139.

29 Roy Porter, *English Society in the Eighteenth Century. The Pelican Social History of Britain* (Harmondsworth: Penguin, 1986), p. 33.

makes frozen food welcome, so a new range of "Donegal Catch Ready Meals"[30] was introduced. The Celtic Tiger consumers "want convenience but are not prepared to compromise on either quality or price". The new range of frozen food combines the natural health-food aspect with the "easy meal solutions that take the hassle out of cooking for the family".[31] Here looms the Celtic Tiger image of the new generation Irish with money on their hands but not always enough time for slow food. The time-poor and money-rich shopper is the new symbol of the Celtic Tiger with a consumer who chooses Irish products, albeit for patriotic reasons. Food consumption must definitely be seen as a means to create a lifestyle, it is invested with a moral significance and is thus politicised, as in the green movements and the slow-food campaign all over the world. Ireland under the Celtic Tiger is maybe a money-ridden society, it is a consumer culture which defines status in society by means of so-called "lifestyle shopping" which satisfies personal tastes and "construct[s] personal itineraries".[32]

The former GDR aimed to establish the classless society according to socialist theory, but nevertheless there existed two classes: those with Deutschmark and those without.[33] The GDR socialist concept of a classless society was the alternative to the consumer society according to Western capitalist ideas. Today in Germany everybody pays with the Euro and the myth of consumerism is that everybody can choose the products he or she wants to buy and thus the peer group he or she wants to belong to. The socialist ideals of a classless society could not live up to really existing conditions of scarcity in the GDR. The frugal comforts of socialism were the conditions under which citizens of the GDR had to live, always confronted with TV images from an affluent West which made life in the GDR arduous, unless you belonged to the party elite and could afford products from the West, for instance a Volvo instead of a Trabi. In GDR ideology it was not the sign-value that was intended to be decisive, but the use-value. The iconography of a capitalist system of products and lifestyles was rejected in East Germany. The GDR did not understand itself as a consumer society but as a culture society in which it was not material possessions but rather the formation of culturally rich individualities, within the socialist ideology, that made all the difference.[34] West German capitalism and consumerism put an end to this chimera.

---

30 Cf. Oram, ed., *Ireland's Superbrands*, p. 45.

31 ibid., pp. 44f.

32 Chaney, *Lifestyles*, p. 18.

33 Cf. Ina Merkel, *Utopie und Bedürfnis. Die Geschichte der Konsumkultur in der DDR* (Weimar: Böhlau Verlag, 1999), p. 245.

34 ibid., p. 26.

Old class hierarchies were abolished by consumer culture, but gender specifications remained: it is woman who is usually associated with consumption. Rachel Bowlby argues: "there is an obvious connection between the figure of the narcissistic woman and the fact of women as consumers."[35] Marketing strategies appeal frequently to woman's need or wish to adorn and create herself. The narcissistic mirror is replaced by the shop window offering woman an idealised image of herself or of what she could become if she bought the products offered. In the 18th and 19th centuries consumption was mainly considered a female activity in middle-class circles. While men were toiling in production, women were enjoying consumption. The rise of the department store in the early 19th century developed a new sphere and public space for women where they could go to shop and where they could find work. Emile Zola's novel *Au bonheur des dames* (1883)[36] is an excellent example of this development. We are all consumers by now and advertising addresses all groups in society. Consumption, just like production, is in our age and time no longer gender-specific. Baudrillard claims "that the heroes of production have been replaced by idols of consumption ('great wastrels') such as movie stars and sports heroes. It is they who fulfil the function of useless and inordinate expenditure". And he continues: "The body has become the object that people lavish more attention *and* money on than any other object."[37] So after all, money does smell, or if you have the money to lavish more attention on your body you might smell of your shaving water or deodorant. 'Stinking rich' gains a new implication when looked at from this point of view. Consumption equals sign-posting which is done by money, but also by taste and so-called cultural capital. Taste is an additional criteria which is celebrated in consumer culture as a means of differentiation. It is not only a question of having enough money, it is also a question of having the proper taste, of being able to show off how the money is spent in the proper, i.e. culturally-coded way.

Consumer culture did not lead to a society without hierarchies and social differences, but these hierarchies and concomitant hegemonies are never stable. We have to fight for our position in society and the consensus has to be newly acquired all the time. Symbolic meanings of lifestyles or brands are transitory in our fast-moving culture. This applies in particular to fashion, but it can also be extended to other features of consumer culture. There is still space for creative autonomy reserved for the social actors in consumer society and identity is never established once and for all. Fashion changes and status symbols lose their sign-

---

35 Rachel Bowlby, "Commerce and Femininity" in *The Consumption Reader*, ed. David B. Clarke et al. (London: Routledge, 2003), pp. 168-172, here: p. 171.

36 Emile Zola, *Au bonheur des dames* (Paris: Charpentier, 1883).

37 Baudrillard, *The Consumer Society*, pp. 5, 14.

value or gain a new one, for instance when the formerly exquisite product develops into a mass-produced commodity used by the majority of consumers. Clothes function as "repertoires of signs that transcend their functional utility and define their wearers in particular images and associations".[38] Clothes display the taste and idiosyncrasies of the label or logo which is transferred to the wearer who thus acquires a certain status and shows his affiliation to specific organisations by wearing the relevant badges or logos of corporations, as for instance university base caps demonstrate. If the communicative decoding process works, the insiders recognize the signs and the feeling of belonging is strong among the peers. Chaney claims that we are living in a "culture of spectacle"[39] and thus expresses in different words what Veblen meant by conspicuous consumption. Spectacle and appearances have gained in importance in consumerism making the sign-value relevant. We have to keep our eyes open to recognize the proper signs of the peer group we would like to belong to. And we have to be aware of changing situations and changing meanings. Money plays an important role in the ability to communicate; not everything is possible, not everything can be paid for. Even though the whole second-hand business and institutions such as eBay have definitely done a lot to even things out and brought a lot of commodities within the reach of many more people than at the time when Veblen wrote his study. In our consumer culture and in the culture of spectacle a lack of money can be equated with social exclusion, unless we decide to belong to a peer group which declares its renunciation of consumption, as far as this is possible in a highly organised society based on money. As a rule money and the status symbols it can buy mean social status and acceptance. Veblen deals in his book with conspicuous consumption, conspicuous waste and with the conspicuous leisure of the leisure class. In his days leisure as such was a status symbol. If you had the money you could buy free time. The wealthy land-owners in the 18th century did not start their day before midday, as a further indication that they did not really have to turn up for work at a certain time. You employed or bought somebody to work for you. You had spare time for leisure, time to waste so to speak.

One of the stereotypes about Ireland used to be that the pace of life was slower, that people had plenty of time to enjoy life. The Celtic Tiger economy made Ireland into the "the second most prosperous country in Europe, after Luxembourg".[40] The question remains of how far consumerism and the Celtic

---

38 Chaney, *Lifestyles*, p. 108.

39 ibid.

40 Pete McCarthy, *McCarthy's Bar. A Journey of Discovery in Ireland* (London: Lir Sceptre, Hodder & Stoughton, 2000), p. 368.

Tiger have changed Ireland and perhaps damaged the tourist image of green Ireland, "time rich and money poor".[41] Clinch et al. argue in their study *After the Celtic Tiger*:

> Ireland has had a great economic run: unprecedented economic growth lasting for nearly a decade, higher incomes, more jobs, more people, more variety. For over ten years it seems as if everything has gone right, both externally and internally. But just as everything can go right, everything can also go wrong. Murphy's Law still waits in the wings to exert its sobering influence.[42]

What has gone right, what has gone wrong and from which perspective do we have to judge the developments? Under Thatcherism credit was considered the symbol of citizenship and the entrance to consumer society. Has something similar happened in Ireland since the mid 1990s and has the Celtic Tiger ravished the old, tourist-industry Ireland? There is definitely more money around in Ireland since the early 1990s and the beginning of the Celtic Tiger phase. Ireland has become a cosmopolitan society with large immigration rates. The flow of the brain drain has been reversed as Clinch et al. claim: "The national self-image has been transformed. Ireland has gone from being a country to get out of to a country to get into." Emigration songs are "like echoes from a distant age".[43] The trend towards a cosmopolitan society is only one side of the coin. The question remains of whether money and the concomitant lifestyles have spoilt the countryside, the environment, maybe the character of the Irish. Clinch et al. claim that this has in fact happened: "In addition, almost a third of people suggest that the Irish have become less friendly during the economic boom as the pace of life, stress and anxiety increase."[44] There are no clear-cut answers as far as the consequences of the economic boom are concerned, but a few points can be raised and a few questions asked when looking into the Ireland of the Celtic Tiger from an outsider's and a tourist's point of view. The travelogues by Pete McCarthy, *McCarthy's Bar. A Journey of Discovery in Ireland* (2000), and Tony Hawks, *Round Ireland with a Fridge* (1998), will function as a textual basis and guideline. McCarthy went on a quest for his roots and very much looked for the old traditional Ireland, the Ireland of his youth and of the tourist industry, but he realized the changes which had taken place.

---

41 Oram, ed., *Ireland's Superbrands*, p. 9.

42 Peter Clinch, Frank Convery and Brendan Walsh, *After the Celtic Tiger. Challenges Ahead* (Dublin: O'Brien Press Ltd., 2002), p. 14.

43 ibid., p. 24.

44 ibid., p. 177.

Ireland needs roughly 50,000 immigrants per year to keep the economy running at the present level. The Celtic Tiger has brought to a lot of people more money and a change of lifestyle. Baudrillard argues: "'Affluence' is, in effect, merely the accumulation of the *signs* of happiness".[45] How about the signs of happiness in today's Ireland? What makes us happy is a personal matter, but we must accept the fact that "throughout the 1990s [Ireland] significantly outperformed all other EU countries". Car ownership has for instance grown by 7% per annum over the 1990s.[46] McCarthy obviously reached the same conclusion, claiming that Ireland is "a nation of actual or newly aspirant BMW drivers". So Ireland has definitely done well as far as the economy goes, but still McCarthy writes: "Despite the much-vaunted Celtic Tiger economy, these people dress and look poorer than people where I live",[47] which is in Lancashire, England. This statement sounds a bit like Thackeray's repeated comments about the poverty of the Irish in his *Irish Sketchbook* (1842) which McCarthy took with him as a travelling companion.

If we are living in a culture of spectacle and affluence is the accumulation of signs of happiness, a lot of people should be happy in Ireland. Has the Celtic Tiger brought more happiness to the Irish? Have they got more spare time for the pub, the *craic* and to go fishing or maybe for holidays abroad? Has conspicuous leisure come to the Irish? The Ireland described in the two bestselling travelogues is the Ireland known to most foreigners who cherish the stereotypes of the Ireland before the Celtic Tiger. Hawks writes "you'll probably be made extremely welcome".[48] The cliché of the Irish pub and Irish hospitality is central to the stereotypical picture of Ireland. Tony Hawks describes the typical Irish pub and its clientele:

> I came to call these establishments the old boys' pubs, where everybody talks to everybody else regardless of who they are, partly because the clientele are very friendly and partly because the clientele are very pissed. Just like an orchestra will have a Lead Violinist, most pubs will have a Lead Drunk. Or Drunk in Residence.[49]

McCarthy uses the same stereotypes:

> The Irish are perceived as young, eloquent, romantic, tuneful, mystical, funny, and expert havers-of-a-good-time. And, as a bonus, in the same way that the English

---

45 Baudrillard, *The Consumer Society*, p. 31.

46 Clinch, Convery, Walsh, *After the Celtic Tiger*, pp. 25, 117.

47 Pete McCarthy, *McCarthy's Bar. A Journey of Discovery in Ireland* (London: Lir Sceptre, Hodder & Stoughton, 2000), pp. 364, 13.

48 Tony Hawks, *Round Ireland with a fridge* (London: Ebury Press, 1998), p. 23.

49 ibid., p. 40.

abroad are made doubly welcome once people realise they're not German, so the Irish are welcomed for not being English.
[...] in Ireland you can still find idiosyncratic, family-owned hovels with no food, or décor, that remain temples to hospitality, conversation and drink.[50]

The pub represents certain Irish values: namely "Sociability and warmth" or "warmth and conviviality"[51] and it is a central feature of stereotypical Irishness in the sense of leisure and good *craic* and it is still there according to these two authors.

Others claim, however, that Irish society has changed within the last few years, it used to be "time rich but money poor" and it is now "money rich but time poor".[52] Clinch et al. argue in the same way: "almost a third of people suggest that the Irish have become less friendly during the economic boom as the pace of life, stress and anxiety increase".[53] If this last statement is considered to be true, then all the affluence, the money and the BMWs, did not bring additional happiness to Ireland. It looks instead as if Ireland has joined the rat race of global capitalism and consumer culture. It is significant that Robin Cook mentioned both the booming economy and the tourist image when he referred to Ireland in his "Chicken Tikka Masala" speech of April 2001.

Ireland joined [the EU] at the same time as Britain. Its period of membership has transformed Ireland into a country with a dynamic economy and a cosmopolitan society. The result has been a new assertiveness of national identity, and confidence in their culture. We can see that for ourselves in Britain through the new affection for Irish music and dance, and the attachment to Irish pubs.[54]

Is Ireland selling its green and Celtic soul by becoming a dynamic economy according to the pattern of the South East Asian tiger states? In the culture of spectacle the shopping mall has taken over the carnivalesque because it functions as a traditional market square where people meet – the rich and the poor alike –, the mall is a site for "communication and interaction".[55] McCarthy argues that the shopping mall has replaced the Celtic Stone Circle: "Proponents of this undeniably imaginative theory make comparisons with shopping malls, which

50 McCarthy, *McCarthy's Bar*, pp. 14, 61.

51 ibid., p. 367.

52 Oram, ed., *Ireland's Superbrands*, p. 9.

53 Clinch, Convery, Walsh, *After the Celtic Tiger*, p. 177.

54 Robin Cook, "The chicken tikka masala speech", April 19, 2001, September 27, 2005, http://www.guardian.co.uk/racism/Story/0,2763,477023,00.html.

55 Rob Shields, ed., *Lifestyle Shopping. The Subject of Consumption* (London: Routledge, 1992), p. 5.

might be seen as the new temples. Shoppers are worshippers, McDonald's is the sacrament, Nike provide the vestments".[56] This sounds like the end of the traditional Irish identity and the beginning of the age of final and conclusive globalisation in consumerism. The lifestyle has changed, Ireland has chosen a different peer group and flaunts the relevant signs of the global village of consumer culture.

But as tourism is still one of the main sectors of the Irish economy, the preservation of the green image and of the cliché of traditional Ireland is of utmost importance from a money-making perspective. In rural parts of Ireland a reduction in population took place due to movements to the industrial urban centres. It is in these rural areas that tourism will be the only industry with growth potential, and tourism needs to keep up the green image of Ireland. The same applies to the food industry: "The food industry at the upper end of international markets depends on Ireland's 'green image' for its competitive advantage."[57] This image is also extensively used in Irish advertising. The Irish chain of Green Isle Foods, part of Northern Foods Group plc. sell under the brand name Goodfellas a cosmopolitan meal, Irishness mixed with American and Italian values:

> Goodfellas is at the apex of pizza values, both Italian (family, food values, warmth etc.) and American (can-do attitude and outgoing nature). [...] Goodfellas has mainstream appeal, targeted at sociable people who enjoy themselves and who want to mark the day with a little event. These people want an easy life – low maintenance, exciting and quality food as a comfort as well as fuel.[58]

The environmental consciousness and the green credentials play also a part in the selling of Inversoft and Kittensoft toilet tissues. Not only does the name come from the river Inver, the emphasis is on the Irish heritage of the company and its kindness to the environment. Key product messages are: "value for money, local manufacture and softness on nature", Inversoft has been active in the "Tree Council of Ireland" to replant native trees in Ireland. The brand's core values combine all the ecologically valuable ingredients needed in advertising products from the region: "soft on nature, recycled, value for money and Irish made".[59]

Clinch et al. fall back on the old and negatively connotated term of "gombeenism" and link it with ecologically disastrous consequences of the Celtic Tiger economy: "The practice of 'gombeenism', of ruthless exploitation of others,

---

56 McCarthy, *McCarthy's Bar*, p. 44.

57 Clinch, Convery, Walsh, *After the Celtic Tiger*, p. 134.

58 Oram, ed., *Ireland's Superbrands*, p. 59.

59 ibid., p. 69.

maximising short-term gain at the expense of the future, has dire consequences [...] there is evidence of 'environmental gombeenism' in much of our recent environmental performance".[60] Affluence might have come to Ireland, conspicuous consumption is reflected in the increasing number of new cars registered, but it is not all happiness, the negative consequences are visible as well. The destruction of the image of a clean environment in Ireland (whether this is true or not) could do great damage to both the tourism and the food industry, because both rely on "environmental pristineness".[61] Tourism is a "significant feature of lifestyle differentiation"[62] and the term ethical tourism with its sensibility towards nature has come in vogue and is used as counterpoint to McDonaldization and Disneyfication.[63] McCarthy describes such traditional values when he sees an old man sitting in front of his cottage and ponders: "The next time I'm here, the old man will be gone and there'll be another holiday home to rent"). He points out the dangers imminent in mass tourism and criticizes the devastation of the countryside by the boom in building industry: "the invasion of the Killer bungalows has swept all before it". The building of bungalows and big new houses are signs of newly acquired affluence and of a new self-confidence: "The self-confident synthetic consumerism of the new houses is a response to this history of deprivation". It is not ethical tourism which McCarthy sees as the danger, but mass tourism and its consequences: "Now the Irish economy is so driven by tourism, will every special little place end up like this, as they see what's to be earned by marketing their idiosyncrasies, leaping aboard the Celtic Tiger, and getting the builders in? A successful tourist industry can quickly turn a place into a parody of itself". Knock has obviously already become a victim of global tourism with "eighteen self-service holy water fountains. [...] One of the consequences of this fly in, pray, buy stuff, fly out conveyor belt is an economy driven by the kitsch souvenir industry."[64] This is merchandising, selling Knock and the Holy Virgin as a brand in a money-spinning industry.

The marketing of Ireland as a brand is big business but the specific Irish combination of friendly people and scenic countryside is under threat by this big business in spite of the enormous sums of money which are generated by tourism.

---

60 Clinch, Convery, Walsh, *After the Celtic Tiger*, p. 135.

61 ibid., p. 143.

62 Chaney, *Lifestyles*, p. 134.

63 Cf. George Ritzer, *The McDonaldization of Society* (London: Sage, 2000); George Ritzer, *The McDonaldization Thesis. Explorations and Extensions* (London: Sage, 1999).

64 McCarthy, *McCarthy's Bar*, pp. 138, 116, 117, 264, 302.

The reference to the "relaxed pace of life" or to "a normalised pace of life"[65] is significant and part of the traditional image of the Irish pub and leisure culture which has been on the wane since the Celtic Tiger took over. The relaxed pace of life in Ireland is also referred to in Jameson's Irish Whiskey advertisements. A campaign was begun in 1999 under the slogan of "What's the Rush?" The stress is on the importance to find the time to enjoy oneself with friends in a fast-moving world. The advertisements depict fashionable young people of the young urban, stylish and cosmopolitan tribe of professionals of both sexes who relax and enjoy a glass of Jameson Whiskey amidst the rush of a big city. The Irish yuppies of the advertising campaign take a break with friends. So Jameson Irish Whiskey also cashes in on the image of Irish sociability. The people depicted are obviously those with money, the young well-off Celtic Tiger generation who still has the time to enjoy a few minutes of *craic* in the buzz of the big cities.

In connection with ethical tourism we can also talk about ethical consumption in general, a not altogether new concept. It can be traced back to an ascetic form of Protestantism, especially Calvinism, and its emphasis on self-control connected with the belief in a better life after death. John Ruskin wrote on the subject of the conscientious consumer and admonished the consumers of his day to spend their resources in a wise and responsible way: "you can never be wrong in employing any labour to produce food, houseroom, clothes and fuel". And then he admonished the consumer not to employ productive energy on the satisfaction of "the frivolous whims and desires of the self-indulgent, idle rich". He expressed a profound distaste for luxury expenditure and exhorted the middle classes about the costs of keeping them by the toil of the labouring poor. Ruskin continued to argue: "It does not cost money only it costs degradation. You do not merely employ people you also tread on them ... It cannot be helped ... but see that you tread as lightly as possible"). In his study *The Seven Lamps of Architecture* Ruskin berated the reader: "we should think of the manner of life which our demand necessitates."[66] Victorian voices such as those of John Ruskin and William Morris emphasised the role of the socially-aware citizen-consumer who has the national well-being in mind and who shows his or her social conscience in consumption habits.

On the other hand increased consumption could also be seen as a patriotic duty of the so-called citizen-consumer, for instance if the Germans began to

[65] Oram, ed., *Ireland's Superbrands*, p. 71.

[66] John Ruskin, quoted in Noel Thompson, "Social Opulence, Private Asceticism: Ideas of Consumption in Early Socialist Thought" in *The Politics of Consumption. Material Culture and Citizenship in Europe and America*, eds. Martin Daunton and Matthew Hilton (Oxford: Berg, 2001), pp. 51-68, here: pp. 67, 65.

spend more money on consumer goods to give the economy a boost and consequently put more money into the coffers of the state. A similar attitude was expressed by patriotic American consumers after 9/11 when they saw it as their national duty to buy American products in order to put money into the American economy.[67] Walmart underlines the concept of buying American goods in contrast to imported goods. Naomi Klein's study *No logo* also calls for the citizen-consumer and delineates the plight of Third-World workers in sweatshops who have to toil for little money so that we can buy cheap Nike trainers.[68] Her argument calls for a social consciousness and feeling of responsibility towards the environment and the workers in those sweat shops. We live in a postmodern age in which the old securities of everlasting values have gone. But the consumer and the human being in general still has a choice which depends not only on money but on the culture we accept for ourselves and on the lifestyles we choose. If the heroes of production are finally replaced by the citizen-consumers, then there is hope, for Ireland and for humanity.

67 Cf. Quart, *Branded*, p. 44.

68 Cf. Naomi Klein, *No logo* (London: HarperCollins, 2001), p. 202.

Contributors' Details

MICHAEL J. BZDAK
is a visiting part-time lecturer in the Art History Department as well as in the School of Communications, Information and Library studies at Rutgers, the State University of New Jersey. His academic studies in art history focus on medieval imagery associated with wisdom and learning as well as the relationship of business to the arts. In addition, Michael is employed by Johnson & Johnson and serves as a Director of Corporate Contributions for the Corporation.

WILLIAM H. CARTER
is a Lecturer in German Studies at Iowa State University. His current book project *Goethe Age Economics* explores various intersections between literature, economics and philosophy beginning in the late eighteenth century.

DICK COLLINS
PhD Trinity, Cambridge, 1998, in Medieval Languages and Literature. Has published on Old French-Latin puns, medieval ghosts and witches; on Pagnol's use of Occitan; on the links between Bram Stoker and Sweeney Todd; and on James Malcolm Rymer, Thomas Peckett Prest and G.W.M. Reynolds. Edited and introduced *The String of Pearls* and Reynolds' *Wagner the Wehr-wolf*, with *The Necromancer* forthcoming from Valancourt; co-translated *La Proie et l'ombre* with Fiona Cox for Penn State. Works on crime/horror literature in Victorian England and contemporary Occitan.

FIONA COX
is a Lecturer in French at UCC – National University of Ireland Cork. Her book *Aeneas Takes the Metro – Virgil's Presence in Twentieth Century French Literature* was published with Legenda in 1999. She has also published numerous articles on Butor, Hugo and Virgil, and with Dick Collins has co-translated Marius Roux's novel *The Substance and the Shadow* (Philadelphia: Penn State University Press, 2007).

SHEILA DICKSON
is a Senior Lecturer in German at the University of Glasgow in Scotland. She has edited Volume 1, *Schriften der Schüler- und Studentenzeit*, of the historical-critical Weimarer Arnim-Ausgabe (2004), and has published articles and edited conference proceedings on German Romanticism, particularly on the works of

Achim von Arnim and E.T.A. Hoffmann. She has also translated a short story by Arnim, *The Marriage Blacksmith* (Hannover: Wehrhahn, 2007).

MICHAEL FODOR

teaches in the Department of French and Italian at Dartmouth College (USA). He has published articles on 18th century French literature and political economy.

JOYCE GOGGIN

is an Associate Professor in Literature, New Media and Film Studies at the Universiteit van Amsterdam. She has published numerous articles on film, video games, gambling, literature and specific authors such as Paul Auster and Nabokov. Dr Goggin is currently working on several book projects including *Playing, Texts and Games: Reading Narrative Stakes* and *Gambling and Representation: Painting, Literature, Film and New Media.*

MICHAEL HUTTER

is Professor of Economics at Witten/Herdecke University in Germany. His research focuses on the economics of media and culture. His most recent publication is titled *Beyond Price. Value and Valuation in Economics, Culture and Art* (Cambridge University Press), edited together with D. Throsby.

EKKEHARD KNÖRER

is a literary and film scholar and freelance film critic. PhD on *The History of Ingenium and Wit* (forthcoming), post-doc project on *The Art of Appropriation in Film, Theatre, Literature and the Arts*. He writes for the German daily newspaper *taz*, teaches at FU Berlin and lives in Berlin. He has recently written articles on Bollywood film, Tod Browning and Edgar Ulmer.

BRIAN MOLONEY

is Emeritus Professor of Italian at the University of Hull. His most recent book is *Italian Novels of Peasant Crisis, 1930-1950. Bonfires in the Night.* (Dublin: Four Courts Press, 2005). He has published extensively on the Triestine Italo Svevo (1861-1928) and is currently engaged in editing vol. 4 of the *Edizione Nazionale delle Opere di Italo Svevo,* which will include Svevo's essays and newspaper articles, as well as autobiographical writings.

CHRISTINA OLDMAN

is a Research Fellow in the Department of Modern Languages at the University of Umea, Sweden. Her research interests include Life Writing.

MARY O'NEILL
completed her PhD, *Ephemeral Art: Mourning and Loss*, in 2007. Two chapters based on that research are published in edited volumes "*Being Lost*" in *Feeling Our Way: Advancing Emotional Geographies*, ed. Joyce Davidson, Liz Bondi, Mick Smith and Laura Cameron (Ashgate, 2007) and "Ephemeral Art: Memory and Loss" in *Im/Permanence: Cultures in and out of Time*, ed. Judith Schachter and Stephen Brockmann, (Carnegie Mellon Center for the Arts in Society in association with Pennsylvania State University Press, 2007).

MARY PIERSE
teaches at the English Department, University College Cork. Editor of *George Moore: Artistic Visions and Literary Worlds* (Cambridge Scholars Press, 2006), she has published articles on Moore's art, Kate Chopin's prose, and on the poetry of Cathal Ó Searcaigh and Dennis O'Driscoll. Her current research into early literary impressionism (begun when IRCHSS Post- Doctoral Research Fellow, 2004-2006) involves establishing a database of artistic reference in Moore's writings.

CORDULA POLITIS
is an IRCHSS Government of Ireland Postdoctoral Fellow in the Department of Germanic Studies at Trinity College Dublin. Her book *The Individualization of Fortune in the Sixteenth-Century Novels of Jörg Wickram* was published with The Edwin Mellen Press in spring 2007.

KIRILL POSTOUTENKO
is an Associate Professor of Literature and Chair of Sociology and Anthropology at Smolny College (Saint-Petersburg). He has published a book *Onegin Text in Russian Literature* (Pisa, 1998) and more than 60 articles on topics ranging from the history of versification to the social analysis of political discourse.

ARNIM SCHÄFER
is Lecturer at the University of Erfurt and member of the Centre of Excellence *Cultural Foundations of Social Integration* at the University of Konstanz. He is author of *Die Intensität der Form. Stefan Georges Lyrik* (2005) and co-edited the volumes *Psychographien* (2005) and *Struktur, Figur, Kontur. Abstraktion in Kunst und Lebenswissenschaften* (2007).

HANS-WALTER SCHMIDT-HANNISA
is Professor of German at the National University of Ireland, Galway. His research interests include German Enlightenment and Romanticism (in particular

Jean Paul, Clemens Brentano, and E.T.A. Hoffmann), the literary and cultural history of dream, historical and intercultural aspects of reading, and media theory. He also translated major contemporary French philosophers like Derrida, Lyotard, Baudrillard, and Sarah Kofman into German.

JOACHIM SCHWEND
is Professor of Cultural Studies in the English Department at Leipzig University, Germany. He has published numerous articles on regionalism in Germany and the British Isles, the nation-state and integration in Europe, identity construction in the regions as opposed to an increasingly globalized culture. He is co-editor of *Political Discourse* (Tübingen, 2005). Consumerism and consumer cultures is a second major field of research with relevant publications – he is co-editor of *Consumption and Consumer Cultures* (Tübingen, 2004).

MICHAEL SHIELDS
is a lecturer in the German Department at National University of Ireland, Galway. He has published on medieval German literature and its music, focusing on the rhetorical interaction of text and melody in political, gnomic and religious lyric. He is currently researching borrowings between German, French and Italian musical and lyric genres ("Spruch" and "Sirventes") in the 13th century.

GUY SNAITH
is a Lecturer in French at the University of Liverpool. He speaks and writes on subjects as diverse as seventeenth-century French theatre, French Canada, architecture, and masculinities. In the Quebec field, his edition of Roch Carrier's novel *La Guerre, yes sir!* was published by Bristol Classical Press in 2000.

NIAMH SWEENEY
is a doctoral student at the Department of French, University College Cork. She was an IRCHSS Government of Ireland Scholar from 2002 to 2005. She is currently completing her thesis on the subject of the decline of Paris as capital of modernism.

AILBHE THUNDER
has a PhD in Critical and Cultural Theory from Cardiff University, where she has also lectured on the BA programmes in Cultural Criticism and English Literature.

SINA VATANPOUR
is a lecturer in American civilisation and history at the applied languages department of university of Lille 3 in France. He has published several articles on

Norman Mailer, on the subject of money in American literature and co-organised an International conference on money in 2004. Currently his research is mainly focused on Paul Auster's work.

MATTHIAS WEISS

is working on his PhD thesis, entitled *The History of Ethical Investing in Germany*, in Social and Economic History at the University of Hamburg, where he also worked as a Lecturer in Fundraising (2005/6) after ten years in business. He has a MA in Cultural Studies and European Ethnology for which he wrote a thesis entitled: *Presenting the Stock Exchange – Three Exhibitions in New York City*.

Marzena Kubisz

Strategies of Resistance

Body, Identity and Representation in Western Culture

Frankfurt am Main, Berlin, Bern, Bruxelles, New York, Oxford, Wien, 2003.
107 pp.
Literary and Cultural Theory. General editor: Wojciech H. Kalaga. Vol. 16
ISBN 978-3-631-50718-6 · pb. € 24.50*

The book is a part of growing literature on human embodiment and attempts to answer the question of the role of the body in the construction of identity in consumer culture. The book examines two related spheres: the centrality and marginality of cultural practices. The phenomena discussed include cosmetic surgery, Modern Primitivism, photographs by Matuschka and projects by French multimedia artist Orlan. The aim of the book is to postulate that in the present conditions of the fragmentation and disintegration of subjectivity, the body may be employed in a strategy of identification. Practices of body modification, performed both in the centre and in the margins of culture, reveal the ways in which identity is constructed, experienced and negotiated. By presenting the body as a site for the construction of identity, the study adds to the ongoing discussion about the status of individual identity and the identity of western culture.

Contents: The Body in the Centre. Surgical (Re)Constructions of the Body · The Body in the Margins. The Body and Resistance: Reclaiming the Self in Non-Mainstream Body Modifications · Mastectomy: Phenomenology of Absence, or Reclaiming the Self in Contemporary Breast Culture · "Identity-Alterity": Orlan's Transient Body · Securing the Self, or Towards an Ontology of the Body

Kolibri 360 GmbH
Ferdinand-Jühlke-Straße 7
99095 Erfurt, Deutschland
produktsicherheit@kolibri360.de

Druck:
CPI Druckdienstleistungen GmbH
im Auftrag der
Kolibri 360 GmbH
Ferdinand-Jühlke-Str. 7
99095 Erfurt